Green Organizations

This book is a landmark in showing how industrial-organizational psychology and related fields contribute to environmental sustainability in organizations. Industrial-organizational psychology embraces a scientist/practitioner model: evidence-based best practice to solve real-world issues. The contributors to this book are experts in science and practice, demonstrating the ways in which human-organization interactions can drive change to produce environmentally beneficial outcomes. Overall, the authors address cogent issues and provide specific examples of how industrial-organizational psychology can guide interventions that support and maintain environmentally sound practices in organizations. *Green Organizations* can be used as a general reference for researchers, in courses on sustainable business, corporate social responsibility, ethical management practices, and social entrepreneurship. The book will provide an excellent overview for anyone interested in sustainability in organizations, and will serve as a valuable guide to industrial-organizational psychology and management professionals.

Ann Hergatt Huffman is Associate Professor of Psychology and Management at Northern Arizona University. Dr. Huffman received her Ph.D. in Industrial-Organizational Psychology from Texas A&M University in 2004. Prior to Texas A&M University, she worked as a principal investigator with the Walter Reed Army Research Institute-Europe. She was awarded the 2009 Northern Arizona University Most Promising New Scholar Award and was selected as a 2007–2008 Sloan Early Career Work-Family Scholar.

Stephanie R. Klein is the Solution Specialist at SHL in Minneapolis, where she has held a variety of roles including change management, product development, assessment and training program development, and client solutions consulting. Most recently, she led post-merger transformational change within the UK and Ireland sales organization. Her areas of professional expertise include transformational change and the ability to balance client logistics, scientific best practices, and technology capabilities to identify solutions to client business needs. Dr. Klein received her M.S. and Ph.D. in Industrial-Organizational Psychology from the Pennsylvania State University in 1998 and 2006, respectively, following her B.A. in Psychology from Kenyon College.

SERIES IN APPLIED PSYCHOLOGY

Series Editors
Jeanette N. Cleveland, Colorado State University
Kevin R. Murphy, Landy Litigation and Colorado State University

Edwin A. Fleishman, Founding series editor (1987–2010)

Winfred Arthur, Jr., Eric Day, Winston Bennett, Jr., and Antoinette Portrey
Individual and Team Skill Decay: The Science and Implications for Practice

Gregory Bedny and David Meister
The Russian Theory of Activity: Current Applications to Design and Learning

Winston Bennett, David Woehr, and Charles Lance
Performance Measurement: Current Perspectives and Future Challenges

Michael T. Brannick, Eduardo Salas, and Carolyn Prince
Team Performance Assessment and Measurement: Theory, Research, and Applications

Neil D. Christiansen and Robert P. Tett
Handbook of Personality at Work

Jeanette N. Cleveland, Margaret Stockdale, and Kevin R. Murphy
Women and Men in Organizations: Sex and Gender Issues at Work

Aaron Cohen
Multiple Commitments in the Workplace: An Integrative Approach

Russell Cropanzano
Justice in the Workplace: Approaching Fairness in Human Resource Management, Volume 1

Russell Cropanzano
Justice in the Workplace: From Theory to Practice, Volume 2

Laura Crothers and John Lipinski
Bullying in the Workplace: Symptoms, Causes and Remedies

David V. Day, Stephen Zaccaro, Stanley M. Halpin
Leader Development for Transforming Organizations: Growing Leaders for Tomorrow's Teams and Organizations.

Green Organizations

Driving Change With I-O Psychology

Edited by

Ann Hergatt Huffman
Northern Arizona University

Stephanie R. Klein
SHL

Routledge
Taylor & Francis Group

NEW YORK AND LONDON

First published 2013
by Routledge
711 Third Avenue, New York, NY 10017

Simultaneously published in the UK
by Routledge
27 Church Road, Hove, East Sussex BN3 2FA

Routledge is an imprint of the Taylor & Francis Group, an informa business

Library of Congress Cataloging in Publication Data
Green organizations : driving change with IO psychology / edited by
Ann Hergatt Huffman & Stephanie R. Klein.
    p. cm. — (Applied psychology series)
    Includes bibliographical references and index.
    1. Business enterprises—Environmental aspects. 2. Psychology, Industrial.
    3. Social responsibility of business. I. Huffman, Ann Hergatt. II. Klein, Stephanie R.
    HD30.255.G7427 2013
    658.4'083—dc23

ISBN: 978–1–84872–974–2 (hbk)
ISBN: 978–0–415–82515–3 (pbk)
ISBN: 978–0–203–14293–6 (ebk)

Typeset in Minion
by Swales & Willis Ltd, Exeter, Devon

In loving memory of our moms,
Jean Green Hergatt
and
Robin Withall Klein

Contents

PART 3   Individuals and Organizations

PART 4   I-O Psychology and Environmental Sustainability for Tomorrow's Workforce

Series Foreword

Jeanette N. Cleveland
Colorado State University

Kevin R. Murphy
Landy Litigation and Colorado State University
Series Editors

The goal of the Applied Psychology Series is to create books that exemplify the use of scientific research, theory and findings to help solve real problems in organizations and society. Huffman and Klein's *Green Organizations: Driving Change with I-O Psychology* accomplishes this goal. Huffman and Klein have assembled an impressive set of chapters that examine the convergence between industrial-organizational (I-O) psychology and environmental sustainability. Their volume demonstrates the potential for I-O psychology to inform and advance the development of green organizations.

The first part of this book introduces key concepts and findings from research on environmental psychology, ethics, and engineering that help to define the problem of environmental sustainability in organizations and the responses of psychologists to this problem. The next part explores the question of why organizations can and do care about environmental sustainability and examines how sustainability can be measured and evaluated. The third part applies familiar theories of individual and organizational behavior to key problems in sustainability, including the responsible management of supply chains, the motivation to engage in sustainability-promoting behaviors, interventions to enhance sustainable behaviors, and the use of recruitment and selection as tools for building sustainability. The final part presents case studies and an evaluation of relationships between consumers, investors, regulatory agencies, trainers and organizations that can influence sustainability.

Green Organizations: Driving Change with I-O Psychology shows how I-O psychology can be used to help organizations develop, implement, evaluate, and maintain environmental sustainability efforts. There has been increasing attention in recent years on documenting the contributions of I-O psychology to solving real-world problems; the current volume represents a great exemplar of how moving I-O psychology beyond its traditional emphases on individual and small-group phenomena can open up new vistas for using the tools of this field to address macro-level problems, such as the relationships between work organizations and the environments in which they are housed. We are very happy to add *Green Organizations: Driving Change with I-O Psychology* to the Applied Psychology Series.

Foreword

The vast majority of new books expand on current knowledge of a topic. Rarely does a book come along that serves as a catalyst and vanguard. It points us in new directions and opens our minds to possibilities unimagined. Such books generate intellectual excitement and energy. In my 40 years as an industrial-organizational (I-O) psychologist I have read very few books with such potential. *Green Organizations* is one of them.

There are five bases to my sense of anticipation. First and foremost, sustainability matters. It matters for us both now and later. It matters for generations yet unborn. It matters to us both in our personal and work lives. It is the paragon of equal opportunity (and equal responsibility) for all segments of society. If we were looking for an exemplar of "practical significance," sustainability would make anyone's short list.

Second, sustainability has emerged as a standard for guiding commerce. The United Nations Global Compact specifies sustainability as one of ten principles for organizations to follow in the conduct of business, taking its place alongside such venerable principles as human rights and the welfare of children. The intent of the Global Compact is to promote good by following these principles.

Third, consideration of sustainability requires I-O psychology to think about a new unit of analysis. Historically, I-O psychology has been directed to three units of analysis: individuals (micro); teams (meso); and organizations (macro). We are now on the threshold of a broader field of vision. I propose the name for this new unit of analysis is *magno* (meaning "expanded," as evidenced in the word "magnification"). We may well discover that some concepts relevant to the micro, meso, and macro units of analysis will also extend to magno. However, I believe the magno unit of analysis will also require consideration of concepts we have yet to identify. As such, sustainability will place I-O psychology in currently unchartered territory.

The names for the units of analysis are but a convenient form of verbal shorthand whose meaning is disciplinary specific. For example, what is micro for I-O psychology is not micro for cell biology. As such, questions about the unit of analysis foreshadow the fourth basis: the interdisciplinary nature of sustainability. Very complex problems will not be solved by singular disciplinary approaches. All of the contributing disciplines must learn to speak a common language. There is no analogue of United Nations interpreters for the various scientific disciplines that address issues of sustainability. Perhaps one contribution that I-O psychology can make will be to facilitate greater cohesion among the scientific disciplines. I-O psychology has been instrumental in achieving organizational change. Our talents will be tested as we seek to enable global change.

Finally, addressing issues of sustainability directly places I-O psychology in a prescriptive role. As a profession, I-O psychology has not traditionally assumed advocacy positions. There will be, by necessity, a closer link between the science and practice of I-O psychology when addressing issues of sustainability. While some may argue that science should be conducted from a position of detachment, the urgency of sustainability no longer permits the luxury of an impartial stance. The famed journalist, Edward R. Murrow, once said, "Some stories don't have two sides." Sustainability is one of them.

The editors of this book and the authors of the chapters are pioneers. It has been said that some scholars have great vision because they stand on the shoulders of giants who preceded them in their research. Pioneers are never so fortunately situated. They are the ones who must open reluctant doors and in so doing provide the shoulders to support those who follow them. We owe these scholars a debt of gratitude for their intellectual courage.

The primary value of *Green Organizations* will not be the specific chapters contained therein. Rather, the book will serve as a clarion call for I-O psychology to have a seat at the sustainability table. *Green Organizations* will spawn deeper investigations into the work psychology of sustainability. As such, the book will be a portal to the future as well as a statement of the present. I believe history will render a most positive verdict on the influence of this book in expanding the scope of I-O psychology to achieve a greater good.

Paul M. Muchinsky, Ph.D., D.Sc.
Joseph M. Bryan Distinguished Professor
University of North Carolina at Greensboro

Preface

We produced this book because we believe that industrial-organizational (I-O) psychology has tremendous opportunity—even an obligation—to reinforce and encourage responsible behaviors in and by organizations. It is unlikely that any individual, or any collective of individuals comprising an organization's decision makers, sets out with the goal of damaging the environment or making the world a worse place. However, the exigencies of business may lead to failure to think through the consequences of actions, or the belief that the benefits (e.g., profit) outweigh presumed costs of engaging in environmental sustainability. Yet just as an initial expenditure of human and operational resources (time and money) to design an effective training program pays off in the long run (employees' time spent in training is not wasted, and they learn what is necessary to work more productively), attention spent on environmental sustainability can also pay off.

We believe in the power of incremental change. The more we demonstrate ways to improve environmental sustainability, and show various beneficial outcomes, the more organizational decision makers will be open to sustainability conversations for the next round of company initiatives. We also deem that although I-O is uniquely placed to drive sustainability change in organizations, scientists and practitioners in many domains can—and do—contribute. Our book is intended for any professional who works with, or works within, organizations. We may not all be placed to design and implement sweeping change, but smaller initiatives can have incremental effects that ultimately do make a significant difference. The purpose of this book, therefore, is to provide a range of ways in which individuals and organizations can drive sustainability-related change.

Through the process of developing this book we have had the opportunity to work with some really incredible people. First, we want to acknowledge and thank Paul Muchinsky, without whom—we say with confidence—this book would not have been possible. He had the insight to bring the two of us together, and has provided mentoring and support throughout this process. Second, we would like to acknowledge the support provided by Anne Duffy, our editor at Psychology Press/Routledge, who patiently helped us navigate this incredible journey.

This book has also allowed us to meet professionals from several fields who share our enthusiasm and concern for our environment, many of whom you will encounter in the following chapters. We chose our chapter authors carefully, desiring a variety of perspectives and, above all, a focus on what professionals might actually *do* to effect change in the organizations they work in, or work with. We are delighted with the contributions from each of our authors, and hope our readers are as well. We especially hope that each reader will take from this book some practical, applicable ideas to drive change in their, or their clients', organizations.

Finally, on a personal level, we each have people we want to thank. From Ann Huffman: I want to thank my partner and husband, Bill, for his support and understanding throughout this lengthy project. I appreciate his patience with my business calls while on vacation, my early morning writing sessions, and my "distracted nature" during key times throughout this project. I also want to thank my parents for instilling some basic values that I believe have influenced the way that I see (and want to respect) our world. From Stephanie Klein: sincere thanks to my family, especially my brother David—always an inspiration—and to my friends, in Minneapolis and around the world. There are countless ways to make the world a better place, and you live many of them.

We thank you for your interest in our work, and wish you all the best in driving environmental sustainability.

About the Editors

Ann Hergatt Huffman is an Associate Professor of Psychology and Management at Northern Arizona University. Dr. Huffman received her Ph.D. in Industrial-Organizational Psychology from Texas A&M University in 2004. Prior to Texas A&M University, she worked as a principal investigator with the Walter Reed Army Research Institute-Europe.

Dr. Huffman's primary research interests include environmental sustainability issues, the work-life interface, high-stress occupations (e.g., police, military), and diversity in the workplace. She has published numerous research articles in journals such as the *Academy of Management Journal, Journal of Occupational Health Psychology, Journal of Business and Psychology, Psychological and Educational Measurement*, and *Human Resource Management*, and has written chapters in several edited books. Dr. Huffman has received grants from the Society for Human Resource Management Foundation, the Society of Industrial-Organizational Psychologist Small Grant Program and the Department of Defense to support her research. She was awarded the 2009 Northern Arizona University Most Promising New Scholar Award and was selected as a 2007–2008 Sloan Early Career Work-Family Scholar.

Stephanie R. Klein is the Solution Specialist at SHL in Minneapolis, where she has held a variety of roles since 2000, including change management, product development, assessment and training program development, and client solutions consulting. Most recently, she led post-merger transformational change within the UK and Ireland sales organization. Dr. Klein's areas of professional expertise include transformational change and the ability to balance client logistics, scientific best practices, and technology capabilities to identify solutions to client business needs. Her professional and research interests align in regard to designing effective programs and measuring outcomes, especially around efficient use of resources (including people, time, money, and the natural environment).

Dr. Klein received her M.S. and Ph.D. in Industrial-Organizational Psychology from the Pennsylvania State University in 1998 and 2006, respectively, following her B.A. in Psychology from Kenyon College. She has presented at the Society for Industrial and Organizational Psychology (SIOP) conference on topics including effective client communication, career pathing, and professional and organizational citizenship, as well as in her core area of interest, environmental sustainability. She recently contributed the article "Organizational Responsibility" to Ricky Griffith (Ed.), *Oxford bibliographies in management* (New York: Oxford University Press, 2013). Dr. Klein is a member of the American Psychological Association (APA), SIOP, and Minnesota Professionals for Psychology Applied to Work (MPPAW). She currently serves as a member of SIOP's Visibility Committee, and recently completed her rotation with the SIOP International Affairs Committee.

About the Contributors

Herman Aguinis is the Dean's Research Professor, Professor of Organizational Behavior and Human Resources, and the Founding Director of the Institute for Global Organizational Effectiveness in the Kelley School of Business, Indiana University. His research, teaching, and consulting activities address human capital acquisition, development, and deployment. Professor Aguinis is a Fellow of the Society for Industrial and Organizational Psychology (SIOP), the American Psychological Association, and the Association for Psychological Science, and currently serves as a SIOP representative to the United Nations Economic and Social Council.

Lance Andrews is the Manager of SHL's Client Solutions consulting practice, where he leads a team of I-O psychologists who serve as scientific and technical advisors to SHL's customers. His professional and research interests focus on assessment system effectiveness, legal defensibility, and innovations in assessment methodology. Mr. Andrews has an M.A. in Industrial-Organizational Psychology from Minnesota State University, Mankato, and is an active member of the Society for Industrial and Organizational Psychology, the American Psychological Association, and Minnesota Professionals for Psychology Applied to Work. His research on assessment and selection practices has been published in peer-reviewed journals and presented at annual conferences.

Marina N. Astakhova is an Assistant Professor in the Management and Marketing Department at the University of Texas at Tyler, where she teaches Strategic Human Resources Management, Organizational Behavior, and Research Methods. Her research interests include person-organization fit, heavy work investment, and organizational sustainability. Dr. Astakhova received her B.A. (2003) in Education from Volgograd Pedagogical University, Volgograd, Russia, and MBA (2007) from Kent State University, Ohio, USA. She earned her Ph.D. (2012) in Human Resources Management and Statistics from Kent State University.

Craig R. Barrett is a leading advocate for improving education in the USA and the world, and is a vocal spokesman for the value technology can provide in raising social and economic standards globally. Dr. Barrett received his B.S., M.S. and Ph.D. in Materials Science from Stanford University. He was a Fulbright Fellow at the Danish Technical University in Denmark and a NATO Postdoctoral Fellow at the National Physical Laboratory in England. Dr. Barrett joined Intel Corporation in 1974, was elected to the Board of Directors in 1992, and became Intel's fourth President in 1997, CEO in 1998, and Chairman of the Board in 2005, retiring in May 2009.

Wendy S. Becker is Associate Professor of Management at the John L. Grove College of Business, Shippensburg University, and Partner, Becker-Dale Consulting. She teaches business ethics, human resource management, and organizational behavior at the undergraduate, Master's, Ph.D., and Executive level. Dr. Becker earned her Ph.D. in Industrial-Organizational Psychology from the Pennsylvania State University. She received the 2010 Research Excellence Award from the Academy of Human Resource Development. She is an officer of METRO, the Metropolitan New York Association of Applied Psychology, and in 2010 completed a three-year editorship of *The Industrial Organizational Psychologist.*

Tara S. Behrend is an Assistant Professor of Industrial-Organizational Psychology at the George Washington University (GWU). She is the director of the Workplaces and Virtual Environments Lab at GWU; the lab's research focuses on understanding and resolving barriers to computer-mediated work effectiveness, especially in the areas of training, recruitment, and selection. Dr. Behrend received her Ph.D. in Psychology from North Carolina State University in 2009. Her research in this area has been published in journals such as *Behavior & Information Technology* and *Computers in Human Behavior,* and she is a member of the Society for Industrial and Organizational Psychology and the Academy of Management.

Mary O'Neill Berry is an Organizational Psychologist and Management Consultant specializing in international survey and evaluation research. Dr. Berry is a non-governmental organisation representative to the United Nations Economic and Social Council from the International Association of Applied Psychology. She is also outgoing Co-Chair of the Global Task Force for Humanitarian Work Psychology. She obtained her Ph.D. in Social Psychology from Columbia University, and co-authored (with Walter Reichman) a chapter in the book *Humanitarian work psychology* edited by S.C. Carr, M. MacLachlan, and A. Furnham (Palgrave Macmillan, 2012).

David E. Campbell is a Professor in Psychology at Humboldt State University. His research has covered a variety of issues in environmental psychology with emphasis on behavioral issues in environmental design. Currently he is addressing the psychological obstacles to achieving a sustainable lifestyle. Dr. Campbell received his Ph.D. in Industrial-Organizational Psychology from the University of Houston. He has prepared and taught over 20 different courses in psychology and business, and chairs or serves on a variety of university committees.

J. Elliott Campbell is Associate Professor in the School of Engineering at University of California, Merced. His research program deals with sustainable bioenergy assessment, chemical transport modeling, ecological design, and carbonyl sulfide/carbon cycle interactions. He maintains an ongoing interest in the application of atmospheric sciences to engineering.

Dr. Campbell received his Ph.D. in Environmental Engineering and Science from the University of Iowa. His professional affiliations include serving as Associate Editor for *Trends in Ecology & Evolution* and membership of the Ecological Society of America, the American Geophysical Union, and Policy Consulting: UN Environmental Programme.

Sean Cruse, Ph.D., provides research and communications support for the United Nations Global Compact. In this capacity, he conducts internal and external evaluation projects for the initiative, such as an annual study of implementation and a long-term brand analysis. He also manages a program to train affiliates in developing markets on how they can actively support implementation of corporate sustainability according to the United Nations Global Compact ten principles. Dr. Cruse received his Ph.D. in Applied Organizational Psychology from Hofstra University; his dissertation focused on individual characteristics that are predictive of success in multinational corporate leadership situations.

Raymond De Young is Associate Professor of Environmental Psychology and Planning and Co-director of the Workshop on Transitions in the School of Natural Resources and Environment, University of Michigan. His work focuses on planning for foundational sustainability by rapidly transitioning to the local and motivating environmental stewardship by drawing on intrinsic satisfaction and behavioral competence. Dr. De Young received his Bachelor's (1974) and Master's (1975) in Engineering from Stevens Institute of Technology and holds a Ph.D. (1984) in Urban, Technological and Environmental Planning from the University of Michigan. He is on the editorial review board of *Environment and Behavior* and co-author of *The localization reader: Adapting to the coming downshift.*

Erich C. Dierdorff is an Associate Professor of Management in the Driehaus College of Business at DePaul University. His research interests include examining the consequences of the green economy for both occupations and individuals, improving the effectiveness of individual- and team-level learning, examining the predictors and consequences of organizational citizenship, and studying contextual factors that impact work analysis and work design. Dr. Dierdorff received his Ph.D. in Industrial-Organizational Psychology from NC State University. He has published numerous articles in academic, industry, and popular press outlets. He has also consulted to both private and public sector organizations in areas such as strategic workforce development and selection system design.

Stephan Dilchert is an Assistant Professor of Management at the Zicklin School of Business, Baruch College, City University of New York. He teaches Master's and doctoral-level human resource management and an MBA course in sustainable organizational behavior. Dr. Dilchert received his Ph.D. in Industrial-Organizational Psychology from the University of Minnesota. His research on creativity received multiple awards, including the S. Rains Wallace Award from the Society for Industrial and Organizational Psychology (SIOP). He co-chaired the 2011 SIOP Theme Track on Environmental Sustainability and the 2012 SIOP Leading Edge Consortium on the same topic, and recently co-edited *Managing HR for environmental sustainability* (SIOP Professional Practice Series; with Susan Jackson and Deniz Ones).

Cathy L. Z. DuBois is the Interim Associate Dean of the College of Business Administration at Kent State University. Prior to her administrative position, she taught human resource management (HRM) and sustainability courses. Her sustainability-related research focuses on the transformational role of HRM in embedding sustainability within organizations, motivating sustainability-related behavior change, and employee health and well-being. Dr. DuBois received her Ph.D. in Industrial Relations from the University of Minnesota. She serves on the Association for the Advancement of Sustainability in Higher Education (AASHE) Editorial Board, as a member of the AASHE Advisory Council, and as a Sustainability Tracking, Assessment and Rating System (STARS) Technical Advisor.

David A. DuBois is an organizational psychologist with a current focus on social design for sustainability. He is the Founding Partner of the Social Design Group, a consulting company, and serves as Director of Research and Development for True Market Solutions, a new venture bringing sustainable business practices to small and medium enterprises. He also consults in sustainability issues related to employee wellness. Dr. DuBois received his Ph.D. in Industrial-Organizational Psychology from the University of Minnesota. He is adjunct faculty at Kent State University and serves as a Technical Advisor for the Association for the Advancement of Sustainability in Higher Education (AASHE).

Jacob Forsman is an Associate Consultant at PDRI. He works in the Human Capital Branch and is a part of the selection and assessment team, where he started in 2012. Prior to that, he worked with international firms conducting leadership assessment and development centers for global clients. His main research focus has been on environmental sustainability and how it relates to the modern workforce. Mr. Forsman has an M.A. in Industrial-Organizational Psychology from Minnesota State University, Mankato. He is a member of the Society for Industrial and Organizational Psychology as well as the American Psychological Association.

Ante Glavas is an Assistant Professor of Organizational Behavior at the University of Notre Dame. His current research activities are focused on the underlying mechanisms of and effects on employees when they work for socially and environmentally responsible companies. Dr. Glavas received his Ph.D. in Organizational Behavior from Case Western Reserve University where he also was on the faculty of the Organizational Behavior department. Prior to going into academia, he worked as an organizational consultant and lived in five countries, working with around 100 companies around the world. Dr. Glavas' work has always focused on using business as a force for world benefit.

Christina M. Gregory is a research consultant with North Carolina State University and the National Center for O*NET Development, where she serves as lead for new and emerging occupations and occupational taxonomy projects, and studies how green economic activities and technologies influence occupational requirements. Dr. Gregory received her Ph.D. in Industrial-Organizational Psychology from North Carolina State University. Her published research appears in *Organizational Research Methods, Journal of Business and Psychology*, and *Computers in Human Behavior*.

David A. Jones is an Associate Professor at the School of Business Administration, University of Vermont. His research focuses on organizational justice, employee volunteerism, and understanding why job seekers and employees tend to respond positively to an organization's community involvement and pro-environmental practices. Dr. Jones obtained his Ph.D. in Industrial and Organizational Psychology from the University of Calgary in 2004. In addition to conference presentations and journal publications, he works with organizations to train managers and executives in the principles of organizational justice, management, and leadership.

Phil M. Lewis is the technical officer for the National Center for O*NET Development, responsible for the program's occupational data collection, career assessment tools, and workforce development products and services. He serves as lead to Center and contract staff in completing all technical projects related to O*NET, the nation's primary source of occupational information. Mr. Lewis' work includes development of innovative data collection strategies/systems, data quality and analyses, technical assistance, training and development, and program evaluation. He was instrumental in developing the Department of Labor's Whole Person Assessment Policy, research on green occupations, and recently released *MyNextMove*, a career site designed for young adults/job seekers with literacy challenges.

Siegwart Lindenberg is a Professor of Cognitive Sociology in the Department of Sociology and the Interuniversity Center for Social Science Theory and Methodology (ICS), University of Groningen, as well as the Tilburg Institute for Behavioral Economics Research, both in the Netherlands. He co-founded the ICS and is a member of the Royal Netherlands Academy of Arts and Sciences. Dr. Lindenberg received his Ph.D. from Harvard University. His interests lie in the development, test and application of theories of social rationality that deal with the influence of the social environment on norms, cooperative behavior, and self-regulation, and their relevance for governance.

Rodney L. Lowman is Distinguished Professor in the Organizational Psychology Programs, California School of Professional Psychology at Alliant International University, and President of Lowman & Richardson/Consulting Psychologists, both in San Diego. He is an internationally recognized authority on professional ethics, career assessment, and work dysfunctions. A Ph.D. graduate of Michigan State University with specializations in Industrial-Organizational (I-O) and Clinical Psychology, Dr. Lowman is a Fellow of American Psychological Association (APA) Divisions 12 (clinical), 13 (consulting) and 14 (I-O) and is a Diplomate of the American Board of Assessment Psychology. He is Past President of the Society of Psychologists in Management and the Society of Consulting Psychology, and has held a variety of positions in the APA.

Megan C. Lytle is completing her Ph.D. in Counseling Psychology at Seton Hall University with a concentration in multicultural counseling. Her primary research interests are multicultural issues, including the impact of religion and culture on gay, lesbian, bisexual, and transgender individuals as well as their families; heterosexism; Christian privilege; ageism; and intersecting identities. Ms. Lytle obtained her M.A. in Counseling and Psychological Studies and her Ed.S. in Mental Health Counseling from Seton Hall University. She recently completed an internship with the International Association of Applied Psychology, a non-governmental organization accredited at the United Nations. She has co-authored two chapters on industrial and organizational psychology.

Gary Niekerk is currently the Director, Global Citizenship in Intel's Corporate Affairs organization, where he works on corporate strategy related to sustainability, stakeholder management and creating shared value. Prior leadership roles in his 18 years at Intel include Regional Environmental Health & Safety Director, HR Communications Manager, and External Affairs Manager. Mr. Niekerk has a Bachelor of Science degree in Occupational Safety and Health from Montana Tech of the University of Montana, and a Master of Science degree in Industrial Hygiene from Texas A&M University. He is an accomplished speaker with expertise in integrating corporate responsibility into the business.

Jennifer J. Norton is a Research Consultant affiliated with North Carolina State University and the National Center for O*NET Development. She has worked on O*NET projects for more than 12 years and has researched areas including work task content, occupational taxonomy issues, high-growth industries, new and emerging technologies, occupational-specific tools and technologies, and cross-occupational work activities. Ms. Norton received an M.S. in Industrial and Organizational (I-O) Psychology from NC State University. She previously conducted I-O psychology research at organizations including Alcatel-Lucent, Nortel Networks, the Army Research Institute and the Naval Air Warfare Center.

Deniz S. Ones is the Hellervik Professor of Industrial Psychology and a Distinguished McKnight Professor at the University of Minnesota. She co-edited *Managing HR for environmental sustainability* (with Susan Jackson and Stephan Dilchert). She also co-chaired the 2011 Society for Industrial and Organizational Psychology (SIOP) Theme Track on Environmental Sustainability and the 2012 SIOP Leading Edge Consortium on the same topic. Dr. Ones received her Ph.D. from the University of Iowa and received numerous awards for her research, including the 1998 SIOP Ernest J. McCormick Award for Distinguished Early Career Contributions. She is a Fellow of the Association for Psychological Science and American Psychological Association Divisions 5 and 14.

Niti Pandey is an Assistant Professor of Management in the Department of Business Administration at Eastern Connecticut State University. Her research interests focus on understanding the employment relationship from the employees' perspective, specifically in terms of employee attitudes and outcomes related to teamwork and work structuring, rewards and compensation, and corporate social responsibility practices. Dr. Pandey received her Ph.D. in Human Resource Management and Industrial Relations from the University of Illinois, Urbana-Champaign, in 2008. She serves on the editorial board of the *Journal of Organizational Behavior* and is an ad hoc reviewer for the *Journal of Management.*

Walter Reichman is Vice President and Partner of OrgVitality, and Emeritus Professor of Psychology at Baruch College and the Graduate Center of the City University of New York. He is the International Association of Applied Psychology's main representative to the Economic and Social Council of the United Nations. Dr. Reichman earned his B.A. and MBA from The City College of New York and his M.S. and Ed.D. from Teachers College, Columbia University. He is a member of the Global Task Force for Humanitarian Work Psychology, and co-authored (with Mary O'Neill Berry) a chapter for *Humanitarian work psychology* edited by S.C. Carr, M. MacLachlan, and A. Furnham (Palgrave Macmillan, 2012). Dr. Reichman is a member of the American Psychological Association, Association for Psychological Science, and Society for Industrial and Organizational Psychology.

David Rivkin is a Technical Officer for the National Center for O*NET Development, where he leads projects in support of the development and dissemination of the U.S. Department of Labor's Occupational Information Network (O*NET). His work includes directing projects to develop occupational information related to the green economy for inclusion in O*NET products and tools. Mr. Rivkin also plays a critical role in national O*NET data collection programs, the development of O*NET websites and O*NET Career Exploration Tools. His work has advanced the field of whole-person, self-directed career exploration. He serves as a key liaison with government sponsors and the O*NET user community.

Deborah E. Rupp is the William C. Byham Chair in Industrial-Organizational (I-O) Psychology in the Department of Psychological Sciences at Purdue University. She has two major research areas: phenomena related to employee justice, behavioral ethics, emotions at work, and corporate social responsibility; and behavioral assessment and development. Dr. Rupp received her Ph.D. in I-O Psychology from Colorado State University. Her behavioral assessment and development research was cited in the Supreme Court proceedings for Ricci v. DeStefano et al., and was a component of the revised Guidelines and Ethical Considerations for Assessment Center Operations (2009).

Dan Sachau is a Professor of Psychology and Director of the Organizational Effectiveness Research Group (OERG) at Minnesota State University. The OERG provides human resource consulting services for local, national, and international organizations. Dr. Sachau's primary research interests include attitudes, intrinsic motivation, impression management, and athletic performance. Dr. Sachau earned a Ph.D. in Social Psychology from the University of Utah. He was the recipient of the Society for Industrial and Organizational Psychology Distinguished Teaching Award and he teaches courses in motivation, organization development, statistics, and consumer behavior.

Linda Steg is Professor of Environmental Psychology at the University of Groningen. She studies individual and corporate behaviors that affect environmental quality from a multidisciplinary perspective, including strategies and conditions for behavior change. Dr. Steg received her M.Sc. and Ph.D. in Behavioural and Social Sciences at the University of Groningen in 1991 and 1996, respectively. She is a member of the scientific board of the Groningen Energy and Sustainability Program at the University of Groningen, and is president of Division 4 (Environmental Psychology) and treasurer of Division 13 (Traffic and Transport Psychology) of the International Association of Applied Psychology. She has organized several international conferences on sustainability issues.

Kurt Strasser is the Phillip I Blumberg Professor of Law at the University of Connecticut Law School where he teaches environmental law, natural resources law, and contracts. His scholarly writing is primarily concerned with the law of corporate groups and with environmental law and policy. Professor Strasser received his B.A. (1969) and J.D. (1972, Order of the Coif) from Vanderbilt University, and earned his J.S.D. from Columbia University (1986). He is a member of the Connecticut and Tennessee bars. In addition to publications in academic journals, he was the Reporter for the Uniform Environmental Covenants Act, adopted by the National Conference of Commissioners of Uniform State Laws in 2003.

Lori Foster Thompson is Professor of Psychology and Director of NC State University's IOTech4D lab, which is devoted to research at the intersection of work, psychology, technology, and global development. Her scholarship focuses on how technology and Industrial-Organizational (I-O) Psychology can enrich and improve work addressing our world's most pressing challenges. Dr. Foster Thompson received her Ph.D. in I-O Psychology from the University of South Florida in 1999. She is a Fellow of the Association for Psychological Science and the Society for Industrial and Organizational Psychology, where she serves on the Executive Board and is a representative to the United Nations Economic and Social Council.

Meghan A. Thornton is a doctoral student at Purdue University. Her primary areas of interest are organizational fairness, which includes third-party justice, justice climate, and corporate social responsibility, the assessment center method, and cross-cultural measurement equivalence. Ms. Thornton received her B.A. from the University of Notre Dame in 2010. She currently serves as the Managing Editor for the *Journal of Management*.

Carol M. Werner is a Professor in the Psychology Department at the University of Utah, Salt Lake City. She developed their Environmental Studies and Sustainability Program and works with local administrators to develop and evaluate effective interventions for "greening" the campus. Her recycling, energy conservation, and transit use research has appeared in social and environmental psychology journals. Professor Werner earned her B.A. at Raymond College, University of the Pacific. She earned her Master's (1970) and Ph.D. (1973) in Psychology at the Ohio State University, with a specialty in Social Psychology. She is on the editorial board of the *Journal of Environmental Psychology* and an Associate Editor for *Environment and Behavior*.

Chelsea R. Willness is an Assistant Professor of Human Resources and Organizational Behavior at the Edwards School of Business, University of Saskatchewan. She is also Associate Faculty with the graduate School of Environment and Sustainability, and a Research Associate with the Community-University Institute of Social Research. Dr. Willness' research focuses on how organizations' social and environmental practices impact organizational reputation, recruiting talent, employee engagement, and consumer behavior. Dr. Willness received her Ph.D. in Industrial and Organizational Psychology from the University of Calgary in 2008. She holds two national research grants for this work through the Social Sciences and Humanities Research Council of Canada.

Part 1

Introduction to
I-O Psychology and
Environmental Sustainability

1

I-O Psychology and Environmental Sustainability in Organizations: A Natural Partnership

Stephanie R. Klein and Ann Hergatt Huffman

Industrial-organizational (I-O) psychology is extremely well positioned to facilitate environmental sustainability (ES) in organizations. I-O psychology experts (e.g., Muchinsky, 2011) have stressed, and we agree, that the nature of our mission (dealing with issues of critical relevance to business) makes our profession a natural fit to be active players to promote and support ES practices in organizations. We believe that our qualifications were established quite early in I-O psychology's history, and contend that facilitation of efficiency is one of the fundamental goals of I-O psychology. Maximum output is no longer the sole purpose of organizations, but efficiency remains critical to the practical application of I-O psychology—and also to ES in organizations. We firmly believe that it is a short, appropriate, and (pun intended) natural step to extend our attention to the efficient use of environmental resources. Efficiency is not the only driver for I-O psychology, nor is it the only avenue to ES. However, the field of I-O psychology is a bit late to the sustainability table, and therefore we have chosen, with this introduction, to help illustrate how closely linked I-O psychology and ES really are.

Although I-O psychology's link to efficiency is one component of ES related to the workplace, we contend that there are many disciplines that help guide and direct employees, organizations, and our society in achieving a sustainable environment. Other areas of I-O psychology, additional psychology fields (e.g., social, clinical), related disciplines such as management, human resources, and more distal disciplines such as law and engineering, are important to fully understand how best to effect ES change in organizations. With this in mind, we recognize the truly interdisciplinary nature of ES, and choose to include diverse perspectives.

The goal of this introductory chapter is threefold. First, we define ES as it applies to organizations, and review I-O psychology's role. Second, we provide a brief history of I-O psychology's roots in efficiency, setting the stage for I-O psychology's opportunity—even obligation—to contribute to ES in the workplace. Finally, we provide a brief introduction to the contents of this book's perspectives on effecting sustainability-related change within organizations.

DEFINING ENVIRONMENTAL SUSTAINABILITY IN ORGANIZATIONS

In order to effect sustainability-related change in organizations, we need to first understand the term "environmental sustainability" (ES) as it applies to organizations. In constructing our definition we adopted the triple bottom line approach, which measures organizational success on three criteria: people, planet, and profit. The three criteria, people, planet, and profit, are viewed as critical stakeholders in the organization's success; people typically include both employees and community, planet reflects the natural environment, and profit represents traditional shareholders. Significant attention in the literature has been given to demonstrations that successes related to the first two are not necessarily detrimental to the last, and in fact may facilitate profit (see, for example, Aguinis & Glavas, 2012, and Orlitzky, Schmidt, & Rynes, 2003). It can also be argued, for instance, that a financially sound business benefits employees and the community by facilitating economic stability.

We also incorporated the United Nations Global Compact ten principles, which provide guidance to businesses that recognize their opportunity to positively affect economies and society; three of the ten principles are specific to ES (United Nations, 2011; see Chapter 14, this book, for the list of principles). We intentionally avoid the commonly used "corporate environmental sustainability" (CES) because the term "corporate" is US-centric and limited to specific legal entities, and would thus exclude many small to medium size, international, and public sector organizations.

Additionally, we ensure that our definition incorporates multiple levels of analysis for sustainability-related action and outcomes. ES often refers to policies and actions by organizations, and also to the behaviors and attitudes of individuals within organizations. Similarly, sustainability outcomes must be evaluated for individuals, business units, and organizations, and sustainability in organizations can certainly cross levels. For example, the organization may implement initiatives to change individual eco-friendly behaviors that can reduce organization-level waste production or energy consumption.

Oskamp (2000), one of the leading contributors in the field of environmental psychology, constructed a general definition of ES as "using the world's resources in ways that will allow human beings to continue to exist on Earth with an adequate quality of life" (p. 496). Extending this definition into the workplace, as follows, we conclude:

> Environmental sustainability in the workplace is defined as measuring organizational success according to triple bottom line criteria, and acting individually and collectively in organizations to maximize effective use of natural resources, and minimize negative impact on the planet.

I-O PSYCHOLOGY'S ROLE IN ENVIRONMENTAL SUSTAINABILITY

Organizational researchers and practitioners encourage ES for many reasons, including financial benefits (e.g., Orlitzky, Schmidt, & Rynes, 2003), employee engagement (e.g., Glavas & Piderit, 2009), candidate attraction (e.g., Behrend, Baker, & Thompson, 2009), or simply because it is the right thing to do (e.g., Huffman, Watrous-Rodriguez, Henning, & Berry, 2009; Lefkowitz, 2008). We propose that because I-O psychologists are already working with and within organizations for the benefit of their (the organizations') people and processes, we are therefore uniquely placed to facilitate a range of improvements related to ES. And we certainly have the expertise to do so.

Although we accept that there are differences in opinion related to environmentally-sustainable business practices, most people will agree that while wholly eliminating consumption of natural resources is unrealistic, there is significant value in reducing waste and maximizing effective use for the resources we must consume. As good stewards of people resources, I-O psychologists have the knowledge, skills, and abilities to design programs that maximize effective use of people's time and are likely to achieve the intended purpose. We are also capable of measuring those outcomes, determining success, and, when appropriate, making adjustments to the programs to further improve effectiveness and achievement of purpose.

Sustainability implications also stem from I-O psychologists' expertise in measurement of outcomes. Organizations implement programs and initiatives for a variety of reasons related to profitability, process improvements, work quality, or new business ventures. Some of these changes to the way an organization does business have secondary outcomes beneficial to the environment. For example, a friend of one of the editors mentioned that the Fortune 500 company where she works had implemented video-based interviews in recruitment of professional staff, reserving in-person interviews for the final stages of candidate selection. The purpose in doing so was to streamline processes, because they were finding that aligning senior-level interviewers' calendars for a single-day candidate visit was adding weeks to their recruiting timeline. As a secondary and unintended side effect, the video-based interviews significantly reduced the carbon footprint associated with their recruitment efforts because fewer candidates were being flown to the company's headquarters.

ES was not the primary driver of the recruitment process change in this example; nevertheless, this is a meaningful benefit that the company should be aware of. If I-O psychologists can help organizations recognize environmental benefits that were not an intended outcome of the initiative, this will help elevate awareness of environmental effects of many business processes, and bring recognition of ES challenges to more areas of the business.

I-O PSYCHOLOGY AND EFFICIENCY

As noted earlier, facilitation of efficiency is a fundamental goal of I-O psychology. Efficiency dates back to the early days of our field (e.g., Munsterberg, 1913) and continues to play a role in how we conceptualize and measure productivity (Pritchard, 1992). Attention has expanded further to include efficient use of operational resources—for example, by demonstrating return on investment of funds spent on I-O psychology-driven programs (Gale, 2012). A dictionary definition tells us that efficiency is "performing or functioning in the best possible manner with the least waste of time and effort; having and using requisite knowledge, skill, and industry; competent; capable" (http://dictionary.com). Although the goals of organizations have evolved beyond the early 20th-century focus on maximum outputs alone, efficiency remains fundamental to the business benefits of many areas of I-O practice. For example, the Society of Human Resource Management (SHRM) Foundation's 2006 *Effective practice guidelines on employee engagement* lists productivity and efficiency as among the most common performance measures linked to employee engagement surveys (Vance, 2006).

Many of the programs I-O psychology practitioners help organizations implement are motivated at least in part by efficiency, including training and employee selection. For example, organizations invest in management training so that managers can perform more effectively, improving management of employees who should in turn perform more effectively in their own jobs. I-O psychologists are able to ensure such management training programs are well designed and well implemented, maximizing outcomes of the program investments (financial costs and managers' time). I-O psychologists are also able to help organizations measure these outcomes, providing objective metrics of improved effectiveness.

Efficiency is similarly embedded throughout the motivation for and design of pre-employment assessment programs. In 2010, the U.S. Department of Homeland Security set out an action plan as part of the Presidential Hiring Reform initiative. Their objectives included improved applicant and hiring manager satisfaction, decreased time to hire, and increased applicant quality; efficiency is both explicit and implicit in these goals. I-O psychologists often implement validated pre-employment assessments to measure or predict designated job requirements (e.g., ability and motivations). As good stewards of people resources, those practitioners will design an assessment program for maximum efficiency not only for the organization's human resources staff (e.g., ease of administration, ease of accessing results) and hiring managers (e.g., more qualified new hires may require less training time), but also for an efficient applicant experience (e.g., completion ease and time). Lahti (2011) provides a case study for retail organization Swarovski, whose assessment system led to significant reductions in both time and financial costs attached to employee turnover, as well as notable improvements in sales performance and in new hires' time to proficiency.

To conclude our brief overview of the link between I-O psychology and ES in organizations, we present two broad areas of environmentally-sustainable behaviors linked to I-O psychology's grounding in efficiency. First, one of the most common behaviors related to ES is *waste reduction.*

In the workplace, reuse and recycling of materials is an efficient mechanism for both small-scale (e.g., daily office) and large-scale work tasks (e.g., manufacturing; Bjorklund & Finnveden, 2007). Recycling is becoming a norm in all aspects of life, including within organizations. Analyses have shown that although recycling is one of the lower impact ES behaviors, it still provides substantial savings to organizations. For example, in 2006, Guardian Automotive (Ligonier Plant) recycled over 13,000 tons of manufacturing products and saved over $360,000 (U.S. Environmental Protection Agency). This is just one example of using recycling as a means of an efficient management practice.

The second area of potential behavior change is *energy consumption.* It makes sense to have business practices designed to save money through decreased energy consumption. For example, telecommuting has become a more common working strategy for many organizations. Telework, or telecommuting, is a flexible work arrangement that allows workers to conduct all or some of their work at a location away from the main worksite. Telecommuting has shown to not only have positive effects on job performance (Gajendran & Harrison, 2007), but it also can provide cost savings to the organization due to decreased operating costs (U.S. General Services Administration, 2006); both of these outcomes suggest that telecommuting is an efficient business practice. Returning to our earlier anecdotal example of the Fortune 500 company that implemented video-based interviewing, the only people who traveled to the company's headquarters had a much higher probability of being hired, so there were fewer wasted trips and the airline fuel was consumed to better purpose.

We should note that our ideas are not new. Many scientists and practitioners have stressed that ES makes good business sense (e.g., Campbell & Campbell, 2005; Molina-Azorin, Claver-Cortes, Lopez-Gamero, & Tari, 2009; Ones & Dilchert, 2012). We assert that efficiency is a critical aspect of both organizational productivity and ES. Therefore, environmentally-sustainable behaviors contribute to the organization's bottom line. Moreover, there are many opportunities to influence organizations to change relative to ES, related to efficiency and also benefiting from the expertise in several disciplines with organizational experience. I-O psychologists have a central role to play in guiding organizations toward improved ES, and—along with other professionals working within organizations—will benefit from multiple disciplines and perspectives in learning how they may help drive those changes.

AN INTERDISCIPLINARY APPROACH TO DRIVING ENVIRONMENTAL SUSTAINABILITY CHANGE IN ORGANIZATIONS

The goal of this book is to present a diverse interdisciplinary review of ES issues germane to I-O psychology. We also recognize that meaningful long-term change rarely "just happens." Rather, individuals and organizations must plan and execute to effect change. To attain our goal we have collected a set of writings from experts in the fields of I-O psychology, social psychology, environmental psychology, management, human resources, engineering, ethics, law, and other related fields. In the following pages, we provide a broad overview of chapter topics and how they contribute to the goals of this book.

Introduction to I-O Psychology and Environmental Sustainability

The authors in this introductory part of the book provide a general overview of key topics in support of our proposed convergence between I-O psychology and ES. Following this chapter (Chapter 1), the authors focus on environmental psychology, ethics, and engineering, providing important context for the rest of the book.

In Chapter 2, Raymond De Young provides an overview of environmental psychology. The author, whose training is in technological and environmental planning, begins with a brief history of the field, noting its relevance for conservation behavior and human-environment interaction. He presents the reasonable person model as an important framework for creation of interventions related to environmental stewardship behaviors; this framework also allows behavior change evaluation metrics that distinguish short-term and long-term effects. De Young also introduces a big problem/small experiment approach, advising that it is possible to begin solving large problems on a smaller scale.

Next, in Chapter 3, clinical and I-O psychologist Rodney L. Lowman explores the ethical values of I-O psychology and consulting psychology as they relate to ES. He reviews the values and ethics code of the American Psychological Association, noting its prohibition against psychologists' practice outside their areas of competence. Lowman then proposes several areas of competence relevant to sustainability issues, including program creation and evaluation, conflict management, decision making, work design, and creation of ethical organizational climates. He also reminds the field of the ethical obligation to contribute pro bono or reduced-fee services to good causes, suggesting that pro-environment and eco-friendly non-profits would be excellent recipients.

The introductory part of the book ends with Chapter 4, engineering perspectives from David E. Campbell (I-O psychology) and J. Elliott Campbell (environmental engineering and science). They note that physical and biological scientists have been developing a description of environmental crises, and studying the behaviors leading to environmental destruction. At the same time, social and behavioral scientists have been refining theories of what motivates people and elicits change. However, very little effort has been expended on integrating the two to understand how one might motivate attitude and behavior changes toward ES. Campbell and Campbell provide perspectives on how environmental engineering and I-O psychology have in the past, and can in the future, worked more effectively together to include human factors in sustainable design projects.

Theory and Methods to Understand Environmental Sustainability in Organizations

This next part of the book provides readers with additional context to understand ES in organizations. The authors discuss key theoretical frameworks that help explain motivation, behavior, and how ES is understood, and they introduce methods for measurement of behaviors and outcomes.

First, in Chapter 5, Niti Pandey, Deborah E. Rupp, and Meghan A. Thornton use their psychology and business backgrounds in developing their argument that environmental issues have become highly moralized, and, therefore, in further need of a more comprehensive examination. Using a psychological lens to investigate ES introduces issues (e.g., perceptual, moral, and ethical) that extend beyond how the environment was once conceptualized in organizations. Based on this thesis, the authors discuss the moral motivational space surrounding two questions. The first is whether ES is sufficiently distinct from the broader domain of corporate social responsibility to warrant its own research literature. The second is how organizational acts of ES influence employee attitudes and behaviors.

In Chapter 6, Siegwart Lindenberg (sociology) and Linda Steg (behavioral and social sciences) propose that experts need to provide organizations with a theory-based multi-faceted strategy to guide organizational players to engage in environmentally-friendly policies and practices. They further propose that due to the complexity that makes up organizational systems (e.g., interdependent corporations, individual actors), it is necessary to identify the key actors, and develop a sound behavioral theory for how these actors behave and interact with each other and other organizational players. They further provide perspectives on adoption of environmentally-friendly policies by market democracy organizations. Goal-framing theory is presented as a microfoundation for understanding factors that influence ES-related behaviors.

Chapter 7 addresses measurement of environmentally-sustainable employee behaviors in the workplace. In this chapter, I-O psychologists Deniz S. Ones and Stephan Dilchert provide an overview of ES in work settings, with a focus on individual behavior. Based on meta-analytic evidence, they demonstrate that the nomological net for corporate social responsibility and ES are distinct. Ones and Dilchert maintain that human resources of organizations are fundamentally at the core of ensuring ES behaviors happen. They describe the relationships between employee green behaviors and constructs related to employee engagement and job performance. These conceptual linkages highlight the relevance of employee green behaviors for task performance, contextual performance, and avoidance of counterproductive work behaviors.

In Chapter 8, the final chapter in the theory and methods part of the book, Lance Andrews, Stephanie R. Klein, Jacob Forsman, and Dan Sachau use their training in I-O psychology (and social psychology for Sachau) to provide an applied perspective on how common business practices can yield environmentally-sustainable outcomes. Based on research and organizational case studies, they discuss costs and benefits of technology-based I-O psychology and human resources practices. Their chapter provides examples and guidance on how organizations might calculate environmental return on investment (ROI), in addition to the more common financial ROI, for a variety of organizational initiatives.

Individuals and Organizations

The next part of the book, "Individuals and Organizations," applies more traditional I-O perspectives to ES-related challenges such as organizational design, attitudes, behavior change, and candidate attraction. It ends with a chapter focusing on a Fortune 500 company that has successfully embedded ES throughout the organization.

First, in Chapter 9, Wendy S. Becker draws on her training in I-O psychology to apply I-O principles to the design of green, socially responsible, sustainable organizations with employees as stakeholders and a focus on long-term returns on investment. This sustainable approach is in contrast to short-term profit methods that position both human and environmental resources as expendable commodities. She also links supply chain management terminology (e.g., zero inventory, flexibility through postponement, free riding, supply chain surplus, outsourcing, and the bullwhip effect) to I-O principles, demonstrating how alignment between the two fields can help create truly sustainable organizations.

In Chapter 10, Cathy L. Z. DuBois, Marina N. Astakhova, and David A. DuBois provide a business and I-O perspective via their framework, which describes how organizations can initiate environmentally-focused change. They suggest that effective change requires a whole-systems perspective incorporating strong executive support, sufficient resources, and engagement of employees at all levels, to accommodate the concerns of multiple stakeholders. Their chapter applies several theories to address how organizations can support and facilitate the attitude and behavior changes necessary for successful implementation and maintenance of ES initiatives, with the goal of empowering employees towards self-determined environmentally-sustainable behavior. To illustrate their framework, the authors provide several examples of organizations that have successfully embedded sustainability into their cultures.

In Chapter 11, Carol M. Werner provides a social psychological perspective on inducing long-term change in support of pro-environmental practices. Werner's model proposes that organizations need to instill change by facilitating processes that create behaviors that become habitual, and/or enjoyable. Although she stresses that there are many approaches to behavior change, she presents four core principles to guide organizations to achieve ES. These principles include the treatment of change as a process, the physical environment that can facilitate or inhibit change, the social environment, and the negative effects of incentives. She draws on applied research to illustrate how these principles can be actualized in organizations.

Next, I-O psychologists Chelsea R. Willness and David A. Jones examine the impact of environmentally-sustainable business practices on recruitment outcomes. They draw from signaling theory to examine factors mediating the relationship between environmentally-sustainable practices and positive recruitment outcomes. Willness and Jones propose that job seekers have limited information concerning specifics about a job, and therefore use signals to help interpret what little information they do possess. Their chapter also provides a research agenda with insightful suggestions for further research to inform how ES can affect organizational recruitment practices. The authors conclude with practical implications, based on the research and theory, for organizations' recruiting strategies.

The final chapter of this part of the book (Chapter 13) is written by Craig R. Barrett, the retired CEO/Chairman of the Board of Intel Corporation, and Gary Niekerk, the current Intel Director of Corporate Citizenship. This chapter provides a case study from a large and successful organization that has won numerous awards based on their environmentally-sustainable business practices. It illustrates the importance of embedding ES into the culture of the organization. The authors describe Intel's program of "design for the environment," which ensures that environmental improvements are integrated in manufacturing and technology processes, in addition to their global efforts to create energy-efficient technologies to address our world's environmental challenges.

I-O Psychology and Environmental Sustainability for Tomorrow's Workforce

The final part of the book focuses on workplace ES at a more macro level. Perspectives include international efforts, technology as a facilitator, how legislation might be best leveraged, and the new green economy. The book closes with suggestions of how ES can drive change for I-O practice.

The first chapter (Chapter 14) of this part of the book was written by Walter Reichman, Mary O'Neill Berry, Sean Cruse, and Megan C. Lytle. These authors, trained in psychology (organizational and clinical), also have an impressive collective resume in international and global issues related to ES. In their chapter, the authors contend that ES is a global issue and requires the worldwide commitment of all corporations, local and national governments, and organizations. They describe the efforts of major international organizations and the largest international psychological organization to promote ES in organizations. This chapter includes some of the key guidelines (e.g., the Ten Principles of the United Nations

Global Compact), which have been (and can be) used to guide businesses in their environmentally-sustainable practices.

In Chapter 15, I-O psychologists Tara S. Behrend and Lori Foster Thompson focus on the influence that technology has on organizations' ES practices. They propose that technology can be used to facilitate more sustainable practices, and they provide suggestions to assist employers and workers to successfully implement, manage, and engage in a host of virtual, "green ICT" work practices. They note that I-O psychologists can ensure that these practices are properly designed to allow for their effectiveness, acceptance, and sustained usage. The authors conclude with a discussion on how I-O psychology can help support impoverished regions of the world in their emersion into technology and ES.

With Kurt Strasser's training in law, Chapter 16 provides a legal perspective for environmentally-sustainable business practices. In this chapter, the author proposes that legislation for business claims of environmentalism focus on accuracy of information, rather than attempting to define what ES is. He argues that businesses need to go beyond regulation, and develop their own initiative and commitment to environmental practices. This commitment should be facilitated by policy requiring that business disclosure be truthful and accurate. Consumers have a right to expect accurate environmental claims from organizations, and it is this expectation that needs to be regulated. The chapter includes a review of what companies are currently doing in regard to business environmentalism and how successful they are at the task at hand.

Erich C. Dierdorff, Jennifer J. Norton, Christina M. Gregory, David Rivkin, and Phil M. Lewis all have extensive background in I-O psychology and in the U.S. Department of Labor's O*NET Resource Center. Chapter 17 provides an overview of the work that the U.S. Department of Labor is undertaking in identifying occupational categories for green jobs. In this chapter, the authors describe the new green economy and how this economy has affected different occupations, including changes in demand for existing occupations, new requirements in roles that are adapting to the green economy, and new occupations. They conclude their chapter with a look at the needs and expectations of the future green job economy.

The closing chapter (Chapter 18) is written by Herman Aguinis (I-O psychology) and Ante Glavas (organizational behavior). The authors draw on their years of international and national experience in corporate social responsibility to provide an alternate yet complementary perspective of our conceptualization of I-O psychology and ES. Whereas we stress that I-O psychology can effect sustainability-related change, Aguinis and Glavas suggest that ES can be a driver of change for I-O psychology. They stress that I-O psychology has two gaps in the field—a science-practice gap and a micro-macro gap—and advise that ES can provide insight on how to narrow these gaps in our field.

CONCLUSION

Molina-Azorin et al. (2009) assert that organizations need to visualize environmental issues in terms of resource productivity and focus on "the opportunity costs of pollution (wasted resources, wasted effort, and diminished product value to the customer)" (p. 1082). I-O psychologists are experts at organizational efficiency. A core goal of this book is to remind our profession that our roots seep deeply into science-based management and that we are skilled in efficient resource utilization, outcome measurement, and change management—all key components to understanding and managing organizational ES.

In this introductory chapter, we have focused primarily on efficiency, just one area in which I-O psychologists contribute to facilitate workplace ES. The authors in this book emphasize how other skills allow I-O psychology to be instrumental in effecting sustainability-related change. It is our hope that this book provides readers with unique insights into how I-O psychologists can integrate ES into our practice and research agenda. We also hope to provide non-I-O consultants and managers with actionable ideas for effecting sustainability-related change into their organizations. And, ultimately, we hope that the ideas that are presented in this book will be built on and expanded in a way that can strengthen the partnership between I-O psychology and ES.

REFERENCES

Aguinis, H., & Glavas, A. (2012). What we know and don't know about corporate social responsibility: A review and research agenda. *Journal of Management, 38,* 932–968.

Behrend, T. S., Baker, B. A., & Thompson, L. F. (2009). Effects of pro-environmental recruiting messages: The role of organizational reputation. *Journal of Business and Psychology, 24,* 341–350.

Bjorklund, A. E., & Finnveden, G. (2007). Life cycle assessment of a national policy proposal—the case of a Swedish waste incineration tax. *Waste Management, 27*, 1046–1058.

Campbell, J. E., & Campbell, D. E. (2005). Eco-I-O psychology? Expanding our goals to include sustainability. *The Industrial-Organizational Psychologist, 43*, 23–28.

Gajendran, R. S., & Harrison, D. A. (2007). The good, the bad, and the unknown about telecommuting: Meta-analysis of psychological mediators and individual consequences. *Journal of Applied Psychology, 92*, 1524–1541. doi:10.1037/0021-9010.92.6.1524

Gale, S.F. (2012). Putting a dollar value on talent. *Workforce*, July. Retrieved July 11, 2012, from http://www.workforce.com/article/20120709/NEWS02/120709967/putting-a-dollar-value-on-talent#

Glavas, A., & Piderit, S. K. (2009). How does doing good matter? Effects of corporate citizenship on employees. *Journal of Corporate Citizenship, 36*, 51–70.

Huffman, A. H., Watrous-Rodriguez, K. M., Henning, J. B., & Berry, J. (2009, October). "Working" through environmental issues: The role of the I/O psychologist. *The Industrial-Organizational Psychologist, 47*, 27–35.

Lahti, K. (2011, November). You've got talent, but for what? *Talent Management, 36–39*. Retrieved December 12, 2012, from http://www.shl.com/assets/11-2011-Talent-Management-Youve-Got-Talent.pdf

Lefkowitz, J. (2008). Explaining the values of organizational psychology to match the quality of its ethics. *Journal of Organizational Behavior, 29*, 1–15.

Molina-Azorin, J. F., Claver-Cortes, E., Lopez-Gamero, M. D., & Tari, J. J. (2009) Green management and financial performance: A literature review. *Management Decision, 47*, 1080–1100.

Muchinksy, P. (2011). *Psychology applied to work* (10th ed.). Summerfield, NC: Hypergraphic Press.

Munsterberg, H. (1913). *Psychology and industrial efficiency*. Boston, MA: Houghton Mifflin Company.

Ones, D. S., & Dilchert, S. (2012). Environmental sustainability at work: A call to action. *Industrial and Organizational Psychology: Perspectives on Science and Practice, 5*(4), 444–466.

Orlitzky, M., Schmidt, F. L., and Rynes, S. L. (2003). Corporate social and financial performance: A meta-analysis. *Organization Studies, 24*, 403–441.

Oskamp, S. (2000). A sustainable future for humanity? How psychology can help. *American Psychologist, 55*, 496–508. doi: 10.1037//0003-066X.55.5.496

Pritchard, R. D. (1992). Organizational productivity. In M. D. Dunnette & L. M. Hough (Eds.), *Handbook of industrial and organizational psychology* (2nd ed., Vol. 2, pp. 444–471). Palo Alto, CA: Consulting Psychologists Press.

United Nations (2011). *Overview of the UN global compact*. Retrieved March 23, 2012, from http://www.unglobalcompact.org/AboutTheGC/index.html

U.S. Department of Homeland Security (2010, August). *2010 DHS hiring reform action plan*. Retrieved December 12, 2012, from http://www.dhs.gov/xlibrary/assets/mgmt/department-of-homeland-security-hiring-reform-action-plan.pdf

U.S. General Services Administration (2006, May). *Task 7: Recommendations to assist cost recovery/ROI strategies and budget planning*. Retrieved from http://www.gsa.gov/graphics/ogp/Task7CostRecoveryROIStrategieswAltTags_508.ppt

Vance, R. J. (2006). *SHRM Foundation's effective practice guidelines: Employee engagement and commitment: A guide to understanding, measuring and increasing engagement in your organization*. Retrieved December 12, 2012, from http://www.shrm.org/about/foundation/research/documents/1006employeeengagementonlinereport.pdf

2

Environmental Psychology Overview

Raymond De Young

Environmental psychology is a field of study that examines the inter-relationship between environments and human affect, cognition, and behavior (Bechtel & Churchman, 2002; Gifford, 2007; Stokols & Altman, 1987). The field has always been concerned with both built and natural environments with early research emphasizing the former (Stokols, 1995; Sundstrom, Bell, Busby, & Aasmus, 1996). However, as environmental sustainability issues became of greater concern to society in general, and the social sciences in particular, the field increased its focus on how humans affect, and are affected by, natural environments. The goals of this chapter are to introduce environmental psychology, explain how it emerged from the study of human-environment interactions and note how it has redefined what we mean by the terms *nature* and *environment*. Special note is made of humans as information-processing creatures and the implications this has for encouraging reasonable behavior under trying environmental circumstances. Finally, two pragmatic approaches to bringing out the best in people are presented.

In an effort to promote durable living on a finite planet, environmental psychology develops, and empirically validates, practical intervention strategies regardless of where the foundational science resides. Thus, the field considers as not useful the sometimes artificial distinction among the fields of cognitive, evolutionary, and social psychology. In so doing, environmental psychology incorporates the work of individuals who might not otherwise initially be identified with the field (consider, for instance, Cone & Hayes, 1980; Geller, Winett, & Everett, 1982; Katzev & Johnson, 1987).

The same integrative approach applies to the level of analysis and scale of intervention. The field explores individual and collective level behavior and seeks interventions that work at all of these scales. In fact, this is one of the strengths of the field. It has always been problem-oriented, using, as needed, the theories, methods, and findings of related disciplines (e.g., anthropology, biology, ecology, psychology, sociology) and the professional schools (e.g., education, public health, social work, urban planning). In this pragmatism, environmental psychology well symbolized one of Kurt Lewin's better known quotes, "There is nothing so practical as a good theory" (1951, p. 169).

More recently, the applied fields of conservation psychology (Clayton & Myers, 2009; Saunders & Myers, 2003) and ecopsychology (Doherty, 2011) have emerged to understand and resolve issues related to human aspects of conservation of the natural world. The former initiative merges the insights, principles, theories, and methods used by conservation biology and a wide range of psychology subfields. The latter initiative is also broad-based and includes a therapeutic approach to enhancing people-environment interactions and personal wellbeing. Both maintain a rich network of researchers and practitioners who share the goals of creating durable behavior change at multiple levels, promoting an environmental ethic and maintaining harmonious human-nature relationships.

Today the fields of environmental psychology, conservation psychology and ecopsychology are helping society to form an affirmative response to emerging environmental and natural resource constraints. This is a grand challenge since the response must plan for, motivate, and maintain environmental stewardship behavior through a period of significant energy and resource descent. The initial focus is to pre-familiarize ourselves with living well within the limits of natural ecosystems (De Young & Princen, 2012).

WHAT IS MEANT BY ENVIRONMENT

Over its nearly half-century of research and practice, the field of environmental psychology has expanded both the definition of what is nature and what is environment. The field still studies to good effect built settings (e.g., wayfinding in subways systems, navigating in distracting environments). But as its research interests and methods matured, the field found the distinction between built and natural settings often unhelpful and unnecessarily limiting.

Clearly, urban settlements devoid of all forms of nature, if they ever existed, are infrequent to the point of being irrelevant to most people. Likewise, pristine wilderness, untouched by human hands, is rare. Environmental psychology understands that humans know nature, in its many forms, as intermixed with built elements. This melding can be seen in urban parks and waterfronts, zoos and aquaria, backyard and meditation gardens, exurban bikeways and wetland boardwalks, fence-lined country lanes and blazed mountain trails. Nature is nearby and viewable from almost any window. Even when not nearby, nature usually contains signs that others have been there before.

Here too is another discovery of environmental psychology. Something counts as nature even if it does not contain DNA. The wind through the leaves, the flow of water, the smell of a spring rainstorm, moonrises, and ocean waves are all experienced as part of nature and have potential psychological effect.

But a perhaps more fundamental insight of environmental psychology comes from its broad conceptualization of what constitutes an environment. It borrows from cognitive psychology the notion that all environments are patterns of information and that people are fundamentally information-processing organisms, deeply motivated to remain informationally, and thus environmentally, competent. In their pursuit of goals, humans need both to understand current environmental patterns and to continuously expand their proficiency by exploring and learning from new patterns.

The shift here is subtle. The focus is not on specific groups, single personality traits or particular psychological mechanisms. Rather, environmental psychology explores the environmental context of human behavior and wellbeing. This context might be physical (e.g., home, office, park), social, conceptual (e.g., design, narrative), vast or small. It might be known from direct experience or from becoming pre-familiarized with something not yet present, something that might be experienced only indirectly though stories or simulations. The latter is possible because one of the astonishing effects of our information-processing capability is our being able to feel at home in a place we do not yet inhabit.

One additional aspect of the subtle shift in perspective reveals a key premise of environmental psychology. To understand behavior we need to study more than just the context of that behavior (i.e., the environment) and more than just the traits and goals of the individual or group whose behavior is of interest. We can understand, and perhaps influence, behavior more effectively by studying the interaction of context and traits, environmental affordances and cognitive inclinations, settings, and goals. It is in the interactions that we can understand the origins of reasonable (and unreasonable) human behavior.

ENCOURAGING AND SUPPORTING REASONABLE PEOPLE

Unreasonable behavior (e.g., being irresponsible, uncooperative, intolerant, unpleasant) seems to be proliferating in fast-paced, high-consuming industrialized societies. One might conclude that such behavior is humans' standard operating condition. Fortunately, many years of psychological research shows this conclusion to be wrong. Environmental psychologists Rachel Kaplan and Stephen Kaplan suggest that the difference between reasonable and infuriatingly unreasonable behavior may be partly explained by the environments in which people find themselves. To this observation that the context of behavior makes a difference, they note two other key facts: that humans have a remarkable facility to process information, and that information and affect are in a close adaptive relationship with each other. Taken together, these provide the basic premise of the reasonable person model—namely, that people are more likely to be reasonable and cooperative in environments that support their informational needs (Kaplan and Kaplan, 2003, 2009).

Before outlining these informational needs, it is useful to make clear what is meant by information. Information, much more than money or social interaction, is the foundation of our lives. As Kaplan, R. (1995) points out, humans are information-based organisms: "… we love it and hate it, we collect it and trade it, we hide it and leak it, we are overwhelmed by it and addicted to it. Information is central to our functioning, to our personal sense of esteem, to our interdependencies, to the basis for distinguishing ourselves from others—for better and for worse." Information surrounds us. While much information comes from spoken and written material, the environment in all its many forms conveys vast amounts of information (e.g., the behavior of others, the array of objects we encounter, the events that unfold).

The reasonable person model focuses on the interrelationships among three major domains of human informational needs. First is the need for *building mental models*. These models address the simultaneous human needs for understanding and exploration. The way in which the environment supports or hinders this need affects everything from behavioral competence to psychological wellbeing. The second domain is about *becoming effective* and also includes two elements: being clear-headed enough to be capable of responding appropriately to the profusion of information around us, and the sense of competence that comes from knowing what may be possible and how to act. Being confused or incompetent does not bring out the best in people; thus restoring and maintaining mental vitality and proficiency is essential to supporting reasonable behavior. Finally, there is the need for *meaningful action*, a need to be an active part of the world around us, to be respected for our role and to do things that matter in the long run. While closely aligned with our inclinations to be helpful, this need can also be fulfilled by the many behaviors where the social relevance may not be obvious or immediate. Each domain can be explored independently. However, as a practical matter they are highly interrelated. Consider how hard it is to take meaningful action without first understanding the situation, how being clear-headed can make our behaviors much more effective, and how exploring natural settings can restore our mental vitality.

Model Building

A mental model is a highly simplified version of reality that humans store in their head and use to make sense of things, to plan, to evaluate possibilities, in short to manage all everyday functioning. These portable models store the knowledge gained from the many experiences people have and are the basis for making decisions. They are foundational to all knowing and acting and people find it useful to be constantly building and testing them against reality. One element of model building, understanding, can be achieved through formal learning. More commonly, however, understanding is gained through direct and indirect experience. The other element of model building, exploration, is about moving about in a space or a concept to learn more about it. Such exploration can take place in the physical world, or virtually, or entirely in one's mind. It can be about the present or about a future time and place. Team-based problem solving and brainstorming are group-based exploration although the models built are contained in the heads of the individual team members; this seems like an obvious observation until we realize that the stored models may not be identical, thus affecting group behavior. Satisfying the need for exploration allows humans to expand their mental models, increasing their understanding.

Being an information-based animal, our survival requires the mental capability to recognize what is happening and to predict what might happen next while there is still time to take suitable action. This need places a high priority on exploration. Yet, while we are motivated to learn more about the environment, we must never go so far that our mental models no longer sufficiently understand the situation. While we are eager to explore, so too are we quick to return to what is familiar. Simultaneously, we need to make sense of our present situation while also acquiring, at our own pace, information that is relevant to our current and future concerns. Thus exploration, if pursued close to the familiar, becomes a powerful means of expanding our understanding.

One of the fascinating aspects of human nature builds upon the role familiarity plays in our cognition. In conversations about behavior change, it is often claimed that people anchor to the status quo and are immune to scientific arguments. One might infer that, if true, this would pose a serious problem for behavior change efforts. After all, to deal with the urgent environmental problems being faced, people may be called upon to make far-reaching changes away from the status quo, toward an unfamiliar life pattern, some promoted by abstract scientific arguments alone. Fortunately, however, the issue here is not a status quo bias but a familiarity bias. A familiarity bias is based on our mental model of a situation and thus mirrors the strengths and weaknesses of our current understanding. This provides great hope since mental models can be formed and altered in a large variety of ways.

Becoming Effective

This domain is about the need to be clear-headed and competent so as to be able to achieve our goals. It is here that we can clearly see the constraints on and limits of human information processing.

First and foremost, becoming effective is about achieving clarity in our thinking by maintaining our mental vitality. This is a formidable challenge since handling all the information we crave, as well as dealing with the onslaught of unbidden information, easily leads to being overwhelmed and mentally exhausted. Yet, while some environments can cause a loss of mental vitality, others can provide for its restoration.

Attention restoration theory (Kaplan, S., 1995, 2001) explains this apparent contradiction. This theory builds on the distinction between two forms of attention called fascination and directed attention. The former, fascination, is involuntary attention; it requires no significant effort and is not under volitional control. Fascination is experienced when, out of innate interest or curiosity, certain objects or processes effortlessly engage our thoughts. William James provided a list of such innately fascinating stimuli: "strange things, moving things, wild animals, bright things, pretty things, blows, blood, etc. etc. etc." (1892/1985). The potential significance of such objects argues for why this form of attention does not fatigue; it is adaptive that such things continue to rivet our attention even if encountered repeatedly.

In contrast to fascination, the capacity to direct attention requires major effort. This directed mental effort is essential for remaining effective in the many situations that lack fascination. In order to contemplate important yet uninspiring objects and processes, we must inhibit competing or peripheral yet perhaps more interesting thoughts and stimuli. Such inhibition allows us to carry out an important plan despite the presence of diversions, listen closely while beset by noise, and feel compassion for and help others despite our own unmet needs. The adaptive significance of directed attention is enormous. Behaviorally, the ability to hold the immediate environment at bay permits humans to insert their own intentions between stimulus and response. Cognitively, this ability allows us to concurrently run multiple models in our head without undue confusion, contemplate alternate explanations for an observation and consider multiple responses.

Unfortunately the capacity to voluntarily direct our attention is finite. When under constant demand our ability to control the inhibitory process tires, resulting in a condition called directed attention fatigue. This mental state greatly reduces our effectiveness. The signs of this mental fog are many: irritability and impulsivity that results in regrettable utterances, impatience that has us quickly jumping to ill-formed conclusions, and distractibility that results in tasks being left unknowingly unfinished (De Young, 2010).

In order to restore the capacity to direct attention, it is necessary to seek out environments that require little of this finite resource or that use other means of maintaining mental focus. Thus recovery can be achieved by pursuing activities that rely heavily on involuntary fascination. As fascination is engaged, the need for directed attention is greatly reduced, which thereby allows for its recovery. Thus an essential feature of restorative environments is their ability to elicit fascination. In principle there are many types of restorative environments. However, research has repeatedly highlighted the role of time spent in natural settings in the effort to remain mentally effective (Berman, Jonides, & Kaplan, 2008, Frumkin 2001, Herzog, Black, Fountaine, & Knotts, 1997, Kaplan & Kaplan, 1989, 2005).

Tending to our mental vitality is essential for achieving clear-headedness. Becoming fully effective, however, requires a second element, which involves achieving and maintaining a sense of competence. Feeling competent depends on knowing how things work in the world, knowing what is possible and appropriate, and having the skills that match the challenges we face. While there is a contentment from being competent, we are also intrinsically motivated by the process of improving and extending the competence we already have.

Meaningful Action

Information can be a source of insight, comfort, and motivation. It also can be fascinating. All too often, however, the information we receive leaves us feeling overwhelmed or feeling that there is nothing we can do to put things right. Such feelings of helplessness, not surprisingly, are demoralizing (Seligman, 1975), hardly a state that leads to reasonable behavior.

Meaningful action, in contrast, is the opportunity to make a useful contribution to a genuine problem. It may involve being effective at a large scale (e.g., the choice of livelihood, a lifelong struggle for environmental justice or food security) but perhaps more often it involves actions at a more modest level (e.g., participating in a stewardship activity, community involvement, voting). The meaningfulness experienced is less about the scale of the effort and more about deriving a sense of making a difference, being listened to and respected, and feeling that we have a secure place within our social group. Reasonable behavior is more likely when people feel that they are needed and that their participation matters. A number of studies indicate that doing something judged worthwhile or making a difference in the long run are primary motives underlying voluntary environmental stewardship behavior (Grese, Kaplan, Ryan, & Buxton, 2000, Miles, Sullivan, & Kuo, 2000). In these studies, the notion of meaningful action emerged as one of the most significant sources of satisfaction.

As mentioned earlier, the elements of the reasonable person model are highly interrelated. Perceiving a sense of competence and achieving respect are deep founts of meaningful action. Just as people who feel confused, mentally exhausted or helpless are rarely at their best, when these concerns are addressed, people are much more likely to be reasonable and cooperative. In short, bringing out the best in people is more likely when the environment supports understanding and exploration, develops competence, promotes a clear head, and enables meaningful action.

TRANSITIONING TO SUSTAINABLE LIVING

As we contemplate the changes that will be needed to address the many environmental issues being faced (e.g., climate disruption, energy descent, environmental injustice, soil depletion), it is heartening that the reasonable person model supports the notions that humans seek meaningfulness more than novelty, that they benefit more from developing a sense of competence, clarity, and mental vitality than from pursuing convenience or hedonic pleasure, and that the mind is better adapted to exploring, problem solving, and sense making than it is to affluence.

The transitions needed to live sustainably within biophysical limits will dramatically alter the context and content of everyday behavior. Surprising to some, the coming downshift may actually stimulate people's natural inclinations to explore and understand, and to pursue acts of meaning. Thus, the transition we will need to make will create many of the very conditions that, environmental psychology research shows, support reasonable behavior.

However, to increase the probability of success, we must encourage experiments on a multitude of options. Citizen and environmental experts alike should constantly tinker with new institutional forms, metaphors, norms, and principles. Perhaps most importantly, we must each become behavioral entrepreneurs, exploring new behaviors and new ways to combine old behaviors. Perhaps a behavioral aesthetics is possible, a way to live our daily lives as a work of art as we adapt-in-place. We may be facing a materially simpler life but it may be possible to live with beauty.

Although our current analytical tools can help make sense of the past (e.g., how did we get to this state of climate disruption and energy descent) and the present (e.g., what is the nature of our environmental predicament), and can extrapolate recent trends into the future, they cannot determine which paths into the future will prove more useful. For this we must adopt an adaptive, experimental approach. Our problem solving must seek a plurality of solutions, not the one right solution or the magic elixir. Emerging plans, policies, and procedures should be viewed as hypotheses in constant need of reality testing. Or, as author and community organizer Pat Murphy puts it, we need to "make a lot of mistakes quickly" (quoted in Cobb, 2009). The "quickly" part of this suggestion comes from the concern that climate disruption and energy constraints are happening at a frequency and intensity thought to be, until recently, many decades away. The anticipation of mistakes comes from a humility that echoes the insights of Meadows, Randers, and Meadows (2004) who argue that in our current state of biophysical overshoot we need to find the right balance between environmental urgency and patience. Achieving this balance will require humility, honesty, and clear-headedness.

THE POWER OF SMALL EXPERIMENTS

To the extent that the response to an environmental dilemma must be place-based, it becomes inappropriate to rely solely upon universal interventions. In fact, the need for a localized response diminishes the effectiveness of outside solutions altogether. Participants struggling to form a localized response will benefit only slightly from generic instructions. And they certainly will not take kindly to being informed by outside practitioners about how they must behave.

In such situations a competent and situation-aware practitioner will see that his or her role has changed. This role becomes suggesting guidelines for how participants might craft their own response and then being prepared to answer the questions that naturally arise from the resulting effort. The urgency and dramatic consequences remain, but the process of responding has changed.

An approach to behavior change under conditions of urgency, great environmental uncertainty, and grave stakes, yet with a need for place-based sensitivity, might start with small steps. As anthropologist and political scientist James Scott advises with respect to interventions for economic development, "Prefer wherever possible to take a small step, stand back, observe, and then plan the next small move" (Scott, 1998, p. 345). Scott's suggestion follows, in part, the small-experiment approach to environmental problem solving outlined by Irvine and Kaplan (2001; see also Kaplan, Kaplan, & Ryan 1998). Small experiments is a framework for supporting problem solving that is based on the innate inclinations that are at the core of the reasonable person model, particularly the building and sharing of mental models. It supports innovation, maintains local relevance and experimental validity all while promoting rapid dissemination of findings. It is also in contrast to the large-scale, bigger-is-better approach that dominates so much of research these days; an experiment need not be intimidating to be useful.

The small experiment framework can help people who are not trained scientists to validate what works in their locality. But while the involvement of the non-expert is possible, is it more likely under this approach? To be effective, the small-experiment framework would need to create greater individual and group engagement.

To enhance engagement, the small experiment framework carefully manages the scale of the activity. Picking the appropriate scale is a crucial step. It was Weick's (1984) insight that people anchor around the scale and structure of the initial problem definition and start to work on solutions that are only at that same scale or structure. If we cast the problems faced as being at a large scale, as is often the case with environmental issues, then it is hard to imagine anything but a large-scale solution sufficing. Furthermore, imagining that solutions as being of only one fundamental type (e.g., political, economic) unnecessarily limits what people can offer. Large-scale problems may seem to demand large-scale solutions, yet the scale of the problem need not dictate the scale of the solution. And not all environmental problems work out to be problems of policy or economics and thus not all solutions need be political or economic in nature.

There are both ethical and motivational issues at work in the small experiment framework. The careful attention to the scale of problems and solutions is well matched to the ancient ethical teaching that while "it is not your responsibility to finish the work [of perfecting the world], you are not free to desist from it either." A key element of small experiments is that people need only focus on what they are better prepared to handle. Others will handle that which they are positioned to solve.

The motivational effect likely comes from the intrinsic satisfaction derived from developing, displaying, and maintaining competence (De

Young, 1996). Since success at a smaller scale can result in an empowering sense of competence, this may result in people being more willing to continue or re-start their problem-solving efforts at a later date or in a different setting (Monroe, 2003). Social benefits also may emerge from keeping the scale small; trust is easier to build and may prove useful when efforts must be repeated.

Small experiments are going on all the time. They are often the basis of stories told by at-home tinkerers, dedicated gardeners, office problem solvers and innovative teachers. They are part of team efforts where experts and citizens combine and apply their talents and knowledge to a problem of mutual concern. Consider also the many pilot programs, field tests, demonstration sites, and trial runs regularly reported in both popular and scientific publications.

Small experiments are so common that they may seem inconsequential to the casual observer, yet they can be a powerful means of behavioral entrepreneurship. Their effectiveness can be enhanced by following a few simple guidelines.

Scale and Expectation

While already an integral aspect of small experiments, smallness can be understood in a variety of ways. Keeping the physical scope small is obvious. Others include keeping the breadth of exploring small and the time-span short as well as involving only a small number of people as participants or respondents. The experiment can also be tentative, tried out for a limited time or on a limited basis. These guidelines help keep the costs of project initiation and management low. So too should expectations be kept in check. The findings of small experiments are unavoidably imperfect and incomplete. Yet small too are the consequences of failure; failure is always a possibility if an experiment is genuine. Nonetheless, as Irvine and Kaplan document (2001), findings from a modest enterprise may prove extraordinarily useful and have broad effects.

Goal and Focus

Keep the focus on only one specific and well-defined problem. While it may be okay to start exploring before having absolutely everything in place, it is essential to first have a clear and concise question. Such a question motivates the effort and makes it easier to avoid distractions no matter how fascinating they may be. Spending too little time on figuring out what you hope to learn is the surest way to fail. Anticipating what you would like to be able to say at the end is an excellent way of formulating your initial question. Here too, modest expectations may be a helpful guide; the aim of the small experiment is to identify reasonable solutions, preferably a multitude of them. The goal is not a search for the ideal answer.

Tracking and Record Keeping

Empirical research, at its core, involves being attentive to what is going on. Whether formal or informal information gathering is used, the objective is to systematically learn what worked and what did not. At the immediate time frame and at the local level, the tracking allows for feedback to the participants. In situations involving behavior change, rapid feedback allows for self-correction; people can learn how the specific choices they made affected the outcome. Without such feedback behavior cannot be changed is a pragmatic and productive way. Over the longer time frame, the information recorded informs next steps and may provide the basis for developing generalizations that might be useful to share with others. Once again, modest expectations can play a role in deciding the amount and form of information to be tracked. The intent is to collect only enough information to allow for feedback and inference; too little information precludes useful learning, but too much information can paralyze the analysis process. Easy to gain information is always preferred in modestly funded small experiments.

Dissemination and Communication

Sharing the successes of a small experiment is an excellent way to let participants know that their efforts mattered. It is also an opportunity to validate the correctness of the proposed changes for the local people who were not directly involved in the small experiment. Finally, communicating with people at a distance may inform and motivate other small experiments; successes in one locality become plausible options to explore elsewhere, while communicating about failures instills caution. The form of communication used can vary with the circumstances. Newsletters, newspaper articles, and presentations at an open-house can work well locally while professional presentations, blogs, journals, and magazines can help with wider dissemination. But regardless of the outlet used, clear, concrete, vivid, and engaging language will help to familiarize others with the findings.

It is noteworthy that nothing in these guidelines restricts small experiments to taking only small steps or to a slow discovery process. A behavior change process called adaptive muddling stresses this subtle but important issue (De Young & Kaplan, 1988). Adaptive muddling adds one important aspect to the small experiment framework. A stability component is used to reduce the costs of failure for the individuals involved. It also makes highly improbable unchecked and disorienting change. With a safety net in place, people need not privilege the status quo by investigating only marginal behavior change. Far-reaching change can be both contemplated and explored. The scale of the experiment may be small but adaptive muddling supports people exploring, and thus pre-familiarizing themselves with life-changing adaptations. Since this modification to the small experiment framework makes the exploration process less intimidating, discovery can occur more quickly as more people become engaged. Furthermore, while the impact from any one group's change may be modest, this process supports simultaneously exploring, and sharing the results of, many changes at once, each drawing on the knowledge and experience people already possess.

Some people may argue that the small experiment framework is a renamed version of the experimenting society proposed by Campbell (1981). The experimenting society suggests that social programs should be designed and implemented as experiments with a built-in evaluation process. However, in Campbell's version, the evaluation is a formal process, one conducted by social scientists using meticulous, expertly designed trials followed by rigorous statistical analyses. Furthermore, the results are intended for use by governmental policy makers and, perhaps, for later publication.

The small experiments approach uses the concept of an experiment in a much less restricted sense. The analysis involved in such experiments is less formal and more compatible with immediate needs and local capabilities. Online accounts, reports by participants or visits by interested individuals would be appropriate additions to whatever formal record keeping is employed. The more expert-based framing of an experiment used by Campbell makes his approach less likely to be tried by, and the results less accessible to, non-experts.

The small experiment framework is a quick and simple way to promote behavior change that is compatible with what environmental psychology has learned about human nature. Such an approach can enable people to build mental models that allow them to view the urgent and serious environmental issues they face in terms of challenge and possibility rather than inevitability and despair.

HUMANS AS ENGAGED AND PURPOSEFUL

There is still much to be learned about human-environment interaction. Nonetheless, the reasonable person model, and the related tools of small experiments and adaptive muddling, provides a context for creating interventions that bring out the best in people. Together they provide a framework for working with people in ways that fulfill a variety of innate inclinations: to explore, to understand, to enhance competence, to be part of a solution, and to pursue meaningful goals.

This framing recognizes humans as active, purposive beings, not as mere recipients of the information patterns generated by environments or experts. But of all these innate inclinations, none is more central than model building. In an effort to explore and understand, people are constantly either building models of their experiences and the environment, or using their existing mental models to effectively function in an environment. There is an affective and motivational aspect here as well, but it does not involve putting people into a positive affective state beforehand. People deeply care about the model-building process. They gain intrinsic satisfaction from exploring, building, and sharing mental models. They are pained by a process that results in confusion or boredom. Thus affect is fundamental to, but derived from, the process of learning and knowledge transfer.

In short, environmental psychology has discovered that by being attentive to the innate need and capability of people to build new mental models and test old ones, we can enhance their knowledge acquisition and wellbeing. We can also better manage and leverage behavior change and thus, quite possibly, repair the world.

REFERENCES

Bechtel, R. B., & Churchman, A. (Eds.) (2002). *Handbook of environmental psychology*. New York, NY: Wiley.

Berman, M. G., Jonides, J., & Kaplan, S. (2008). The cognitive benefits of interacting with nature. *Psychological Science, 19*, 1207–1212.

Campbell, D. T. (1981). Introduction: Getting ready for the experimenting society. In L. Saxe and M. Fine (Eds.), *Social experiments: Methods for design and evaluation* (pp. 41–62). Beverly Hills, CA: Sage.

Clayton, S., & Myers, O. E., Jr. (2009). *Conservation psychology: Understanding and promoting human care for nature*. New York, NY: Wiley-Blackwell.

Cobb, K. (2009, March). We must make a lot of mistakes quickly. *Resource Insight*. Retrieved May 30, 2012, from http://resourceinsights.blogspot.com/2009/03/we-must-make-lot-of-mistakes-quickly.html.

Cone, J. D., & Hayes, S. C. (1980). *Environmental Problems/Behavioral Solutions*. Monterey, CA: Brooks/Cole.

De Young, R. (1996). Some psychological aspects of reduced consumption behavior: The role of intrinsic satisfaction and competence motivation. *Environment and Behavior, 28*, 358–409.

De Young, R. (2010). Restoring mental vitality in an endangered world. *Ecopsychology, 2*, 13–22.

De Young, R., & Kaplan, S. (1988). On averting the tragedy of the commons. *Environmental Management, 12*, 283–293.

De Young, R., & Princen, T. (2012). *The localization reader: Adapting to the coming downshift*. Cambridge, MA: MIT Press.

Doherty, T. J. (2011). Psychologies of the environment. *Ecopsychology, 3*, 75–77.

Frumkin, H. (2001). Beyond toxicity: Human health and the natural environment. *American Journal of Preventative Medicine, 20*, 234–240.

Geller, E. S., Winett, R. A., & Everett, P. B. (1982). *Preserving the environment: New strategies for behavioral change*. New York, NY: Pergamon Press.

Gifford, R. (2007). *Environmental psychology: Principles and practice* (4th ed.). Canada: Optimal Books.

Grese, R. E., Kaplan, R., Ryan, R. L., & Buxton, J. (2000). Psychological benefits of volunteering in stewardship programs. In P. H. Gobster and R. B. Hill (Eds.), *Restoring nature: Perspectives from the social sciences and humanities* (pp. 265–280). Washington, D.C: Island Press.

Herzog, T. R., Black, A. M., Fountaine, K. A., & Knotts, D. J. (1997). Reflection and attentional recovery as distinctive benefits of restorative environments. *Journal of Environmental Psychology, 17*, 165–170.

Irvine, K. N., & Kaplan, S. (2001). Coping with change: The small experiment as a strategic approach to environmental sustainability. *Environmental Management, 28*, 713–725.

James, W. (1982/1985). *Psychology: The briefer course*. Notre Dame, IN: University of Notre Dame Press.

Kaplan, R. (1995). Informational issues: A perspective on human needs and inclinations. In G. A. Bradley (Ed.), *Urban forest landscapes: Integrating multidisciplinary perspectives* (pp. 60–71). Seattle, WA: University of Washington Press.

Kaplan, R., & Kaplan, S. (1989). *The experience of nature: A psychological perspective*. New York, NY: Cambridge University Press.

Kaplan, R., & Kaplan, S. (2005). Preference, restoration, and meaningful action in the context of nearby nature. In P. F. Barlett (Ed.), *Urban place: Reconnecting with the natural world* (pp. 271–298). Cambridge, MA: MIT Press.

Kaplan, R., Kaplan, S., & Ryan, R. L. (1998). *With people in mind: Design and management of everyday nature*. Washington, DC: Island Press.

Kaplan, S. (1995). The restorative benefits of nature: Toward an integrative framework. *Journal of Environmental Psychology, 15,* 169–182.

Kaplan, S. (2001). Meditation, restoration and the management of mental fatigue. *Environment and Behavior, 33,* 480–506.

Kaplan, S., & Kaplan, R. (2003). Health, supportive environments, and the reasonable person model. *American Journal of Public Health, 93,* 1484–1489.

Kaplan, S., & Kaplan, R. (2009). Creating a larger role for environmental psychology: The Reasonable Person Model as an integrative framework. *Journal of Environmental Psychology, 29,* 329–339.

Katzev, R. D., & Johnson, T. R. (1987). *Promoting energy conservation: An analysis of behavioral research.* Boulder, CO: Westview Press.

Lewin, K. (1951). *Field theory in social science: Selected theoretical papers.* D. Cartwright (Ed.). New York, NY: Harper & Row.

Meadows, D. H., Randers J., & Meadows, D. L. (2004). Tools for the transition to sustainability. In *Limits to growth: The 30-year update* (pp. 265–284). White River Junction, VT: Chelsea Green Publishing Company

Miles, I., W. C. Sullivan, & Kuo, F. E. (2000). Psychological benefits of volunteering for restoration projects. *Ecological Restoration, 18,* 218–227.

Monroe, M. (2003). Two avenues for encouraging conservation behaviors. *Human Ecology Review, 10,* 113–125.

Saunders, C., & Myers, O. E., Jr. (Eds.) (2003). Conservation psychology [Special edition]. *Human Ecology Review, 10*(2).

Scott, J. C. (1998). *Seeing like a state: How certain schemes to improve the human condition have failed.* New Haven, CT: Yale University Press.

Seligman, M. E. P. (1975). *Helplessness: On depression, development, and death.* San Francisco, CA: Freeman.

Stokols, D. (1995). The paradox of environmental psychology. *American Psychologist, 50,* 821–837.

Stokols, D., & I. Altman (Eds.) (1987). *Handbook of environmental psychology.* Volumes 1 and 2. New York: John Wiley and Sons.

Sundstrom, E., Bell, P. A., Busby, P. L., & Aasmus, C. (1996). Environmental psychology 1989–1994. *Annual Review of Psychology, 47,* 482–512.

Weick, K. (1984). Small wins: Redefining the scale of social problems. *American Psychologist, 39,* 40–49.

3

Is Sustainability an Ethical Responsibility of I-O and Consulting Psychologists?

Rodney L. Lowman

> We do not inherit the earth from our ancestors, we borrow it from our children.
>
> —Native American proverb

When I was an undergraduate student studying psychology at the University of Oklahoma in the early 1970s, a biology professor who taught my introductory zoology course was a staunch advocate of sustainability. Only then it was not called sustainability. The popular term then as I recall was "ecology" but the concerns about what even then were our misuse of resources and the threat to our collective environment raised similar, if less comprehensive, issues as now.

Almost 40 years later, the pace of acceleration of our environmental degradation has greatly increased and there are few people anywhere who have not at least heard about environmental concerns. By most accounts (see, for example, Gore, 2007), we (collectively) are toasting the planet at a pace that may sooner rather than later affect the ability of the environment to sustain life as we know it, including that of our own kind. We (humans) by our actions are wiping out entire species and destroying the delicate balance of the food chain in the process. And although society has made modest progress in some areas of cutting back on our environmentally-destructive actions and improving our good ones—including the recognition that these issues are real, not manufactured—we are rendering change at a rate that even our remarkably resilient and self-correcting environment seems ill equipped to be able to accommodate.

Although "global warming" is considered to be a major component of our environmental challenges, the broader term, the focus of this book, is sustainability. Various definitions have been offered for this term but its major parameters can be summarized succinctly. The United Nations World Commission on Environment and Development (WECD) offered one of the most widely used definitions of sustainability. In *Our common future,* the WCED (1987, IV.2) defined sustainability as being able to "meet present needs without compromising the ability of future generations to meet their needs." This view implies that doing problematic things to the environment in the name of sustaining current economic needs is not a sustainable practice. Sustainability has a positive connotation because it forces us to recognize that there are longer term consequences to decisions made today, and that we need to be thinking of those when making decisions in the present.

Because humans live for a very short period of time but have the ingenuity to impact the world in profound ways—both good and bad—the concept of environmental fragility is often difficult to comprehend. As Hawking (1988) put it:

> The earth was initially very hot and without an atmosphere. In the course of time it cooled and acquired an atmosphere from the emission of gases from the rocks. This early atmosphere was not one in which we could have survived. It contained no oxygen, but a lot of other gases that are poisonous to us, such as hydrogen sulfide … There are, however, other primitive forms of life that can flourish under such conditions. It is thought that they developed in the oceans, possibly as a result of chance combinations of atoms into large structures, called macromolecules, which were capable of assembling other atoms in the ocean into similar structures. The first primitive forms of life consumed various materials, including hydrogen sulfide, and released oxygen. This gradually changed the atmosphere to the composition that it has today and allowed the development of higher forms of life such as fish, reptiles, mammals, and ultimately the human race (pp. 120–121).

By this description, life was accidentally created and developed, through evolution, into the phenomenal diversity that we know today. Yet, the miraculous nature and diversity of life forms mask the fragility of the balance with the environment on which life depends, and the ease with which major changes in the environment can have an impact on life forms. What they do not mask is the extraordinary indifference of nature to whether or not our planet—much less our life form—continues to exist. We somehow believe that the whole complicated environmental system on which we depend for our existence will somehow self-correct no matter what we do to it and, through denial, we keep out of focal awareness the real possibilities that life as we know it will not—cannot—continue without radical reform.

There are of course many reasons for the rapid desecration of our environment. Industrialization is certainly one of these with the concomitant increase in carbon emissions. When industrialization was the province of a few rich nations that generally felt it their destiny to be the unilateral decision makers about environmental issues, that was one thing. The emergence of booming new economies in large, some would argue overpopulated, countries like China, India, and Brazil, is another. The rate of accelerated pollution and carbon emissions, combined with the exporting of manufacturing functions from richer to less rich nations, has created huge and growing consequences that any concerned citizen anywhere in the world has a legitimate basis about which to be concerned (see, for example, Franzen, 2003; Opotow & Weiss, 2000).

Predictably, those who have raised the alarm buttons about global warming (see Weart, 2008) and pollution have been met, among other reactions, with the derision and ridicule that commonly is afforded radical innovators and inconvenient truth tellers. From the early days of what has become an environmental movement, activists like Rachel Carson, who in 1962 published the remarkable and, against odds, impactful volume called *Silent spring* (Carson, 1962), raised frankly alarmist concerns about what we were doing to Earth. Although Carson is regarded as being one of the founders of the contemporary environmentalist movement, there were many others who before her had similarly raised important issues about environmental preservation. These included John Muir (Teale, 2001), Theodore Roosevelt (Brinkley, 2009), Aldo Leopold (1949), and less "household word" contributors such as scientists Roger Revelle and Charles Keeling (Keeling, 1970), who are attributed with credit for first documenting the rising levels of carbon dioxide in the ocean.

Concern with the environment and humankind's impact on it is not new (see, for example, Kates et al. 2001) but the interest in has accelerated dramatically. Increasingly, environmental issues are brought into curricula of business and there are so-called "Green MBAs" that aim to combine business and environmentalism. Clearly, also, there is now money to be made from positioning one's company as environmentally sensitive (see, for example, Lash & Wellington, 2007).

Current concerns about the environment can be succinctly, if crudely and non-comprehensively, summarized as follows: (a) we (society) now have far greater awareness of environmental impact than ever before; (b) the degradation of the environment has accelerated more rapidly than our apparent ability to reverse its adverse consequences; (c) we have made notable progress in reversing some effects of mistreatment of the environment (as with the detoxification of certain rivers and lakes, the preservation of certain species, and reductions of air pollution in certain areas); (d) in some countries, notably the United States, a "conspiracy theorist" minority persists that espouses the beliefs that the issues are not real, the science behind the conclusions about serious environmental function wrong, and the goals of the sustainability "movement" primarily political; and (e) there is a recognition among many experts that catastrophic collapse of the environment will occur sooner rather than later.

If there is somewhat unstable and fluctuating agreement among many nations that these issues are real, not manufactured, there are still those who believe that all issues of global warming and sustainability are made up and that there is no cause for alarm (see Jaques, Dunlap, & Freeman, 2008). Such skeptics claim environmental concerns about sustainability and global warming are all part of a grand hoax. The denial of global warming has itself been studied as a psychological phenomenon (see, for example, Armitage, 2005). A research base has also begun to develop (e.g., Feygina, Jost, & Goldsmith, 2010) about how people make decisions about environmental threats and the perceived need for action or inaction.

I-O AND CONSULTING PSYCHOLOGY AND SUSTAINABILITY

What does all this have to do with industrial-organizational psychology (IOP), consulting psychology (CP) and, for that matter, with psychology in general? I will argue in this chapter that the relative disinterest of IOP and CP in issues of sustainability relates, especially, to issues of ethics and values, and, I contend, is part of a larger theme of ambivalence toward value-driven issues but is coupled with the reality that concern with these issues are, I conclude, neither directly ethically mandated by the ethics of the profession nor by the values of I-O, consulting or psychology more generally. I will also suggest, however, that they are implied by some of the ethical principles of psychologists.

DO PSYCHOLOGISTS HAVE ETHICAL OBLIGATIONS REGARDING SUSTAINABILITY INITIATIVES?

I will make the case later in the chapter that engagement with sustainability issues is both a good use of our profession and a purpose for which we have much relevant expertise that is potentially relevant. But first I want to examine the evidence about whether there is an ethical mandate to be involved with such issues and, if not, whether there should be.

The idea that I-O psychology should "drive change" for a "social purpose" such as advancing a "green agenda" is perhaps one not likely to be readily accepted by mainstream I-O or consulting psychology. Both I-O and consulting psychology are pridefully "science based" but also perceived, not inappropriately, as being focused more on the needs and issues of management than of other aspects of organizations (Brief, 2000; Lefkowitz, 2003, 2005).

Still, the question of whether there are any ethical obligations of psychologists to be concerned with environmental issues is somewhat complicated. Ethics, I argue (Lowman, 2011) is one of the major characteristics that defines any profession as a profession. A profession encompasses a particular body of knowledge, a particular set of applications (that may or may not be regulated by governments) and agreement to behave in a certain way when functioning as a member of the profession.

In the case of IOP and CP, the ethics code of the American Psychological Association (APA) (2002) is the governing ethical standards for I-O psychologists who are members of the APA and the Society for Industrial-Organizational Psychology (SIOP) as well as for I-O psychologists licensed in the United States who may not be members of those organizations. Those practicing, teaching or researching I-O psychology in other countries may be governed by other ethical codes but the APA Code has been widely used as the conceptual model for psychological codes in other countries and there is more alike than different about the various codes governing the practice of psychology around the world.

In considering whether there is an ethical requirement to address sustainability issues, it is appropriate to begin by consulting the APA Ethical Principles and Code of Conduct (American Psychological Association, 2002) as a starting place for considering whether I-O psychologists have any ethical obligation to focus on sustainability issues. The 2002 version of the Code (modified slightly in 2010 to address the issue of psychology's involvement in terrorism) consists of several general principles and a number of specific, enforceable standards organized in ten categories (*Ethical principles*, 2002; American Psychological Society, 2010). The ethical principles are aspirational guidelines, those to which psychologists are morally obligated to aspire and consider in making judgments as psychologists, but they are not per se enforceable. The standards of the APA Ethics Code are enforceable and increasingly relate to the practice of psychology in organizational and consulting contexts.

A careful review of the current APA Ethics Code, however, shows that nowhere in the current APA Code is there any direct ethical admonition to take up sustainability issues. Indeed, psychologists are admonished not to practice outside their areas of competence (Standard 2.01, American Psychological Association, 2002, pp. 1063–1064).

It is in the broad and overarching aspirational standards that a case might better potentially be made that there is an ethical obligation to address sustainability issues. So I will examine each of those in turn to see if there is an implied ethical obligation to address these issues as a "higher purpose" emerging issue.

The first of these principles concerns beneficence and nonmaleficence. It states:

Principle A: Beneficence and Nonmaleficence

Psychologists strive to benefit those with whom they work and take care to do no harm. In their professional actions, psychologists seek to safeguard the welfare and rights of those with whom they interact professionally and other affected persons, and the welfare of animal subjects of research. When conflicts occur among psychologists' obligations or concerns, they attempt to resolve these conflicts in a responsible fashion that avoids or minimizes harm. Because psychologists' scientific and professional judgments and actions may affect the lives of others, they are alert to and guard against personal, financial, social, organizational, or political factors that might lead to misuse of their influence. Psychologists strive to be aware of the possible effect of their own physical and mental health on their ability to help those with whom they work. (American Psychological Association, 2002, p. 1062)

The admonition of Principle A is, essentially, to do good, avoid doing harm, and avoid conflicts of interest. There's little here that would drive an obligation to be concerned with sustainability issues except in the context of "those with whom they work" if that happens to include, for I-O or consulting psychologists, organizations that are dealing with such matters and the organizational or consulting psychologist has that work in the professional practice portfolio. On the other hand, the I-O psychologist interested in sustainability advocacy may find him/herself at odds with client organizations whose agendas, in the name of profitability, for example, do not include a focus on the environment. The definition of the nature of the client-organization relationship is applicable here.

The next principle, B, relates to responsibilities and professional codes of ethics. The ethical principle states:

Principle B: Fidelity and Responsibility

Psychologists establish relationships of trust with those with whom they work. They are aware of their professional and scientific responsibilities to society and to the specific communities in which they work. Psychologists uphold professional standards of conduct, clarify their professional roles and obligations, accept appropriate responsibility for their behavior, and seek to manage conflicts of interest that could lead to exploitation or harm. Psychologists consult with, refer to, or cooperate with other professionals and institutions to the extent needed to serve the best interests of those with whom they work. They are concerned about the ethical compliance of their colleagues' scientific and professional conduct. Psychologists strive to contribute a portion of their professional time for little or no compensation or personal advantage. (American Psychological Association, 2002, p. 1062)

Here we see the articulation of professional and scientific ethical responsibilities and to the "communities" in which psychologists work. However, there is little specification of any obligation to such issues as sustainability or to the broader ecological or environmental context in which psychologists work.

The next principle, C, concerns integrity. This is conceptualized mostly as a responsibility of the psychologist to be honest, to keep promises. It states:

Principle C: Integrity

Psychologists seek to promote accuracy, honesty, and truthfulness in the science, teaching, and practice of psychology. In these activities psychologists do not steal, cheat, or engage in fraud, subterfuge, or intentional misrepresentation of fact. Psychologists strive to keep their promises and to avoid unwise or unclear commitments. In situations in which deception may be ethically justifiable to maximize benefits and minimize harm, psychologists have a serious obligation to consider the need for, the possible consequences of, and their responsibility to correct any resulting mistrust or other harmful effects that arise from the use of such techniques. (American Psychological Association, 2002, p. 1062)

Principle D, concerning justice, does raise some potential connections to sustainability issues. It states:

Principle D: Justice

Psychologists recognize that fairness and justice entitle all persons to access to and benefit from the contributions of psychology and to equal quality in the processes, procedures, and services being conducted by psychologists. Psychologists exercise reasonable judgment and take precautions to ensure that their potential biases, the boundaries of their competence, and the limitations of their expertise do not lead to or condone unjust practices. (American Psychological Association, 2002, pp. 1062–1063)

Even with the implied concern for social justice, however, Principle D does not apparently obligate psychologists to address societal concerns. The focus is more on equality in treatment of individuals and access to service. It does not establish a social justice agenda for psychologists that would address concerns about the environment we all share.

Finally, Principle E addresses issues of psychologists' needs to respect people's rights and dignity. It states:

Principle E: Respect for People's Rights and Dignity

Psychologists respect the dignity and worth of all people, and the rights of individuals to privacy, confidentiality, and self determination. Psychologists are aware that special safeguards may be necessary to protect the rights and welfare of persons or communities whose vulnerabilities impair autonomous decision making. Psychologists are aware of and respect cultural, individual, and role differences, including those based on age, gender, gender identity, race, ethnicity, culture, national origin, religion, sexual orientation, disability, language, and socioeconomic status and consider these factors when working with members of such groups. Psychologists try to eliminate the effect on their work of biases based on those factors, and they do not knowingly participate in or condone activities of others based upon such prejudices. (American Psychological Association, 2002, p. 1063)

All of these are admirable concerns to avoid discrimination and to protect the rights and welfare of "persons or communities" whose ability to make autonomous decisions has been impaired. Psychologists are admonished to be aware of, and to respect, individual differences.

The specific enforceable standards of the APA similarly identify ethical obligations to do and not to do in a wide assortment of professional practice areas but there is no requirement to engage in any pro- or avoidant actions concerning sustainability.

Not only is there little in the APA Ethics Code to suggest that psychologists have an ethical responsibility to address sustainability issues but also there are several standards that might disincline I-O psychologists to be engaged with them. Foremost among these, perhaps, is Standard 2.04 Bases for Scientific and Professional Judgments, which states: "Psychologists' work is based upon established scientific and professional knowledge of the discipline" (American Psychological Association, 2002, p. 1064). To date, there is very little scientific and professional knowledge about sustainability issues in the discipline of psychology, much less in IOP or CP.

Additionally, the mandate that psychologists practice or research only within their areas of competence places restrictions on getting into new areas, ones that were not in their area of training or scope of practice. In particular, the APA Ethics Code, in Standard 2.01 Boundaries of Competence mandates:

(a) Psychologists provide services, teach, and conduct research with populations and in areas only within the boundaries of their competence, based on their education, training, supervised experience, consultation, study, or professional experience. (American Psychological Association, 2002, p. 1063)

The Code further states in 2.01 (c) that:

Psychologists planning to provide services, teach, or conduct research involving populations, areas, techniques, or technologies new to them undertake relevant education, training, supervised experience, consultation, or study. (American Psychological Association, 2002, p. 1064)

Finally, the APA Ethics Code Standard 2.01 (e) states that:

In those emerging areas in which generally recognized standards for preparatory training do not yet exist, psychologists nevertheless take reasonable steps to ensure the competence of their work and to protect clients/patients, students, supervisees, research participants, organizational clients, and others from harm. (American Psychological Association, 2002, p. 1064)

Thus, to the extent that psychologists are scientists-practitioners (see Lefkowitz, 1990; Lowman, 2012), their ethics code mandates that they practice within their areas of professional competence, that their work be science-based, and that they get appropriate training to transition to new areas (such as sustainability). It is therefore entirely understandable, if unfortunate, that IOP and CP have not to date really engaged with sustainability issues in any substantive way. However, this underestimates the value that IOP could, potentially, bring to these issues (see, for example, Campbell & Campbell, 2005; Klein, Sanders, & Huffman, 2011).

There is another sense in which the APA Code might be interpreted as implying psychologists should be concerned with sustainability issues. It is in the (non-enforceable) Preamble to the APA Code, which states: "Psychologists are committed to increasing scientific and professional knowledge of behavior and people's understanding of themselves and others and to the use of such knowledge to improve the condition of individuals, organizations, and society (American Psychological Association, 2002, p. 1062).

Improving the condition of society and individuals, in today's society, certainly would include sustainability issues. And, as in many areas (e.g., multicultural) that were once viewed, at best, as being tangential to psychology's mission, once there is focused attention of psychological research and practice on these issues, they often in time become part of the obligatory focus of psychologists. Additionally, cases can be made that sustainability issues affect minority groups and at-risk populations (see Principle E of the Code; American Psychological Association, 2002; see also American Psychological Association, 2003) more than others, so there might be an implied obligation to be concerned about these issues.

OTHER ETHICS CODES

The ethics codes of other countries' psychological associations also suggest little direct concern with sustainability issues. Perhaps the ethics code with the greatest concerns expressed about the obligations of psychology to society is that of the Canadian Psychological Association (CPA). This code includes four broad overarching standards that include Principle I: Respect for the Dignity of Persons; Principle II: Responsible Caring; Principle III: Integrity in Relationships; and Principle IV: Responsibility to Society. Concerning the latter, the Code explicitly identifies a social contract, stating that "By virtue of this social contract, psychologists have a higher duty of care to members of society than the general duty of care that all members of society have to each other" (Canadian Psychological Association, 2000, p. 2). "Society" is defined in the Canadian Code "... in the broad sense of a group of persons living as members of one or more human communities, rather than in the limited sense of state or government" (Canadian Psychological Association, 2000, p. 28).

The CPA Code elaborates in its value statement about responsibility to society, stating that:

> Psychology functions as a discipline within the context of human society. Psychologists, both in their work and as private citizens, have responsibilities to the societies in which they live and work, such as the neighbourhood or city, and to the welfare of all human beings in those societies. Two of the legitimate expectations of psychology as a science and a profession are that

it will increase knowledge and that it will conduct its affairs in such ways that it will promote the welfare of all human beings. (p. 28)

IV.22 Speak out, in a manner consistent with the four principles of this *Code*, if they possess expert knowledge that bears on important societal issues being studied or discussed. (Canadian Psychological Association, 2000, p. 31)

In its "extended responsibilities," Canadian psychologists have as an enforceable standard, "IV.30 Encourage others, in a manner consistent with this *Code*, to exercise responsibility to society" (Canadian Psychological Association, 2000, p. 32).

All that said, in the CPA Code, the four overarching principles are prioritized and Principle IV is listed as being least important when there is conflict between it and any of the other three. In discussing this prioritization, the Code states:

Although it is necessary and important to consider responsibility to society in every ethical decision, adherence to this principle must be subject to and guided by Respect for the Dignity of Persons, Responsible Caring, and Integrity in Relationships. When a person's welfare appears to conflict with benefits to society, it is often possible to find ways of working for the benefit of society that do not violate respect and responsible caring for the person. However, if this is not possible, the dignity and well-being of a person should not be sacrificed to a vision of the greater good of society, and greater weight must be given to respect and responsible caring for the person. (Canadian Psychological Association, 2000, p. 2)

Reviews of the ethics codes of other psychological societies (e.g., the British Psychological Society, 2011) and of other professional groups (e.g., the Society of Human Resource Management, 2007, and the OD Network, 2011) found no direct or indirect mention about any ethical responsibilities to be concerned with environmental issues.

Values

Values, those principles thought to underlie and guide actions, are another way in which a profession can identify its commitments. The APA (undated) has issued a statement of values, *Our values*, but they seem to relate more to organizational values (e.g., open communication, resiliency) for the APA than for the profession. I-O psychology appears never to have promulgated an official values statement. Yet, as Lefkowitz (2005) noted (see also Alderfer, 2011), even without a specifically adopted set of values, the field still has real and implicitly espoused values. His article both identified a pro-management, pro-science, pro-effectiveness approach to I-O psychology's espoused values. There is little reason to think that those values would drive IOP into roles emphasizing sustainability. Indeed, Lefkowitz (2003, 2005) paints a rather dim view of the degree to which IOP has reached out beyond a narrow, somewhat technocratic, role.

Ethical and Values-Driven Opportunity

Summarizing, to date there is no apparent direct ethical or values-driven mandate for I-O psychologists to take environmental issues into account, or for these issues to be at the forefront of their work. Yet, environmental issues are part of a much broader concern that are of such great potential importance that it is important to think of ways that the values and competencies of I-O psychologists can be made use of in the mission. Rather than thinking about sustainability as an ethical obligation, it perhaps makes more sense to think of it as an ethical opportunity (see, for example, Aguinis, 2011). And the question naturally arises as to whether IOP and CP, even if not driven to do so by their ethics or values, have anything to offer the sustainability movement (see Klein et al., 2011).

THE POTENTIAL CONTRIBUTIONS OF IOP TO SUSTAINABILITY INITIATIVES

What do sustainability issues have to do with IOP and CP? The short answer is: so far, not much—but, potentially, a lot.

An analogy is relevant. I was born just after the end of World War II. My father served as a fighter pilot in that war and, in contrast to many of the wars that were to follow, in that war, men and women of all ages were eager to contribute positively to the war effort. Psychologists who were part of the nascent discipline of industrial psychology (see Koppes, 2007;

Lowman, Kantor, & Perloff, 2007) were also important to the war effort. Their talents were used in selection and classification, training, work motivation, and human factors roles. Few were experts in war or aspired to military careers but most all wanted to make a difference in something greater than themselves. Similarly, important contributions to psychology were made immediately after the war, with psychology contributing greatly to the mental health needs of returning war veterans and the needs of the post-war society.

Thus, even though from an ethical standpoint, psychologists of all stripes are admonished not to practice outside their areas of competence, their expertise can ethically and appropriately be used for many legitimate and worthy purposes. That is the beauty of an applied field like IOP and CP; their applications are essentially unlimited. IOP and CP can be used to make organizations and managers more effective and successful, and they can be used (though generally are not: see Lefkowitz, 2003, 2005) to make labor unions stronger and, perhaps, more effective adversaries to management.

Additionally, to effectively serve the organizations and corporations that are our clients or employers, we generally cannot ignore sustainability issues. Huffman, Watrous-Rodriguez, Henning, and Berry (2009) reviewed websites of Fortune 500 companies and found that 71% of those companies had sustainability initiatives. Whether it is an ethical imperative or just a good business practice, psychologists who work with organizations have good reason to be fluent in these concerns. Similarly, the management literature has devoted considerable attention to sustainability (see, for example, Aguinis & Glavas, 2012; Pandey, Rupp, & Thornton, this book). Indeed, many of the chapters in this book (e.g., Ones & Dilchert; Willness & Jones), demonstrate how concern with sustainability issues can be value added for I-O and consulting psychologists.

It is in the uses to which the core discipline of IOP can be put that, I argue, there is the greatest opportunity to make significant contributions to sustainability issues. This implies that psychologists working in these areas do not need to master, for example, the complex chemistry and biology of environmental issues beyond that which any citizen should know, but they can usefully apply their knowledge base to what, I argue, is a greater good and a cause.

Toward a New Vision for I-O Psychology's Role in Sustainability

Assume that sustainability really is the ominous issue that it is portrayed to be by scientists and environmentalists. As with World War II, wouldn't psychologists want to be part of the process of saving the world? If so, how can IOP make a difference in sustainability? In this section I will identify several possibilities more as examples than a comprehensive listing of possibilities.

Helping Organizations Keep Sustainability Issues in Their Evaluation Parameters

As with diversity issues, which corporations and employers did not come readily to embrace, sustainability issues have not been at the forefront of powerful corporations. Creating eco-sensitive products, even when it is the right thing to do for the environment, can add to costs and adversely affects profits. Yet there are long-term and short-term costs with not addressing environmental issues. Helping translate sustainability issues into cost-and-benefit terms and helping to incorporate environmental costs into managerial thinking can at least bring such issues into consideration.

Using Their Expertise to Help Create Sustainability Initiatives Within Organizations

I-O psychologists are experts in employee involvement and engagement. Employees become more connected to organizations when they can identify with and be enthusiastic about their actions. Sustainability efforts such as creating recycling programs, incentivizing ideas that result in a greener organization, and celebrating successes that move positively forward on environmental issues are all examples of actions by which IOP can be useful (see DuBois, Astakhova, & DuBois, this book; Werner, this book, for a more in-depth discussion on how organizations can implement environmental sustainability programs).

Persuasion

The problem of sustainability is, arguably, especially centered on building awareness and shared understanding of the nature and dimensions of the issues. The enormity of the concerns (worldwide) takes the concept of superordinate goals to a new level. However, psychologists are experts in persuasion methods (see, for example, Cacioppo, Petty, Kao, & Rodriguez, 1986; Aronson, 1999) that work and those that don't, and that knowledge can be applied to sustainability awareness.

Conflict Management

Increasingly, sustainability initiatives reflect conflict between local and more global issues (e.g., Buckles, 1999; Clapp & Mortenson, 2011; Ukeje, 2008). Political and governmental issues are inevitably about managing conflicts of interests.

Measurement of Sustainability Goals and Outcomes

I-O and consulting psychologists are experts in assessment and evaluation. As sustainability efforts become less something "nice to do" than "must do," it becomes important to analyze the impact of initiatives on a variety of outcome members. I-O psychologists are well qualified for such work (see Singh, Murty, Gupta, & Dikshit, 2012). (See Ones and Dilchert, this book, for a more in-depth discussion on ES organizational assessment issues.)

Studying Decision Making About Sustainability Issues

Psychologists are experts in examining how and why people make decisions (see, for example, Kahneman, 2011). Lewin, for instance, in World War II, performed classic, action-based research about how homemakers could be encouraged to decide to use "undesirable" cuts of meat during wartime shortages (Lewin, 1948). I-O psychology's work in focus groups (e.g., Krueger & Casey, 2009) is legendary. The decision-making process by which certain people and groups have concluded (or publicly pronounced) that global warming and other sustainability issues are politically motivated hoaxes is also worthy of study, including the process by which such views may (and may not) influence public opinion and legislative and governmental decision making; this is also worthy of IOP's attention.

Helping Eco-Friendly Organizations Develop

There are a number of pro-environment organizations, largely not-for-profits. They are organizations like any others and face the same, if not more, challenges in being underfunded and less able to attract top management skills. I-O and consulting psychologists can help such organizations become more effective through the use of organizational development and other methods (see, for example, Dunphy, Griffiths, & Benn, 2007). They should consider doing so on a pro bono or reduced fee basis consistent with the ethical obligation to contribute a portion of one's services to good causes (American Psychological Association, 2002).

Attitudes Toward Sustainability Issues

What influences people to hold attitudes, pro or con, toward sustainability issues and how to change those attitudes is well within the province of IOP and CP. Psychologists are experts in attitudes (see, for example, Fazio & Olson, 2003) and attitude change (e.g., Petty, 1989; Visser & Cooper, 2007), and can effectively assess attitudes on an individual, group, and organizational (or societal basis).

Executive Assessment

Selecting organizational leaders who support eco-friendly policies and who are willing to integrate sustainability issues into organizational decision-making processes makes it significantly easier to effectively address these issues on the local level. Psychologists are the experts in executive and managerial assessment (see, for example, Lefkowitz & Lowman, 2010; Silzer & Jeanneret, 2011). We can certainly devise valid and reliable ways to make such assessments.

A number of other potential contributions to sustainability initiatives could be identified that are well within the province of psychologists. Even if concern with sustainability is not an ethically oriented or values-driven requirement of I-O and consulting psychologists, we have significant contributions to make to what, I argue, is a cause with which all of us should rightfully be concerned.

Design of Work

Increasingly work must be redesigned to meet environmental standards (see, for example, Campbell & Campbell, 2005). Human factor psychologists are an important part of the team that redesign work in a way that is both environmentally appropriate and appropriate for the needs of people.

Helping to Create Ethical Organizational Climates

Evidence suggests that organizations can make a difference in the ethical behavior of their employees, vendors, and customers by creating and sustaining an ethical environment (see Adams, Tashchian, & Shore, 2001; Kish-Gephart, Harrison, & Treviño, 2010; McKinney, Emerson, & Neubert, 2010; Wimbush, Shepard, & Markham, 1997). Who better than I-O and consulting psychologists to help in this task?

ABOVE ALL, BE A PSYCHOLOGIST

We are self-selected and selected by others into the profession of psychology to use our science and our craft as a force for good in the world (Aguinis, 2011). By our ethics and the strong tradition we inherit from those who preceded us, we are predisposed to make a positive difference in the world. We, but not organizations, have an ethical obligation to use our knowledge for worthwhile, beneficent purposes. Whatever our particular areas of specialization, it is likely that we can apply the knowledge and practice of I-O and consulting psychology to contribute positively to the sustainability movement. Nothing less than the future of our planet may be at stake—if not in our lifetimes, then in those of the not-so-future generations of humans.

REFERENCES

Adams, J. S., Tashchian, A., & Shore, T. H. (2001). Codes of ethics as signals for ethical behavior. *Journal of Business Ethics, 29,* 199–211.

Aguinis, H. (2011). Organizational responsibility: Doing good and doing well. In S. Zedeck

(Ed.), *APA handbook of industrial and organizational psychology* (Vol. 3, pp. 855–879). Washington, DC: American Psychological Association.

Aguinis, H., & Glavas, A. (2012). What we know and don't know about corporate social responsibility: A review and research agenda. *Journal of Management, 38,* 932–968. doi: 10.1177/0149206311436079

Alderfer, C. P. (2011). *The practice of organizational diagnosis.* New York, NY: Oxford University Press.

American Psychological Association (2002). Ethical principles of psychologists and code of conduct. *American Psychologist, 57,* 1060–1073. doi: 10.1037/0003-066X.57.12.1060

American Psychological Association (2003). Guidelines on multicultural, education, training, research, practice, and organizational change for psychologists. *American Psychologist, 58,* 377–402.

American Psychological Association (2010). Ethical principles of psychologists and code of conduct. Adopted August 21, 2002. Effective June 1, 2003. With the 2010 Amendments. Adopted February 20, 2010. Effective June 1, 2010. *American Psychologist, 58,* 377–402. Retrieved January 14, 2013, from http://www.apa.org/ethics/code/principles.pdf

American Psychological Association (n.d.). *Our values.* Washington, DC: Author.

Armitage, K. C. (2005). State of denial: The United States and the politics of global warming. *Globalizations, 2,* 417–427. doi: 10.1080/14747730500368064

Aronson, E. (1999). The power of self-persuasion. *American Psychologist, 54,* 875–884.

Brief, A. P. (2000). Still servants of power. *Journal of Management Inquiry, 9,* 342–351.

Brinkley, D. (2009). *The wilderness warrior: Theodore Roosevelt and the crusade for America.* New York, NY: HarperCollins.

British Psychological Society (2011). *Code of ethics and conduct. Guidance published by the Ethics Committee of the British Psychological Society.* London: British Psychological Society. Retrieved July 18, 2011, from http://www.bps.org.uk/sites/default/files/documents/code_of_ethics_and_conduct.pdf

Buckles, D. (1999). *Cultivating peace: Conflict and collaboration in natural resource management.* Washington, DC: World Bank.

Cacioppo, J. T., Petty, R. E., Kao, C. F., & Rodriguez, R. (1986). Central and peripheral routes to persuasion: An individual difference perspective. *Journal of Personality and Social Psychology, 51,* 1032–1037.

Campbell, J.E., & Campbell, D.E. (2005). Eco-I-O psychology? Expanding our goals to include sustainability. *The Industrial-Organizational Psychologist, 43*(2), Retrieved December 17, 2012, from http://www.siop.org/tip/backissues/Oct05/04campbell.aspx

Canadian Psychological Association (2000). *Canadian code of ethics for psychologists.* Ottawa, Canada: Author.

Carson, R. (1962). *Silent spring.* New York, NY: Houghton Mifflin.

Clapp, R., & Mortenson, C. (2011). Adversarial science: Conflict resolution and scientific review in British Columbia's Central Coast. *Society & Natural Resources, 24,* 902–916. doi: 10.1080/08941921003801505

Dunphy, D., Griffiths, A., & Benn, S. (2007). *Organizational change for corporate sustainability: A guide for leaders and change agents of the future* (2nd ed.). London: Routledge.

Fazio, R. H., & Olson, M. A. (2003). Attitudes: Foundation, functions and consequences. In M.A. Hogg & J. Cooper (Eds.), *Sage handbook of social psychology* (Concise student edition, pp. 123–145). Thousand Oaks, CA: Sage.

Feygina, I., Jost, J. T., & Goldsmith, R. E. (2010). System justification, the denial of global warming, and the possibility of "system-sanctioned change". *Personality and Social Psychology Bulletin, 36*(3), 326–338. doi: 10.1177/0146167209351435

Franzen, A (2003). Environmental attitudes in international comparison: An analysis of the ISSP Surveys 1993 and 2000. *Social Science Quarterly, 84,* 297–308.

Gore, A. (2007). *An inconvenient truth: The crisis of global warming.* New York, NY: Penguin.

Hawking, S. (1988). A brief history of time. From the big bang to black holes. New York, NY: Bantam Books.

Huffman, A. H., Watrous-Rodriguez, K. M., Henning, J. B., & Berry, J. (2009, October). "Working" through environmental issues: The role of the I/O psychologist. *The Industrial-Organizational Psychologist, 47,* 27–35.

Jaques, P. J., Dunlap, R. E., & Freeman, M. (2008). The organisation of denial: Conservative think tanks and environmental skepticism. *Environmental Politics, 17,* 349–385.

Kahneman, D. (2011). *Thinking, fast and slow.* New York, NY: Farrar, Straus and Giroux.

Kates, R. W., Clark, W. C., Corell, R., Hall, J., Jaeger, C. C., Lowe, I., McCarthy, J. J., Schellnhuber, H. J., Bolin, B., Dickson, N. M., Faucheux, S., Gallopin, G. C., Gruebler, A., Huntley, B., Jager, J., Jodha, N. S., Kasperson, R.E., Mabogunje, A., Matson, P., Mooney, H., Moore III, B., O'Riordan, T., & Uno, S. (2001). Sustainability science. *Science, 292*(5517), 641–642. doi: 10.1126/science.1059386

Keeling, C. (1970). Is carbon dioxide from fossil fuel changing man's environment? *Proceedings of the American Philosophical Society, 114,* 10–17.

Kish-Gephart, J. J., Harrison, D. A., & Treviño, L. (2010). Bad apples, bad cases, and bad barrels: Meta-analytic evidence about sources of unethical decisions at work. *Journal of Applied Psychology, 95,* 1–31. doi: 10.1037/a0017103

Klein, S. R., Sanders, A. M., & Huffman, A. H. (2011). Green outcomes: Partnering with organizations to demonstrate unintended eco-benefits. *The Industrial-Organizational Psychologist, 48,* 39–46.

Koppes, L. L. (Ed.) (2007). *Historical perspectives in industrial and organizational psychology.* Manwah, NJ: Lawrence Erlbaum.

Krueger, R. A., & Casey, M. (2009). *Focus groups: A practical guide for applied research* (4th ed.). Thousand Oaks, CA: Sage.

Lash, J., & Wellington, F. (2007). Competitive advantage on a warming planet. *Harvard Business Review, 85,* 94–102.

Lefkowitz, J. (1990). The scientist-practitioner model is not enough. *The Industrial-Organizational Psychologist, 28*(1), 47–52.

Lefkowitz, J. (2003). *Ethics and values in industrial and organizational psychology.* New York, NY: Erlbaum (Francis & Taylor).

Lefkowitz, J. (2005). The values of industrial-organizational psychology: Who are we? *Industrial-Organizational Psychologist, 43*(2), 13–20.

Lefkowitz, J., & Lowman, R.L. (2010). Ethics of employee selection. In J.L.Farr & N. Tippins (Eds.), *Handbook of employee selection* (pp. 571–590). New York, NY: Psychology Press (Taylor & Francis).

Leopold, A. (1949). *A Sand County almanac, and sketches here and there.* New York, NY: Oxford University Press.

Lewin, K. (1948). Group decision making. In T.M. Newcomb & E.L. Hartley (Eds.), *Readings in social psychology* (pp. 330–341). New York, NY: Henry Holt.

Lowman, R. L. (2011, March 5). *Creating impact through assessment, coaching, and ethics.* Presentation at the annual IO-OB national conference, San Diego, CA.

Lowman, R.L. (2012). The scientist-practitioner consulting psychologist. *Consulting Psychology Journal: Practice and Research, 64*, 151–156. doi: 10.1037/a0030365

Lowman, R. L., Kantor, J., & Perloff, R. (2007). History of I-O psychology educational programs in the United States. In L. L. Koppes (Ed.), *Historical perspectives in industrial and organizational psychology* (pp. 111–137). Manwah, NJ: Lawrence Erlbaum.

McKinney, J. A., Emerson, T. L., & Neubert, M. J. (2010). The effects of ethical codes on ethical perceptions of actions toward stakeholders. *Journal of Business Ethics, 97*, 505–516. doi: 10.1007/s10551-010-0521-2

OD Network (2011). *Organization Development Network announces vision and mission.* Retrieved January 15, 2013, from http://c.ymcdn.com/sites/www.odnetwork.org/resource/resmgr/files/strategic_plan_1_pager_final.pdf

Opotow, S., & Weiss, L. (2000). New ways of thinking about environmentalism: Denial and the process of moral exclusion in environmental conflict. *Journal of Social Issues, 56*, 475–490. doi: 10.1111/0022-4537.00179

Petty, R. E. (1989). Attitude change. In A. Tesser (Ed.), *Advanced social psychology* (pp. 195–255). Boston, MA: McGraw-Hill.

Silzer, R., & Jeanneret, R. (2011). Individual psychological assessment: A practice and science in search of common ground. *Industrial and Organizational Psychology: Perspectives on Science and Practice, 4*, 270–296. doi: 10.1111/j.1754-9434.2011.01341.x

Singh, R., Murty, H. R., Gupta, S. K., & Dikshit, A. K. (2012). An overview of sustainability assessment methodologies. *Ecological Indicators, 15*(1), 281–299. doi: 10.1016/j.ecolind.2008.05.011

Society of Human Resource Management (SHRM) (2007). SHRM code of ethics. Retrieved December 17, 2012, from http://www.shrm.org/about/Pages/code-of-ethics.aspx

Teale, E. W. (Ed.) (2001). *The wilderness world of John Muir.* New York, NY: Houghton Mifflin Harcourt.

Ukeje, C. (2008). Globalization and conflict management: Reflections on the security challenges facing West Africa. *Globalizations, 5*, 35–48. doi: 10.1080/14747730701574510

United Nations World Commission on Environment and Development (WECD) (1987). *Report of the World Commission on Environment and Development: Our common future* (Report A/42/427). New York, NY: Author. Retrieved January 14, 2013, from http://www.un-documents.net/our-common-future.pdf

Visser, P. S., & Cooper, J. (2007). Attitude change. In M. A. Hogg & J. Cooper (Eds.), *Sage handbook of social psychology* (Concise student edition, pp. 197–218). Thousand Oaks, CA: Sage.

Weart, S. R. (2008). *The discovery of global warming* (2nd ed.). Cambridge, MA: Harvard University Press.

Wimbush, J.C., Shepard, J.M., & Markham, S.E. (1997). An empirical examination of the relationship between ethical climate and ethical behavior from multiple levels of analysis. *Journal of Business Ethics, 16*, 1705–1716.

4

Engineering Sustainability

David E. Campbell and J. Elliott Campbell

Scientists (primarily physical and biological) have been developing a description of evolving anthropogenic environmental trends that are completely new to human experience. The facts regarding these emerging ecological crises are so stark and disturbing that it is difficult to present them in a college classroom without leaving the students in a blue funk with a collective "doomster" outlook. Other scientists (primarily social and behavioral) have been refining theories of what motivates people to persist in environmentally-damaging actions, what maintains human lifestyle decisions, and what is needed to elicit change in environmental attitudes and behavior. Each group of scientists addresses a part of the problem—the problem of encouraging widespread individual and corporate environmental sustainability (CES). Physical and biological scientists are working out in detail the ways in which our actions as managers, workers, and consumers are leading to excessive greenhouse gas (GHG) emissions and destructive environmental pollution. But the research literature reveals little inclination for these scientists to address the task of redirecting human decisions and actions towards mitigation. Social and behavioral scientists, on the other hand, are centrally concerned with the human choices, social influence, organizational norms, emotions, habits, and individual aspirations. But their research literature shows only sporadic and limited concern for how to shift the mass of humanity in the direction of environmentally-sustainable lifestyles. This chapter addresses that gap. We review the perspective of environmental scientists with emphasis on environmental engineering, and identify ways in which a few of them are beginning to voice an inclination to engage in interdisciplinary work so as to include the human factor in their sustainable design projects. Our intent is to pave the way for industrial-organizational (I-O) psychologists to work more effectively with environmental engineers—and we begin by describing a time when engineers and I-O psychologists actually *were* effective in learning from each other.

A BIT OF HISTORY

During the latter part of the 19th century, Frederick Winslow Taylor, an American industrial engineer, developed the basic principles for combining tool design, rest breaks, and compensation schedules to optimize worker performance on jobs requiring manual labor. His work and resulting book, *Principles of scientific management* (Taylor, 1911), were lauded by the first true I-O psychologist, Hugo Munsterberg. In his *Psychology and industrial efficiency* (precursor to comprehensive I-O textbooks), he devoted a full section to Taylor's contributions (Munsterberg, 1913). In the early years of the 20th century, Lillian and Frank Gilbreth, two industrial engineers, applied time-and-motion analysis in their work to develop recommendations regarding the "one best way" to conduct most jobs. During the 1920s and 1930s, a series of engineering-inspired experiments at the Hawthorne Works in Cicero, Illinois, sought to optimize lighting levels, rest breaks, and compensation for factory workers. All of these early efforts to apply an engineering perspective to worker motivation and performance were given recognition in the first comprehensive I-O textbooks authored by Morris Viteles, *Industrial psychology* (1932) and *Science of work* (1934) and have been dutifully included in nearly all subsequent I-O textbooks of an introductory nature (based on the first author's personal observation over 40 years of teaching).

During the 1940s, a different form of workplace-oriented engineering was developed. Operating under the labels human engineering, human factors, and ergonomics, this specialty focused on the design of tools and workplaces to optimize worker (and consumer) safety, efficiency, convenience, and job performance (Spector, 2008). By taking into account anthropometrics, human information capacity, and other human limitations, tendencies, and capabilities (the *human* factor in the performance equation), industrial designers were able to make improvements in tools, displays, machine controls, workplaces, and consumer products. Beginning with early efforts to standardize military cockpit controls and by doing so reduce aircraft accidents, the field of human engineering has expanded to make improvements in nearly all areas of work, study, and play. It represents perhaps the only long-lasting established hybrid specialty encompassing both I-O psychology and a field of engineering.

At this point we have accounted for two historically significant areas of research activity linking I-O psychology and fields of engineering. But building on these two established areas of collaboration will not further the CES interests of this book. Industrial engineering tends to be closely allied with business and management (in fact, industrial engineering and production-operations management are sometimes considered synonymous) and neither deals specifically with environmental issues (Salvendy, 2001). And while the hybrid specialty "human factors engineering" addresses a specific set of human-machine and human-environment criteria, the list of criteria does not include environmental sustainability as a prominent item. We have to look further to find engineers with a central interest in environmental issues, and this will take us into engineering specialties with little sensitivity to psychological concepts and little or no training in the behavioral sciences.

SPECIALTIES WITHIN ENGINEERING

The U.S. Department of Labor Statistics lists 17 different engineering specialties, four of which deal fairly directly with the environment (Bureau of Labor Statistics, 2009). Most obvious is *environmental engineering*, which applies knowledge from biology and chemistry to environmental problems such as industrial wastewater treatment and the comparison of difference transportation modes on global warming. If engineering in general is understood as providing the link between scientific discoveries and economically viable social applications, then environmental engineering provides the link between environmental science findings and programs to achieve ecologically sustainable lifestyles. Historically, environmental engineering has been more concerned with mitigating human damage of natural environments (e.g., wastewater treatment facilities) than with the general issue of environmental sustainability. However, environmental engineering is evolving to a much broader focus on sustainability (Mihelcic et al., 2003). *Civil engineers* deal with the design and construction of structures such as factories and office buildings. In recent years they have become more concerned with ways to design and build in an environmentally-responsible manner (e.g., using recycled materials, working with passive solar principles). *Industrial engineers* combine management of employees, manufacturing technology, and information systems to maximize work performance and efficiency. They are well positioned to incorporate sustainability criteria into management programs. Finally, *mechanical engineers* work with mechanical devices of all kinds in the workplace. They can promote sustainability goals in the design and maintenance of tools and machinery involved in factory and office settings.

EMERGING INTEREST IN SUSTAINABILITY

While each of the above-mentioned engineering specialties are connected in some way to environmental issues, specific concern with environmental threats like global warming has emerged fairly recently in engineering science. Roots of this recent environmental sensitivity can be found in the work of Victor Papanek (1972) who referred to our throw-away society as a Kleenex culture. At about the same time, ecologist Howard Odum was arguing for the formation of an *ecological engineering* field with the goal of designing and constructing (or reconstructing) sustainable ecosystems to serve human needs (Mitsch, 1993). The primary focus here was on applying engineering knowhow to alter the world for human ends—*adapting* to global ecosystems in a sustainable way was a refinement in thinking that was to come later. Anton Moser added to the early calls for action by arguing that engineers should learn from nature as they approach the design of ecosystems. After all, ecological systems are inherently sustainable, so the task of the engineer is to identify and mimic the principles of natural sustainability (Moser, 1996). As the 20th century came to a close, voices in the engineering community (such as those just mentioned) were beginning to address more seriously the need to make environmental sustainability a requirement for engineering projects. But exactly how to accommodate this requirement is turning out to be a challenge for both practicing engineers and those involved in engineering education. An understanding of this application problem is relevant for the I-O psychologist who might hope to collaborate effectively with engineers and other design specialists to achieve outcomes involving sustainable organizational practices.

SUSTAINABILITY IN THE ENGINEERING EDUCATION CURRICULUM

Liv Haselbach, writing as editor for a special journal edition on sustainability, reminds us that ten years ago there were very few engineering programs in the United States that offered courses in sustainability or even mentioned sustainability in the curriculum (Haselbach, 2011). A parallel argument was made by Campbell and Campbell (2005) when they discussed the lack of interest in sustainability issues among faculty and students in I-O programs.

At this time, it appears that the various fields of engineering are taking the lead in making sustainability issues a prominent part of the curriculum. Kevern (2011) reviewed the available literature on engineering education and found that sustainability issues were often presented via case studies suggesting ways in which students could integrate green engineering concerns into capstone projects. Issues involving environmental sustainability were typically integrated into environmental engineering courses while the *social* aspects of sustainability (psychological, social, economic, and political) were associated with service learning courses such as the senior capstone requirement. Some of Kevern's observations could be taken as a warning to I-O psychologists and others who intend to engage in interdisciplinary relationships with engineers—especially civil engineers. He notes that many civil engineers express positive attitudes about sustainability as a general concept but have little idea what it really means in practice. The community of professional engineers is interested in becoming greener but at the same time reveals suspicion of new work concepts and resistance to changes in traditional practices. It doesn't help that sustainability is an evolving concept with no fixed definition; today's principles for achieving sustainability in new construction will not be the same as those of tomorrow as technology, building codes, and social support change. For civil engineers, this means being flexible, being uncomfortable, working with other professions, and being accommodating to new ideas (Kevern, 2011). The problem of organizational inertia and professional resistance to change is not new to I-O psychologists. However, it represents a complication if the two disciplines are expected to collaborate in CES-related projects while each side is dealing with its own issues of internal change and adaptation to new sustainability pressures.

The assertion that sustainability is a relatively recent addition to the engineering literature is supported by the 2003 call for a *new* metadiscipline of sustainability science and engineering—a new field integrating industrial, social, and environmental processes (Mihelcic et al., 2003). In essence, the authors were arguing that it is time to take environmental sustainability seriously—making it a featured goal and not just an added concern of the applied sciences that can be integrated into their usual activities. What is interesting about the Mihelcic article is the development of the social concept. The importance of social concerns in designing for sustainability was emphasized several years earlier in the Brundtland Commission Report. This influential document defined the three pillars of the modern sustainability movement as environmental, social, and economic (World

Commission on Environment and Development, 1987). Mihelcic et al. provide an expanded analysis of the social and economic pillars as they call for increased understanding of social and psychological processes on the part of engineers. They argue that engineers must consider the broad economic and social implications of their projects and take into account individual, household, and corporate decision processes. Using the "What would Jesus drive?" automobile ad campaign as an example, they urge engineers to attempt to understand individual and household belief systems when pursuing the objective of motivating the selection and design of greener products (such as energy-efficient modes of transportation). Of course this argument cuts both ways. Just as the engineering professions need greater awareness of consumer values, political realities, and social processes within institutions, the non-engineering public (particularly managers and administrators) require a better understanding of engineering fields for effective collaboration to occur.

The Brundtland Report and Mihelcic paper put pressure on the engineering community to take into account human thought processes and social forces while addressing sustainability goals in society. This same concern was applied to the design process by Blevis (2007) using the term *sustainable interaction design* (SID). However, SID is much more than a call to action—it includes a set of principles and an evaluation rubric for scoring a given design based upon sustainability criteria. For example, does the design result in the disposal of physical material? Does the design make possible the recovery of previously discarded physical material? Does the design make use of recycled physical materials or provide for the future recycling of physical materials when no longer needed? The SID approach promotes reuse and recycling. What the I-O psychologist can add is an understanding and a set of principles to motivate users or occupants of a SID to reliably engage in sustainable actions associated with reuse and recycling.

ACCEPTANCE OF SUSTAINABILITY AMONG ENGINEERS

Discussion of sustainability in the literature can result in the impression that the need to adopt sustainability goals is widespread within the community of engineering professionals. Unfortunately this may not be the case—at least, not yet. Chong et al. (2009) conducted a survey of members of the American Society of Civil Engineers (ASCE) who were associated with the construction industry. The findings revealed that fewer than a third of the respondents considered sustainability to be "very important," most did not know how to initiate sustainability in their work, only a few had participated in sustainability-related meetings (11%), and over 70% reported that less than 10% of their employees participated regularly in sustainability-related activities. In short, very few of the employees in the ASCE members' organizations were interested in and had participated in sustainability activities.

Mechanical Engineer provided slightly more positive findings in its latest annual survey of attitudes towards sustainability and green technology among mechanical engineers and mechanical engineering (ME) students (Brown, 2011). Two-thirds of the respondents reported that their organizations are "somewhat" or "extremely" involved in sustainability efforts (but one-fifth indicated little or no interest). The ME professionals generally endorsed designs and manufacturing processes that used less energy, reduced emissions, used renewable or recyclable materials and reduced waste, produced less pollution, and had smaller carbon footprints. However, a common comment was that sustainable engineering is nothing more than "good engineering." In other words, sustainability is really just the latest "flavor of the month"; responsible engineers have been designing with sustainability in mind all along—otherwise their firms would not have remained economically viable. For example, competent engineers know that including a fairly expensive but energy-efficient pump in a design will result in long-term savings because the capital costs are small relative to the operating costs. But Brown notes that capital budgets and operating budgets are often kept separate in organizations so the sustainable option becomes a tough sell for the manager who is pressured to keep capital costs down. Failure to effectively address this budget divide may result in an organizational decision to go with less-sustainable design options. One interesting finding from the survey is that sustainability is reported by 27% of ME students to be a core part of their curriculum (and 61% report that it is an elective). This appears to conflict with the finding covered earlier in this chapter on the need to emphasize sustainability in the engineering curriculum.

ACCEPTANCE OF SUSTAINABILITY CONCERNS WITHIN ORGANIZATIONS

While the engineering community is examining ways to define, support, and implement sustainability objectives, a similar discussion is occurring among management scholars. For example, Altman (2009) reports that one of the biggest issues facing corporations today is the problem of remaining financially viable while addressing social and environmental values within the organization. Drawing on a McKinsey global survey report, he claims that the main challenge facing businesses, government, and non-profit organizations today is how to stabilize GHG emissions and the global warming problem while maintaining economic growth. This is the same concern expressed by engineering practitioners—the professional (manager or engineer) must find a way to maintain sustainability objectives while maintaining a profitable business or consulting firm. This would not pose a problem if accommodating to sustainability objectives added value (or cut costs) for the organization in an obvious way. The problem arises with the perception that sustainability comes with its own costs—that is, adding sustainability to the set of current business objectives amounts to adding to the cost of doing business. Any proposal that raises business costs and threatens the viability of an organization is likely to be rejected by managers and administrators unless a persuasive argument can be mounted to accept and work with those added costs. See DuBois, Astakhova, and DuBois (this book) for a discussion of gaining acceptance for sustainability initiatives within organizations.

IMPLICATIONS FOR THE I-O PSYCHOLOGIST

We have represented engineering in this chapter as a varied group of specialties that hold in common an interest in application of science and technology to societal needs. The specific focus of engineering ranges from concern with ecological systems (e.g., environmental engineering) to manufacturing processes (industrial engineering) and office construction (civil engineering). (Dierdorff, Norton, Gregory, Rivkin, and Lewis, this book, provide a comprehensive listing of engineering and other jobs related to the green economy.) An underlying implication of our discussion is the conviction that engineers and I-O psychologists must understand the perspectives, biases, and internal issues of their respective disciplines if they are to effectively work together towards CES objectives. We conclude our discussion with a brief consideration of several suggestions for how engineers and I-O psychologists might initiate collaboration for the good of the environment.

First, it would help in any sustainability project to agree on just what the sustainability concept means. We prefer the definition provided by Mihelcic et al. (2003): Sustainability refers to:

> the design of human and industrial systems to ensure that humankind's use of natural resources and cycles do not lead to diminished quality of life due either to losses in future economic opportunities or to adverse impacts on social conditions, human health and the environment. (p. 5315)

A more specific definition could be worked out. However this is done, all parties must operate with a common understanding of what is meant by "sustainability" so that the ultimate outcome for a project is agreed upon from the outset.

Second, it must not be assumed that employees will occupy and use green designs in the intended sustainable manner. Instead, project designers should be alert for unanticipated and undesired use of the workspaces they construct. Jones (2011) provides a number of examples of energy-efficient buildings designed for living, learning, and working that actually resulted in *greater* energy use than would have been the case with conventional designs. For example, schools have been designed following passive-solar principles with large windows on sun-exposed walls to capture natural light for work and warmth. The result has been use of shades and blinds throughout the day with indoor lights constantly on and the heater turned up. The designers had failed to account for the occupants' response to glare, need to view information projected on large screens, tendency to leave blinds in position when no longer needed, and so on. Technical solutions for energy reduction that ignore human expectations, habits, and preferences run the risk of leaving us worse off than we were at the outset of the project.

Third, don't expect to fix all problems at the outset. All too often, projects are evaluated for sustainability at the conclusion of the design phase—before the users or occupants have arrived. The first author of this paper works in a building that was awarded the LEED gold certification and named "best overall sustainable design project in the UC/CSU system" for 2005. This was accomplished *before* the occupants had been allowed into their offices and labs. In other words, the building was evaluated and the builders were long gone before it was known exactly how the building would actually "work." As it turned out, there were numerous problems from the commuter showers for bicyclists that have yet to be used (no lockers or other secure spaces for valuables while in the shower) to unresponsive room thermostats (resulting in open windows with the heating system running). It is not possible to evaluate the building's energy-saving performance without taking into account occupant behavior. This can only be done by means of a post-occupancy evaluation (POE) with subsequent retrofitting and/or user training. Given the high cost of large office buildings and manufacturing facilities, the added cost of an interdisciplinary POE study seems small and is the only way to establish principles of use so that sustainability goals can be achieved (Gifford, 2007).

Fourth, concentrate first on projects where collaboration is likely to be successful. Construction of green office buildings and industrial facilities should be prominent on this list. Engineers are involved in the design and construction of buildings while I-O psychologists can play a role in assessment of occupant needs prior to construction, training of occupants at initial occupation, and evaluation of facilities post-occupation. I-O psychologists involved in such projects must understand that engineers and architects will focus on energy efficiency and use of recycled building materials in attaining green construction goals. Consequently I-O psychologists should have some familiarity with LEED certification. LEED stands for Leadership in Energy Efficiency and Design, and LEED certification is provided by the U.S. Green Building Council using a rating system that emphasizes energy efficiency and clean energy (2011). I-O psychologists should also understand sustainability-related business and industry concepts such as cradle-to-grave, life cycle assessment, and triple bottom line (corporate profitability, social responsibility, and environmental sustainability) in order to communicate with designers and managers on questions of environmental sustainability (McDonough & Braungart, 2002; Elkington, 1998; Horne, Grant, & Verghese, 2009).

Fifth, recognize that no matter how elegant the engineering solution is, human tendencies can undermine it. Among the psychological barriers to sustainable behavior change are a tendency to respond to short-term consequences while ignoring long-term outcomes, distrust of change, distrust of experts and other authority figures, and attachment to a worldview that precludes change in the direction of sustainability (Gardner & Stern, 2002; Gifford, 2011; Koger & Winter, 2010). (For more on motivations underlying sustainability, see Lindenberg & Steg, this book.) I-O psychologists have the responsibility of anticipating such barriers to sustainability and finding appropriate solutions.

Engineers and I-O psychologists working in the ergonomics tradition have had 60 years of success in addressing human tendencies to promote efficiency in work environments. Dealing effectively with the environmental challenges facing us will require even broader interdisciplinary efforts if we are to make substantial progress in the direction of CES. As Stern put it, psychologists must "stretch beyond the discipline, collaborate with experts in other areas, and combine psychological insights with those of other fields" if we are to avoid environmental catastrophes in the not so distant future (Stern, 2011, p. 311). We view collaboration between I-O psychology and environmentally-oriented fields of engineering as a potentially fruitful way to promote CES research.

REFERENCES

Altman, W. (2009). Carbon consultant. *Engineering & Technology, 4,* 76–79.

Blevis, E. (2007, April–May). *Sustainable interaction design: Invention and disposal, renewal and reuse.* Proceedings of the SIGCHI Conference on Human Factors in Computing Systems. San Jose, CA. doi: 10.1145/1240624.1240705

Brown, A. S. (2011). Sustainability. *Mechanical Engineering, 133,* 36–41.

Bureau of Labor Statistics (2009). *Occupational outlook handbook* (2010–11 edition, Architecture and engineering). United States Department of Labor. Retrieved December 17, 2012, from http://www.bls.gov/oco/ocos027.htm

Campbell, J. E., & Campbell, D. E. (2005). Eco-I-O psychology? Expanding our goals to include sustainability. *The Industrial-Organizational Psychologist, 4,* 23–28.

Chong, W. K., Kumar, S., Haas, C. T., Beheiry, S. M. A., Coplen, L., & Oey, M. (2009). Understanding and interpreting baseline perceptions of sustainability in construction among civil engineers in the United States. *Journal of Management in Engineering, 25,* 143–154.

Elkington, J. (1998). *Cannibals with forks: The triple bottom list of 21st century business.* Stony Creek, CT: New Society.

Gardner, G. T., & Stern, P. C. (2002). *Environmental problems and human behavior* (2nd ed.). Boston, MA: Pearson Custom.

Gifford, R. (2007). *Environmental psychology: Principles and practice* (4th ed.). Colville, WA: Optimal Books.

Gifford, R. (2011). The dragons of inaction: Psychological barriers that limit climate change mitigation and adaptation. *American Psychologist, 66*, 290–302.

Haselbach, L. (2011). Special issues on sustainability in civil and environmental engineering education. *Journal of Professional Issues in Engineering Education and Practice, 137*, 49–50.

Horne, R., Grant, T., & Verghese, K. (2009). *Life cycle assessment: Principles, practice, and prospects*. Collingwood, Australia: CSIRO.

Jones, G. (2011). Energy conserving buildings: The human factor. Scientists for Global Responsibility (SGR) *Newsletter, 40*, 17.

Kevern, J. T. (2011). Green building and sustainable infrastructure: Sustainability education for civil engineers. *Journal of Professional Issues in Engineering Education and Practice, 137*, Special Issue: Sustainability in civil and environmental engineering education, 107–112.

Koger, S. M., & Winter, D. D. N. (2010). *The psychology of environmental problems*. New York, NY: Psychology Press.

McDonough, W., & Braungart, M. (2002). *Cradle to grave*. New York: NY. North Point.

Mihelcic, J. R., Crittenden, J. C., Small, J. M., Shonnard, D. R., Hokanson, D. R., Zhang, Q., Chen, H., Sorby, S. A., James, V. U., Sutherland, J. W., & Schnoor, J. L. (2003). Sustainability science and engineering: The emergence of a new metadiscipline. *Environmental Science & Technology, 37*, 5314–5324.

Mitsch, W. J. (1993). Ecological engineering: A cooperative role with the planetary life-support system. *Environmental Science & Technology, 27*, 438–445.

Moser, A. (1996). Ecotechnology in industrial practice: Implementation using sustainability indices and case studies. *Ecological Engineering, 7*, 117–138.

Munsterberg, H. (1913). *Psychology and industrial efficiency*. Boston, MA: Houghton Mifflin.

Papanek, V. (1972). *Design for the real world: Human ecology and social change*. New York, NY: Pantheon.

Salvendy, G. (Ed.) (2001). *Handbook of industrial engineering: Technology and operations management* (3rd ed.). New York, NY: Wiley.

Spector, P. E. (2008). *Industrial and organizational psychology*. Hoboken, NJ: Wiley.

Stern, P. C. (2011). Contributions of psychology to limiting climate change. *American Psychologist, 66*, 303–314.

Taylor, F. W. (1911). *The principles of scientific management*. New York, NY: Harper & Row.

U.S. Green Building Council (2011). *LEED rating systems*. Retrieved December 17, 2012, from http://www.usgbc.org/DisplayPage.aspx?CMSPageID=222

Viteles, M. S. (1932). *Industrial psychology*. New York, NY: Norton.

Viteles, M. S. (1934). *Science of work*. New York: NY: Norton.

World Commission on Environment and Development. (1987). *Our common future*. New York, NY: Oxford University Press.

Part 2

Theory and Methods to Understand ES in Organizations

5

The Morality of Corporate Environmental Sustainability: A Psychological and Philosophical Perspective

Niti Pandey, Deborah E. Rupp, and Meghan A. Thornton

> **Alternatively Empowered** means making business decisions based on minimizing environmental impact, encouraging the growth of our employee owners, and being a socially responsible contributor to our community. It's rewarding, challenging, and educational. It's what makes us New Belgium.
>
> We believe to be environmental stewards we need to:
>
> 1. Lovingly care for the planet that sustains us.
> 2. Honor natural resources by closing the loops between waste and input.
> 3. Minimize the environmental impact of shipping our beer.
> 4. Reduce our dependence on coal-fired electricity.
> 5. Protect our precious Rocky Mountain water resources.
> 6. Focus our efforts on conservation and efficiency.
> 7. Support innovative technology.
> 8. Model joyful environmentalism through our commitment to relationships, continuous improvement, and the camaraderie and cheer of beer.
>
> —(New Belgium, undated, a)

The moral motivational space for corporate environmental sustainability (CES) efforts is a complex and nuanced one. Corporate social responsibility (CSR) has been defined as the responsibility of businesses encompassing "the economic, legal, ethical, and discretionary expectations that society has of organizations at a given point in time" (Carroll, 1979, p. 500). The ecological dimension of CSR is corporate environmental responsibility (de Bakker & Nijhof, 2002) and typically includes efforts aimed at environmental sustainability such as environmental concerns in business operations, environmental stewardship, and a cleaner environment (Dahlsrud, 2008). In broader terms, CES may be defined as "meeting the needs of the present generation without compromising the needs of the future generation" (Sarkis, 2001, p. 666).

Following Carroll's (1979) early model of CSR, CES efforts may also be viewed to exist as economic, legal, ethical, and discretionary responsibilities. At the lowest levels of CES are organizations that might be motivated by self-interest manifested in environmental concerns in business operations. At the very highest level of CES are firms like New Belgium Brewing Company, where the entire culture of the organization is organized around environmental sustainability principles aimed at high-impact stewardship imbued with deeply internalized social values. Recently, on the basis of an extensive review and analysis of the literature on CSR, Aguinis and Glavas (2012) propose that CSR be categorized as either peripheral ("focusing on activities that are not integrated into the daily strategies and operations") or embedded ("integrated into strategy and daily operations by using the firm's core competencies"). Synthesizing these ideas with Carroll's classical model, we can think about peripheral activities as motivated by economic and legal responsibilities and embedded activities as motivated by ethical and discretionary responsibilities. Aguinis and Glavas hold that embedded CSR requires an organization to build into its very culture the idea that social responsibility principles be the core competency in building and delivering products, supply chains, and services.

This continuum provides a useful starting point for talking about CES. We would expect organizations with peripheral CES activities to be motivated by economic and legal interests, and would interpret their actions through a lens of self-interest (enlightened or otherwise). [Enlightened self-interest is the "recognition that business can operate in a socially conscious manner without forsaking the economic goals that lead to financial success" (Werther & Chandler, 2011)]. Organizations with more embedded CES would be expected to develop a deep culture of environmental responsibility motivated by ethical and discretionary values and felt responsibilities. For such organizations, virtue ethics and principles of justice will drive a synchronization of strategic choices with a goal of creating an environmental values-based culture, whose strategic choices and actions are evident from their sustainability values statement (such as New Belgium's at the beginning of this chapter). Virtue ethics is described as:

> addressing itself to the question, "What sort of person should I be?" rather than to the question, "What sorts of actions should I do?" … as rejecting the idea that ethics is codifiable in rules or principles that can provide specific action guidance.

It includes virtues such as respectfulness, non-malevolence, benevolence, and justice or fairness (Hursthouse, 1999). Moving from peripheral to embedded activities would require a shift in organizational culture and values, as espoused by the top leadership and decision makers. Such large shifts in an organization's culture and values seldom occur and these sorts of internalization processes take time (Rupp & Williams, 2011). It should be noted, however, that some organizations "start up" with embedded CES as a defining element—the case of New Belgium later in the chapter will illustrate this. However, such organizations seem to be less prevalent than organizations that are making efforts to move along the peripheral/embedded continuum.

Cultural shifts in organizations require not just commitment from top management but also value identification from all employees. Culture is a social construction that cannot be imposed by organizational policies or mandates; rather, it is the product of interactions between individuals within organizations (see Alvesson, 2010). This is what makes CES a crucial and important topic for industrial-organizational (I-O) psychologists. Indeed, research has just begun to argue for the study of "the psychology of corporate social responsibility" (Aguinis & Glavas, 2012; Rupp, Williams, & Aguilera, 2011). We feel that CES in particular is further ripe for psychological investigation given that, within the public discourse, environmental issues have become highly moralized. This creates myriad perceptual, moral, and ethical issues for scholars of the environmental side of CSR (i.e., CES) to consider. For example, environmental sustainability as a highly moralized and ethical issue can have strong influences on employee attitudes and behaviors. In fact, research on organizational culture by Cardador and Rupp (2010) suggests that ethical culture encourages meaningful work experiences for employees through the pursuit of moral values and norms. Consequently, organizational CES actions can influence both employee and employer outcomes and the peripheral/embedded nature of CES in an organization can impact its ability to attract, motivate, and retain talent.

In this chapter we explore two key questions surrounding CES: Is CES a distinct enough part of the broader domain of CSR to warrant its own research literature? (e.g., does it have unique antecedents and consequences?) and, How do organizational acts of CES influence employee attitudes and behaviors? In order to answer these questions we explore the moral motivational space that surrounds these issues.

IS CES AN IMPORTANT AND DISTINCT ENOUGH PART OF THE BROADER DOMAIN OF CSR AND DOES IT HAVE ANTECEDENTS AND CONSEQUENCES DISTINCT FROM GENERAL CSR PHENOMENA?

Issues of environmental sustainability have become increasingly moralized in the public discourse. In the Western philosophical tradition, the concept of ecological ethics is fairly new and proposes that ethical questions must embrace not just other human beings but also the natural world (Curry, 2006). Moralizing an issue can have the effect of inculcating in people strong negative emotions and attitudes about behaviors that violate the expectations surrounding the moralized issue (Lindenberg & Steg, 2007; Horberg, Oveis, Keltner, & Cohen, 2009; Mulder & Rupp, 2012).

The Moralization of Environment Sustainability

When considering whether CES is unique from traditional discussions of CSR, it helps to reflect on the relative novelty, at least for Western moralities, of including the natural world within the domain of the moral. Rachel Carson's *Silent spring* (1962) is thought to have launched the environmental movement. This moralization of the environment stands in opposition to a theme in Western religious and philosophical traditions (i.e., the traditional engines of moral consciousness and judgment) emphasizing a division between human beings and nature. For example, the Bible presents humans as having been given the authority to "subdue" nature and to "have dominion" over everything on the earth (*Holy Bible*, Genesis 1:28). In the philosophical tradition, Immanuel Kant, whose thoughts are the bedrock of modern theories of rights, justice, and liberal democracy, states that it is "man, and in general every rational being" that exists "as an end in himself and not merely as a means to be arbitrarily used by this or that will" (Kant, 1996). The implication of such a view is that everything that is not a rational being is a mere means to be used arbitrarily according to human will.

Exceptions to this division between moral and rational humans and the non-moral domain of nature have existed, most notably among the American Transcendentalists (e.g., Ralph Waldo Emerson). However, a dilemma remains in moral philosophy as to the scope of this component of transcendental thought. Is the environment itself a phenomenon with moral status that should be considered an "end in itself" and not merely a "means to an end"? Or is it something that we should be morally concerned with only derivatively because of the consequences of environmental degradation on human beings?

Traditionally, the CSR literature has taken the latter approach. For example, the integrative social contracts theory approach of Donaldson and Dunfee (1995) construes CSR as what is minimally morally required by rational agents in a hypothetical social contract. Classic normative conceptions of stakeholder theory argue that a business ought to be concerned with the rights and/or wellbeing of all the individuals or groups who benefit from or are harmed by its actions (Evan & Freeman, 1988). We might interpret the fact that the majority of the CSR literature focuses on links between social and economic performance as suggestive of the non-moral status of social responsibility in the zeitgeist of management. Both views can regard the environment to be of moral concern only insofar as humans are harmed or have their rights ignored. But this derivative moral status insufficiently protects the environment, ignoring a host of values that surround moral concerns for the environment such as respect for wilderness, environmental beauty, and concern over limited natural resources. Traditional approaches do not view the scarcity of natural resources as relevant if such scarcity does not impact current and future generations. In fact, as stated earlier, CES has been defined as "meeting the needs of the present generation without compromising the needs of the future generation" (Sarkis, 2001). This limited definition can thus be seen to align with the environmentally-insufficient traditional approaches to corporate responsibility. Thus, the idea of environmental stewardship needs to underscore the importance of viewing CES (and in fact, CSR) through a much broader moral motivational lens.

Philosophers as different from each other as Thomas Aquinas and Friedrich Nietzsche have written that Western moral thinking evolves out of the notions of fair or just economic exchanges—relations that differ in tone from the idea of environmental ethics. Aquinas states that the moral virtue of justice only concerns "external actions and things … in so far as one man is related to another through them" ("Summa Theologica Q 58"). Right and just actions are those that are "adjusted to another person according to some kind of equality" either by a natural proportionality ("a man gives so much that he may receive equal value in return") or according to a contract or agreement ("Summa Theologica Q 57"). Likewise, Nietzsche (1998) argues that the very notion of moral obligation comes from "the oldest and most primitive relationship among persons there is, in the relationship between buyer and seller, creditor and debtor". More recently, the anthropologist David Graeber (2011) has argued similarly, stating that the basic language of right and wrong is based in economic transactions. Conceptualizing CSR with traditional Western moral notions, which appear to be themselves modeled on economic relations, leaves little space for environmental concerns.

The unique, non-anthropocentric theoretical foundations of environmental ethics suggest that CES should be differentiated from the ordinary set of stakeholder relations that characterize theorizing about CSR. But setting aside questions of the philosophical justification of moral and environmental concern, it seems that in contemporary life we are nearing the achievement of consensus that the environment is of significant moral concern, especially with younger generations, even as our moral theories lag behind. Moral judgments can be viewed simply as matters of past experiences of moral right and wrong, of harms and injustices, applied to new cases (Jonsen & Toulmin, 1988). Given that we all basically share the same moral experiences, the question before us is how, in practice, the emerging moral consensus of environmental concerns, as evidenced in public reactions to CES, is penetrating the workplace from the top down (in the form of organizational strategies and decisions) and consequently influencing employee attitudes, emotions, and behaviors.

Environmental sustainability is so moralized today that new terminology has been created to define the unethical actions of corporations. For example, "greenwashing" (Werther & Chandler, 2011) has entered the CSR lexicon. It refers to purely marketing-based motives for informing stakeholders of (real or construed) acts of CSR. It is a term imbued with immorality, and a strategy that has been shown to seem inauthentic and morally inappropriate by consumers. Further evidence of the public moralization of CES is illustrated by the public outcry following corporate acts of environmental irresponsibility. Take for example the case of Shell's Brent Spar oil drilling platform, where, upon discovering environmental irresponsibility, the public fallout was so serious that it required Shell to essentially reevaluate its culture, values, and decision-making processes.

On April 20, 1995, Shell announced that after considerable research the company had decided to dispose of Brent Spar by sinking it in the ocean. At the time, Shell was given approval by the U.K. Department of Trade and Industry and Department of Environment to tow the platform to an undisclosed location and sink it. It was believed that contaminants from the platform would become rapidly diluted and would have an insignificant impact on the environment. Greenpeace responded by occupying the platform, which, inactive since 1991, was being used to store waste from nearby drilling operations. Intense media and public outcry and scrutiny followed, including a boycott of Shell products by Germany. On June 20, 1995, just two months after their initial decision announcement, Shell announced that it was reconsidering sinking the platform and would instead seek a license for onshore disposal (Klein & Greyser, 1997).

The case of Brent Spar indicates that mere legal compliance is no longer sufficient to assuage the ethical standards society holds for environmental protection—even though Shell was following existing legislation regarding the assessment and disposal of the defunct oil rig, public opinion and environmental activism were strongly opposed to the company's actions and its perceived impact on the environment (Brent Spar, 1998). A highly moralized issue such as environmental sustainability is likely to engender strong emotions and attitudes in society. Environmental sustainability can, thus, create strong emotions in employees who are affiliated with the values, culture, and actions of their organization.

Differentiating CES from CSR

Based on the moralization arguments presented earlier, it is now possible in some ways to differentiate CES from traditional CSR. Classic definitions of

CSR have traditionally not included environmental or ecological concerns (Carroll, 1999), and typical definitions of CSR tend to focus on stakeholders (interactions with stakeholders, treatment of stakeholders) and society (contribution to betterment of society, integrating social concerns with business operations, considering the impact of business on communities), and not ecology per se. Having said that, it should be noted that in-depth explanations of CSR do often make reference to environmental issues (Dahlsrud, 2008), and we see that increasing importance is being placed on the environmental dimension of CSR as evidenced by the existence of organizational performance metrics like the triple bottom line. The triple bottom line is an "evaluation of businesses by comprehensively assessing their financial, environmental, and social performance" (Werther & Chandler, 2011).

Such change is stemming not just from stakeholder concerns at a societal level, but also at a supranational level in the form of the directives of bodies like the United Nations (see Reichman, Berry, Cruse, and Lytle, this book, for a review of international organizations' contributions to environmental sustainability). The most salient example of this is the United Nations Global Compact, which is "an initiative intended to increase and to diffuse the benefits of global economic development through voluntary corporate policies and actions" (Williams, 2008). It focuses, among other issues, on concern for the environment through principles that state "businesses should support a precautionary approach to environmental challenges; undertake initiatives to promote greater environmental responsibility; and encourage the development and diffusion of environmentally friendly technologies." CES has become increasingly relevant as a distinct feature of broader CSR in areas such as supply chain management (Kovacs, 2008), product innovation (Dangelico & Pujari, 2010), and manufacturing in general (Sarkis, 2001). There is even a call for integrating environmental management in organizations with human resource management systems to ensure the effectiveness of CES efforts (Jabbour & Santos, 2008).

Traditional CSR research has tended to focus on the impact of organizational decisions on external stakeholders such as stockholders, partners, customers, and society in general. And while employees are acknowledged as organizational stakeholders, CSR theory has traditionally overlooked the impact of CSR-related decisions on employees. We propose that the moralization of CES in public discourse makes CES a distinct part of CSR for I-O psychology to pursue since it is likely to impact employees as a key stakeholder category. Additionally, organizations are increasing their efforts at environmental sustainability, driven by complex motives ranging from peripheral (such as legal compliance) to embedded (such as virtues of environmental stewardship) strategies. In the next section we will discuss these complex motives and how mechanisms such as self-determination, value internalization, and/or justice-based identification translate organizational-level CES into employee attitudes and behaviors.

HOW DOES CES AT THE ORGANIZATIONAL LEVEL INFLUENCE EMPLOYEE-LEVEL ATTITUDES AND BEHAVIOR?

Most of the research on CSR tends to be at the institutional/firm/organizational level of analysis. It focuses on the actions and reactions of external stakeholders (e.g., customers, shareholders, suppliers, vendors, government, NGOs, society), and often studies the interrelationships between a firm's social and financial performance (Aguinis & Glavas, 2012). Yet, as pointed out by Bansal and Roth (2000), firms may choose to engage in CSR for value-based (as opposed to strictly instrumental) reasons. Regardless of the justifications behind institutional decision making, organizations create a values culture, an ethos, which we can assume informs employee attitudes. This has been evidenced by extant I/O psychology research (e.g., research on organizational culture and climate, Ashkanasy, Wilderom, & Peterson, 2010; attraction-selection-attrition, Schneider, 1987; and person-environment fit, Kristof-Brown, Zimmerman, & Johnson, 2005). It is not difficult to imagine that an institution's values and principles can be edifying for employees, which, through work experience, might narrow or broaden their circle of moral regard (Reed & Aquino, 2003). But at the same time, employees also come to work with independent moral compasses, with which they are able to judge the social responsibility of organizational acts. Such perceptions can have an impact on their identification with the organization as well as their job satisfaction, organizational commitment, citizenship behaviors, work engagement, turnover intentions, and job performance (Rupp, Ganapathi, Aguilera, & Williams, 2006; Rupp, Thornton, Bielski Boris, & Bruno, 2012).

CES offers a unique frame through which to view how the culture of an institution informs employees' perceived alignment between their own values and those of their employing organization. Shifting moral attitudes towards the environment are to be expected given the already noted novelty of environmental ethics. This suggests a developmental perspective on both individual employee and organizational CES values. Just as organizations could potentially move, over time, from peripheral acts of CES to more embedded ones, so too could employee values shift as environmental issues become increasingly infused within the public discourse, and as employees are increasingly exposed to CES issues at work.

Rupp and Williams (2011) provided an illustrative case of this phenomenon in their description of how the Equator Principles have changed the moral landscape surrounding environmental protection in the field of project finance. In 2000, Citigroup was targeted by the Rainforest Action Network (RAN) for financing infrastructure projects that harmed the environment and the indigenous people living near such projects. After RAN-sponsored protests and publicity campaigns began to threaten its reputation, Citigroup worked with RAN to review its policies, and agreed to a set of guidelines to manage the social and environmental impact of capital projects in the developing world (Werther & Chandler, 2011). These guidelines, launched in 2003, became known as the Equator Principles and were based on the International Finance Corporation's original guidelines for funding projects in developing countries (Sevastopulo, 2006).

It is now estimated that 75% of project finance is carried out by banks that have adopted the Equator Principles as a voluntary code of conduct, and many of the global banks that have adopted these principles have, over time, introduced similar environmental sustainability initiatives into other aspects of their business (i.e., beyond project finance alone; Conley & Williams, 2011). Rupp and Williams (2011) provide evidence of a "contagion effect," resulting in a shift over time from environmental motives that were largely self-serving (i.e., reputational threats, in addition to the fact that project finance involves non-recourse loans, and thus there is no party responsible for payback in the event of a natural disaster), to motives that were more relational (i.e., industry norms developed surrounding environmental sustainability), to motives that were more truly ethics-based (e.g., as evidenced by the evolution and widespread adoption of the Equator Principles).

Now that we have begun to explicate the motive structures both firms and employees may hold for implementing or reacting to CES, we will further this discussion by presenting the specific psychological mechanisms that may undergird CES. Our full theoretical model is presented in Figure 5.1. In this model, we see CES actions along the continuum of peripheral actions (reducing pollution, minimizing waste, legal compliance) to intermediate actions (developing green products, better reputation, following industry norms and "softer" forms of regulation) to embedded actions (genuine environmental stewardship). In the remainder of the chapter, we present the psychological mechanisms we expect to operate on employee attitudes and behaviors, and provide illustrative case studies to support our inferences.

Peripheral CES and Employee Self-Determination

We propose that CES actions of organizations at the peripheral level are motivated by economic and legal responsibilities and will include such actions as reducing pollution, minimizing waste, and compliance with legal standards. Society expects businesses to produce goods and services that are in demand and sell these for a profit while adhering to society's laws and regulations (Carroll, 1979). This is what is known in the legal

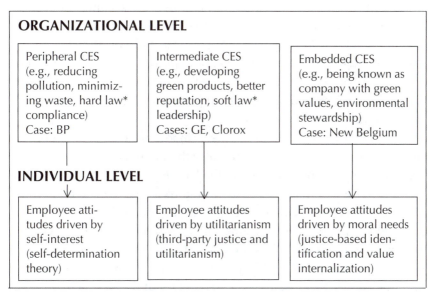

FIGURE 5.1
Multi-level, multi-motive model of corporate environmental sustainability (CES).

* Hard laws are prescriptive standards while soft laws are voluntary governance initiatives (Williams, 2004)

literature as compliance to *hard law* (Rupp & Williams, 2011). We assume that most legitimate organizations in our society are upholding the minimum legal standards pertaining to the environment, and, consequently, are engaged in some peripheral level of CES actions. However, as the Brent Spar case described earlier reveals, an organization's primary focus for its economic responsibilities, even if undertaken within the scope of the law, can have dire environmental consequences.

The recent BP oil spill is another example. On April 20, 2010, an explosion on Deepwater Horizon, a BP-operated oil-drilling facility, exploded and killed 11 employees. Between then and July 15, when the underwater rupture was finally capped, around 4.9 million barrels of crude oil leaked into the surrounding ocean and only 800,000 barrels were captured during the containment operations ("BP leak," 2010). The consequent devastation of the marine and coastal environment has been well documented. The administration's oil spill commission's final report concluded that a series of cost-cutting decisions were made by both BP and its partners that eventually led to the accident ("Obama oil spill," 2011). The report stated that "whether purposeful [and we would add legal] or not, many of the decisions that BP, Halliburton, and Transocean made that increased the risk of the Macondo blowout clearly saved those companies significant time (and money)" and that "the root causes are systemic and, absent significant reform in both industry practices and government policies, might well recur." Ultimately, BP may be required to pay billions of dollars in fines as civil penalties under the Clean Water Act, of which President Obama has recommended a significant proportion be allocated to ecological restoration ("Task Force," 2011).

Significant from the perspective of our model of CES is BP's response to the spill. Then CEO Tony Hayward called the amount of oil and dispersant "relatively tiny" in comparison with the "very big ocean" ("BP boss," 2010) and that the environmental impact would likely be "very, very, modest" ("BP doubles," 2010). Despite this, the subsequent media and public relations fallout resulted in BP creating a new division to handle the response and spent millions of dollars on ad campaigns to salvage the company image ("BP's television," 2010). BP even bid on and bought several search terms on Google that would direct searches about the oil spill to the company website ("BP buys," 2010). These links lead searchers to the company's efforts and policies for addressing the environmental impact of the spill. Ultimately, Tony Hayward quit as CEO and the culture at BP was criticized as having played a huge role in how the events unfolded ("Our view," 2010).

We propose that organizations where leadership and culture are motivated by economic self-interest or enlightened self-interest (driven by legal necessities, such as BP, or by RAN activism in the case of Citigroup) will display very perfunctory CES actions. Environmental sustainability values at such organizations are largely motivated by issues of image, reputation, or economic and legal viability. We expect the employees at these organizations to have corresponding motive structures—that is, CES motives that are based more on self-interest than virtue ethics. A psychological theory of motivation that may help us unpack these predictions is self-determination theory (Deci & Ryan, 1985).

Self-determination theory holds optimal human behavior to be predicated on motivation and responsibility, and that in certain contexts optimal human behavior might be compromised (Ryan & Deci, 2000). Rejecting the requirements of law would be considered non-optimal human behavior under this model. The theory posits that individual behaviors can be explained as reactions to social environments and the conditions under which humans are able to live up to their potential (Gagne & Deci, 2005). Thus, employees' reactions to environmental issues (which are manifested in their attitudes and behaviors) could be attributed to the social context they function in—their firm's culture and predominant CES values. In organizations with peripheral CES actions, employees are expected to be primarily motivated by the threats of non-compliance (i.e., the avoidance of punishment). For example, a company might institute a green initiative in response to bad publicity or legal issues. Such a culture might create a compliance attitude in employees and behaviors, leading to their participation in the initiative more to avoid negative repercussion than to actually help to protect the environment. This would be especially the case if the company instituted accountability measures for compliance (such as through performance evaluations, which is gaining popularity in many companies; Collier & Esteban, 2007).

Intermediate CES and Utilitarianism-Based Third-Party Justice

We propose that CES actions of organizations at the intermediate level will be motivated by ethical responsibilities that are based in enlightened self-interest. These are organizations that realize that in order to gain competitive advantage in the long run they can no longer choose to ignore CES issues. These organizations actively make the choice to change their business strategy and culture and focus at least some of their resources on efforts such as developing green products, adopting voluntary sustainability standards, or developing and maintaining a reputation for being environmentally conscious. Organizations might see economic opportunity in the increasing concern for the environment (Werther & Chandler, 2011) and see opportunities for an overlap between enlightened self-interest and utilitarian values. In these cases, firms are more likely to sign on to voluntary codes of conduct and follow industry-level standards (these non-legal forms of regulation are often referred to as *soft law*; Williams, 2004), as a way to signal to stakeholders environmental concern that they (the organization) may or may not have actually internalized.

For example, in 2002 GE appointed a vice president of corporate citizenship and in 2005 launched its Ecomagination program, which centered on creating solutions for renewable energy, water services, and clean technology, and which has amassed a revenue of $17 billion (Kamenetz, 2009). Environmental sustainability has become a key driver of innovation for many firms today and executives no long need to necessarily choose between social/environmental benefits and developing financially viable products or processes (Nidumolu, Prahalad, & Rangaswami, 2009). Nidumolu et al. contrast the cases of automobile manufacturers and Hewlett-Packard (HP) to illustrate how enlightened self-interest can motivate organizations to view legal compliance as an opportunity for innovation. For example, unlike their competitors, GM, Ford, and Chrysler did not embrace California Air Resources Board's fuel consumption and emission standards when they were proposed in 2002, thus putting them several design cycles behind their rivals. The California guidelines are set to become U.S. law by 2016, thus providing early adopters a competitive advantage. On the other hand, HP realized in the 1990s that most governments would soon ban the use of lead in solders. Consequently, the company invested in innovating alternatives and by 2006 had created a product that was able to comply with the European Union's Restriction of Hazardous Substances Directive as soon as it came into effect.

A voluntary and proactive approach to environmental strategies (i.e., CES activities that go beyond regulatory requirements) has been said to pay off in terms of social reputation, customer preferences, continuous innovation, and employee motivation (Aragon-Correa & Rubio-Lopez,

2007). Thus, while at the peripheral CES level, firms might commit only superficially to sustainability (or do so to get themselves out of trouble), at the intermediate level, organizations can be expected to commit via actions such as financial investments in sustainability-related innovation. At these organizations, the culture and values support the attainment of profitability and success in conjunction with sustainability principles rather than subverting one for the other.

Another example is Clorox, a manufacturer and marketer of premium-branded consumer products. Clorox was founded in 1913 and a Centennial Strategy was devised to honor the company's 100th anniversary in 2013 through the achievement of accelerated growth and key metrics for measuring success. Clorox decided to focus on two "megatrends"—health and wellness, and environmental sustainability. Consequently, Clorox successfully rebranded Brita (a water filtration system), acquired Burt's Bees (a natural personal care line), and launched Green Works (a natural cleaning product line). In spite of the challenging business environment, Clorox has been meeting or exceeding success targets under this initiative, with sales in 2010 of $5.5 billion. And although these initiatives accounted for just 10% of Clorox revenues, they contributed to most of the company's sales growth over the recent years (Ofek & Barley, 2011).

Companies like GE and Clorox are examples of intermediate CES—while they make certain strategic choices and actions aimed at environmental sustainability, these choices stem from economic self-interest at the least and utilitarianism at the most. In these cases CES only pervades (strategically chosen) aspects of the organization's operations. However, at both GE and Clorox, accountability measures have been put into place to strongly institutionalize sustainability practices. With such CES actions, organizations create divisions, positions, and jobs that require CES capabilities and make environmental sustainability a strategic part of the organizational structure. These organizations formalize goals of environmental sustainability and put in place metrics for measuring successful achievement of these goals in financial terms. Thus, the culture in such organizations is likely to promote employee attitudes aimed at utilitarian solutions—creating products and services for the greater good of society and making them profitably so.

We hold that at organizations with intermediate CES, employee attitudes will be shaped via utilitarian values and third-party justice perceptions. Utilitarianism as an ethical theory holds that the moral worth of actions should be determined by the resulting outcomes—specifically, increasing the greater good. Jeremy Bentham (1907) wrote that:

> by utility is meant that property in any object, whereby it tends to produce benefit, advantage, pleasure, good, or happiness, (all this in the present case comes to the same thing) or (what comes again to the same thing) to prevent the happening of mischief, pain, evil, or unhappiness to the party whose interest is considered: if that party be the community in general, then the happiness of the community: if a particular individual, then the happiness of that individual. (See p. 4, section 1.4)

John Stuart Mill (1951) extended on Bentham's concept and claimed that all outcomes are not equal and that the quality of outcomes matter in his "greatest happiness principle," which holds that "actions are right in proportion as they tend to promote happiness; wrong as they tend to produce the reverse of happiness" (p. 7).

While this ethical philosophy does disregard the environment as a party of interest, and in Mill's case applies to only sentient beings, the moralization of environmental issues today requires us to apply ethical theories to better understand human attitudes. As such, utilitarian values work in congruence with the notion of third-party justice perceptions, a recent extension of the organizational justice literature (Skarlicki & Kulik, 2005). This research suggests that employees form perceptions about how others are treated by organizations, as well as the levels of dignity and respect bestowed to external groups by firms (Rupp, 2011). Perceptions of justice can and do exist independent of individual self-interest, and individuals are likely to feel moral unease when they witness unfair treatment of others (Folger, 1998, 2001). Rupp et al. (2006) concluded that "justice is a universal norm of interpersonal conduct and people have an automatic morality-driven response upon witnessing injustice, even when they are not themselves the victim of the unfair act" (p. 538). Although the justice literature has largely applied this theoretical reasoning to the study of how employees react to the unfair treatment of coworkers, CSR scholars have extended this line of inquiry to explore how employees react to situations where their employing firm acts unethically toward external social groups and the environment (e.g., Rupp et al., 2012). Creating environmentally-safe or green products and services can be seen as an essentially utilitarian outcome—it provides the greatest good. Additionally, an organizational culture and strategy centered on environmental sustainability innovation signals a degree of concern for environmental issues to employees. Consequently, at organizations with intermediate CES, we can assume that actions aimed at the environment as an external stakeholder group will impact employee justice perceptions, job attitudes, and their own citizenship behaviors within the firm. Employees that value environmental protection will be attracted to and remain with organizations with such CES initiatives in place (Rupp & Thornton, in press; Schneider, 1987).

Embedded CES and Justice-Based Moral Identification

Embedded CES exists in organizations that grew out of a sustainability vision. These are organizations that are motivated by their role as environmental stewards and their core mission statement is first and foremost one of CES. For example, Patagonia states that its "reason for being" is to "build the best product, cause no unnecessary harm, use business to inspire and implement solutions to the environmental crisis" (Patagonia, 2012). Burt's Bees, an independently operated part of Clorox, states about their culture: "In the stewardship of our brand and the environment, we set high standards, build for the future and never compromise quality" (Burt's Bees, 2012). The company Tom's of Maine has a stewardship model as part of their organizational values, which includes standards for sustainability such as to:

> contribute to environmental and economic sustainability; environmentally friendly products and packaging; establish safety and efficacy in our products and ingredients without testing on animals; renewable and recyclable resources; biodegradability; promote sustainable harvesting practices; and accountable to present and future generations. (Tom's, 2012)

We began this chapter with New Belgium's sustainability values statement. New Belgium was started by Jeff Lebesch as a home-brewing family operation that went commercial in 1991 and became immensely well known for famous brands such as Fat Tire beer. As of 2010, New Belgium is the third largest craft brewery and the seventh largest overall brewery in the USA. (Brewers, undated). The founding cultural values of New Belgium include beliefs such as kindling social, environmental, and cultural change as a business role model, and environmental stewardship—

honoring nature at every turn of the business, among others. New Belgium is wholly owned by its employees and stresses both employee ownership and eco-friendly practices as their cornerstones. In 1998 the employee owners voted to convert all operations to being completely wind powered ("New Belgium," undated, b). The company has set up an environmental stewardship grants program, the purpose of which "is to serve and connect with the communities where we sell our beers ... cultivate relationships and support those making an impact ... improve the health of the planet and inspire others to joyously embrace sustainable choices" (New Belgium, undated, c).

New Belgium is the perfect example of an organization with embedded CES. Employees who seek employment, engagement, and ownership in such organizations are driven by deep moral needs. In our model, we propose that justice-based identification and value internalization are strong explanatory mechanisms for employee attitudes and behaviors in such organizations. For instance, we can expect that the employee owners in the New Belgium case have extremely strong congruence with their organization's CES culture and values. Their attitudes and behaviors are thus embedded in nature as well—they make decisions (moving to wind power) based on this value congruence and not in response to economic or legal responsibilities.

Justice-based identification suggests that there is a deontic approach to understanding employee attitudes (Rupp & Cropanzano, 2002; Rupp & Bell, 2010; Rupp, 2011). (The term "deontic" is derived from the Greek term *deon*, meaning duty or obligation.) Moral philosophers have long held justice as a moral imperative and, increasingly, I-O psychologists are starting to apply this understanding to organizational justice and employee attitudes (Folger & Skarlicki, 2008). Early research has established that people are willing to sacrifice their own interests in response to perceptions of injustice and allocate their own resources to uphold justice (Kahneman, Knetsch, & Thaler, 1986). This was seen in the case of New Belgium where employees chose to use their bonus to subscribe to a wind energy program in order to reduce their carbon footprint (New Belgium, undated, d). People also have a tendency to want to punish those who commit injustice against others (Truxillo, Folger, Lavelle, Umphress, & Gee, 2002), with those high in moral maturity tending more toward punishment (Rupp, 2003).

Employees with justice-based identities are likely to believe that fair and just actions are an end in themselves because they are the right things to do, and that injustices are often discretionary and unethical actions against undeserving parties (Rupp, 2011). This deontic approach can be applied to organizational actions that impact the environment. The moralized social discourse today has made the environment and the planet a key entity undeserving of injustice and unethical treatment that harm, deplete, or destroy the environment. Thus, from a CES perspective, employees motivated by deontic justice as a core value will be attracted and engaged in organizations that exist to sustain the environment and defray the harmful impact of their existence through conscious, proactive, strategic means.

WHAT LEADS TO THE MOST ENVIRONMENTAL SUSTAINABILITY?

As environmental sustainability becomes moralized in the public discourse, there is greater pressure on organizations to engage in CES practices. However, as the cases discussed in this chapter illustrate, organizations can have varying motives for engaging in CES. Similarly, the moral motivation for employees to respond positively to, advocate for, and participate in their organizations on CES issues will vary as well. Our discussion illustrates that organizational CES creates a social context in which employees function and that employees' motivation to be engaged in their organizations is actively shaped by this context (Rupp et al. 2011). Our model proposes that we will see varying levels of CES efforts depending on how organizations create their CES context and how this motivates employees. People tend to comply with rules only to the extent to which they feel psychological identification with the governing entity (Tyler, 2009). Employees, over time, develop attitudes based in identification with their organization's values (Rupp & Williams, 2011).

We are likely to see the least CES efforts from organizations engaged in peripheral actions with employees motivated by self-interest, such as in the case of BP. In such organizations, the focus of CES will be on legal compliance and/or salvaging or repairing reputation. Many CES actions today are driven by corporate enlightened self-interest, and a corresponding employee attitude of utility and third-party justice. These types of organizations are engaged at an intermediate level of CES. In such cases, organizations are likely to leverage employee engagement to innovate and create profitable products and services, such as at HP. We are likely to see the most environmental sustainability efforts from organizations with embedded CES, whose employees are driven by virtue ethics and justice-based morals and who identify with the sustainability culture of their organization. These are the organizations like New Belgium, where employees are willing to sacrifice their self-interests in order to realize the CES potential of their organization. And while it is true that many organizations with embedded CES are so since their inception because of the values and culture of the founders, it is possible for organizations to move along the continuum from peripheral to intermediate to embedded CES, over time.

The decisions organizations make do not operate in isolation—rather they actively create the context in which employee attitudes are shaped. Employees hold mixed motives beyond self-interest and organizations must find ways of meeting these values (Cropanzano, Stein, & Goldman, 2007). If indeed employees' moral motives are closely related to organizational sustainability actions, the study of CES takes on great relevance for I-O psychology. We can assume that employees' values-based identification with their organization's CES culture will likely impact the organization's ability to attract, engage, and retain desirable employees, thus making this topic an exciting new area of study.

REFERENCES

Aguinis, H., & Glavas, A. (2012). What we know and don't know about corporate social responsibility: A review and research agenda. *Journal of Management, 38*, 932–968. doi: 10.1177/0149206311436079

Alvesson, M. (2010). Organizational culture: Meaning, discourse, and identity. In N. M. Ashkanasy, C. P. M. Wilderom, & M. F. Peterson (Eds.), *The handbook of organizational culture and climate* (2nd ed., pp. 11–28). Thousand Oaks, CA: Sage.

Aragon-Correa, J. A., & Rubio-Lopez, E. A. (2007). Proactive corporate environmental strategies: Myths and misunderstandings. *Long Range Planning, 40*, 357–381.

Ashkanasy, N. M., Wilderom, C. P. M., & Peterson, M. F. (Eds.) (2010). *The handbook of organizational culture and climate* (2nd ed.). Thousand Oaks, CA: Sage.

Bansal, P., & Roth, K. (2000). Why companies go green: A model of ecological responsiveness. *Academy of Management Journal, 43*, 717–736.

Bentham, Jeremy (1907). *An introduction to the principles of morals and legislation.* Library of Economics and Liberty. Retrieved December 16, 2012, from http://www.econlib.org/library/Bentham/bnthPML.html

BP boss admits job on the line over Gulf oil spill. (2010, May 14). *The Guardian.* Retrieved December 14, 2012, from http://www.guardian.co.uk/business/2010/may/13/bp-boss-admits-mistakes-gulf-oil-spill

BP buys "oil" search terms to redirect users to official company website. (2010, June 5). ABC News. Retrieved December 14, 2012, from http://abcnews.go.com/Technology/Broadcast/bp-buys-search-engine-phrases-redirecting-users/story?id=10835618#.TwExN9XIDSg

BP doubles estimate for oil captured from spill. (2010, May 18). Bloomberg News. Retrieved December 14, 2012, from http://www.bloomberg.com/news/2010-05-18/bp-doubles-its-estimate-for-amount-of-oil-being-captured-in-gulf-of-mexico.html

BP leak the world's worst accidental oil spill. (2010, August 3). *The Telegraph.* Retrieved December 14, 2012, from http://www.telegraph.co.uk/finance/newsbysector/energy/oilandgas/7924009/BP-leak-the-worlds-worst-accidental-oil-spill.html

BP's television ad blitz. (2010, June 4). CNN. Retrieved December 14, 2012, from http://money.cnn.com/2010/06/03/news/companies/bp_hayward_ad/?postversion=2010060321

Brent Spar gets chop. (1998, November 25). BBC World News. Retrieved December 14, 2012, from http://news.bbc.co.uk/2/hi/europe/221508.stm

Brewers Association releases 2010 top 50 brewers list. (2012). Brewers Association. Retrieved December 14, 2012, from http://www.brewersassociation.org/pages/media/press-releases/show?title=brewers-association-releases-2010-top-50-breweries-lists

Burt's Bees (2012). *Our Culture.* Retrieved January 4, 2013, from http://www.burtsbees.com/c/story/culture.html

Cardador, M. T., & Rupp, D. E. (2010). Organizational culture, multiple needs, and the meaningfulness of work. In N. M. Ashkanasy, C. P. M. Wilderom, & M. F. Peterson (Eds.), *The Handbook of organizational culture and climate* (2nd ed., pp. 158–180). Thousand Oaks, CA: Sage.

Carson, R. (1962). *Silent spring.* New York, NY: Houghton Mifflin.

Carroll, A. (1999). Corporate social responsibility: Evolution of a definitional construct. *Business and Society, 38,* 268–295.

Carroll, A. B. (1979). A three-dimensional conceptual model of corporate performance. *Academy of Management Review, 4,* 497–505.

Collier, J., & Esteban, R. (2007). Corporate social responsibility and employee commitment. *Business Ethics: A European Review, 16,* 19–33.

Conley, J. M., & Williams, C. (2011). Global banks as global sustainability regulators? The Equator Principles. *Law and Policy, 33,* 542–575.

Cropanzano, R., Stein, J., & Goldman, B. M. (2007). Individual aesthetics: Self-interest. In E. H. Kessler & J. R. Bailey, (Eds.), *Handbook of Organizational and Managerial Wisdom.* Thousand Oaks, CA: Sage.

Curry, P. (2006). *Ecological ethics: An introduction.* Cambridge, UK: Polity Press.

Dahlsrud, A. (2008). How corporate social responsibility is defined: An analysis of 37 definitions. *Corporate Social Responsibility and Environmental Management, 15,* 1–13.

Dangelico, R. M., & Pujari, D. (2010). Mainstreaming green product innovation: Why and how companies integrate environmental sustainability. *Journal of Business Ethics, 95,* 471–486.

De Bakker, F., & Nijhof, A. (2002). Responsive chain management: A capability assessment framework. *Business Strategy and Environment, 11,* 63–75.

Deci, E. L., & Ryan, R. M. (1985). *Intrinsic motivation and self-determination in human behavior.* New York, NY: Plenum Press.

Donaldson, T., & Dunfee, T. (1995). Integrative social contracts theory: A communitarian conception of economic ethics. *Economics and Philosophy, 11,* 85–112.

Evan, W., & Freeman, R. E. (1988). A stakeholder theory of the modern corporation: Kantian capitalism. In T. Beauchamp and N. Bowie (Eds.), *Ethical theory and business* (4th ed., pp. 77–84). Englewood Cliffs, NJ: Prentice-Hall.

Folger, R. (1998). Fairness as a moral virtue. In M. Schminke (Ed.), *Managerial ethics: Moral management of people and processes* (pp. 13–34). Mahwah, NJ: Lawrence Erlbaum.

Folger R. (2001). Fairness as deonance. In S. W. Gilliland, D. D. Steiner, & D. P. Skarlicki (Eds.), *Research in Social Issues in Management* (pp. 3–33). Greenwich, CT: Information Age.

Folger, R., & Skarlicki, D. P. (2008). The evolutionary bases of deontic justice. In S. W. Gilliland, D. D. Steiner, & D. P. Skarlicki (Eds.), *Justice, morality, and social responsibility* (pp. 29–62). Greenwich, CT: Information Age.

Gagne, M., & Deci, E. L. (2005). Self determination theory and work motivation. *Journal of Organizational Behavior, 26*, 331–362.

Graeber, D. (2011). *Debt: The first 5,000 years.* Brooklyn, NY: Melville House Publishing.

Holy Bible, The. Authorized King James Version. Iowa Falls, IA: World Bible Publishers.

Horberg, E. J., Oveis, C., Keltner, D., & Cohen, A. B. (2009). Disgust and the moralization of purity. *Journal of Personality and Social Psychology, 97*, 963–976.

Hursthouse, R. (1999). *On virtue ethics.* Oxford, UK: Oxford University Press.

Jabbour, C. J. C., & Santos, F. C. A. (2008). Relationship between human resource dimensions and environmental management in companies: Proposal for a model. *Journal of Cleaner Products, 16*, 51–58.

Jonsen, A., & Toulmin, S. (1988). *The abuse of casuistry: A history of moral reasoning.* Berkeley and Los Angeles, CA: University of California Press.

Kahneman, D., Knetsch, J. L., & Thaler, R. H. (1986). Fairness and the assumption of economics. *Journal of Business, 59*, 285–300.

Kamenetz, A. (2009). GE's new ecomagination. *Fast Company*, February, 71.

Kant, I. (1996). Groundwork of the metaphysics of morals (1785). In M. J. Gregor (Ed.), *Practical philosophy.* Cambridge, UK: Cambridge University Press.

Klein, N., & Greyser, S. A. (1997). *The Brent Spar incident: "A shell of a mess."* Harvard, MA: Harvard Business School Publishing.

Kovacs, G. (2008). Corporate environmental responsibility in the supply chain. *Journal of Cleaner Products, 16*, 1571–1578.

Kristof-Brown, A. L., Zimmerman, R. D., & Johnson, E. C. (2005). Consequences of individuals' fit at work: A meta-analysis of person-job, person-organization, person-group, and person-supervisor fit. *Personnel Psychology, 58*, 281–342.

Lindenberg, S., & Steg, L. (2007). Normative, gain, and hedonic goal frames guiding environmental behavior. *Journal of Social Issues, 63*, 117–137.

Mill, John Stuart (1951) Considerations on representative government. In H.B. Action (Ed.), *Utilitarianism, liberty, and representative government.* London, UK: Dent.

Mulder, L., & Rupp, D. E. (unpublished manuscript). When snacking is sinful: The moralization of obesity and its effects on healthy eating among high and low weight individuals.

New Belgium. (undated, a). Alternatively empowered. Retrieved December 14, 2012, from http://www.newbelgium.com/culture/alternatively_empowered.aspx

New Belgium (undated, b). We'll set the scene. Retrieved December 14, 2012, from http://www.newbelgium.com/culture/our-story.aspx

New Belgium (undated, c). Environmental stewardship grants program 2012. Retrieved December 15, 2012, from http://www.newbelgium.com/Community/local-grants.aspx

New Belgium (undated, d). Corporate sustainability report. Retrieved December 14, 2012, from http://www.newbelgium.com/culture/alternatively_empowered/sustainable-business-story/planet/energy-and-greenhouse-gas-emission.aspx

Nidumolu, R., Prahalad, C. K., & Rangaswami, M. R. (2009). Why sustainability is now the key driver of innovation. *Harvard Business Review*, September, 57–64.

Nietzsche, F. (1998). *On the genealogy of morality*. Indianapolis, IN: Hackett Publishing.

Obama oil spill commission's final report blames disaster on cost-cutting by BP and partners. (2011, January 5). *The Telegraph*. Retrieved December 16, 2012, from http://www.telegraph.co.uk/finance/newsbysector/energy/oilandgas/8242557/Obama-oil-spill-commissions-final-report-blames-disaster-on-cost-cutting-by-BP-and-partners.html

Ofek, E., & Barley, L. (2011). *The Clorox company: Leveraging green for growth*. Harvard Business School Publishing.

Our view on disaster in the Gulf: Boycott BP? Feels good, but it hurts the innocent. (2010, June 23). *USA Today*. Retrieved December 16, 2012, from http://www.usatoday.com/news/opinion/editorials/2010-06-24-editorial24_ST_N.htm

Patagonia company info. (2012). Retrieved December 14, 2012, from http://www.patagonia.com/us/patagonia.go?assetid=2047&ln=140

Reed, A., & Aquino, K. F. (2003). Moral identity and the expanding circle of moral regard toward out-groups. *Journal of Personality and Social Psychology, 84*, 1270–1286.

Rupp, D. E. (2003). *Testing the moral violations component of fairness theory: The moderating role of value preferences*. Paper presented at the 18th annual conference of the Society for Industrial and Organizational Psychology, Orlando, FL.

Rupp, D. E. (2011). An employee-centered model of organizational justice and social responsibility. *Organizational Psychology Review, 1*, 72–94.

Rupp, D. E., & Bell, C. H. (2010). Extending the deontic model of justice: Moral self-regulation in third-party responses to injustice. *Business Ethics Quarterly, 20*, 89–106.

Rupp, D. E., & Cropanzano, R. (2002). The mediating effects of social exchange relationships in predicting workplace outcomes from multifoci organizational justice. *Organizational Behavior and Human Decisions Processes, 89*, 925–946.

Rupp, D. E., Ganapathi, J., Aguilera, R. A., & Williams, C. A. (2006). Employee reactions to corporate social responsibility: An organizational justice framework. *Journal of Organizational Behavior, 27*, 537–543.

Rupp, D. E., & Thornton, M. (in press). Fairness and justice, climate and culture. In B. Schneider & K. M. Barbera (Eds.), *Handbook of organizational climate and culture: An integrated perspective on research and practice*. Oxford University Press.

Rupp, D. E., Thornton, M., Bielski Boris, M., & Bruno, R. (2012). *Employee perceptions of corporate social responsibility: The moderating effects of benevolence and labor context*. Paper presented at the 27th Society for Industrial and Organizational Psychology, San Diego, CA.

Rupp, D. E., & Williams, C. A. (2011). The efficacy of regulation as a function of psychological fit: A re-evaluation of hard and soft law in the age of new governance. *Theoretical Inquires in Law, 12*, 581–602.

Rupp, D. E., Williams, C. A., & Aguilera, R. V. (2011). Increasing corporate social responsibility through stakeholder value internalization (and the catalyzing effect of new governance): An application of organizational justice, self-determination, and social influence theories. In M. Schminke (Ed.), *Managerial ethics: The psychology of morality*. New York, NY: Routledge/Psychology Press.

Ryan, R. M., & Deci, E. L. (2000). Self-determination theory and the facilitation of intrinsic motivation, social development, and well-being. *American Psychologist, 55,* 68–78.

Sarkis, J. (2001). Manufacturing's role in corporate environmental sustainability: Concerns for the new millennium. *International Journal of Operation and Production Management, 21,* 666–686.

Schneider, B. (1987). The people make the place. *Personnel Psychology, 40,* 437–453.

Sevastopulo, D. (2006). Revisions raise social hurdles. *Financial Times,* May 31, 158–163.

Skarlicki, D. P., & Kulik, C. (2005). Third party reactions to employee (mis)treatment: A justice perspective. In B. Staw and R. Kramer (Eds.), *Research in organizational behavior.* Greenwich, CT: JAI Press.

Summa Theologica Q 57. Retrieved December 16, 2012, from http://www.newadvent.org/summa/3057.htm (*Summa Theologica* Secunda Secundae Partis, Q 57, A. 2)

Summa Theologica Q 58. Retrieved December 16, 2012, from http://www.newadvent.org/summa/3058.htm (*Summa Theologica* Secunda Secundae Partis, Q 58, A. 8)

Task force says BP oil spill fines should go to Gulf restoration. (2011, December 5). *The New York Times.* Retrieved December 14, 2012, from http://www.nytimes.com/2011/12/06/science/earth/panel-says-bp-oil-spill-fines-should-go-to-gulf-restoration.html

Tom's of Maine (2012). Our company. Retrieved 16 December, 2012, from http://www.tomsofmaine.com/business-practices/values-beliefs/stewardship-model

Truxillo, D. M., Folger, R., Lavelle, J. J., Umphress, E., & Gee, J. (2002). Is virtue its own reward? Self-sacrificial decisions for the sake of fairness. *Organizational Behavior and Human Decisions Processes, 89,* 839–865.

Tyler, T. (2009). New approaches to justice in the light of virtues and problems of the penal system. In M. E. Oswald, S. Bieneck, & J. Hupfeld-Heinemann (Eds.), *Social Psychology of Punishment of Crime.* Chichester, UK: Wiley.

Werther, W. B., & Chandler, D. (2011). *Strategic corporate social responsibility: Stakeholders in a global environment* (2nd ed.). Thousand Oaks, CA: Sage.

Williams, C. A. (2004). Civil society initiatives and "soft law" in the oil and gas industry. *New York University Journal of Law and Politics, 36,* 457–502.

Williams, O. F. (2008). The UN global compact: The challenge and the promise. In G. Flynn (Ed.), *Leadership and business ethics.* Springer Science.

6

What Makes Organizations in Market Democracies Adopt Environmentally-Friendly Policies?

Siegwart Lindenberg and Linda Steg

Firms, especially large firms, are powerful players in the economy but also in the political arena. Their behavior can make much difference with regard to the environment, in terms of pollution and waste. There have been many suggestions about directing firms in an environmentally-friendly direction, ranging from environmental agreements between organizations (e.g., to reduce packaging; organizations may be motivated to do so in order to avoid governmental regulations developed beyond their control), government enforcement with fiscal instruments (Hepburn, 2006), market instruments like emission trading schemes (e.g., the European Union Emissions Trading Scheme, see http://ec.europa.eu/clima/policies/ets/index_en.htm; see also Ellerman & Buchner, 2007), to the switch from a shareholder to a stakeholder perspective of value creation (Clarkson, 1995), and appeals to the business ethics of the corporate leaders themselves (Crane & Matten, 2007). Many of these works are about describing the "right" policies. However, even assuming we would know what the "right" policies are, we are still left with the question about the adoption of these policies. Firms are governed by people, and the questions are: What can make these people use their power and influence to direct their firms towards environmentally-friendly policies? Is it likely that firms can be turned into ethically responsible actors? Is state intervention necessary? If so, is it sufficient? Clearly, the government has much influence. But would appeals to business ethics not work better? Where would ethical appeals have the largest effect? What is needed to provide theory-driven answers to such questions, we claim, is a two-pronged approach: because firms are embedded in a system of interdependent corporate and individual actors, we need a macro perspective, but, in order to identify and understand motivations and actions of the relevant actors in the system and to say something about the way they influence each other, we need a micro perspective—that is, a good behavioral theory for such actors. The result will be a micro theory-driven macro (including meso) analysis of the processes that impact the decision of firms with regard to adopting environmentally-friendly policies. As we will claim in this chapter, we should thus not merely look inside firms for the answer as to when and why their leaders would adopt environmentally-friendly policies. Rather, leaders of firms react to constraints, to some degree from the inside (if environmentally-committed employees make it difficult to ignore their wishes, see DuBois, Astakhova, and DuBois, this book), but mainly to constraints imposed from salient players on the outside. So, we have to look at processes that generate these kinds of constraints, and whole systems of influence.

Our micro-macro approach to analyzing systems is based on the premise that institutional orders (such as market orders, state constitutions and democratic institutions, institutions governing science, free speech) heavily influence the basic orientation of people who are playing roles in these institutional orders. This means that we also need a micro theory that can help us identify the relevant players in these institutional orders, their basic orientations, and interrelations under various system conditions (Abell, Felin, & Foss 2008; Lindenberg, 2006a). In past work of ours and others, goal-framing theory has proved to be a good basis for such microfoundations for the purpose of explanations on the meso and macro level (see Etienne, 2011; Lindenberg, 1992; Lindenberg & Foss 2011; Lindenberg & Steg, in press). For this reason, we begin with an overview of goal-framing theory, after which we will discuss how this theory can be fruitfully applied to the explanation of factors that promote the adoption of pro-environmental policies by organizations.

GOAL-FRAMING THEORY

The Power of Goals

Goal-framing theory (Lindenberg, 2006b, 2008; Lindenberg & Steg, 2007) is based on the evidence that human perception, thinking, and deciding can change when goals change. A goal is a mental representation of a desired future state with both cognitive and motivational components. Among others, goals govern what situational information one is sensitive to, how one processes the information, what knowledge is activated, what one likes and dislikes at the moment. Take as an example the effect of being hungry. Somebody very hungry is likely to have a strong focal goal to eat something. This makes the hungry individual particularly sensitive to cues in the environment that something is edible, making it easy to imagine what something would taste like, increasing the liking for objects that are edible and tasty, and suppressing attention to goal-irrelevant or possibly distracting aspects (such as monetary costs, or possible negative long-term effects of what you eat). Goals can become activated ("focal") as an automatic reaction to cues, without deliberation (see Bargh, Gollwitzer, Lee-Chai, Barndollar, & Trötschel, 2001).

Three Overarching Goals

If we are looking for the most inclusive flexible goals, we must look at overarching goals each of which comprising a great number of subgoals and representations of means and causal relations among them. When an overarching goal is activated, its effects on cognitions and motivation are even stronger than with lower level goals. Once activated, it can "frame" one's orientation towards a particular situation by making cognitions and motivations subservient to the pursuit of this goal. A "goal-frame" is an overarching goal that is more strongly activated than its rival overarching goals. Goal-frames make one act in a one-sided way. If situational factors keep activating the same goal-frame, it will thus resemble a personality trait, even though it is upheld by the situation.

Which are the most important overarching goals? Here, it helps to look at evolutionary developments. There are three most important domains of life: satisfying one's fundamental needs, acquiring or maintaining resources to satisfy these needs, and relating to others and the collectives they represent (Lindenberg, in press). In humans, three overarching goals seem to have evolved accordingly: a goal "to improve the way one feels right now" (related to the satisfaction of fundamental needs); a goal "to guard and improve one's resources"; and a goal to "act appropriately" in terms of the collective (dyad or group).

Of these three, the most basic overarching goal is related to how one feels right now and how one can improve the way one feels at this moment. This is called a hedonic goal. When this goal is the "goal-frame," it will sharpen the sensitivity towards opportunities for need satisfaction (such as a piece of cake left on the kitchen counter) and towards events that affect the way one feels (such as exerting effort, mood swings, pain, the friendliness or unfriendliness of people at this moment, mishaps, and losses).

One of the main features of the added brain power of humans (Dunbar, 2003) provides the basis for the other two overarching goals: the improved ability to put oneself into the shoes of others, including of oneself in the future. When people are able to put themselves into the shoes of themselves in the future, they can make plans, invest, and generally be focused on the goal to increase their resources. This focus on increasing or maintaining one's resources is called a gain goal. When it is focal (i.e., a goal-frame), it sharpens one's sensitivity for opportunities to increase one's monetary (e.g., profit) and non-monetary (e.g., status) resources and for aspects of cost, while aspects that are unrelated to resources, such as fun, effort, or normative considerations, are pushed into the cognitive background.

Being able to put oneself into the shoes of the collective (be that a dyad or a whole group) makes it possible that goals of the collective become focal. Then the goal is to act appropriately with regard to group goals. Because what is appropriate is often codified in terms of social norms, this goal is called a normative goal. When the goal is the goal-frame, it is likely to make situationally relevant norms cognitively more accessible. This accessibility makes people particularly sensitive to information about what is expected, thus activating the modules to process information on gaze and on certain facial expressions of approval and disapproval, response tendencies and habitual behavioral sequences concerning conformity to norms (such as facial expression, shaking hands, keeping a certain distance from the other person, and helping others in need), and positive evaluations of the means to reach the goal (Ferguson & Bargh, 2004).

All three overarching goals are chronically influential, but which of the three goals is focal (i.e., which is the goal-frame?) and thus has the greatest influence on cognitive and motivational processes depends on internal and especially on external cues that trigger the goal and give it temporarily a weight that is stronger than that of the other two. In other words, people can often choose to expose themselves to such cues, but often they cannot directly choose to have one or the other overarching goal to be focal, since this is subject to automatic priming effects.

Overarching goals that are pushed into the cognitive background can still exert some influence and either increase the strength of the goal-frame (when they are compatible with the goal-frame, such as getting a social reward for conforming to a norm, in which case hedonic goals in the background strengthen a focal normative goal), or weaken the goal-frame (when they are incompatible with the goal-frame, such as having to make sacrifices for conforming to a norm, in which case gain goals weaken the focal normative goal). Because satisfying fundamental needs is a priori more important than caring for resources or the collective, the hedonic goal is a priori the strongest overarching goal. Since showing concern for the collective is less directly related to the satisfaction of fundamental needs than being concerned about resources for the satisfaction of needs, the normative goal is a priori the weakest. Thus unless the normative goal gets extra support, it will be sidelined by the hedonic or the gain goal. This means that, in order to be socially oriented, human beings need considerable support from their social surroundings.

MARKET DEMOCRACIES AND THE DYNAMICS OF GOAL-FRAMES RELEVANT FOR ENVIRONMENTALLY-FRIENDLY BEHAVIOR

In the following, we will restrict our discussion to market democracies in order to trace the effect of such societies on the dynamics of goal-frames and thereby on the conditions under which leaders of market organizations (firms) are likely to adopt environmentally-friendly policies. The term "market democracies" refers in principle to societies that have a free market and functioning democratic institutions (parliaments, political parties, regular and free elections). Clearly, there cannot be categorical distinctions because both the freedom of the market and the functioning of the democracy are sliding scales. Our arguments apply the better, the closer a society approaches the ideal type of a free market and a system of functioning democratic institutions. There are many such societies in the world and their number is increasing rather than decreasing.

Goal-framing theory is well suited as microfoundation for meso and macro analyses of market democracies because it allows one to look for systematic influences of the social and institutional environment on goal-frames and thus on classes of behavior that are governed by specific goal-

frames (see Lindenberg, 2006a). With the help of this theory, we can identity the goal-frame of the firms' leaders, which, in turn, allows us to trace
actors (and their goal-frames) that influence decisions of firms to adopt
or not adopt (or only seemingly adopt) environmentally-friendly policies.
Due to restrictions in space, we have to focus on the main lines of the
argument, leaving out the finer details about such things as the influence
of local governments, committed employees, and increasing scarcity of
resources.

Firms

In a market democracy, firms have to make a profit in order to maintain
themselves. Profit-making of firms is thus built into the system of functioning markets. In terms of goal-framing theory, one can say that in market societies leaders of firms that partake in the market are systematically
pushed into a gain goal-frame. A gain goal-frame implies that environmental concerns enter decision making only to the degree that they affect
expected profits. Notice that this implies that solutions to conflicting values will be chosen in favor of profit. In some cases, there is no conflict
because it is possible that environmentally-friendly policies of the firm are
also those that maximize profit. Also, of course there can be gain goal-
driven environmentally-friendly adaptations, such as changes in energy
policy due to rising prices of non-renewable resources. This implies that
technological innovations or rising prices of environmentally-unfriendly
means might help reduce the conflict to some degree. But in many cases
there will be a conflict in the sense that at least the short- and medium-
term profit is (or is thought to be) incompatible with environmentally-
friendly policies in terms of the ruling patterns of cost-benefit analysis.
So, we argue that due to the dominant gain goal-frame, if environmental
policies are not compatible with the gain goal-frame, they will by and large
not be adopted (Babiak & Trendafilova, 2011; Sarkar, 2008). In the literature, corporate social responsibility (CSR) is often used as an indicator that
includes environmentally-friendly behavior. But this indicator includes
taking into account stakeholders' expectations and the triple bottom line
of economic, social, and environmental performance (see Aguinis & Glavas, 2012). The direct compatibility of social and environmental corporate
responsibility (CR) with corporate financial performance may be highest
for the social aspects (such as good stakeholder relations, transformational

leadership, team work, and trust; see Barnett & Salomon, 2012; Lindenberg & Foss, 2011; Surroca, Tribo, & Waddock, 2010), though even there one finds that firms engage in CR "primarily due to instrumental reasons such as expected financial outcomes" (Aguinis & Glavas, 2012). It is much less likely that policies concerning the sustainability of the environment will be compatible with corporate financial performance (see e.g., Walls, Berrone, & Phan, 2012). Seeming compliance with stakeholder wishes about environmentally-friendly policies is often just symbolic (David, Bloom, & Hillman 2007). As Ditlev-Simonsen and Midttun (2011, p. 35) conclude after having studied managers' motives for engaging in corporate responsibility: "The relatively low ranking of ethics as a CR motivator in current business practice could be taken as an indication of the view that the corporate world has adopted CR mainly for pragmatic or functional reasons."

Thus, appeals to the environmental "conscience" of CEOs are not likely to make much of a difference, even if there may be incidental cases of leaders who are personally so strongly committed that they withstand the institutional pressure on goal-frames and are willing to sacrifice some profit for the sake of environmentally-friendly policies of their firms, and even though some environmentally-friendly policies may yield clear economic profits as well. In short, because of the prevalent gain goal-frame among business leaders, strategies to get a firm's leadership to adopt environmentally-friendly policies must affect profit rather than conscience or concern. Appeals to business ethics (i.e., to the normative goal-frame) will by and large not have much effect. Emissions trading might be a way to get CEOs to adopt environmentally-friendly policies on the basis of self-interest, because this implies that polluting costs money. However, as ingenious as this instrument may be, it is highly restricted in the range of potentially polluting substances and it tends not to control the largest polluters. Also, it is challenging to decide upon the best allocation rules, and to establish predictable prices (Ellerman & Buchner, 2007; National Audit Office, 2009). Furthermore, emission trading may reduce the likelihood of realizing emissions beyond the limits set, and are only successful when valid and comprehensible monitoring systems are in place.

Consumers

In principle, consumers could make the difference. They could boycott goods or services by environmentally-unfriendly firms. However, even if valid information about firms' policies towards the environment were available (which often it is not; see Strasser, this book), here too the asymmetric a priori strengths of the goal-frames favor the predominance of a gain goal-frame. The normative goal-frame is not very steadfast against a continued barrage of decisions that involve sacrifices in terms of a gain goal. Environmentally-friendly production is often accompanied by higher costs (and thus higher prices) because extra measures have to be taken and additional investments need to be made to make the products "green." For example, the production of organic produce like vegetables and fruit is frequently more costly than regular produce because no insecticides and other cheap but dangerous chemicals can be used, and crop harvest tend to be lower. Flying in organic products from afar in order to make use of cheap labor or cheap warmth is a typical profit-oriented measure in which the firm only seemingly accommodates the consumers' preference for green produce while in fact it contributes to serious pollution by flying products over great distances (see Pollan, 2007).

Products or services from firms that do not make these extra costs are advantaged in the price competition of the market. Given that the normative goal-frame is a priori weaker than the gain goal-frame, lower prices for environmentally-unfriendly products will favor price comparisons and thus shifts towards gain goal-frames in consumers, even when consumers endorse the importance of environmentally-friendly policies of firms (this is also covered by the so-called low-cost hypothesis, see Diekmann & Preisendörfer, 2003; Kirchgässner, 1992). As Bhattacharya and Sen (2004, p. 18) observe after studying consumers: "For the most part, our respondents say that if CSR plays a role at all in purchases, it matters at the margin and they are unwilling, even if they view the CSR initiatives positively, to trade-off CSR for product quality and/or price." Of course there may be customers with very strong views who are able to uphold a normative goal-frame (e.g., Collins, Steg, & Koning, 2007), but by and large, the majority can be expected to be in a gain goal-frame with regard to the purchase of goods and services when there is a considerable price difference in favor of environmentally-unfriendly goods and services.

Government and Law-Making Bodies

Since the gain goal-frame of the firms' leaders is particularly sensitive to external constraints that affect profit, and since these are not likely to come from customers in sufficient strength, the most relevant source of external constraints left is the government and the law-making bodies. It is regulation that creates the external constraints. This is also supported by recent results. Having found a large discrepancy between what actually motivates managers to assume corporate responsibility (CR) and what they themselves think should motivate them, Ditlev-Simonsen and Midttun (2011, p. 35) conclude that "more formal regulations are necessary to close the gap between positivistic, or actual, and normative, ideal, CR behaviour," suggesting that governments should play a key role in encouraging pro-environmental behavior of firms. Governments can use their lawmaking and repressive apparatus to get firms to adopt environmentally-friendly policies. They can, for example, establish laws, tax advantages, or expensive pollution rights that directly reduce the profits of environmentally-unfriendly production (see Strasser, this book, for a more expansive review of the role of government in environmental protection). This shifts the question to the conditions under which governments are likely to take and enforce such measures. In democratic market societies, governing coalitions have to be reelected to stay in power, which favors a predominance of gain goal-frames in political decision making and thus restricts the kind of pro-environmental policies they can push. One of the important factors that influence reelection is economic growth and the image of being able to make it happen. Economic growth creates a widespread feeling of satisfaction by promoting a preponderance of optimism and of being able to cater to short-term interests in consumption and security. Thereby it favors a hedonic goal-frame in voters (see later). In times of economic decline, fear of threats of one's way of life will make a hedonic goal-frame for voters even more likely. Pro-environmental governmental policies are generally believed to hurt economic growth, at least in the short term, because they are likely to lead to higher production costs and possibly lowered competitiveness of national firms in the international arena. Except in special circumstances (which will be taken up in the next section), ruling coalitions are likely to be reluctant to push policies that are believed to reduce economic growth, fearing that thereby they increase the chance that competing parties who promise growth will be voted into power. The upshot of all this is that governing coalitions are likely to look at environmental policies with a gain goal-frame, notwithstanding the occasional politician who is personally deeply committed to environmental concerns. This leaves mainly cosmetic pro-environmental measures that are believed to have little influence on economic growth. How, then, can governments be influenced to stand for essential pro-environmental policies? Clearly, on the basis of what has been said, the answer must be: if such policies do not negatively affect the chances of reelection. When can this be the case? Our answer lies in what we call "the embedded-value process of political influence," which involves many important players and their systematic inter-relations. In the following, we will present this process in some detail.

THE EMBEDDED-VALUE PROCESS OF POLITICAL INFLUENCE

Voting in an election is a process in which people can make a choice at relatively low cost. This makes it possible that many voters are not drawn into a gain goal-frame while they vote. Research also shows that, by and large, people do not vote in their rational financial interests and thus are not in a gain goal-frame when they vote, even when they vote for parties that promise job security or increased economic growth (Sears, Lau, Tyler, & Allen, 1980). This means that voting is one channel of political influence that reduces the power of the gain goal-frame that is otherwise so prominent in market societies. The importance of this process for environmentally-friendly policies can hardly be overestimated, especially in times of economic prosperity.

For casting a vote, feelings (linked to a hedonic goal) or convictions (linked to a normative goal) play the most important role. There is empirical evidence for both kinds of influence (Brader, 2006; Kangas, 1997). People in a hedonic goal-frame are particularly sensitive to threats to one's way of life (based on a feeling of fear), whereas people in a normative goal-frame would give obligations to help preserve important collective goods (such as one's country, humanity, future generations, and the environment) center stage. What activates these goal-frames in such a way that they relate to environmental concerns? We argue that "biospheric" (i.e., strong pro-environmental) values play a key role in this respect. Values are guiding principles in the life of a person or other social entity (Schwartz, 1992). Biospheric values pertain to a focus on the interests of non-human species and the biosphere, and thereby also to interests of future human generations (Steg & De Groot, 2012). Such values help activate either a hedonic or a normative goal, or both. If one of these goals is strongly activated and in the foreground (i.e., the goal-frame), the other goal can still exert some influence from the background, adding to the effect of the foreground goal. For example, if following pro-environmental norms is in the foreground, then action based on these norms is even more likely if fear of ecological disasters, such as epidemics that are related to food-production and dangerous shifts in climate, are in the background. Biospheric values are thus likely to align threats to one's way of life (due to a belief in the threat of environmental sustainability) with collective concerns about sustainability. Voters with strong biospheric values will thus be more likely to vote for political parties that promise sustainability policies, and there is empirical evidence for this claim (see Steg, De Groot, Dreijerink, & Abrahamse, & Siero, 2011; Verplanken & Holland, 2002). Such voters are also more likely to use alternative ways of influencing politics in favor of biospheric values, such as signing petitions, protesting, and supporting environmental organizations (Steg et al., 2011; Stern, Dietz, Abel, Guagnano, & Kalof, 1999). The influence of voters on green politics may often not be very strong, but it is likely to be the most prominent source of green pressure on political decision making. Economic, security, and political power concerns are so dominant in politics that, without green parties or green parts of party programs, parliaments will not have any incentives to pass laws that will pressure firms to adopt environmental-friendly policies. The stronger and more widespread biospheric values are in the society, the stronger the pressure on political decision making in parliament and governments to support environmentally-friendly policies. The question then is how biospheric values can become strong enough to play this role, both in the sense of being stronger than alternative values and in the sense of being easily activated.

There seems to be a trend towards the formation of biospheric values as a separate group of values (De Groot & Steg, 2007, 2008; Steg, Dreijerink, & Abrahamse, 2005; see Steg & De Groot, 2012, for a review). But where do these values come from and what feeds their intensity? If environmentally-friendly behavior of firms needs to be directed by governments, and if governments need to be pushed by voters in that direction, this values question becomes central to the focal question of this chapter. We suggest that in market democracies the creation and maintenance of values is embedded in a process that involves players whose role is particularly relevant for the awareness of threats to our way of life. In the following, we will sketch this embedded value process and identify the important players (see boxed part of Figure 6.1 for an overview).

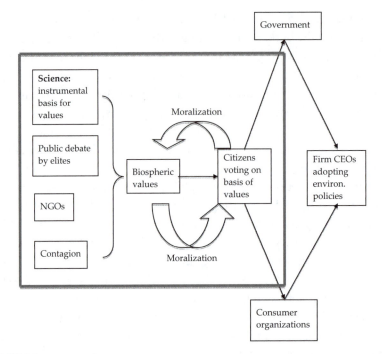

FIGURE 6.1
The major players and influence relations in the embedded-value process of political influence.

Values are not just private guiding principles in people's lives but reflect socially shared evaluations of behavior or states of the world (Lindenberg, 2009). In contrast to goals, values transcend situations. Goal-framing theory would suggest that values can be grouped according to the same three spheres of life as overarching goals: feelings, resources, and the collective. Thus, there are hedonic values (related to enjoyment of life), gain values (related to material welfare and status), and normative values (related to the collective). Note that even though hedonic goals (related to fear) can lead to environmentally-friendly behavior, by and large hedonic values (in which enjoyment of life is the focus) are not conducive to such behavior. Indeed, research in the environmental domain has shown that environmental beliefs and norms, policy acceptability, intentions, and behavior are positively related to normative (i.e., altruistic and biospheric) values, whereas they are negatively related to hedonic and gain values (e.g., De Groot & Steg, 2007, 2008; Gärling, Fujii, Gärling, & Jakobsson, 2003; Honkanen & Verplanken, 2004; Nordlund & Garvill 2003; Steg & De Groot, 2012; Steg, Perlaviciute, Van der Werff, & Lurvink, in press).

As with the overarching goals, hedonic values can be considered to be the a priorily most salient values, which means that the other two spheres of values must get support from the social context in order to be more influential in a particular situation than hedonic values. Ways of life reflect more or less hedonic, gain, and collective aspects. Values thus relate first and foremost to aspects of a way of life (Lindenberg, 2009). For values to be created, evaluations have to be shared on a wide basis in society. For example, if freedom of expression has become a way of life, it is very likely also positively evaluated by people who share this way of life. Social influence (especially during a child's period of socialization) plays an important role in the spreading of values, but what is most effective in creating a broad basis for shared values (that potentially trump hedonic values) is a common threat to a shared way of life (Lindenberg, 2009). For instance, the shared experience of hyperinflation or of a strong economic depression (especially during one's pre-adult years) is likely to make people value thrift and material welfare (Abramson & Inglehart, 1995). Inglehart (1990) has also argued that threats to material welfare are likely to push materialistic values. However, contrary to Inglehart's claim, this does not mean that rising material welfare would automatically increase the significance of norm-related values in choices people make. Rather, goal-framing theory would suggest that rising material welfare would weaken the significance of gain-related values and thereby increase the relative weight of hedonic values, unless there are simultaneously other factors that would push and support norm-related values. We would argue that only an increasing threat to our way of life would make norm-related values stronger than hedonic values.

Science as a Major Player

Where would we get believable information of ecology-related threats to our way of life? In modern societies, the major source of believable facts is science (Luhmann, 1996). If scientists argue convincingly that certain economic or consumption practices threaten our way of life, they push values that relate to the preservation or sustainability of our way of life and devalue the practices that create the greatest threat for it (see Steg & Nordlund, 2012; Stokman, 2009a). In this way, scientists can be a prime source of value creation and of arguments that will ultimately lead to prioritization of biospheric values and environmentally-friendly behavior. This holds for psychological arguments (e.g., Kasser & Kanner, 2004) and even more for arguments from natural sciences about CO_2 emissions, climate change, pollution, resource depletion, and the like. Biospheric values are very likely the result from such a process. In the light of biospheric values, scientific evidence can make certain practices become valuable in themselves (such as the preservation of natural variety) and devalue other practices (such as the use of polluting fossils). The role of science is thus double: it helps establishing biospheric values and it supplies guides to concrete do's and don'ts and thus to norms that people can or should follow if and when they are motivated to engage in environmentally-friendly behavior due to their goal-frame. The influence of science on politics thus runs mainly via the influence of values and norm creation of voters who, in turn, can translate this influence into pressure on political decision making.

Additional Players

Science by itself is not equipped to also deal with all the contrary influences of other values and interests and push a reordering of value priorities. The process of value creation and concrete norm creation thus needs input also from a variety of other actors for purposes of value prioritization. Because of ambiguities in the interpretation of scientific information, social values that may or may not be compatible with biospheric values, and because of possibly contrary gain-related interests of powerful economic players, other actors enter the scene of value creation and prioritization. There is first of all an important role of public debate (Lindenberg, 2009), in which the various elites (in addition to scientific elites) generate arguments for or against priorities in political and private decision making (e.g., on the basis of the values they endorse), thereby channeling the scientific arguments in various directions (Lowe, 2006). For example, in addition to the controversy about scientific results themselves (say about the environmental impact of certain ways of generating electricity), the public debate can focus on the question whether or not electricity should be centrally or locally produced. This is much more than a technical question about what is more efficient in terms of resources. One may argue that decentralized production increases engagement in energy issues, and promotes energy savings. It can also involve the argument that decentralized production of electricity may create more solidarity than central production, because local production creates neighborhood initiatives and interconnected networks of people who are both consumers and producers (Stokman, 2009b). The question then becomes: Is local solidarity in a market democracy a threatened part of our way of life? Here, arguments for or against may touch important ambiguities about priorities in our way of life.

In addition to the public debate among elites, non-governmental organizations (NGOs) aimed at pushing environmentally-friendly policies can help in the process of creating and prioritizing values. Environmental NGOs have made it their business to pressure governments and public opinion, on the basis of scientific results, and use their own means to sway both the public and the government. This means the NGOs can even play this role when their leaders are more or less gain oriented themselves. By partisan intervention, NGOs ideally help translate abstract arguments (from science) into value prioritization in practice. For example, they do not only try to influence public opinion (say, about "wrong" food that has been produced in a non-sustainable way) but also intervene on behalf of what they see as threats to the sustainability of natural resources based on "wrong" priorities of short-term economic interests (such as Greenpeace acting as a lobby organization at international climate conferences). NGOs can also get investors to pressure firms' leadership to adopt environmentally-friendly policies because investors are interested in positive reputation effects. It is, however, not certain that such pressure really furthers environmentally-friendly policies (see David, Bloom, & Hillman 2007).

Finally, there is the process of contagion that acts as an important player in value creation and prioritization. People who are very committed to certain values tend to influence others in the same direction unless they are perceived as outgroups. For example, people who strongly disapprove of wasting paper as a way of threatening sustainability are likely to influence others to do likewise. By contrast, people who chain themselves to train rails, in order to prevent transport of ecologically dangerous material, may be seen as outgroups and thus lose influence (cf. Abrams, Wetherell, Cochrane, Hogg, & Turner, 1990; Smith & Louis, 2008).

In sum, the embedded value process involves the special role of science (due to the centrality of internal contradictions in the way of life in Western market democracies) and the derived roles of public debate, NGOs, and contagion of the highly committed to the less committed citizens. The motives for the various players are decoupled from a market-related gain goal-frame. This means that even though scientists, leaders in the public debate, leaders of NGOs, and role models about environmentally-friendly behavior may be in part motivated by gain aspects, such as status (Griskevicius, Tybur, & Van den Bergh, 2010), or hedonic aspects, such as a warm glow from being on the right side of biospheric values (Bolderdijk, 2010; Bolderdijk, Lehman, & Geller, 2012), they are not likely to be heavily distracted by contrary economic (i.e., gain) motives. This is a consequence of the way Western market democracies work. Heavy and obvious conflicting interests are by and large neutralized by the scientific system and the way the media work. This does not mean that occasional mishaps may not happen, but there is no likely systematic bias.

MORALIZATION

This process of value creation, prioritization, and maintenance can result in especially powerful values if value-incongruent practices are coupled to a process of moralization (Lindenberg, 1983; Rozin, 1999). Moralization means that people who act against particular values are considered not just to show their contempt for these values but are considered bad people. Going against moralized practices comes close to having a faulty character rather than a deviant set of values. Moralization has a strong effect on behavior because in that case values are more likely chronically accessible in the minds of people, and because people feel more ashamed acting against moralized conduct and more angry when others act against this conduct.

The likelihood of moralization is higher the larger the perceived threat to the way of life. This can be a threat from the outside, a threat to the collective identity, or a threat derived from internal contradictions in the way of life. Because the latter is central to market democracies and because the threats may be contested, moralization depends on consensus about the threats. For example, today, in Western market democracies, dumping poisonous waste in the fields around our cities is on its way of being moralized, meaning that people who do this are seen as criminal and of bad character because they threaten biospheric values. However, dumping Western waste in poor non-Western countries is not yet moralized in this way, even though it may be done on a much larger scale than dumping around our own cities, and it is thus a larger threat to sustainability and threatens the same values. Again, in this scientists play an important role.

To the degree that they identify threats of actions for key values and to the degree that their findings are less controversial, to that degree moralization will be more likely achieved. Achieving consensus is hampered by contrary economic interests, but progress has been made. For example, Al Gore's campaign around the world had these two aims: show how large the threat is and convince people that it is real, given the scientific evidence. He was largely successful, but the fact that he is charged with not living up to the biospheric values he preaches reduced his influence again (*New York Times*, 2009). Because there are considerable interests at stake, any weakness in the advocacy of the threat and the concomitant value change will be focused on right away and fuel a further round of the public debate. However, there is good evidence that in Western market democracies biospheric values have becomes a complex of values by themselves, that consensus on the significance of these values is growing in the public in Western countries, and that these values are even spreading to developing countries (Hansen, Steg, & Suhlmann, in preparation; Steg & De Groot, 2012). Thus, there is some indication that moralization of biospheric values will increase (for a continued discussion on mortality and environmental sustainability, please see Pandey, Rupp and Thornton, this book).

GOVERNMENTS AND THE EMBEDDED VALUE PROCESS

If we combine what has been said about the influence on firms by governments with the embedded value process, then we get a more complete picture of the complex way in which leaders of firms may be brought to implement pro-environmental policies. The embedded value process increases the number of voters who are likely to vote with a normative goal-frame (related to obligation to contribute to sustainability) or a hedonic goal-frame (related to fear of threat) and thus favor political parties that promote environmental-friendly legislation and measures, even in the face of contrary economic interests. In turn, political parties need voters in order to become part of governing coalitions and thus are more likely to add such aspects to their party programs; more voters are therefore influenced by biospheric values. Finally, environmentally-friendly government policies will get leaders of firms to change their policies in the same direction.

Because leaders of firms in market democracies are likely to be in a gain goal-frame, there is a high likelihood that they will try to pretend to follow all the rules but in fact find ways to get around them when that would increase their profit. So, in a gain goal-frame, moral hypocrisy is very likely, in which firms try to appear moral without engaging in costly moral behavior (Lindenberg & Steg, 2012). Government controls tend to fall short, because that is very costly and because expenses for control have to compete with measures that are likely to increase success in elections. Control activities are complex, not easily controlled themselves, and thus systematic infractions also are not likely to be brought to the attention of voters. This creates an important role for private not-for-profit watchdog organizations (NGOs), such as consumer organizations, investigative reporting for television or newspapers etc. Such (semi-) private watchdog activities are also positively influenced by stronger and more widespread biospheric values among the public. Their activity is an important complement to environmentally-friendly government policies.

DISCUSSION

Under what conditions are firms in market societies likely to adopt environmentally-friendly policies? To answer this question, one quickly gets into queries about other players. Are firms likely to be impressed by ethical appeals and act on their own, or are they only likely to adopt green policies when governments and consumer organizations exert pressure? If so, what makes governments exert such pressure? In this chapter, we adopted a micro-macro approach for answering such questions: on the macro level, there are institutional orders (such as markets and political institutions) that influence basic orientations of people on the micro level, making them systematically act in certain directions. For identifying these influences, the relevant players, and their interrelations, we need the right kind of behavioral theory as microfoundations for meso and macro level predictions. On the basis of goal-framing theory (as our microfoundational theory), we looked at firms in market democracies as basically gain-oriented actors who are unlikely to adopt voluntarily environmentally-friendly policies that hurt profitability. Next we used goal-framing theory to identify the chains of influence that generate pressure on firms to adopt environmentally-friendly policies. We identified government pressure as the central source of pressure for environmentally-friendly policies of firms. In turn, we identified value-based voting by citizens as the most important source of pressure on governments to do so. This puts a heavy burden on the development, maintenance, and prioritization of biospheric values in the citizenry. The center piece of our argument is what we call *the embedded-value process*. We argue that in modern societies, values, especially biospheric values, and value-congruent actions heavily depend on uncontroversial scientific information on contradictions in our way of life with regard to sustainability. Such information identifies threats to important aspects of our way of life, and it is such threats that help create or prioritize values and promote value-congruent actions (as things to be preserved). The influence of science in this respect is aided by public debate, NGOs, and processes of sheer contagion in which people with more intense values influence people with less intense values. Finally, we identified consumer organizations and NGOs that are influenced by the values citizens hold, as vital for controlling whether or not firms actually conform to government policies.

The overall drift of our argument is that the macro (system) aspects are crucially important and that at the same time we need good micro theories to specify the likely workings and weaknesses of the system. In this way, we complement environmental psychology with attention to systems, without losing the focus on behavioral theory.

REFERENCES

Abell, P., Felin, T., & Foss N. J (2008). Building micro-foundations for the routines, capabilities, and performance links. *Managerial and Decision Economics, 29*, 489–502.

Abrams, D., Wetherell, M., Cochrane, S., Hogg, M. A., & Turner, J. C. (1990). Knowing what to think by knowing who you are: Self-categorization and the nature of norm formation, conformity, and group polarization. *British Journal of Social Psychology, 29*, 97–119.

Abramson, P.R., & Inglehart, R. (1995). *Value change in global perspective.* Ann Arbor, MI: Michigan University Press.

Aguinis, H., & Glavas, A. (2012). What we know and don't know about corporate social responsibility: A review and research agenda. *Journal of Management, 38*, 932–968. doi: 10.1177/0149206311436079

Babiak, K., & Trendafilova, S. (2011). CSR and environmental responsibility: Motives and pressures to adopt green management practices. *Corporate Social Responsibility and Environmental Management, 18*, 11–24.

Bargh, J. A., Gollwitzer, P. M., Lee-Chai, A., Barndollar, K., & Trötschel, R. (2001). Automated will: Nonconscious activation and pursuit of behavioral goals. *Journal of Personality and Social Psychology, 81,* 1014–1027.

Barnett, M. L., & Salomon, R. M. (2012). Does it pay to be *really* good? Addressing the shape of the relationship between social and financial performance. *Strategic Management Journal, 33.* doi: 10.1002/smj.1980

Bhattacharya, C. B., & Sen, S. (2004). Doing better at doing good: When, why and how consumers respond to corporate social initiatives. *California Management Review, 47,* 9–24.

Bolderdijk, J. W. (2010). *Buying people: The persuasive power of money.* Doctoral dissertation, University of Groningen, Faculty of Behavioural and Social Sciences, The Netherlands.

Bolderdijk, J.W., Lehman, P. K., & Geller, E. S. (2012). Promoting pro-environmental behavior with rewards and penalties. In L. Steg, A. E. van den Berg, & J. I. M. De Groot (Eds.), *Environmental psychology: An introduction* (pp. 233–242). Oxford: Wiley Blackwell.

Brader, T. (2006).*Campaigning for hearts and minds: How emotional appeals in political ads work.* Chicago, IL: University of Chicago Press.

Clarkson, M. B. E. (1995). A stakeholder framework for analyzing and evaluating corporate social performance. *Academy of Management Review, 20*(1), 92–117.

Collins, C. M., Steg, L., & Koning, M. A. S. (2007). Customers' values, beliefs on sustainable corporate performance, and buying behavior. *Psychology & Marketing, 24*(6), 555–577.

Crane, A., & Matten, D. (2007). *Business ethics* (2nd ed.). Oxford: Oxford University Press.

David, P., Bloom, M., & Hillman, A. J. (2007). Investor activism, managerial responsiveness, and corporate performance. *Strategic Management Journal, 28,* 91–100.

De Groot, J. I. M., & Steg, L. (2007). Value orientations and environmental beliefs in five countries: Validity of an instrument to measure egoistic, altruistic and biospheric value orientations. *Journal of Cross-Cultural Psychology, 38,* 318–332.

De Groot, J., & Steg, L. (2008). Value orientations to explain beliefs related to environmental significant behavior: How to measure egoistic, altruistic, and biospheric value orientations. *Environment and Behavior, 40,* 330–354.

Diekmann, A., & Preisendörfer, P. (2003). Green and greenback. The behavioural effects of environmental attitudes in low-cost and high-cost situations. *Rationality and Society, 15*(4), 441–472.

Ditlev-Simonsen, C. D., & Midttun, A. (2011). What motivates managers to pursue corporate responsibility? A survey among key stakeholders. *Corporate Social Responsibility and Environmental Management, 18,* 25–38.

Dunbar, R. I .M. 2003. The social brain: Mind, language, and society in evolutionary perspective. *Annual Review of Psychology, 32,* 163–181.

Ellerman, A. D., & Buchner, B. K. (2007). The European Union emissions trading scheme: Origins, allocation, and early results. *Review of Environmental Economics and Policy, 1*(1), 66–87.

Etienne, J. (2011). Compliance theory: A goal-framing approach. *Law & Policy, 33,* 305–333.

Ferguson, M. J., & Bargh, J. A. (2004). Liking is for doing: The effects of goal pursuit on automatic evaluation. *Journal of Personality and Social Psychology, 87,* 557–572.

Gärling, T., Fujii, S., Gärling, A., & Jakobsson, C. (2003). Moderating effects of social value orientation on determinants of proevenvironmental intention. *Journal of Environmental Psychology, 23,* 1–9.

Griskevicius, V., Tybur, J., & Van den Bergh, B. (2010). Going green to be seen: Status, reputation, and conspicuous conservation. *Journal of Personality and Social Psychology, 98*, 392–404.

Hansen, N., Steg, L., & Suhlmann, M. (in preparation). Combating global climate change by acting locally: The impact of biospheric values on pro-environmental behavior in developing countries.

Hepburn, C. (2006). Regulation by prices, quantities, or both: A review of instrument choice. *Oxford Review of Economic Policy, 22*, 226–247.

Honkanen, P., & Verplanken, B. (2004). Understanding attitudes towards genetically modified food: The role of values and attitude strength. *Journal of Consumer Policy, 27*, 401–420.

Inglehart, R. F. (1990). *Culture shift in advanced industrial society.* Princeton, NJ: Princeton University Press.

Kangas, O. E. (1997). Self-interest and the common good: The impact of norms, selfishness and context in social policy opinions. *Journal of Socio-Economics, 26*, 475–494.

Kasser T., & Kanner, A. D. (Eds.) (2004). *Psychology and consumer culture: The struggle for a good life in a materialistic world.* Washington, DC: American Psychological Association.

Kirchgässner, G. (1992). Towards a theory of low-cost decisions. *European Journal of Political Economy, 8*(2), 305–320.

Lindenberg, S. (1983). Utility and morality. *Kyklos, 36*(3), 450–468.

Lindenberg, S. (1992). An extended theory of institutions and contractual discipline, *Journal of Institutional and Theoretical Economics, 148*, 125–154.

Lindenberg, S. (2006a). How social psychology can build bridges to the social sciences by considering motivation, cognition and constraints simultaneously. In P. A. M. Van Lange (Ed.), *Bridging social psychology: The benefits of transdisciplinary approaches* (pp. 151–157). Hillsdale, NJ: Erlbaum.

Lindenberg, S. (2006b). Prosocial behavior, solidarity, and framing processes. In D. Fetchenhauer, A. Flache, A.P. Buunk, & S. Lindenberg (Eds.), *Solidarity and prosocial behavior. An integration of sociological and psychological perspectives* (pp. 23–44). New York, NY: Springer.

Lindenberg, S. (2008). Social rationality, semi-modularity and goal-framing: What is it all about? *Analyse & Kritik 30*, 669–687.

Lindenberg, S. (2009). Values: What do they do for behavior? In M. Cherkaoui & P. Hamilton (Eds.), *Boudon: A life in Sociology* (Vol. 3, pp. 59–89). Oxford: Bardwell Press.

Lindenberg, S. (in press). Social rationality, self-regulation and well-being: The regulatory significance of needs, goals, and the self. In R. Wittek, T. A. B. Snijders, and V. Nee (Eds.), *The handbook of rational choice social research.* Stanford, CA: Stanford University Press.

Lindenberg, S., & Foss, N. (2011). Managing joint production motivation: The role of goal-framing and governance mechanisms. *Academy of Management Review, 36*, 500–525.

Lindenberg, S., & Steg, L. (2007). Normative, gain and hedonic goal frames guiding environmental behavior. *Journal of Social Issues, 65*(1), 117–137.

Lindenberg, S., & Steg, L. (in press). Goal-framing theory and norm-guided environmental behavior. In H. van Trijp (Ed.), *Encouraging sustainable behaviour.* London: Psychology Press.

Lowe, B. M. (2006). *Emerging moral vocabularies: The creation and establishment of new forms of moral and ethical meanings.* Landham, Md.: Lexington Books.

Luhmann, N. (1996). *Social systems.* Stanford, CA: Stanford University Press.

National Audit Office (2009). *European Union emissions trading scheme: A review by the National Audit Office.* London: National Audit Office.

New York Times (2009). Gole's dual role: Advocate and investor. November 3.

Nordlund, A. M., & Garvill, J. (2003). Effects of values, problem awareness, and personal norm on willingness to reduce personal car use. *Journal of Environmental Psychology, 23*, 339–347.

Pollan, M. (2007). *The omnivore's dilemma. A natural history of four meals*. London: Bloomsbury Publishers.

Rozin, P. (1999). The process of moralization. *Psychological Sciences, 10*, 218–221.

Sarkar, R. (2008). Public policy and corporate environmental behaviour: A broader view. *Corporate Social Responsibility and Environmental Management, 15*, 281–297.

Schwartz, S. H. (1992). Universals in the content and structures of values: Theoretical advances and empirical tests in 20 countries. In M. Zanna (Ed.), *Advances in experimental psychology* (Vol. 25, pp. 1–65). Orlando, FL: Academic Press.

Sears, D. O., Lau, R. R., Tyler, T. R., & Allen, H.M., Jr. (1980). Self-interest versus symbolic politics in policy attitudes and presidential voting. *American Political Science Review, 74*, 670–684.

Smith, J., & Louis, W. (2008). Do as we say and as we do: The interplay of descriptive and injunctive group norms in the attitude–behaviour relationship. *British Journal of Social Psychology, 47*, 647–666.

Steg, L., & de Groot, J. I. M. (2012). Environmental values. In S. Clayton (Ed.), *The Oxford handbook of environmental and conservation psychology*. New York, NY: Oxford University Press.

Steg, L., De Groot, J. I. M., Dreijerink, L., Abrahamse, W., & Siero, F. (2011). General antecedents of personal norms, policy acceptability, and intentions: The role of values, worldviews, and environmental concern. *Society and Natural Resources, 24*(4), 349–367.

Steg, L., Dreijerink, L., & Abrahamse, W. (2005). Factors influencing the acceptability of energy policies: Testing VBN theory. *Journal of Environmental Psychology, 25*, 415–425.

Steg, L., & Nordlund, A. (2012). Models to explain environmental behaviour. In L. Steg, A.E. van den Berg, & J.I.M. de Groot (Eds.), *Environmental psychology: An introduction* (pp. 185–195). Oxford: John Wiley & Sons.

Steg, L., Perlaviciute, G., Van der Werff, E., & Lurvink, J. (in press). The significance of hedonic values for environmentally-relevant attitudes, preferences and actions. doi: 10.1177/0013916512454730

Stern, P. C., Dietz, T., Abel, T., Guagnano, G. A., & Kalof, L. (1999). A value-belief-norm theory of support for social movements: The case of environmentalism. *Human Ecology Review, 6*, 81–97.

Stokman. F. N. (2009a). Climate change and peak oil: An analysis of (false) beliefs regarding two 21st century world challenges. In M. Cherkaoui & P. Hamilton (Eds.), *Raymond Boudon: A life in sociology* (pp. 123–143). Oxford: Bardwell Press.

Stokman. F. N. (2009b). *The two faces of James Lovelock: An alternative social and political view*. Groningen: C8Foundation. Retrieved January 3, 2012, from http://www.stokman.org/artikel/09Stok.TwofacesLovelock.pdf

Surocca, J., Tribo, J. A., & Waddock, S. (2010). Corporate responsibility and financial performance: The role of intangible resources. *Strategic Management Journal, 31*, 463–490.

Verplanken, B., & Holland, R. W. (2002). Motivated decision making: Effects of activation and self-centrality of values on choices and behaviour. *Journal of Personality and Social Psychology, 82*, 434–447.

Walls, J. L., Berrone, P., & Phan, P. (2012). Corporate governance and environmental performance: Is there really a link? *Strategic Management Journal, 33*. doi: 10.1002/smj.1952

7

Measuring, Understanding, and Influencing Employee Green Behaviors

Deniz S. Ones and Stephan Dilchert

We would like to thank our colleagues and students for their contributions to the research, concepts, theories, and empirical findings highlighted in this chapter: Brenton Wiernik, Rachael Klein, Susan D'Mello, Lauren Hill, Andrew Biga, and Sarah Semmel.

Organizations are a "function of persons behaving in them" (Schneider, 1987, p. 438). This is why all discussions of environmental sustainability in organizations must start with an understanding of individual behaviors—including those of leaders, employees, and even job applicants. As organizational members pursue common goals, behaviors of individuals determine organizational direction, structures, and processes. The implication for environmental sustainability research and practice in organizational settings is that scientific explanations must rest on an understanding of people at work and not only the consequences of their behaviors (e.g., organizations' environmental impacts).

Yet, many discussions of environmental sustainability in organizations center on improving product design for environmental sustainability; creation of more efficient as well as less impactful processes (e.g., supply chains, manufacturing); and impacts on water, land, natural resources, biodiversity, energy availability, and so forth. But products and processes are created by people, adopted by people, and used by people. Embedding environmental sustainability into the organizational DNA requires workforce involvement. Leaders choose strategic goals to pursue on behalf of the organization. Managers make decisions that determine the degree to which organizational products, services, and processes will take environmental sustainability into consideration. Employees participate in the creation of products and services that vary in their degree of environmental sustainability. They also support practices and initiatives as organizational citizens. This is true for all functional areas of organizations, from manufacturing to logistics to marketing to sales to accounting. Employees give rise to organizational culture (Schneider, 1987), including culture that is mindful of the natural environment. Without employees and their deep involvement in environmentally-responsible work practices, organizations cannot fulfill their responsibility in sustaining the natural environment of our planet.

In this chapter, we first highlight evidence that environmental sustainability and responsibility are increasingly valued by many corporations. Second, we delineate environmental sustainability constructs at both the organizational and individual levels of analysis. At the organizational level, we distinguish environmental performance from social responsibility, and highlight how each is related to organizational financial performance. At the individual level, we distinguish between general pro-environmental behaviors and employee green behaviors. We also discuss how employee green behaviors relate to constructs such as employee engagement, task performance, organizational citizenship behaviors, counterproductive work behaviors, and organizational tenure. Third, we describe a taxonomy of employee green behaviors, noting functional and motivational differences among categories. Fourth, we review person-based approaches (recruiting, staffing) and intervention-based approaches (training, motivational interventions) that can be used to influence employee green behaviors in organizations. We conclude by highlighting streams of employee-focused research that will contribute to improving environmental sustainability of organizations.

THE ENVIRONMENT FOR ENVIRONMENTAL RESPONSIBILITY IS CHANGING

Since the 1970s, organizations have gone through major changes that have brought about fundamental transformations of organizational goals. Increasingly, businesses are recognizing the interconnectedness of economic, social, and environmental sustainability as contributors to long-term organizational viability. Ones and Dilchert (2012b) summarized evidence that environmental sustainability is gaining in importance. Here, we highlight three of the relevant trends: (1) an increased prevalence of sustainability reporting, (2) pervasiveness of proactive environmental initiatives on behalf of organizations, and (3) organizational leaders' increasingly positive environmental attitudes.

First, in the past, corporate environmental sustainability reporting lagged behind reporting initiatives for corporate social responsibility initiatives. Moreover, instead of reporting on change-oriented, proactive initiatives, much of the corporate reporting relating to environmental impact focused on *outcomes* (lagging indicators in the form of readily available metrics; see, for example, recommendations of the Global Environmental Management Initiative, 1998). However, increasing consumer scrutiny as well as the pressure from external rating agencies (non-governmental organizations [NGOs], governments, certification programs) has recently led to a shift in emphasis towards more comprehensive organizational reporting, both in North America and the European Union (Hedberg & von Malmborg, 2003; Kolk, 2008; Rikhardsson, Anderson, & Bang, 2002; van Wensen, Broer, Klein, & Knopf, 2011). This includes an increasing push for reporting leading indicators, rather than only outcomes and impacts.

Second, there appears to be a genuine increase in pro-environmental efforts that organizations can now report on. In research conducted with our colleagues, we examined websites and sustainability reports of the 635 largest U.S. companies, and found that the overwhelming majority engages in and reports on environmental sustainability efforts. For example, the average Fortune 500 company reported on ten different initiatives (D'Mello, Ones, Klein, Wiernik, & Dilchert, 2011). While the nature of pro-environmental initiatives appears to differ across industries, the majority involves recycling programs, reduction of energy use, and conservation of natural resources (see Accenture, 2011; SHRM, BSR, & Aurosoorya, 2011; Zibarras & Ballinger, 2011).

Third, organizational leadership has experienced a substantive change in attitudes and resulting behaviors relating to the natural environment. For example, the 2009 Global CEO survey (PriceWaterhouseCoopers, 2009) showed that two-fifths of chief executives think that water scarcity will negatively impact their company's long-term success. This finding is notable, because it links environmental outcomes to concrete business outcomes, not the other way around. It is one indicator that businesses are recognizing the interconnectedness between environmental sustainability and economic viability. As a further illustration of this trend, two-thirds of business executives in a recent Accenture (2011) survey indicated that they regard spending on sustainability initiatives as an investment, not a cost. Our own research among organizational leaders indicates that these attitudes are also reflected in concrete on-the-job behaviors. Executives participate more actively in organizational pro-environmental initiatives, an effect that we observed across several hierarchical levels and organizations (Ones, Dilchert, Biga, & Gibby, 2010). Finally, commitment to environmental sustainability is becoming more formalized on the organizational level. Part of this trend is the establishment of top-level positions with oversight of environment-specific issues (e.g., Chief Sustainability Officer; see Deutsch, 2007), as well as the establishment of formal environmental sustainability policies among a majority of organizations (see SHRM et al., 2011).

DELINEATING ENVIRONMENTAL SUSTAINABILITY CONSTRUCTS

The study of environmentally-relevant individual behavior has only a brief history in workplace settings. Aguinis and Glavas (2012) conducted a content analysis of the corporate responsibility literature published in 17 journals and reported that only 4% of articles (8 out of 181), some presumably separating social and environmental responsibility, focused on an individual level of analysis. In contrast, a much more vast literature in environmental, ecological, and conservation psychology has investigated many related phenomena outside the world of work. Dilchert and Ones (2012) provided a summary of the many different labels used to refer to specific yet related constructs (e.g., ecological, environmental, pro-environmental, environmentally conscious, sustainable, and green; see their Table 1). These constructs have been used to refer to specific individual-level behaviors including pollution reduction, waste management, energy conservation, household energy use, recycling, and environmental activism, among others. Accordingly, scholars have typically defined them as behaviors that protect, benefit, or contribute to the protection of the environment. *Pro-environmental behaviors* are environmentally-relevant "individual behaviors that contribute to environmental sustainability" (Mesmer-Magnus, Viswesvaran, & Wiernik, 2012, p. 169)—that is, they have a positive impact on the natural environment. However, most pro-environmental behaviors that have been investigated in psychological research so far are "undertaken as part of one's personal life" (Ones & Dilchert, 2012a).

When environmentally-relevant behaviors are undertaken in relation to individuals' jobs, they become *employee green behaviors*. The first key distinction between pro-environmental behaviors and employee green behaviors thus lies in the settings and roles in which they occur. A second key distinction relates to the degree of control organizations exert over such behaviors. As discussed in Ones and Dilchert (2012a), employee green behaviors are under greater scrutiny and might even be required by organizations as part of individuals' job duties. Pro-environmental behaviors have an entirely individual volitional basis. Finally, employee green behaviors also constitute a more comprehensive construct that includes behaviors with both a positive and negative impact on the natural environment (Ones & Dilchert, 2009, 2010).

Employee green behaviors are defined as "scalable actions and behaviors that employees engage in that are linked with and contribute to or detract from environmental sustainability" (Ones & Dilchert, 2012a, p. 87). By focusing on employee behaviors and actions (versus the outcomes of such actions), our definition is intentionally close to contemporary definitions of job performance (e.g., Campbell, 1990; Viswesvaran & Ones, 2000). We argue that as organizations increasingly consider organizational environmental performance as a goal alongside economic performance, individual-level models of job performance should also take employee green behaviors into account.

On the organizational level, corporate environmental performance is the degree of success with which organizations manage natural resources in the production, manufacture, distribution, and eventual disposal of their products and services. Hence, organizational environmental performance goes beyond the environmental "footprint" (i.e., ecological impact) of operations, and also includes proactive initiatives (Ones & Dilchert, 2012b).

DISTINGUISHING ENVIRONMENTAL PERFORMANCE, SOCIAL RESPONSIBILITY, AND FINANCIAL PERFORMANCE AT THE ORGANIZATIONAL LEVEL

The burgeoning interest in corporate environmental performance in applied psychology is often met with the question of whether environmental performance should be subsumed under the umbrella of corporate social responsibility (CSR). CSR "encompasses both how companies generate their profits and what they do with them" (Ones & Dilchert, 2012b). Orlitzky, Schmidt, and Rynes' (2003) influential quantitative review of this topic reflects the commonly held notion that CSR includes both corporate *social* and *environmental* performance. In this view, organizations are accountable to both their shareholders (financial performance) and stakeholders (CSR)—with the natural environment being one stakeholder among many. However, there is empirical evidence that the nomological networks for CSR and corporate environmental performance differ.

Table 7.1 summarizes the relationships of CSR and environmental performance with different measures of firm financial performance. In compiling this information, we relied on meta-analytic reviews of the research literature that summarized the relationship between the three measures of success that are part of the "triple bottom line" (Margolis, Elfenbein, & Walsh, 2007; Orlitzky, 1998; Orlitzky et al., 2003—two meta-analyses that analyzed the same relationships but did not provide the relevant output in correlational form were excluded: Horváthová, 2010; Orlitzky, 2001). The data show that there is a moderate relationship between corporate social responsibility and firm financial performance (uncorrected correlations ranging from .09 to .23, with a maximum corrected correlation of .47 across 249 effects). The corresponding values for environmental performance are significantly lower (mean *r*s from .06 to .08; $\rho = .12$). While companies that excel financially also display higher levels of CSR, the association between firm performance and environmental responsibility is notably weaker.[1]

In addition to the empirical evidence, there are theoretical and conceptual reasons for a distinction between corporate social responsibility and environmental performance. Despite the fact that human well-being is closely tied to the sustained integrity of the biosphere, these two aspects of organizational performance are of a different nature, based on distinct objectives, and call for unique interventions. As we have previously argued (Ones & Dilchert, 2012b), CSR aims to improve the safety, health, and well-being of individuals (employees, customers, and external stakeholders) directly (e.g., by contributing to social causes, ensuring proper working conditions, or investing in training and education). Environmental performance involves the responsible management of natural resources in business operations to ensure the sustainability of the natural environ-

TABLE 7.1

Relationships of Corporate Environmental Performance and Social Responsibility With Measures of Firm Financial Performance

	Source	Corporate social responsibility				Environmental performance			
		k	N	r	ρ	k	N	r	ρ
Financial performance, mixed measures	Orlitzky et al. (2003)[a]	249	'24055'	.23	.47	139	'9823'	.06	.12
Financial performance, accounting-based	Margolis et al. (2007)[b]	75		.14		15		.06	
Financial performance, market-based	Margolis et al. (2007)[b]	125		.09		28		.08	
Firm risk (variance in earnings, stock returns)	Orlitzky (1998)[a]	60	'6186'	-.15	-.21	6	108	-.20	-.21

Note. k = number of effects summarized. N = number of companies. r = mean, sample-size weighted observed correlation. ρ = corrected correlation. [a] Values for CSR represent results for "pure" measures that did not include environmental performance. [b] Values for environmental performance represent results for objective measures, excluding company self-reports.

ment, in order to sustain organizational economic viability, as well as all future life on this planet.

This theoretical distinction is of particular practical importance when managing employees in occupational settings. Encouraging social versus environmental responsibility among employees requires different interventions and incentives. For example, the knowledge and skill required to support organizational social and environmental goals differ. Furthermore, the motives that drive employees to behave in socially responsible versus environmentally sustainable ways might vary. It is likely that employees will differ in terms of their potential to support these different types of organizational goals, based on their unique individual differences and attitudinal profiles. Management and human resources systems and initiatives (e.g., leadership, recruitment, training) that take these differences into account can better encourage relevant attitudes and elicit correct behaviors among their workforces.

GREEN BEHAVIORS AND THEIR RELATIONSHIPS WITH OTHER CRITERIA AT THE EMPLOYEE LEVEL

Sustainable organizations require a systems approach for ensuring a careful balance of environmental, social, and economic performance (Jackson, 2012), and employee behaviors are a major contributor to organizational environmental performance. In this section, we describe conceptual and empirical relationships between employee green behaviors and employee engagement and tenure as well as job performance.

Employee Engagement

What does the field of industrial, work, and organizational psychology know about the relationships between work attitudes, job performance, and employee green behaviors? Quantitative reviews have reported various benefits of employee engagement (e.g., Brown, 1996; Cooper-Hakim & Viswesvaran, 2005), including relationships with task performance and organizational citizenship behaviors (Crawford, LePine, & Rich, 2010). Engaged employees display more extra-role behaviors at work (Diefendorff, Brown, Kamin, & Lord, 2002). However, none of these investigations have included employee behaviors related to environmental sustainability. Recent research has started to address both engagement for sustainability and the impact of general employee engagement on employee green behaviors.

In a case study of Caribou Coffee, Muros, Impelman, and Hollweg (2012) found that specific indicators of employee environmental sustainability perceptions were strongly and positively related to general engagement among more than 4,000 employees. Observed correlations were in the .40s. General employee engagement has also been linked to employee green behaviors (total N > 20,000 employees; McCance, Biga, Gibby, & Massman, 2012). Employees who are more engaged with their work appear to perform more green behaviors on the job. In a series of studies across multiple years of data collection, employee engagement correlated in the .29 to .35 range (corrected for unreliability) with various aspects of individual level environmental sustainability such as working sustainably, conserving, as well as overall employee green behaviors (Biga, Dilchert, McCance, Gibby, & Oudersluys, 2012).

In their case study, Muros et al. (2012) also found that better perceptions of environmental efforts correlated in the .32 to .35 range with intent to remain with the organization for longer than one year. Furthermore, Biga, Ones, Dilchert, and Gibby (2010) reported that among employees working for a multinational organization with an established environmental sustainability program, organizational tenure was positively related to employee green behaviors. That is, employees who had been with the organization longer reported engaging in more employee green behaviors.

Job Performance

There are both conceptual and empirical linkages between employee green behaviors and job performance. Theoretically, employee green behaviors can be part of task performance, organizational citizenship behaviors, and even counterproductive work behaviors (Ones & Dilchert, 2012b). When employees perform green behaviors as part of their core job tasks and duties, employee green behaviors constitute task performance. Typically, green jobs and jobs in green industries (e.g., renewable energy generation or green construction; see Dierdorff, Norton, Gregory, Rivkin, & Lewis, this book) will include employee green behaviors as part of task performance. However, employees from all sorts of industries and jobs can have green behaviors among their regular job tasks. For example, as organizations undertake efforts to green their products, processes, and services, traditional tasks may be redesigned. Creation and adoption of eco-innovations redefine traditional tasks as eco-friendly ones. Our research across a variety of jobs and multiple U.S. and European industries (not just green jobs or green industries) has found that between 13% and 29% of employee green behaviors are required as part of job duties or organizational expectations (Ones & Dilchert, 2009, 2012a; Hill et al., 2011).

On the other hand, some employee green behaviors are clearly discretionary and are similar to pro-social or organizational citizenship behaviors (cf. Hoffman & Dilchert, 2012). These behaviors might not be part of core performance but nonetheless helpful for broader aspects of organizational functioning. Employee green behaviors that involve individual initiative, altruism, and rule compliance directed at environmentally-relevant goals outside of core job duties fall under the umbrella of organizational citizenship behaviors.

Conceptually, we have previously made the case that employee behaviors can also detract from environmental sustainability. This includes both inhibition of eco-friendly behaviors (such as refraining from recycling) and active performance of harmful behaviors (e.g., polluting). Such irresponsible employee green behaviors are part of the counterproductive work behavior domain (Ones & Dilchert, 2012a). Across our two U.S.-based critical incidents studies, we found that about 25% of the behavioral examples provided were environmentally irresponsible (Dilchert et al., 2010). For European data, about 18% of the critical incidents described were environmentally-irresponsible behaviors (Hill et al., 2011).

In sum, employee green behaviors can contribute to different job performance domains (task, contextual, or counterproductive). Empirical relationships among employee green behaviors and performance constructs support this position. Dilchert (2012) and Ones (2012) both presented data from multiple organizations where expected relationships were documented using non-self-report data (i.e., supervisory ratings). However, Ones (2012) noted that relationships, especially for task performance, appeared to be weaker in an organization that did not have a strong culture of environmental sustainability. Regardless of the performance domains employee green behaviors fall into, identifying their determinants and ways of improving them through interventions is essential for increasing organizational environmental performance. In the next section, we describe a working taxonomy of employee green behaviors, with the goal to further the understanding of this important criterion domain. We then discuss avenues to enhancing employee green behaviors in work settings.

LOOKING UNDER THE HOOD OF EMPLOYEE GREEN BEHAVIORS

The scant empirical literature available on the relationship between green behaviors and work-related outcomes is in part due to a lack of a comprehensive taxonomy of environmentally-relevant behaviors among employees. Much of the psychological literature on environmental sustainability (in both work and non-work settings) has focused on individual behaviors such as recycling or energy conservation. Even popular measurement scales that take a more comprehensive approach suffer from a lack of discriminant validity with constructs such as social responsibility (e.g., see Kaiser's [1998] General Ecological Behavior scale, which assesses several distinct behaviors such as garbage inhibition and volunteering, but also includes pro-social behaviors as well as social and ethnic stereotypes).

As applied psychologists, our interests lie in the explanation, prediction, and modification of behaviors in the workplace, including behaviors that have a positive or negative impact on organizational environmental performance. For this purpose, a behaviorally based taxonomy of environmental performance at the employee level is essential. We have previously summarized our own work on a taxonomy of employee green behaviors (Ones & Dilchert, 2012a), which serves as a model of classifying employee behaviors into psychologically meaningful categories. This working taxonomy was developed based on extensive critical incidents data collections (Ones & Dilchert, 2009), including domestic and international replications (Ones & Dilchert, 2010; Hill et al., 2011). The result is a hierarchical model with five broad functional categories, each distinguished by several facets that differ in target or content of the specific behaviors they describe (see Table 5.1 and Figure 5.1 in Ones & Dilchert, 2012a).

First, the *Conserving* category of employee green behaviors encompasses those actions that most lay people and scholars recognize as the core of pro-environmental behaviors: reducing, reusing, repurposing, and recycling. While analogous behaviors in individuals' personal lives focus mainly on waste reduction, marker behaviors in the workplace include avoiding wastefulness, sensible use of raw materials, and conservation of energy and natural resources. In our research, we found that about half of all employee green behaviors can be classified into this category.

The next category of behaviors not only occurs in the workplace, but relates directly to the work itself. *Working Sustainably* refers to an environmentally-oriented way of performing one's job duties and organizational responsibilities. This includes both changing work products and processes to minimize environmental impact, as well as inventing or creating new products and services (see Table 5.1 in Ones & Dilchert, 2012a, for additional facets and explanations).

Next, the behavior category of *Avoiding Harm* describes avoidance and inhibition of negative environmental behaviors at work. Like other categories in our model, it includes negative behaviors. However, these negative behaviors can also be active (e.g., pollution), compared with the previously described categories where negative green behaviors are mostly defined by refusing to engage in a positive act (e.g., not recycling, not conserving a resource). The positive side of this category encompasses behaviors that prevent pollution or even enhance ecosystems and the biosphere (e.g., planting trees to offset greenhouse gas emissions). While negative behaviors in this category are often driven by a lack of cautiousness (and sometimes motivated by financial gain), positive employee green behaviors that avoid environmental harm tend to be driven by altruism, feelings of responsibility to future generations, and a general concern for the natural environment (Klein, Ones, et al., 2012).

Influencing Others describes the degree to which employees engage, educate, and encourage other individuals to minimize environmental impact or participate in pro-environmental initiatives. These behaviors can be targeted at a variety of organizational stakeholders (including customers)—but by definition they are performed in the employee role. While these behaviors often do not have a direct or immediate environmental benefit, and our own work shows them to occur with relatively low base-rates, they have the potential to significantly impact the environmental bottom line of organizations through influencing the behaviors of multiple organizational members.

The final category, *Taking Initiative*, is defined by a willingness to take risks for environmental benefit. Behaviors in this category reflect the initiating, entrepreneurial spirit of the employee action as the seed for a respective initiative or program. Actions that involve self-sacrifice are also found here. Taking Initiative behaviors can be directed at other behavioral categories. For example, employees who lobby for or organize an organizational recycling program are not simply conserving resources—they are taking an active step to make a bigger, longer lasting change than what they could achieve by engaging in the behavior on their own. Employees who engage in these kinds of activities are change agents, not only on an interpersonal but also organizational level.

The five broad categories of employee green behaviors described here are conceptually and empirically distinguishable. Many of the conceptual distinctions arise from the functions that behaviors in each category serve as well as the psychological basis of the respective behaviors. Moreover, functional motives and individual difference characteristics that determine people's engagement in each type of employee green behavior vary. Of course, even though the different types of green behaviors can be distinguished, and even though employees within the same organization and job will differ in terms of which behaviors they typically engage in, they are positively intercorrelated, in part due to common antecedents (Dilchert & Ones, 2011). Nonetheless, focusing on the content and conceptual distinctions provides utility in designing workplace interventions targeted at increasing green behaviors among employees, and thus contributes not only to an increased understanding in the scientific community, but is useful to applied psychological work as well.

INFLUENCING EMPLOYEE GREEN BEHAVIORS

Employee behaviors can be shaped through two complementary approaches: person-based and intervention-based. Person-based approaches capitalize on individual differences and aim to shape organizational behavior through targeted staffing decisions. In contrast, intervention-based approaches take workforce composition as a given and focus on altering employees' behaviors using educational, motivational, and other organizational strategies. They utilize principles that relate to learning, training, development, and organizational change.

Person-Based Approaches

Organizational behaviors are shaped by individuals who are attracted, selected, and retained by organizations (Schneider, 1987). Personal tendencies and psychological characteristics that are associated with employee green behaviors may be harder to address once employees are on the job. Thus, an important component of enhancing environmental sustainability in organizations is through recruitment and selection strategies.

Recruiting

Organizations are increasingly recruiting job applicants for jobs that include green tasks and duties (Schmit, Fegley, Esen, Schramm, & Tomassetti, 2012). Schmit (2011) reported that a survey of 1,705 human resource professionals indicated that 40% of organizations were creating green jobs or adding green tasks and duties to existing positions, and a further 5% were intending to do so in the future.

Some recent articles have addressed the role of recruitment in environmental sustainability. As Muros (2012) notes, organizations can incorporate environmental sustainability in a variety of ways into their recruitment efforts. These include developing materials that convey information about organizations' environmental goals, values, and initiatives. Furthermore, recruiters themselves can be trained to enable them to properly address environmental sustainability-related questions and to highlight organizational commitment using recruiting messages that include relevant statements. Finally, in recruiting, organizations can specifically target sources that provide environmentally-passionate job applicants. For a detailed discussion of leveraging green business practices to attract talent, see Willness and Jones, this book.

Studies have documented the effect of pro-environmental messages and green organizational reputation on positive outcomes (Bauer, Erdogan, & Taylor, 2012). For example, in an early lab study, Bauer and Aiman-Smith (1996) found that including a pro-environmental message in a recruiting brochure related positively to perceived attractiveness of, intentions to pursue employment with, and acceptance of a job offer from the organization ($N = 303$). A more recent lab study found that job pursuit intentions were directly affected by perceptions of organizational reputation, which in turn was influenced by pro-environmental messages (Behrend,

Baker, & Thompson, 2009). At the organizational level, a study using data from 10,840 French organizations found that those that subscribed to voluntary environmental standards such as organic labeling, fair trade practices, and so forth, reported having an easier time recruiting employees, even after controlling for a host of recruitment-relevant variables such as organizational size and wages offered (Grolleau, Mzoughi, & Pekovic, 2012).

Staffing

Organizations can also affect employee green behaviors through their selection practices. By hiring those individuals who are more likely to be environmentally friendly, responsible, and passionate, organizations can procure human resources that influence environmental sustainability at the organizational level. Despite some existing case studies, there is little published research from organizational settings that can offer guidance about the characteristics of individuals related to employee green behaviors. Therefore, we now draw upon the research on pro-environmental behaviors in general.

Psychological individual differences. Meta-analyses have identified three psychologically based individual differences that relate to pro-environmental behaviors. Locus of control and future time perspective both display moderate positive relationships (Hines, Hungerford, & Tomera, 1986–1987; Milfont, Wilson, & Diniz, 2012). In contrast, past-present time perspective is related negligibly to pro-environmental behaviors (Milfont et al., 2012). More detailed results from these quantitative reviews are summarized in Table 7.2.

Primary research has also revealed moderate to strong relationships between some of the Big Five dimensions of personality and related traits with environmental concern, attitudes, as well as values. Individuals *concerned* about the environment appear to be more extraverted, enthusiastic, and conscientious (Borden & Francis, 1978). In a community sample of 2,690 individuals, Hirsh (2010) reported that environmental concern was related to higher scores on neuroticism, openness, agreeableness, and conscientiousness. These findings are in line with an earlier study reporting that environmentalism was positively related to agreeableness and openness in a student sample (Hirsh & Dolderman, 2007). Similarly, pro-environmental *attitudes* have been connected to sincerity (an agreeableness-related trait) and conscientiousness (Pettus & Giles, 1987). *Values* relating

TABLE 7.2

Individual Differences Correlates of Pro-Environmental Behaviors at the Individual Level

Variables	N	k	ρ	Source
Pro-environmental behavior (general/unspecified)				
Locus of control	—	14	.37	Hines et al. (1986/87)
Future time perspective	5,261	13	.26	Milfont et al. (2012)
Past-present time perspective	3,875	4	.06	Milfont et al. (2012)
Educational level	—	11	.19	Hines et al. (1986/87)
Income	—	10	.16	Hines et al. (1986/87)
Economic orientation	—	6	.16	Hines et al. (1986/87)
Gender[a]	—	4	.08	Hines et al. (1986/87)
Age	—	10	−.15	Hines et al. (1986/87)
Age	50,185	182	.05	Wiernik et al. (in press)
Pro-environmental behavior (specific aspects)				
Age				
Conserving	9,646	18	.12	Wiernik et al. (in press)
Conserving—prior to 1995	2,288	6	−.11	Wiernik et al. (in press)
Conserving—1995 and later	7,358	12	.18	Wiernik et al. (in press)
Avoiding harm	4,037	5	.17	Wiernik et al. (in press)
Making responsible product choices	8,357	7	−.01	Wiernik et al. (in press)
Influencing and educating for sustainability	687	2	.01	Wiernik et al. (in press)
Political behaviors	4,279	2	.03	Wiernik et al. (in press)
Engaging with nature	3,912	4	.20	Wiernik et al. (in press)

Note. N = total sample size (— indicates not reported). k = number of effects summarized. ρ = corrected correlation. [a] Hines et al.'s manuscript refers to results for gender, but most likely analyzed sex differences. The authors did not clarify the direction of positive or negative effect sizes (i.e., the question of whether men or women scored higher on average). They only interpreted the low magnitude of the effect, concluding "there appears to be no relationship between gender and responsible environmental behavior based on the studies coded."

to environmental protection are also correlated positively with agreeableness and conscientiousness (N = 6,507; Milfont & Sibley, 2012).

Shifting focus from concern, attitudes, and values to actual pro-environmental *behaviors*, personality linkages remain remarkably consistent. Wiseman and Bogner (2003) report that individuals low on agreeableness and conscientiousness (as measured by high scores on Eysenck's psychoticism scale) tend to exploit environmental resources more than others. Furthermore, lower impulsivity and emotional stability (i.e., higher neuroticism) relates to conserving behaviors and preservation. Agreeableness and conscientiousness have been found to relate to self-reported electricity conservation (Milfont & Sibley, 2012). Finally, openness to experience, conscientiousness, and extraversion appear to relate to pro-environmental behaviors among students, and openness correlates with general conservation and adopting habits and behaviors (Markowitz, Goldberg, Ashton, & Lee, 2012). We expect personality to also relate to pro-environmental behaviors through environmentally-relevant values (e.g., altruistic, egoistic, anthropocentric, traditional; Dunlap & Van Liere, 1978; Stern & Dietz, 1994), connectedness to nature (Mayer & Frantz, 2004), and environmental perspective taking (Schultz, 2000). However, all of these variables await investigation in organizational settings.

These reviewed findings make it clear that personality variables are relevant to environmental concern, attitudes, values, and behaviors in general. In occupational settings, in our recent empirical research we have found that openness, agreeableness, and conscientiousness relate to employee green behaviors (Dilchert & Ones, 2011). Thus, personality variables would be valuable to take into account in these settings as well. Additional studies are needed before precise point estimates of these traits' potencies in the prediction of both pro-environmental behavior and employee green behaviors can be established meta-analytically.

Other individual differences. As discussed earlier, person-based approaches to enhancing environmental sustainability in organizational settings rely on individual differences as key determinants of employee behaviors. Staffing decisions (i.e., recruitment, selection, placement, exiting) that utilize individual differences that relate to pro-environmental behaviors can yield workforces that are environmentally sensitive and more responsible, and thus benefit organizations' environmental performance.

There are also non-psychological individual differences that have been examined in relation to pro-environmental behaviors. Klein, D'Mello, and Wiernik (2012) have provided a concise summary of demographic variables in relation to individual level environmental sustainability. Of course, not all of these individual differences can or should be taken into account in staffing decisions, based on both legal and ethical considerations. Nonetheless, knowledge of some of these relationships can be valuable in planning and targeting human resources interventions and thus furthering both employee, organizational, and environmental well-being.

Table 7.2 summarizes meta-analytic findings for these variables as well. For example, educational level has been found to relate to pro-environmental behavior ($\rho = .19$; Hines et al., 1986–1987). The Hines et al. meta-analysis also reported moderate positive relations with economic orientation and income; a small relationship was reported for gender.

The relationship between age and pro-environmental behaviors was the subject of two meta-analyses. In earlier research, Hines et al. (1986–1987) reported a moderate negative relationship with pro-environmental behavior, leading to the general conclusion that younger individuals tend to behave in more environmentally-sustainable ways. This assumption was challenged by Wiernik, Ones, and Dilchert (in press) based on results from their expanded meta-analysis that included more than 150 additional effect sizes and utilized a more nuanced breakdown of the criterion space. Wiernik et al. reported that although most age-behavior relationships were negligible, small to moderate and generalizable relationships were found for engaging with nature, avoiding harm, and conserving resources. Older individuals appear to be more likely to engage with nature and avoid environmental harm. Perhaps more interestingly, although prior to 1995, younger individuals tended to perform more conserving behaviors than older individuals, this trend appears to have reversed. Based on data from the last two decades, older individuals engage in more conserving behaviors. Corresponding data for employee green behaviors have not been reported in the scientific literature to date. Klein, Ones, Dilchert, Biga, and McCance (under review) and Wiernik, Ones, Dilchert, and Biga (under review) are examining these links with employee gender and age, respectively.

Intervention-Based Approaches

A complementary approach to recruiting and staffing is the use of interventions and environmental initiatives to influence environmental performance of organizations. In a recent study, D'Mello, Ones, Klein, Wiernik, and Dilchert (under review) analyzed environmental initiatives undertaken by Fortune 500 and Newsweek Green 500 companies. There were two distinct dimensions: changed-oriented initiatives and compliance-oriented initiatives. The former category included initiatives that made products and/or processes more environmentally sustainable (e.g., creating, devising, or adopting more environmentally-friendly products or processes); conserving resources (e.g., energy, water, raw materials) by directly reducing consumption, waste reduction, re-using, and recycling; as well as influencing and improving their own or others' pro-environmental behaviors. Compliance-oriented initiatives targeted prevention of pollution, monitoring for environmental impact, strengthening eco-systems (when harm cannot be prevented), as well as lobbying efforts. D'Mello et al.'s analyses indicated that change-oriented initiatives were more progressive and more closely related to economic indicators of success. Regardless, the authors observed that all organizational initiatives targeting environmental sustainability must operate through employees. That is, both change-oriented initiatives and compliance-oriented initiatives require employee action and behavior. Organizational initiatives provide the behavioral targets whereas interventions are the approaches that can be utilized to ensure the performance of targeted behaviors by employees.

A key question is how individuals can be influenced or affected such that their behavior supports organizational environmental initiatives. Unfortunately, much of the research on the effectiveness of interventions for enhancing pro-environmental behavior has been conducted in non-work settings. We will describe these limited findings organized around two major themes: (a) informational and instructional interventions and (b) psycho-social and motivational interventions. In describing the effectiveness of various interventions on pro-environmental behaviors, we will rely on the meta-analytic research summarizing improvement among those targeted by intervention in terms of standardized mean differences.

Informational and Instructional Interventions

These interventions provide either instructions or information to enable the performance of desired pro-environmental behaviors. The goal is to enable performance through knowledge. This can range from providing simple prompts to signal the appropriateness and desirability of a given pro-environmental behavior, to informational training, to providing feedback. Table 7.3 presents a description and summary of informational and instructional interventions and their relative effectiveness, albeit based on research conducted mostly in lab settings.

For the interventions presented here, the goal is to increase the occurrence of pro-environmental behaviors by providing information about (a) when and where it is appropriate to perform a given behavior (*prompt* interventions), (b) the reasons for engaging in the pro-environmental behavior (*justification* interventions), (c) how to perform various pro-

TABLE 7.3

Informational and Instructional Interventions for Pro-Environmental Behaviors and Their Effectiveness

Intervention/Variable	Explanation	k	Mean effect	Pro-environmental behavior measurement method	Source
Interventions: Experimental research evidence			δ		
Prompts	Reminders and prompts inform individuals about the appropriateness and desirability of the pro-environmental behavior in context	44	**0.62**	objective, non–self-report	Osbaldiston & Schott (2012)
Justifications	Justifications inform individuals about the reasons for engaging in pro-environmental behavior	44	**0.43**	objective, non–self-report	Osbaldiston & Schott (2012)
Instructions	Instructions provide procedural knowledge about performing pro-environmental behaviors	50	**0.31**	objective, non–self-report	Osbaldiston & Schott (2012)
Information	Information provides environmental sustainability relevant declarative and/or procedural knowledge to individuals	8	**1.07**[a]	self-report and objective	Hines et al. (1986/1987)
Feedback	Feedback provides information to individuals about the impact and consequences of environmental behaviors	60	**0.31**	objective, non–self-report	Osbaldiston & Schott (2012)
		13	**0.58**[a]	self-report and objective	Hines et al. (1986/1987)
Knowledge-based variables: Correlational research evidence			ρ		
Environmental problem awareness	General information on environmental problems	18	**0.19**	self-report and objective	Bamberg & Möser (2007)
Environmental knowledge	General declarative and procedural knowledge about environmental problems and environmental sustainability	17	**0.30**	self-report and objective	Hines et al. (1986/1987)

Note. k = number of effects summarized. δ = meta-analytic, standardized mean difference (Cohen's *d* and Hedge's *g*). ρ = corrected correlation.
[a] Obtained by converting corrected correlations reported by Hines et al. (1986/1987) into *d* values.

environmental behaviors (*instruction* interventions), (d) environmental sustainability as well as declarative and procedural knowledge to enable pro-environmental behaviors (*information* interventions), and (d) the impact and consequences of behaviors (*feedback* interventions).

The standardized effect sizes from meta-analyses in the environmental psychology literature listed in Table 7.3 suggest moderate effectiveness of each of the informational or instructional interventions. The unreliability corrected standardized mean differences are in the .30 to .60 range. Information interventions provide an exception (mean effect size = 1.07, based on eight studies). The small number of studies contributing to this estimate (the lowest k across analyses tabulated) and the mixture of self-report and objective criteria in assessing pro-environmental behaviors may explain this outlier.

Though it may be tempting to compare the effectiveness of different interventions listed in Table 7.3, direct comparisons are not possible. First, as noted earlier, various meta-analyses have treated pro-environmental behavior measurement differently. Hines et al. (1986–1987) appear to have combined self-reported and objective criteria whereas Osbaldiston and Schott (2012) included only objective, non-self-reported behavioral outcomes. Second, Osbaldiston and Schott aimed to produce very conservative estimates of effectiveness. Therefore, they made a number of decisions about the effect sizes included in their meta-analysis not shared by others. For example, for studies reporting non-significant effects, they substituted 0.00 as the estimated effect size. They also reduced the influence of outliers at the high end of the effect size distribution. Thus, the meta-analytic findings in Table 7.3 should be taken as one indicator of the moderate effectiveness of instructional and informational interventions. However, they do not provide appropriate point estimates for comparisons.

The lower part of Table 7.3 lists findings from meta-analyses that have examined knowledge-based correlates of pro-environmental behaviors: environmental problem awareness and environmental knowledge. Although these data do not speak to whether or not interventions can increase environmental problem awareness or environmental knowledge among participants, they indicate whether these two knowledge-based variables covary with pro-environmental behaviors. The meta-analytic evidence suggests that environmental knowledge is more strongly related to pro-environmental behavior ($\rho = .30$) than environmental problem awareness ($\rho = .19$).

Psycho-Social and Motivational Interventions

In contrast to instructional and informational interventions that enable the performance of desired pro-environmental behaviors via improvements in knowledge, psycho-social and motivational interventions aim to modify and improve the intensity, direction, and persistence of individual efforts. Hence, the goal is to enable performance through motivation. This includes a broad variety of approaches. Table 7.4 provides a description and summary of psycho-social and motivational interventions and a summary of the meta-analytic evidence for their relative effectiveness in improving pro-environmental behaviors.

Consistent with traditional definitions of motivation (see, for example, Pinder, 1998, p. 11), motivation for pro-environmental behaviors can be described as a set of energetic forces to initiate such behaviors and to determine their form and direction, intensity, and duration. The interventions listed in Table 7.4 all aim to influence pro-environmental behavior by (a) directing effort to pro-environmental behaviors, (b) intensifying directed effort, and (c) sustaining persistence. These interventions are not the only psycho-social and motivational interventions that can be undertaken for environmental sustainability. However, they are the only ones on which a substantial amount of research has been conducted.

Increasing the ease of pro-environmental behaviors is perhaps the motivationally weakest intervention, because it targets direction and duration of effort, but not intensity. Nonetheless, making pro-environmental behaviors convenient and easy to perform appears to result in about half a standard deviation increase in pro-environmental behaviors (Osbaldiston & Schott, 2012). These findings are consistent with Schultz and Oskamp's (1996) conclusion that effort likely moderates the relationship between concern/attitude and pro-environmental behavior. *Appeals* aim to work through intrinsic motivational forces and to increase the psychological salience and valence of pro-environmental behaviors. *Rewards* and *incentives*, on the other hand, focus on extrinsic motivational forces. *Social modeling* interventions rely on demonstrations of the desired pro-environmental behaviors, such that both vicarious learning and self-efficacy perceptions are enhanced. *Cognitive dissonance* interventions work because individuals alter their pro-environmental behaviors to address discomfort and dissonance created by discovering misalignments between preexisting environmental beliefs or attitudes and new environmental informa-

TABLE 7.4

Psycho-Social and Motivational Interventions for Pro-Environmental Behaviors and Their Effectiveness: Experimental Research Evidence

Intervention	Explanation	k	δ	Pro-environmental behavior measurement method	Source
Increasing ease	Increasing convenience and ease of pro-environmental behavior	19	0.49	objective, non-self-report	Osbaldiston & Schott (2012)
Appeals	Increasing psychological salience of pro-environmental behavior	16	2.00[a]	self-report and objective	Hines et al. (1986/87)
Rewards	Increasing extrinsic motivation associated with pro-environmental behavior	36	0.46	objective, non-self-report	Osbaldiston & Schott (2012)
Incentives	Increasing extrinsic motivation associated with pro-environmental behavior	47	1.91[a]	self-report and objective	Hines et al. (1986/1987)
Social modeling	Increasing self-efficacy of individuals to engage in pro-environmental behavior	26	0.63	objective, non-self-report	Osbaldiston & Schott (2012)
Cognitive dissonance	Increasing discomfort and dissonance in individuals by highlighting misalignments between preexisting environmental beliefs or attitudes and new environmental information and knowledge	13	0.94	objective, non-self-report	Osbaldiston & Schott (2012)
Commitment	Increasing commitment to pro-environmental behavior by stating intention and commitment (e.g., signing pledges)	32	0.40	objective, non-self-report	Osbaldiston & Schott (2012)
Goal setting	Regulating pro-environmental behavior by setting goals	15	0.64	objective, non-self-report	Osbaldiston & Schott (2012)

Note. k = number of effects summarized. δ = meta-analytic, standardized mean difference (Cohen's *d* and Hedge's *g*). [a] Obtained by converting corrected correlations reported by Hines et al. (1986/1987) into *d* values.

tion and knowledge. *Commitment* interventions aim to motivate pro-environmental behavior through declarations of intentions and commitment. Finally, *goal setting* utilizes goals as the motivational mechanism by which individuals regulate their environmentally-relevant behaviors.

A review of the meta-analytically derived effect sizes summarized in Table 7.4 indicates considerable effectiveness of these interventions. If the findings of Hines et al. (1986–1987) are excluded because of the mélange of self-report and objective criteria they summarized, effect sizes range from .40 to .94. As we described earlier, the meta-analytic source of these estimates (Osbaldiston & Schott, 2012) is likely overly conservative due to several methodological choices. Thus, clearly, psycho-social and motivational interventions result in increases in pro-environmental behaviors, at least in lab settings. A precise comparison of relative effectiveness of the various psycho-social and motivational interventions is not meaningful due to the apparent differences in the specific behavioral criteria that contributed to each meta-analytic estimate (Osbaldiston & Schott, 2012). However, we can conclude that based on objective, non-self-report behavioral criteria, psycho-social and motivational interventions appear to be generally more effective than instructional and informational interventions (see Table 7.3). The unweighted average effect sizes are .42 (standardized mean-score difference; from Table 7.3) and .59 (from Table 7.4), respectively.

Interventions in Work Settings

Although the results summarized here are promising with regard to the usefulness of interventions for pro-environmental behaviors, there are two limitations concerning this research literature. First, as we discussed earlier in this chapter, pro-environmental behavior in general is not the same as employee green behavior. To date, only a very limited set of studies has examined the effectiveness of interventions on environmental sustainability in work settings, and more specifically on employee green behaviors (Semmel, Klein, Ones, Dilchert, & Wiernik, 2012). Second, there is a multitude of green behaviors that employees can engage in (see the taxonomy of employee green behaviors described previously). Most workplace interventions are targeted at specific behavioral categories (e.g., increasing recycling, reducing energy use, adopting eco-friendly technologies). The effectiveness of various interventions ought to be examined separately for the behavioral categories they were intended to influence.

For their preliminary review, Semmel et al. (2012) sought research from organizational settings to be included in a meta-analysis. They were able to identify only 16 samples for which individual level pro-environmental behavior was assessed. The weighted, average observed effect size was .72 (standardized mean-score difference). However, this estimate spans four different intervention types (instructions, prompts, commitment, and combined interventions) and three domains of employee green behaviors (reducing use, recycling, and putting environmental interests first). An examination of effect sizes from the individual studies suggests that psycho-social and motivational interventions produce somewhat larger effect sizes than instructional and informational interventions, parallel to the conclusions we have drawn from non-work settings. Interventions focusing on conservation of resources appear to have greater impact than those targeting recycling and putting environmental interests first. It is important to stress that much more research on interventions in organizational settings needs to be conducted before a sufficient understanding can be reached regarding (a) which employee green behaviors are most responsive to interventions, and (b) which interventions are most effective.

MODELING PSYCHO-SOCIAL DETERMINANTS OF PRO-ENVIRONMENTAL BEHAVIOR

Although environmental sustainability and employee green behaviors are now drawing attention from human resources management and industrial, work, and organizational psychology researchers, there is a much richer literature in environmental psychology, which has developed over the last 40 years. Much of this literature focuses on psycho-social and motivational determinants of pro-environmental behaviors. It contributes to our understanding of individual pro-environmental behavior, and how psycho-social and motivational determinants could potentially be leveraged to increase it. Next, we briefly review and summarize major findings from this literature in the hope that it will inform organizational practices (e.g., employee surveys, motivational interventions) and further stimulate applied psychological research.

Three major theories underlie social-psychological explanations for why individuals engage in pro-environmental behaviors: the Norm Activation Model (NAM; Schwartz, 1977), Value-Belief Norm theory (VBN; Stern,

Dietz, Abel, Guagnano, & Kalof, 1999), and Theory of Planned Behavior (TPB; Ajzen, 1991). The major difference between the latter and the former two theories lies in the sources motivating pro-environmental behavior. Both NAM and VBN view pro-social motives (e.g., concern for others, including the next generation, concern for other species, and concern for the planet's ecosystems) to be major determinants. These models use the altruistic and social nature of individuals as an explanatory process. TPB, on the other hand, views pro-environmental behavior as the result of a rational choice process whereby individuals aim to maximize their own self-interests. Important variables across the three social-psychological models are environmental problem awareness, causal attributions, concerns, beliefs, norms (personal, subjective, social, and moral), perceived behavioral control, attitudes, intentions, and behavioral commitment. Several meta-analyses have investigated bivariate relationships between these variables and pro-environmental behaviors. Table 7.5 organizes and summarizes this quantitative evidence.

Meta-analytic techniques can be combined with structural equations modeling (see Viswesvaran & Ones, 1995) to examine causal mechanisms implicated in the various models of pro-environmental behavior (see, for example, Bamberg & Möser, 2007; Han & Hansen, 2012). An integrative analysis shows that many of the listed variables are only distally related to pro-environmental behaviors. The only proximal, direct determinant of pro-environmental behavior is behavioral intention. These empirical findings confirm Mesmer-Magnus et al.'s (2012) assertion that commitment to the environmental is a main pillar of environmental sustainability in work settings. Moral norms, perceived behavioral control, and attitudes exert their influence on pro-environmental behaviors more distally, via behavioral intentions (i.e., fully mediated). The zero-order relationships for these sets of distal determinants are in the .36-.40 range. Personal responsibility, as well as personal and social norms, are even further removed, and exert their influence via moral norms, perceived behavioral control, and attitudes, which are in turn mediated through intentions. The zero-order relationships for these distal determinants are weaker than those for moral norms, behavioral control, and attitudes. Finally, problem awareness, attributions, concerns, and beliefs are even further removed from pro-environmental behaviors and tend to be only weakly related.

In sum, the overall environmental performance of organizations can be enhanced by increasing employee green behaviors, and this process can also benefit from knowledge garnered from social-psychological models of pro-environmental behavior. Goal-setting interventions at the individual,

TABLE 7.5

Determinants of Individual Pro-Environmental Behaviors

Variable	N	k	ρ	Source
Distal determinants via social norms and guilt feelings				
Environmental problem awareness	8,276	18	.19	Bamberg & Möser (2007)
Internal causal attributions	1,866	6	.24	Bamberg & Möser (2007)
Environmental sustainability & ecological concerns*	547	1	.66	Han & Hansen (2012)
Health Concerns*	547	1	.47	Han & Hansen (2012)
Beliefs about environmental impact of food production practices*	1,557	3	.38	Han & Hansen (2012)
Distal determinants via perceived behavioral control, moral norms, and attitudes				
Personal responsibility	—	6	.33	Hines et al. (1986/87)
Personal norms*	2,130	3	.70	Han & Hansen (2012)
Guilt feelings	3,203	5	.30	Bamberg & Möser (2007)
Social norms	7,325	18	.31	Bamberg & Möser (2007)
Subjective norms*	1,903	3	.53	Han & Hansen (2012)
Distal determinants via intentions and commitment				
Moral norms	6,840	11	.39	Bamberg & Möser (2007)
Perceived behavioral control	8,029	18	.30	Bamberg & Möser (2007)
Perceived behavioral control*	2,450	9	.38	Han & Hansen (2012)
Attitudes	—	51	.35	Hines et al. (1986/87)
Attitudes	6,751	17	.42	Bamberg & Möser (2007)
Attitudes*	2,787	3	.58	Han & Hansen (2012)
Proximal determinants				
Verbal commitment	—	6	.49	Hines et al. (1986/87)
Pro-environmental behavior intentions	5,654	15	.52	Bamberg & Möser (2007)
Pro-environmental behavior intentions†	4,253	12	.54	Schwenk& Möser (2009)
Sustainable food consumption intentions*	1,918	3	.46	Han & Hansen (2012)

Note. N = total sample size for the effect sizes summarized. k = number of effects summarized. ρ = corrected correlation. * Pro-environmental behavior measures limited to sustainable food consumption. † Pro-environmental behavior measures assessed recycling, eco-friendly travel mode, and general eco-friendly behavior.

team, unit, and organizational level seem particularly suited in light of the relationship between behavioral intentions and pro-environmental behaviors in general. Other organizational initiatives (e.g., employee surveys) can also benefit from knowledge about how psycho-social variables are related to one another and to employee behaviors.

CONCLUSIONS

In this chapter, we distinguished among similar yet distinct constructs that relate to environmental sustainability in organizational contexts (e.g., environmental performance versus CSR at the organizational level; pro-environmental behaviors versus employee green behaviors at the individual level). We then discussed how environmentally-relevant behaviors can be understood, managed, and influenced through both person-based approaches and interventions. We recognize that the empirical evidence that supports most of these interventions does not guarantee their adoption or long-term success in organizational settings. As others have noted for other organizational efforts (e.g., Lawler & Mohrman, 1987), there is always the danger that environmental sustainability interventions, which may be initiated with great enthusiasm, might fail at implementation. It may be worthwhile to remember that top management support is one of the most important ingredients in ensuring success of most workplace programs (Rodgers, Hunter, & Rogers, 1993). We do not expect employee-focused environmental sustainability programs to be any different.

There are great opportunities for industrial, work, and organizational psychologists and human resources professionals in embedding environmental sustainability into what employees do every day. Field research, including descriptive studies, is needed to advance scientific knowledge and improve applied practices relating to employee-based environmental sustainability programs.

NOTE

1. An interesting relationship is observed for measures of firm financial risk. Risk can be operationalized in a variety of ways, but is often measured as variance in earnings or periodic stock returns (indexed by the standard deviation or coefficient of variation).

This relationship is negative for both CSR and environmental performance, indicating that more responsible corporations are associated with less financial risk. Explanations offered for this effect include the decreased threat of lawsuits and public relations debacles for organizations with active CSR and environmental programs, as well as the decreased likelihood of market interventions by regulatory agencies in the presence of responsible business practices (Orlitzky, 1998).

REFERENCES

Accenture (2011). Decision maker attitudes and approaches towards sustainability in business in 2011. Retrieved December 15, 2012, from http://www.accenture.com/us-en/Pages/insight-decision-maker-attitudes-sustainability.aspx

Aguinis, H., & Glavas, A. (2012). What we know and don't know about corporate social responsibility: A review and research agenda. *Journal of Management, 38*, 932–968.

Ajzen, I. (1991). The theory of planned behavior. *Organizational Behavior and Human Decision Processes, 50*, 179–211.

Bamberg, S., & Möser, G. (2007). Twenty years after Hines, Hungerford, and Tomera: A new meta-analysis of psycho-social determinants of pro-environmental behaviour. *Journal of Environmental Psychology, 27*, 14–25.

Bauer, T. N., & Aiman-Smith, L. (1996). Green career choices: The influence of ecological stance on recruiting. *Journal of Business and Psychology, 10*, 445–458.

Bauer, T. N., Erdogan, B., & Taylor, S. (2012). Creating and maintaining environmentally sustainable organizations. In S. E. Jackson, D. S. Ones, & S. Dilchert (Eds.), *Managing HR for environmental sustainability* (pp. 222–240). San Francisco, CA: Jossey-Bass/Wiley.

Behrend, T., Baker, B., & Thompson, L. (2009). Effects of pro-environmental recruiting messages: The role of organizational reputation. *Journal of Business and Psychology, 24*, 341–350.

Biga, A., Dilchert, S., McCance, A. S., Gibby, R. E., & Oudersluys, A. D. (2012). Environmental sustainability and organization sensing at Procter & Gamble. In S. E. Jackson, D. S. Ones, & S. Dilchert (Eds.), *Managing HR for environmental sustainability* (pp. 362–374). San Francisco, CA: Jossey-Bass/Wiley.

Biga, A., Ones, D. S., Dilchert, S., & Gibby, R. E. (2010, April). Perceptions of organizational support and employee sustainability. In D. S. Ones & S. Dilchert (Chairs), *Shades of green: Individual differences in environmentally responsible employee behaviors*. Symposium conducted at the annual conference of the Society for Industrial and Organizational Psychology, Atlanta, Georgia.

Borden, R. J., & Francis, J. L. (1978). Who cares about ecology? Personality and sex differences in environmental concern. *Journal of Personality, 46*, 190–203.

Brown, S. P. (1996). A meta-analysis and review of organizational research on job involvement. *Psychological Bulletin, 120*, 235–255.

Campbell, J. P. (1990). Modeling the performance prediction problem in industrial and organizational psychology. In M. D. Dunnette & L. M. Hough (Eds.), *Handbook of industrial and organizational psychology* (Vol. 1, pp. 687–732). Palo Alto, CA: Consulting Psychologists Press.

Cooper-Hakim, A., & Viswesvaran, C. (2005). The construct of work commitment: Testing an integrative framework. *Psychological Bulletin, 131*, 241–259.

Crawford, E. R., LePine, J. A., & Rich, B. L. (2010). Linking job demands and resources to employee engagement and burnout: A theoretical extension and meta-analytic test. *Journal of Applied Psychology, 95,* 834–848.

D'Mello, S., Ones, D. S., Klein, R. M., Wiernik, B. M., & Dilchert, S. (2011, April). *Green company rankings and reporting of pre-environmental efforts in organizations.* Poster presented at the annual conference of the Society for Industrial and Organizational Psychology, Chicago, Illinois.

D'Mello, S., Ones, D. S., Klein, R. M., Wiernik, B. M., & Dilchert, S. (under review). *What companies are doing to save the planet: Pro-environmental initiatives, their dimensionality, nomological network, and links to human resources.*

Deutsch, C. H. (2007, July 3). Companies giving green an office, *The New York Times.*

Diefendorff, J. M., Brown, D. J., Kamin, A. M., & Lord, R. G. (2002). Examining the roles of job involvement and work centrality in predicting organizational citizenship behaviors and job performance. *Journal of Organizational Behavior, 23,* 93–108.

Dilchert, S. (2012, April). Eco-innovation at work. In D. S. Ones (Chair), *Assessing and advancing environmental sustainability.* Symposium conducted at the annual conference of the Society for Industrial and Organizational Psychology, San Diego, California.

Dilchert, S., & Ones, D. S. (2011, April). Personality and its relationship to sustainable and unsustainable workplace behaviors. In S. Dilchert (Chair), *Focusing on employees to achieve environmentally sustainable organizations.* Symposium conducted at the annual conference of the Society for Industrial and Organizational Psychology, Chicago, Illinois.

Dilchert, S., & Ones, D. S. (2012). Measuring and improving environmental sustainability. In S. E. Jackson, D. S. Ones, & S. Dilchert (Eds.), *Managing HR for environmental sustainability* (pp. 187–221). San Francisco, CA: Jossey-Bass/Wiley.

Dilchert, S., Ones, D. S., Wiernik, B., Hill, L., D'Mello, S., & Klein, R. M. (2010, April). Understanding environmentally unfriendly behaviors of employees. In A. Sanders and A. Huffman (Chairs), *Earth and I/O: Implications for a sustainable workforce.* Symposium conducted at the annual conference of the Society for Industrial and Organizational Psychology, Atlanta, Georgia.

Dunlap, R. E., & Van Liere, K. D. (1978). The "New Environmental Paradigm": A proposed measuring instrument and preliminary results. *Journal of Environmental Education, 9,* 10–19.

Global Environmental Management Initiative (1998). *Measuring environmental performance: A primer and survey of metrics in use.* Washington, DC: Author.

Grolleau, G., Mzoughi, N., & Pekovic, S. (2012). Green not (only) for profit: An empirical examination of the effect of environmental-related standards on employees' recruitment. *Resource and Energy Economics, 34,* 74–92.

Han, Y., & Hansen, H. (2012). Determinants of sustainable food consumption: A meta-analysis using a traditional and a structural equation modelling approach. *International Journal of Psychological Studies, 4,* 22–45.

Hedberg, C.-J., & von Malmborg, F. (2003). The Global Reporting Initiative and corporate sustainability reporting in Swedish companies. *Corporate Social Responsibility and Environmental Management, 10,* 153–164.

Hill, L., Ones, D. S., Dilchert, S., Wiernik, B. M., Klein, R. M., & D'Mello, S. (2011, April). Employee green behaviors in Europe: A cross-cultural taxonomic investigation. In S. Dilchert (Chair), *Focusing on employees to achieve environmentally sustainable organi-*

zations. Symposium conducted at the annual conference of the Society for Industrial and Organizational Psychology, Chicago, Illinois.

Hines, J. M., Hungerford, H. R., & Tomera, A. N. (1986–1987). Analysis and synthesis of research on responsible environmental behavior: A meta-analysis. *Journal of Environmental Education, 18,* 1–8.

Hirsh, J. B. (2010). Personality and environmental concern. *Journal of Environmental Psychology, 30,* 245–248.

Hirsh, J. B., & Dolderman, D. (2007). Personality predictors of consumerism and environmentalism: A preliminary study. *Personality and Individual Differences, 43,* 1583–1593.

Hoffman, B. J., & Dilchert, S. (2012). A review of citizenship and counterproductive behaviors in organizational decision-making. In N. Schmitt (Ed.), *The Oxford handbook of personnel assessment and selection.* New York, NY: Oxford University Press.

Horváthová, E. (2010). Does environmental performance affect financial performance? A meta-analysis. *Ecological Economics, 70,* 52–59.

Jackson, S. E. (2012). Melding Industrial-Organizational scholarship and practice for environmental sustainability. *Industrial and Organizational Psychology: Perspectives on Science and Practice, 5*(4), 477–480.

Kaiser, F. G. (1998). A general measure of ecological behavior. *Journal of Applied Social Psychology, 28,* 395–422.

Klein, R. M., D'Mello, Susan, & Wiernik, Brenton M. (2012). Demographic characteristics and employee sustainability. In S. E. Jackson, D. S. Ones, & S. Dilchert (Eds.), *Managing HR for environmental sustainability.* San Francisco, CA: Jossey-Bass/Wiley.

Klein, R. M., Ones, D. S., Dilchert, S., Biga, A., & McCance, A. S. (under review). *Gender differences in employee green behaviors: Explaining cross-cultural variation.*

Klein, R. M., Ones, D. S., Wiernik, B. M., Dilchert, S., D'Mello, S., & Hill, L. (2012). *Understanding the causes of environmentally responsible and irresponsible behavior at work.* Poster presented at the Sustainability Preconference of the annual conference of the Society for Personality and Social Psychology, San Diego, California.

Kolk, A. (2008). Sustainability, accountability and corporate governance: Exploring multinationals' reporting practices. *Business Strategy and the Environment, 17,* 1–15.

Lawler, E. E., & Mohrman, S. A. (1987). Quality circles: After the honeymoon. *Organizational Dynamics, 15,* 42–54.

Margolis, J. D., Elfenbein, H. A, & Walsh, J. P. (2007). *Does it pay to be good? A meta-analysis and redirection of research on the relationship between corporate social and financial performance.* Paper presented at the annual conference of the Academy of Management.

Markowitz, E. M., Goldberg, L. R., Ashton, M. C., & Lee, K. (2012). Profiling the "proenvironmental individual": A personality perspective. *Journal of Personality, 80,* 81–111.

Mayer, F. S., & Frantz, C. M. (2004). The connectedness to nature scale: A measure of individuals' feeling in community with nature. *Journal of Environmental Psychology, 24,* 503–515.

McCance, S. A., Biga, A., Gibby, R. E., & Massman, A. (2012, April). *Environmental sustainability from the employees' perspective: Organization sensing at P&G.* In S. Dilchert (Chair), *Human resources and its role in environmental sustainability: Case studies.* Symposium conducted at the annual conference of the Society for Industrial and Organizational Psychology, San Diego, California.

Mesmer-Magnus, J., Viswesvaran, C., & Wiernik, B. M. (2012). The role of commitment in bridging the gap between organizational sustainability and environmental sustainability. In S. E. Jackson, D. S. Ones & S. Dilchert (Eds.), *Managing HR for environmental sustainability* (pp. 155–186). San Francisco, CA: Jossey-Bass/Wiley.

Milfont, T. L., & Sibley, C. G. (2012). The Big Five personality traits and environmental engagement: Associations at the individual and societal level. *Journal of Environmental Psychology, 32*, 187–195.

Milfont, T. L., Wilson, J., & Diniz, P. (2012). Time perspective and environmental engagement: A meta-analysis. *International Journal of Psychology*, 1–10.

Muros, J. P. (2012). Going after the green: Expanding Industrial-Organizational practice to include environmental sustainability. *Industrial and Organizational Psychology: Perspectives on Science and Practice, 5*(4), 467–472.

Muros, J. P., Impelman, K., & Hollweg, L. (2012). Sustainability in coffee sourcing and implications for employee engagement at Caribou Coffee. In S. E. Jackson, D. S. Ones, & S. Dilchert (Eds.), *Managing HR for environmental sustainability*. San Francisco, CA: Jossey-Bass/Wiley.

Ones, D. S. (2012, April). *Extending the nomological network of employee green behaviors*. In D. S. Ones (Chair), *Assessing and advancing environmental sustainability*. Symposium conducted at the annual conference of the Society for Industrial and Organizational Psychology, San Diego, California.

Ones, D. S., & Dilchert, S. (2009, August). Green behaviors of workers: A taxonomy for the green economy. In S. Dilchert & D. S. Ones (Chairs), *Environmentally friendly worker behaviors, senior leader wrongdoing, and national level outcomes*. Symposium conducted at the annual meeting of the Academy of Management, Chicago, Illinois.

Ones, D. S., & Dilchert, S. (2010, April). A taxonomy of green behaviors among employees. In D. S. Ones and S. Dilchert (Chairs), *Shades of green: Individual differences in environmentally responsible employee behaviors*. Symposium conducted at the annual conference of the Society for Industrial and Organizational Psychology, Atlanta, Georgia.

Ones, D. S., & Dilchert, S. (2012a). Employee green behaviors. In S. E. Jackson, D. S. Ones, & S. Dilchert (Eds.), *Managing HR for environmental sustainability* (pp. 85–116). San Francisco, CA: Jossey-Bass/Wiley.

Ones, D. S., & Dilchert, S. (2012b). Environmental sustainability at work: A call to action. *Industrial and Organizational Psychology: Perspectives on Science and Practice, 5*(4), 444–466.

Ones, D. S., & Dilchert, S. (forthcoming 2013). Counterproductive work behaviors: Concepts, measurement, and nomological network. In N. R. Kuncel (Ed.), *APA handbook of testing and assessment in psychology*. Washington, DC: American Psychological Association.

Ones, D. S., Dilchert, S., Biga, A., & Gibby, R. E. (2010, April). Managerial level differences in eco-friendly employee behaviors. In S. Dilchert (Chair), *Organizational and group differences in environmentally responsible employee behaviors*. Symposium conducted at the annual conference of the Society for Industrial and Organizational Psychology, Atlanta, Georgia.

Orlitzky, M. (1998). *A meta-analysis of the relationship between corporate social performance and firm financial performance*.Unpublished doctoral dissertation, University of Iowa, Iowa City, IA.

Orlitzky, M. (2001). Does firm size confound the relationship between corporate social performance and firm financial performance? *Journal of Business Ethics, 33*, 167–180.

Orlitzky, M., Schmidt, F. L., & Rynes, S. L. (2003). Corporate social and financial performance: A meta-analysis. *Organization Studies, 24,* 403–441.

Osbaldiston, R., & Schott, J. P. (2012). Environmental sustainability and behavioral science: Meta-analysis of proenvironmental behavior experiments. *Environment and Behavior, 44,* 257–299.

Pettus, A. M., & Giles, M. B. (1987). Personality characteristics and environmental attitudes. *Population and Environment, 9,* 127–137.

Pinder, C. C. (1998). *Work motivation in organizational behavior.* New York, NY: Psychology Press.

PriceWaterhouseCoopers. (2009). 12th annual global CEO survey: Redefining success. Retrieved December 15, 2012, from http://www.pwc.ch/user_content/editor/files/publ_corp/pwc_12th_annual_global_ceo_survey_e.pdf

Rikhardsson, P. M., Anderson, A. D. J., & Bang, H. (2002). Sustainability reporting on the internet: A study of the Global Fortune 500. *Greener Management International, 40,* 57–76.

Rodgers, R., Hunter, J. E., & Rogers, D. L. (1993). Influence of top management commitment on management program success. *Journal of Applied Psychology, 78,* 151–155.

Schmit, M. J. (2011, April). Sustainability business practices in the workplace: Prevalence, methods, and outcomes. In S. Dilchert (Chair), *Green HR: Environmentally sustainable organizations, jobs, and employees.* Symposium conducted at the annual conference of the Society for Industrial and Organizational Psychology, Chicago, Illinois.

Schmit, M. J., Fegley, S., Esen, E., Schramm, J., & Tomassetti, A. (2012). Human resource management efforts for environmental sustainability: A survey of organizations. In S. E. Jackson, D. S. Ones, & S. Dilchert (Eds.), *Managing HR for environmental sustainability* (pp. 61–79). San Francisco, CA: Jossey-Bass/Wiley.

Schneider, B. (1987). The people make the place. *Personnel Psychology, 40,* 437–453.

Schultz, P. W. (2000). Empathizing with nature: The effects of perspective taking on concern for environmental issues. *Journal of Social Issues, 56,* 391–406.

Schultz, P. W., & Oskamp, S. (1996). Effort as a moderator of the attitude-behavior relationship: General environmental concern and recycling. *Social Psychology Quarterly, 59,* 375–383.

Schwartz, S. H. (1977). Normative influences on altruism. In L. Berkowitz (Ed.), *Advances in experimental social psychology* (Vol. 10, pp. 221–279). New York, NY: Academic Press.

Schwenk, G., & Möser, G. (2009). Intention and behavior: A Bayesian meta-analysis with focus on the Ajzen–Fishbein Model in the field of environmental behavior. *Quality and Quantity, 43,* 743–755.

Semmel, S., Klein, R. M., Ones, D. S., Dilchert, S., & Wiernik, B. M. (2012). A meta-analytic review of interventions aimed at greening our workforce. Poster presented at the annual conference of the Society for Industrial and Organizational Psychology, San Diego, California.

SHRM, BSR, & Aurosoorya (2011). Advancing sustainability: HR's role. Washington, DC: Society for Human Resource Management.

Stern, P. C., Dietz, T., Abel, T., Guagnano, G. A., & Kalof, L. (1999). A Value-Belief-Norm Theory of support for social movements: The case of environmentalism. *Research in Human Ecology, 6,* 81–97.

Stern, P. C., & Dietz, T. (1994). The value basis of environmental concern. *Journal of Social Issues, 50,* 65–84.

van Wensen, K., Broer, W., Klein, J., & Knopf, J. (2011). *The state of play in sustainability reporting in the EU* (report commissioned under the European Union's Programme for Employment and Social Solidarity – PROGRESS).

Viswesvaran, C., & Ones, D. S. (1995). Theory testing: Combining psychometric meta-analysis and structural equations modeling. *Personnel Psychology, 48*, 865–885.

Viswesvaran, C., & Ones, D. S. (2000). Perspectives on models of job performance. *International Journal of Selection and Assessment, 8*, 216–226.

Wiernik, B. M., Ones, D. S., & Dilchert, S. (in press) Age and environmental sustainability: Meta-analytic findings and implications for management and organizations. *Journal of Managerial Psychology.*

Wiernik, B. M., Ones, D. S., Dilchert, S., & Biga, A. (under review). Age differences in green work behaviors across 11 countries.

Wiseman, M., & Bogner, F. X. (2003). A higher-order model of ecological values and its relationship to personality. *Personality and Individual Differences, 34*, 783–794.

Zibarras, Lara, & Ballinger, Catrin (2011). Promoting environmental behaviour in the workplace: A survey of UK organizations. In D. Bartlett (Ed.), *Going green: The psychology of sustainability in the workplace* (pp. 84–90). Leicester, UK: British Psychological Society.

8

It's Easy Being Green: Benefits of Technology-Enabled Work

Lance Andrews, Stephanie R. Klein, Jacob Forsman, and Dan Sachau

Teleconferencing and electronic mail have reduced the need for employees to travel between offices, homes, and stores. The internet has thus shortened the distances between businesses and employees. It has also reduced business's dependence on paper. Emails replace memos, envelopes, and letters. A single hard drive can store a warehouse full of manuals, receipts, and records. It would appear that the internet is more environmentally friendly than traditional ways of doing business. However, it does not operate resource free. The computer industry produces a mountain of desktops, laptops, monitors, wires, storage devices and tablets every day. Google alone uses more than 260 megawatts of electricity per year. This is about the same as 200,000 U.S. homes would use in a year (Glanz, 2011). So is there an environmental saving associated with the use of virtual travel and electronic paper?

In this chapter we discuss the costs and benefits of two recent applications of the internet to traditional human resource practices: pre-employment assessments and organizational surveys (see Behrend and Foster Thompson, this book, for a more general review of the application of technology and environmental sustainability). We also examine the broader context by considering the environmental impact of telecommuting. An analysis of telecommuting is informative because it illustrates the complexity involved in disentangling resource use. Ultimately, we show that the internet can save natural resources and lower pollution, but it also redistributes and masks its carbon footprint rather than eliminating it altogether.

THE ELECTRONIC COMMUTE

In the last 20 years, technology has enabled an increasing portion of the workforce to work from home. Between 2005 and 2008, the number of employees working at home one day a month or more increased by 74% (WorldatWork, 2009). By 2010, 26.2 million Americans worked from home (or remotely) for an entire day at least once a month (WorldatWork, 2011, p. 3). Twenty-six million represents nearly 20% of the U.S. working adult population of 139 million (as of fourth quarter 2010) (U.S. Bureau of Labor Statistics, 2011).

Certainly, working from home can reduce the fuel consumption and carbon emission associated with commuting. Consider the employees in a study by Andrews and Klein (2011). The authors gathered data from employees of a large financial services organization as they made the transition from traditional on-site employees to remote workers. All of the employees in the pilot study had worked full-time on-site at the corporate headquarters. When they entered the pilot program, they were moved into remote roles, where they performed the same job they had performed on-site, but now did so from home. Once they had moved, they completed a survey containing questions about commuting. Four hundred and eight employees completed surveys and were included in the final analyses.

Environmental Benefits

Andrews and Klein found the collective impact for just 408 employees was meaningful. Had the employees commuted rather than stayed home for the year, they would have driven an extra 4,010,650 miles. Using conservative U.S. Department of Transportation data to estimate the average (city or highway) fuel economy for cars at 25.2 miles per gallon (U.S. Department of Transportation, 2009), employees collectively saved 159,152 gallons of gasoline per year. According to the U.S. Environmental Protection Agency (EPA), consuming 1 gallon of gasoline releases 8,788 grams or 19.4 pounds (U.S. Environmental Protection Agency, 2011) of CO_2. Over one year, the work at home program reduced CO_2 emissions by 3,087,548 pounds.

It would appear that the results of the Klein and Andrews study provide direct measures of the extent to which a remote work program leads to environmental benefits. However, in order to estimate the overall environmental benefits of working from home, researchers need to examine all of the trade-offs. For example, to calculate the net benefit of working from home rather than working in an office building, researchers will need to address the energy use associated with widely dispersed employees each working in a small building and compare this with the energy use associated with a concentrated group of employees all working in the same large building. Employees who work from home may run their furnace at a higher temperature and their air conditioning at a lower temperature than they would if they were away all day at an office. Heating and cooling multiple homes may not be as efficient as heating and cooling one large building.

Kitou and Horvath (2008) examined the environmental effects of telecommuting using two complex modeling programs that accounted for heating, cooling, lighting, transportation, equipment installation, car occupancy, state of residence, climate conditions, commute distances, and number of days per week commuting. The authors show that telework programs have the potential to lower overall energy use and environmental costs by decreasing tailpipe emissions from commutes and energy use in the office. However, the authors caution that the implementation can "make or break the success of the programs" (p. 164).

A more detailed analysis of the trade-offs associated with working at an office versus working from home would include the impact of dining at home versus dining at restaurants; the use of home televisions and appliances; and the impact of the purchase, use, cleaning and disposal of business clothing versus casual clothing. In addition, researchers also need to consider some of the efficiencies of a commute. That is, a commute can include errands, shopping and day-care delivery or pickup. Stay-at-home employees will still have to travel to make these trips.

Researchers also need to consider whether people act in a more environmentally-friendly way at home or at work. Amel, Manning, and Scott (2009) examined six sustainable actions including recycling/reusing, conserving water, conserving energy, minimizing transportation, minimizing food impact, and avoiding flying at home and at work. The authors found that only 6% of the participants indicated that they performed more environmentally-friendly behaviors at work than at home. Consistent with the Amel et al. study, 96% of the respondents in the Andrews and Klein study either agreed or strongly agreed with the statement, "Working from home benefits the environment." As Table 8.1 illustrates, the benefits of working

TABLE 8.1

Percentage of Respondents Performing Environmentally-Friendly Behaviors

	Don't do either	More at home	Both	More at work
Recycling/Reusing	1.1	34.7	57.9	6.3
Conserving Water	5.3	36.8	52.6	5.3
Conserving Energy	2.1	41.1	50.5	6.3
Minimizing Transportation	18.1	29.8	43.6	8.5
Minimizing Food Impact	8.4	51.6	36.8	3.2
Avoiding Flying	39.6	29.7	25.3	5.5
Average	12.43	37.28	44.45	5.85

from home go beyond limited commuting. Employees may be acting more sustainably at home than at work.

Cost Savings

In addition to the potential environmental benefits from working at home, there may be economic benefits for the employee and the organization as well. In the study of financial services employees, Andrews and Klein found:

- Prior to joining the remote work pilot program, the average round-trip daily commute for an employee in the sample was 40.1 miles.
- The average employee in the sample spent a total of 74 minutes per day commuting to and from work. Thus, once employees began working at home, each employee saved an average of 6 hours per week.
- A typical employee in the pilot study saved $141.76 on gasoline each month by not commuting. This translates to $1,700 per year in fuel savings. If the Internal Revenue Service (IRS) reimbursement rate for mileage is used as an estimate of total travel costs (maintenance and depreciation), an employee who avoided a year's worth of traveling (9,000 miles), would save over $4,500 in commuting costs.
- When presented with the statement, "Working from home saves me money," 94.7% of the employees in the sample either agreed or strongly agreed.

In larger scale studies, AT&T enjoyed a 30% increase in cash flow ($550 million) by allowing enough employees to work from home to cut down on office use (Apgar, 1998). In other words, AT&T was able to reduce enough office space to save a substantial amount of money. California could save $1.5 billion per year if state government employees with telework-compatible jobs worked at home just two days a week (Telework Research Network, 2011). IBM saves 100 million dollars a year in its IBM North America sales and distribution unit by encouraging telecommuting (Apgar, 1998).

The future of telecommuting is exciting. Companies like Cisco are developing teleconference equipment with multiple screens, multiple cameras, and multiple microphones. Cisco is also working on three-dimensional hologram conferencing equipment (http://www.cisco.com). This new technology may further reduce the need for commuting and business travel. This new equipment is, however, power hungry, and, unlike a computer, does not have multiple uses. Again, if business leaders are interested in lowering their net environmental impact using telecommuting and teleconferencing technology, then they need to be cautious about the environmental trade-offs associated with the use of the equipment.

INTERNET TESTING

The internet is moving many job applications from the workplace to the home. It is also allowing prospective employees to complete pre-employment tests away from the workplace. Not only are these tests convenient, but online, unproctored, assessment programs provide environmental benefits over traditional in-person pre-employment screening methods. The primary environmental benefit of an online application and selection system is the reduction in miles traveled by job candidates. Of course, unproctored assessments are not necessarily administered at home, but it is highly likely that individuals completing a remote assessment away from home will choose a location (library, coffee shop, job center, etc.) that is closer than the job site.

To test the benefits of online pre-employment tests, Klein, Andrews, and Smith (2010) examined archival data from two organizations that use online pre-employment assessments: a Fortune 500 telecommunications company, and a large retail organization.

Fortune 500 Telecommunications Company

The first sample included 4,566 candidates who had applied for positions at a Los Angeles call center. The candidates applied between October 2001 and December 2007. They completed an online application and a short, unproctored screening assessment. The assessment included job-relevant biodata and personality scales. Seventy-three percent of the candidates met minimum qualifications and were eligible to advance to an on-site (proctored) assessment.

To investigate the environmental impact of the online assessment, the authors found the geo-coordinates (latitude and longitude) for each applicant's home address. Then they calculated the distance between the home addresses and the testing location. This was a straight-line distance so it was a conservative estimate of driving distance.

The authors found that the average distance between an applicant's home and test site was 14.945 miles. Round trip, 4,566 job candidates would have traveled a total of 136,490 miles if they had completed the application and assessment on-site.

Of the 4,566 local candidates, 1,253 failed to meet the minimum requirements for the screening assessment. Of those who passed, 1,288 did not complete the on-site assessment for a variety of reasons including the use of a top-down selection approach (first contacting candidates with the highest scores). Some candidates were no longer interested in the opportunity, others provided incorrect contact information, some had schedule conflicts, and others were simply no-shows.

For the 1,253 candidates whose initial assessment results rendered them ineligible to take the on-site assessment, the round-trip distance averaged 28.7 miles, totaling an estimated 35,912 miles not traveled. Additionally, the 1,288 candidates who were eligible based on screening results, but did not take the on-site assessment, would have traveled 35.47 miles round-trip on average, totaling an estimated 45,692 miles.

Of the candidates who passed the initial assessment, 2,025 candidates completed an on-site assessment sitting, traveling 27.1 miles round-trip on average. The total mileage traveled was therefore estimated at 54,888 miles, instead of the 136,490 that would have been traveled if all candidates had completed their assessment on-site. Online assessment saved 81,602 driving miles.

Large Retail Organization

The second sample included 11,996 candidates who applied for retail positions at 271 stores across the United States between April 2006 and May 2007. As in the call center sample, candidates completed an online application and an unproctored selection assessment that included job-relevant biodata and personality scales. Just as for the call centers, candidates meeting minimum assessment scores were eligible to advance to an on-site interview.

Of the 11,996 candidates in this sample, 8,203 candidates passed the online assessment and were eligible for the next stage of the selection process. Unfortunately, the authors did not have access to the addresses of the applicants who actually traveled to the stores for interviews (because a second, on-site pre-employment assessment did not take place), so they estimated how many candidates traveled on-site. This estimate was based on the number of candidates who passed the assessment (8,203) and the percentage of candidates who traveled on-site for the call center (61%). By their estimate, 5,003 candidates were invited on-site for an interview *and* would have traveled there. The candidates who traveled on-site would have traveled 129,569 miles. In contrast, had everyone who had applied for the jobs traveled to the stores to complete an application, they would have traveled 328,158 miles. Online assessment saved 198,589 miles.

Environmental Benefits

Across both samples, candidates who completed the unproctored assessment but not the on-site assessment or interview would have traveled a combined 280,191 miles round-trip to the testing location. Based on the Journey to Work Trends report (McGuckin & Srinivasan, 2003), 91.5% of all of these miles would likely have been driven in a single-passenger vehicle. This results in a total of 253,698 miles across all metropolitan areas in the study (see Table 8.2). Thus, online assessment saved 253,698 driving miles.

Table 8.2 describes the fuel consumption savings for the candidates who would have driven on-site if they had not been screened out by the unproctored assessment. U.S. Department of Transportation data were used to estimate the average combined (city and highway) fuel economy

TABLE 8.2

Estimated Miles and CO_2 Savings

	Mean Miles	N All	Miles All	N On-site	Miles On-site Candidates	Miles Saved All Transport	% Drive Car	Miles Saved By Car	Car Fuel Saving (Gal.)	Car CO_2 Saving (Pounds)
Los Angeles, CA	29.89	4,566	136,490	2,025	54,888	81,602	87.6	71,483	2,837	55,030
Mpls/St. Paul, MN	21.02	3385	71,166	1,430	30,219	40,947	88.3	36,156	1,435	27,834
Memphis, TN	44.30	569	25,206	232	10,181	15,025	93.9	14,108	560	10,860
Nashville, TN	40.27	1382	55,649	580	22,957	32,692	93.5	30,567	1,213	23,531
St. Louis, MO	26.59	1854	49,296	747	17,517	31,779	92.5	29,396	1,166	22,630
Louisville/Lexington, KY	25.98	2140	55,605	909	21,701	33,904	92.9	31,497	1,250	24,247
Columbus, OH	27.42	1535	42,092	626	15,361	26,731	91.6	24,486	972	18,850
Cincinnati, OH/ Northern KY	25.77	1131	29,144	479	11,633	17,511	91.4	16,005	635	12,321
Total		16,562	464,648	7,028	184,457	280,191	91.5	253,698	10,067	195,303

for new cars produced between 2001 and 2007 at 25.2 miles per gallon (U.S. Department of Transportation, 2009). Thus, the unproctored assessment and application saved a combined 10,067 gallons of gasoline. The resulting reduction in carbon dioxide output is 195,303 pounds (Pacific Gas and Electric, 2009). These fuel savings are significant and the estimate is especially conservative, given the unlikelihood that all candidates had new cars with maximum average fuel economy. For additional information, leading to less conservative calculations that would suggest even greater fuel savings, the U.S. EPA provides estimates of the average fuel economy for actual passenger vehicles in use (U.S. Environmental Protection Agency, 2009).

Cost Savings

Hiring organizations can experience cost savings by reducing the number of candidate miles traveled during their selection processes. Some companies reimburse candidates for travel expenses associated with on-site testing and interviews. If this policy were in place for the organizations included in the analysis, a minimum of $87,526 in mileage reimbursement would not have been necessary because of those 253,698 miles not driven. This is again the most conservative estimate, using the standard mileage rate of 34.5 cents per mile provided by the IRS for 2001 (corresponding with the oldest of our candidate data) (U.S. Internal Revenue Service, 2009). Using the less conservative estimate, the standard mileage rate for 2007 (the most recent candidate data) was 48.5 cents per mile, which would bring the organizations' cost savings to $123,044 that might otherwise have been spent on mileage reimbursements.

The results of these studies provide an easy way to quantify the impact of unproctored testing on fuel consumption. Although there are a number of assumptions and estimates, the data presented clearly indicate that organizations can use unproctored pre-employment tests and substantially decrease the amount of fuel consumed by candidates applying for positions. If the employers in the studies had conducted only proctored on-site tests, all of the candidates in these samples would have traveled a total of 464,649 miles round-trip for a single on-site event. Online pre-employment testing saved 253,698 miles and this was for fewer than just 167,000 job hunters.

Obviously the widespread use of online tests could save millions of miles of driving. As of November 2011, there were over 140,000,000 people employed in the United States and 13,900,000 people looking for work (U.S. Bureau of Labor Statistics, 2011). If each of the unemployed people would travel 28 miles round-trip (the average for the sample) searching for work, they would collectively travel 389,200,000 miles. If 91.5% traveled by car to look for work (average nationally), they would drive 356,118,000 miles and would burn 14,131,666 gallons of gas; and this is if each unemployed person traveled to only one job site. This translates to 274,154,320 pounds of CO_2. Internet job applications and remote pre-employment screening tests could have a meaningful impact on gas consumption and pollution if the tests only reduced one trip per applicant.

One important caveat is that one cannot know how many candidates would not apply for a given job if the initial stage of the application process had required traveling on-site to the job location. Unproctored screening assessments may actually result in candidates from further distances applying for a job, and becoming eligible for the second, on-site stage of the selection process. Some of these candidates may subsequently accept a job requiring a much longer commute than might have occurred had the entire application and selection process required on-site travel. In 2004, the Bureau of Transportation Statistics reported a national household travel survey indicating that over 3 million Americans travel 50 miles or more to work each way, though they did note that these "stretch commutes" are disproportionately rural (U.S. Department of Transportation, 2004).

It is also unclear how many applicants in the Klein et al. study might not have applied in person had there not been an internet application option. It is relatively effortless to apply online and it is difficult to predict how much the availability of an online process inflates the estimates of cost savings (i.e., by including applicants who would have not travelled on-site to apply).

The study was intended as a preliminary guide to help organizations recognize the multiple levels at which they may realize return on their investment with a validated, unproctored online assessment system. Further analyses would be improved by directly measuring (rather than estimating) the number of candidates who traveled on-site for further selection processes by tracking the number of on-site visits before a hiring decision is made. Organizations and industrial-organizational (I-O) psychologists may also wish to factor in more traditional measures of return on investment (ROI) such as the increased likelihood that individuals who travel on-site actually get hired, to demonstrate that the candidate miles traveled are less likely to be "wasted."

INTERNET SURVEYS

One of the most important changes to occur in the field of survey research has been the introduction of the internet survey. Not since the advent of the telephone survey has a technology so dramatically changed the field (Dillman, 2000). An online survey is a questionnaire administered via the internet that allows respondents to complete a survey on their computer. For the typical online survey, employees are sent an email containing an invitation to complete the survey. The email contains a link that takes the respondent to the survey. Once the participant completes the survey, they simply click a button and submit the survey electronically. Responses are automatically stored in a database. People who have not completed the survey within a fixed period receive an email notice reminding them to complete the survey. Online survey programs include reporting functions allowing the survey administrator to easily create and distribute summary reports. A potential benefit of online surveys, one that has received very little attention, is that they may be more environmentally friendly than traditional paper-and-pencil surveys.

Environmental Benefits

In a summary of 14 studies completed by postal agencies, CO_2 emissions per letter handled ranged from 10 to 30 grams. The median of the 14 studies was 17.9 grams per letter (Pitney Bowes, 2008). This includes CO_2 emissions associated with (1) mail design; (2) manufacturing the writing paper and envelope; (3) production of the letter; (4) distribution of the letter; (5) use; and, (6) disposal and recycling. The typical survey is somewhat larger than the standard letter and the survey needs to be returned via mail. If we assume a larger envelope, then the CO_2 emissions associated with the typical mail survey is about 20 grams per survey mailed. The impact varies with the length (weight) of the survey, response rate, use of reminder letters, and reports.

Google claims that an average query uses .0003 kwh, which is equivalent to about 200 milligrams of CO_2 (Google, 2009). Their calculation is consistent with researchers who estimate that every second spent on the web generates roughly 20 milligrams of CO_2 (Connolly, 2009), and every hour spent on the internet generates between 40 and 80 grams of CO_2. If we assume 60 grams per hour, 15 minutes' completion time for an online survey, and that the computer would not otherwise be used to perform a different function, then completing an internet survey has an impact of 15 grams of CO_2.[1] Just as for mailed surveys, the impact varies by the length of the survey (time), response rates, reminder emails, and reports.

We created three scenarios adjusting length of survey, response rates, and reminders. We set a short survey at two pages and assumed it would take five minutes to complete. The medium survey was ten pages and 15 minutes to complete. The long survey was 20 pages and 30 minutes to complete. We also factored in lower response rates for long surveys and mail surveys (Yun & Trumbo, 2000). Table 8.3 illustrates that, in general, internet-based surveys are more environmentally friendly than paper surveys, but the difference shrinks as the length of the survey increases. For long surveys, the difference in the carbon footprint is so small that simply eliminating a mailed reminder or shortening the paper survey nearly equates electronic and paper surveys. An interesting possibility is, as Don McPherson of Modern Survey points out, "because Internet surveys are relatively easy to develop and inexpensive to distribute, organizations might be surveying more frequently and using larger samples than they would have had they used printed surveys" (D. McPherson, personal com-

TABLE 8.3

CO_2 Emission Associated With Mail and Internet Survey Distribution

	Type of Survey					
	Mail	Internet	Mail	Internet	Mail	Internet
Length of Survey	Short		Medium		Long	
Participants	1,000	1,000	1,000	1,000	1,000	1,000
CO_2 for a Survey	10	3	20	15	30	30
CO_2 for a Reminder	10	3	10	3	10	3
Response Rates	25%	35%	20%	30%	15%	25%
CO_2 to Return a Survey	10	0.5	20	0.5	30	0.5
Total Grams CO2	22,500	6,175	34,000	18,150	44,500	33,125

munication, 2011). If this is the case, the increase in the number of surveys may offset the environmental benefit of using the internet.

It is surprising that the difference in the environmental impact of electronic and mail surveys is not greater. It *feels* as though mail should have a much larger impact than email, but this could be because mail is so much more tangible. One can hold a letter. You cannot touch an email. We see mail trucks on a regular basis and it is easy to imagine a letter's journey to one's building. In contrast, the electricity associated with an email is hidden within a much larger stream of electricity pouring into the office.

Cost Savings

Table 8.4 includes a list of the steps involved in the development, implementation, and reporting of the typical, large paper-based organizational survey. Patti Nass, who is part of a nationwide consortium of organizations that conduct yearly employee opinion surveys, estimated costs for a medium-size survey. She contrasts this with the steps involved in developing and implementing an electronic survey. The costs are conservative and are better used to make comparisons across survey types than across companies. As the table shows, internet surveys are less expensive to produce than paper surveys. They simply require less printing, postage, and labor; but the major environmental impact of surveys is tied to the materials and distribution of the surveys. We will note that it is difficult to estimate the environmental impact of printed and internet-based surveys because the surveys are at the end of a long string of processes, all of which have environmental effects. It is also difficult to compare the two types of surveys because they are intertwined. For example, some surveys are offered in both an electronic and paper format. Further, the results of paper-and-pencil surveys are often posted on the internet, and many internet surveys are accompanied by paper reports, or people print their electronic copies. Nonetheless, we attempted to contrast the environmental impact of the two types of surveys by examining research on the CO_2 emissions associated with postal mail and email.

There are many companies selling survey software (SurveyMonkey, Qualtrics, KeySurvey, Zoomerang, Question Pro, etc.) and countless businesses offering survey-consulting services. Proponents of online surveys suggest that the surveys offer a variety of benefits over paper-and-pencil surveys. For instance, online surveys allow researchers to quickly create, distribute,

TABLE 8.4

Steps Involved in Paper and Internet Survey

Paper Survey				Electronic Survey	
Step	Printed Sheets	Materials Cost	Labor Hours	Labor Hours	Step
Development					**Development**
If new survey					If new survey
• meet with client			4	4	• meet with client
• hold focus groups with employees			20	20	• hold focus groups with employees
• research similar surveys			4	4	• research similar surveys
• write items			8	8	• write items
• select items with client			2	2	• select items with client
• design the survey			16	8	• program the survey software
• submit to client			1	1	• submit to client
• revise survey			4	4	• revise survey
• finalize with client			1	1	• finalize with client
If existing survey					If existing survey
• meet with leaders			3	3	• meet with stakeholders
• suggest changes			3	3	• suggest changes
• rewrite survey			2	2	• rewrite survey
• submit to client			1	1	• submit to client
• finalize with client			1	1	• finalize with client
• design the survey			8	4	• program the survey
Design envelopes			2		
Ask leader to write cover letter/invitation			8	8	Ask leader to write cover letter/invitation
Update mailing labels			8	8	Update email addresses distribution lists
Obtain logo files/photos			1	1	Obtain logo files/photos

Printing

Task	Quantity	Cost
Check preprint proofs of surveys, letter, and envelopes	4	
Print surveys (10,000) × 6 pages	60,000	$6,000
Print cover letter	10,000	$1,000
Print supplemental questions on separate sheets for various lines of business (one set with each of the 10,000 surveys)	20,000	$2,000
Print distribution envelopes	10,000	$1,500
Print postage paid return envelopes	10,000	$1,500
Print reminder post paid postcards	10,000	$1,000

Survey Administration

Task	Quantity	Cost
Stuff envelopes	16	
Attach mailing labels	2	
Test survey with small group	5	
Mail survey and prepaid reminder $1.50 envelope	2	$15000
Mail reminder	2	$2,900

Data Collection

Task	Quantity
Surveys returned to central office	2
Surveys sorted and stored	8
Surveys scanned or entered by hand	30
Comments typed, screened and content coded	100

Analysis

Task	Quantity
Data files created	20
Analysis for each leader	40

Reporting

Task	Quantity	Cost
Print and bind reports. 1,000 Leader Reports (approx. 40 pages each)	40,000	$4,000

Printing

Task	Quantity
Check survey	4

Survey Administration

Task	Quantity
Load email addresses	1
Send letter from leader announcing survey	1
Test survey with small group	5
Send email invite with survey link	1
Send reminder	1

Data Collection

Task	Quantity
Returned to server	2
Comments screened and content coded	50

Analysis

Task	Quantity
Data file created	20
Analysis for each leader	40

Reporting

Task
Make report for each leader

TABLE 8.4 Continued

	Paper Survey				Electronic Survey	
Step	**Printed Sheets**	**Materials Cost**	**Labor Hours**	**Labor Hours**	**Step**	
Development					**Development**	
Print and bind 500 comment reports (ranging in pages from 20—several hundred for large departments)	15,000	$1,500			Make report for each leader	
Print and bind survey support materials/instructions (1,000—approx. 20 pages of support materials)	20,000	$2,000				
Print report envelope	1,000	$100				
Proof and assemble reports for distribution (some year's reports have errors and many need to be re-printed)			40	20		
Mail reports to (1,000)		$1,500	2		Email the reports	
Total	196,000	$40,000	273 to 337	143 to 198	Total	

and collect questionnaires. In addition, online surveys make responding and returning the survey easy. Perhaps the most compelling advantage of online surveys over paper-and-pencil surveys for business is that online surveys are less expensive to administer. Online surveys lower printing, postage, and data entry costs (Tuten, 2010; Yun & Trumbo, 2000).

In sum, a closer examination of the relative impacts of paper and electronic mail shows that it is not always the case that paper surveys have a greater environmental impact than internet surveys. The use of internet-based surveys represents a redistribution of energy consumption rather than a simple elimination.

CONCLUSION

Working from home rather than commuting by car can save energy and reduce an employee's carbon footprint. Remote, online, unproctored, pre-employment tests can eliminate applicant travel and make the selection process more environmentally friendly. Online surveys use fewer resources than traditional paper-and-pencil surveys. Table 8.5 contains a list of the CO_2 emissions associated with a variety of work-related activities and processes. As the table illustrates, the environmental benefits of all three innovations could easily be overstated if we ignore the environmental impact of computer use, long-distance business travel, and the environmental costs of simply staying home.

Work from home, remote testing, and internet surveys were neither invented nor adopted because of their environmental benefits. Businesses use them because they save time and money. Nonetheless, these three innovations offer environmental advantages and business leaders would be wise to measure and broadcast these benefits. Employee engagement is higher in organizations with a strong climate of corporate social responsibility (CSR) (Herman, 2010). Behrend and colleagues (Behrend, Baker, & Thomson, 2009) demonstrated that having a pro-environmental recruitment message was positively related to intentions to seek employment in a hypothetical organization, regardless of the applicant's personal environmental stance. Willness and colleagues (Willness, Jones, & Chapman, 2009; Willness & Jones, this book) demonstrated that actual job seekers' perceptions of an organization's CSR is positively related to intentions to seek employment

TABLE 8.5

CO_2 Emissions From Work-Related Sources

Source CO2	Emissions (Grams)	Reference
1 Gallon of Gas	8,788.00	http://www.epa.gov/oms/climate/
Snail Mail	20	http://blog.gaiam.com/blog/is-e-mail-really-greener-than-snail-mail/
Spam Email	0.3	http://www.guardian.co.uk/environment/green-living-blog/2010/oct/21/carbon-footprint-email
Typical Email	4	http://www.guardian.co.uk/environment/green-living-blog/2010/oct/21/carbon-footprint-email
Email (Large Attachment)	50	http://www.guardian.co.uk/environment/green-living-blog/2010/oct/21/carbon-footprint-email
1 Google Search	0.02	http://googleblog.blogspot.com/2009/01/poweringgoogle-search.html
1 Ream of Paper	4,940.00	http://www.epa.vic.gov.au/climate-change/carbon-management/Worksheet_4-Paper.pdf
4-Person House-hold (year)	83,000.00	http://www.epa.gov/climatechange/emissions/ind_calculator.html
One-way Cross-country Plane Trip (2,470 miles)	1,193,000.00	http://www.carbonify.com/carbon-calculator.htm
One-way Cross-country Train Trip (2,470 miles)	553,500.00	http://www.carbonify.com/carbon-calculator.htm
1 Mile on the Inner City Bus (per passenger)	299.4	http://www.carbonfund.org/site/pages/carbon_calculators/category/Assumptions
1 Long Distance Mile on the Bus (per passenger)	81.6	http://www.carbonfund.org/site/pages/carbon_calculators/category/Assumptions
Average Emissions for Year of Elevator Use	90,000.00	http://www.guardian.co.uk/environment/blog/2009/sep/04/lifts-energy-take-the-stairs
One Night in an Average Hotel	29,530.00	http://www.epa.gov/chp/documents/hotel_casino_analysis.pdf
One Night in an Upscale Hotel	33,380.00	http://www.epa.gov/chp/documents/hotel_casino_analysis.pdf

as well as attraction to the organization beyond other aspects of the job, including pay. However, it should be noted that technology-enabled work is not sufficient to demonstrate eco-focus, although it is a contributor.

Clear demonstrations of organizations benefiting from their own environmental friendliness may serve to strengthen their focus on green initiatives, especially if researchers are able to showcase previously unknown benefits of programs that are already in place and providing value. Moreover, I-O psychologists' ability to shed light on an issue as critical and wide-ranging as environment-focused CSR also has the potential to contribute to the field's visibility and perceived value. As noted in the July, 2009, issue of *The Industrial-Organizational Psychologist*, the goals of the Society for Industrial and Organizational Psychology's Visibility Committee include "better differentiating ourselves from a multitude of others that occupy this space," and updating our brand image to reflect the business-savvy and forward-thinking contributions of I-O psychologists (Rotolo, 2009). We believe that I-O psychology can be more self- and/or field-serving, as well as world-serving, by elevating our focus to the "magno" (worldwide) level (Huffman, 2009).

I-O psychologists have a unique opportunity—even responsibility—to help organizations demonstrate and quantify the environmental sustainability outcomes of their business practices. I-O psychologists are accustomed to measuring individual, team, and organizational performance, and environmental sustainability is a performance dimension that should not be overlooked. As scientist-practitioners, we are uniquely suited to help organizations demonstrate and showcase "green outcomes"—regardless of whether the business practice or process change was implemented with sustainability in mind, or even whether these outcomes result from formal I-O interventions (Sanders & Keim, 2011). Because of our expertise in measuring and articulating organizational outcomes, I-O professionals have the opportunity to facilitate companies' awareness of—and encourage their continued attention to—environmental sustainability.

NOTE

1. Another way to estimate the carbon footprint of electronic surveys is to examine tasks rather than time. A spam email generates about .3 grams, a standard email about 4 grams, and a long email with a large attachment (photo, file, etc.) about 50 grams of CO_2, (*Guardian*, 2010). Because survey invitations do not usually involve large attachments, it is reasonable to use time online as a metric of carbon production.

REFERENCES

Amel, E. L., Manning, C. M., & Scott, B. A. (2009, April). Employee perceptions and organizational opportunities on the path to going green. In A. H. Huffman (Chair), "Working" through environmental issues: The role of the I-O psychologist. Symposium for the annual meeting of the Society for Industrial and Organizational Psychology, New Orleans, Louisiana.

Andrews, L., & Klein. S. R. (2011, April). Green jobs: Environmental benefits of the virtual office. Poster presented at the Thursday Theme Track, *Green HR: Environmentally Sustainable Organizations, Jobs, and Employees,* at the 26th Annual Conference of the Society for Industrial and Organizational Psychology, Chicago, IL.

Apgar, M. (1998). The alternative workplace: Changing where and how people work. *Harvard Business Review, 76*(3), 121–137.

Behrend, T. S., Baker, B. A., & Thomson, L. F. (2009). Effects of pro-environmental recruiting messages: The role of organizational reputation. *Journal of Business and Psychology, 24,* 341–350.

Connolly, Mary V. (2009). *What does a Google search really cost?* Retrieved January 14, 2013, from http://www.ascue.org/files/proceedings/2009/p84.pdf

Dillman, D. A. (2000). Mail and internet surveys: The tailored design method (2nd ed.). New York, NY: John Wiley & Sons.

Glanz, J. (2011). Google details, and defends, its use of electricity. *New York Times.* Retrieved December 15, 2012, from http://www.nytimes.com/2011/09/09/technology/google-details-and-defends-its-use-of-electricity.html?_r=0

Google (2009) Powering a Google search. Retrieved January 14, 2013, from http://google-blog.blogspot.com/2009/01/powering-google-search.html#!/2009/01/powering-google-search.html

Guardian. (2010). What's the carbon footprint of email? Retrieved December 16, 2012, from http://www.guardian.co.uk/environment/green-living-blog/2010/oct/21/carbon-footprint-email

Herman, A. E. (2010). How corporate responsibility and environmentally friendly business practices return the investment. Kenexa Research Institute/HR.com webinar presented 3/23/2010. Retrieved December 15, 2012, from http://www.hr.com/en/communities/organizational_development/how-corporate-responsibility-and-environmentally-f_g5zkqpxn.html

Huffman, A. H. (2009). Chair, "Working" through environmental issues: The role of the I-O Psychologist. Symposium presented at the 24th Annual SIOP Conference, New Orleans, LA.

Kitou, E. & Horvath, A. (2008). External air pollution costs of telework. *International Journal of Life Cycle Analysis, 13*(2), 155–165.

Klein, S. R., Andrews, L., & Smith, W. (2010, April). It's easy being green: How environmentally friendly business practices affect recruitment. In S. R. Klein (Chair), *Green matters: Corporate Social Responsibility (CSR) in recruiting and selection.* Symposium presented at the 25th Annual Conference of the Society for Industrial and Organizational Psychology, Atlanta, GA.

McGuckin, N. A. & Srinivasan, N. (2003). Journey to work trends in the United States and its major metropolitan areas, 1960–2000. Retrieved November 11, 2011, from ftp://ftp.abag.ca.gov/pub/mtc/census2000/JTW_Trends/PDF/FullReport.pdf

Pacific Gas and Electric (2009). PG&E Corporation and Pacific Gas and Electric Company

2009 annual report. Retrieved November 15, 2011, from http://www.annualreports. com/HostedData/AnnualReports/PDFArchive/pcg2009.pdf

Pitney Bowes. (June, 2008). *The environmental impact of mail: A baseline.* Retrieved 19 January, 2013, from: http://www.pb.com/mailimpact

Rotolo, C. T. (2009). Making I-O psychology more visible: "Mommy, I want to be an I-O psychologist when I grow up." *The Industrial-Organizational Psychologist, 47*(1), 111–115.

Sanders, A. M. & Keim, C. (2011). Online recruiting: Providing organizational and environmental benefits. In J. Pierce (Chair), *Online recruiting: Taking it to the next level.* Symposium to be conducted at the 26th Annual Conference of the Society for Industrial and Organizational Psychology, Chicago, IL.

Telework Research Network. (2011). California telework savings could be huge. Retrieved November 27, 2011, from http://www.teleworkresearchnetwork.com/ california-telework-savings-could-be-huge/6372

Tuten, Tracy L. (2010) Conducting online surveys. In Samuel D. Gosling and John A. Johnson, (Eds.), *Advanced methods for conducting online behavioral research* (pp. 179–192). Washington, DC: American Psychological Association.

U.S. Bureau of Labor Statistics (2011). Databases, tables & calculators by subject. Retrieved January 14, 2013 from http://www.bls.gov/data/#employment

U.S. Department of Transportation (2004). Transportation Statistics Annual Report. Retrieved December 15, 2011, from http://www.bts.gov/publications/transportation_ statistics_annual_report/2004

U.S. Department of Transportation (2009). Transportation Statistics Annual Report. Retrieved November 14, 2011, from http://www.bts.gov/publications/transportation_ statistics_annual_report/2009/

U.S. Environmental Protection Agency (2009). Retrieved November 8, 2011, from http:// www.epa.gov/oms

U.S. Environmental Protection Agency (2011). Calculations and references. Retrieved January 14, 2013, from http://www.bls.gov/data/#employment

U.S. Internal Revenue Service. (2009) Retrieved January 14, 2013, from http://www.irs. gov/pub/irs-drop/rp-00-48.pdf

Willness, C. R., Jones, D. A., & Chapman, D. C. (2009). Attracting applicants through corporate social responsibility: A real world test. Presented at the 24th annual meeting of the Society for Industrial and Organizational Psychology, New Orleans, LA.

WorldatWork (2009). Telework Trendlines. Retrieved January 14, 2013, from http://www. workingfromanywhere.org/news/Trendlines_2009.pdf

WorldatWork (2011). Telework 2011: A WorldatWork special report. Retrieved November 14, 2011, from http://www.worldatwork.org/waw/adimLink?id=53034

Yun, G. W. & Trumbo, C. W. (2000). Comparative response to a survey executed by post, e-mail, and web form. *Journal of Computer-Mediated Communication, 6*(1). Retrieved December 15, 2012, from http://jcmc.indiana.edu/vol6/issue1/yun.html

Part 3

Individuals and Organizations

9

Socially Responsible and Sustainable Supply Chains

Wendy S. Becker

> We've been presented with a false choice: either great economic performance or great environmental performance. But through innovation, we can solve both challenges.
>
> —Mark L. Vachon, V.P., Ecomagination, GE
> ("The World's Greenest Companies," 2011)

Social and environmental responsibility is increasingly important to psychological research and practice (Aquinis & Glavas, 2012; Oskamp, 2000). According to 95% of CEOs participating in the United Nations Global Compact, society increasingly expects companies to assume greater public responsibility (Bielak, Bonini, & Oppenheim, 2007). Moreover, investing in sustainability and green initiatives is proposed to offer such benefits as increases in public opinion, customer relations, and the ability to attract and retain talent (Fox, 2008). Further, it is employees who are key agents of change and innovation in the timely identification and response to environmental issues (Fugate, Stank, & Mentzer, 2009). As such, new insight into social responsibility and sustainable organizations is important to the research, teaching, and practice of industrial-organizational (I-O) psychology.

However, I-O psychology has been focused on the profit-side of business (see Lefkowitz, 2008). An economic focus on short-term profit positions employees and the environment as expendable commodities, weakening organizations in at least three fundamental ways. First, as noted in the quote above, a sole focus on cost sets up a false dichotomy between profit and the environment. Second, a sole focus on cost positions employees and the environment simply as inventory without regard for the consequences. Finally, a sole focus on cost does not acknowledge the deep legacy of I-O research relating employee knowledge and skills to the development of healthy and effective organizations, relevant to and imperative for a shift from traditional business practices to sustainable operations. The legitimacy of relevant I-O psychology research and practice should not be ignored or marginalized.

Central to this argument is that motivated and engaged workers provide the innovations needed for social responsibility and sustainability—specifically with regard to the environment. The emphasis is on the *value* offered by employees—the intellectual capital of the organization. While costs to implement socially responsible initiatives may initially appear higher, ultimately society reaps greater benefits through sustainable development (Shrivastava & Berger, 2010).

The objective of this chapter is to examine social responsibility and sustainability through the lens of an operational (supply chain management) perspective. For the purposes of this discussion, exemplars from the supply chain management literature are positioned as extremes—from a short-term approach that focuses solely on profit to a longer term approach that emphasizes justice and sustainability. Concepts gleaned from supply chain management—zero inventory, flexibility through postponement, free riding, supply chain surplus, and the bullwhip effect—are used to emphasize a "bigger picture" approach to social responsibility and sustainability. A sole focus on short-term self-interest compromises goals of social responsibility and sustainability.

DEFINING SOCIAL RESPONSIBILITY AND SUSTAINABILITY

Scholars have noted various definitions of social responsibility—that is, the responsibility that business has to society (Carroll, 1999; Carroll & Shabana, 2010; Porter & Kramer, 2006). Early discussions of the responsibility of business to society considered this a *social responsibility* rather than *corporate social responsibility* (Carroll, 1999). For example, Bowen (1953) defined social responsibility as: "obligations ... to pursue those policies, to make those decisions, or to follow those lines of action which are desirable in terms of the objectives and values of our society" (p. 6). In this context, business has a responsibility for the consequences of actions beyond profit and loss: in other words, a "social consciousness" (Bowen, 1953, p. 44). It is interesting to note that 93.5% of business managers surveyed at the time agreed with this statement (Bowen, 1953; Carroll, 1999).

The term *social responsibility* is retained in this chapter (rather than the term *corporate social responsibility*) for three reasons. First, the science and practice of I-O often takes place in the public sector where the term *corporate* is not really relevant. That is, issues of social responsibility—responsibility to society—are just as important in public sector organizations as in the private sector. For example, public sector crime laboratories have social responsibilities to society, including victims of crimes, defendants, communities, as well as within their own agencies. Second, I-Os often work in industries that include small to medium size organizations that are *not* corporate legal entities; indeed, these smaller organizations bring important business challenges to I-Os. Third, the word *corporate* has an American legal connotation that does not reflect the international context of I-O psychology. Since I-O psychologists work in the public sector, in small and medium size organizations, and in international settings, the more inclusive concept of *social responsibility* will be used in this chapter.

The environment is an important albeit neglected component of social responsibility; often the environment is subsumed in the social component of responsibility (Sekerka & Stimel, 2011; World Business Council for Sustainable Development, 2005). Issues of the environment are critical to the boardroom agenda because they can fatally damage or disrupt sustainable supply chains of energy, food, and raw material (Lindgreen, Sen, Maon, & Vanhamme, forthcoming 2013). Expanding the environmental (green) components of social responsibility to focus on managing *people* (specifically, employees) is well within the realm of I-O psychology. Socially responsible and sustainable I-O psychology can build upon the management imperative to balance the triple bottom line of *people, planet,* and *profit* (Hart, 2005, Hart & Milstein, 2003). In this regard, all stakeholders are treated ethically and in a responsible manner (Fenwick & Bierema, 2008). Further, *sustainability* has been broadly defined as "development that meets the needs of the present without compromising the ability of future generations to meet their own needs" (World Commission on Environment and Development, 1987, p. 8; Shrivastava & Berger, 2010). Throughout this chapter, the general term *sustainability* and the more specific *environmental sustainability* will be used. Positive examples of sustainability and social responsibility focus on the integration of the social (people), environment (planet), and economic (profit) goals over the long term.

SHIFTING FOCUS TO *JUSTICE AND RIGHTS* RATHER THAN *SHORT-TERM PROFIT*

Social responsibility and sustainability require a focus on *justice* and *fairness*—policies and practices that take equity, reciprocity, and impartiality into consideration (Treviño & Nelson, 2010; Pandey, Rupp, & Thornton, this book). Socially responsible and sustainable organizations advocate moral rights and justice. Focusing solely on short-term profit sends a message to employees that the organization views people and environmental issues as commodities (Becker, Carbo, & Langella, 2010; Marcus & Fremeth, 2009). Violating these stakeholders' rights can have negative consequences; for example, Nike's third-world labor practices generated negative publicity that ultimately hurt its business:

> The way it hurt our business was that it hurt our people. Individual employees at Nike started to wonder what kind of a company they were working for and what message was being sent about the people who worked there. (Nike Vice President, Maria Eitel, cited in Williams, 2002, p. 38)

By attending to and reforming its own business practices, Nike was able to positively influence labor standards throughout the third world (Zadek, 2004).

Focusing on justice and rights has implications for designing organizational systems such as recruitment. Applicant perceptions of an organization's responsibility to the environment can affect the attractiveness of key jobs (see Willness and Jones, this book). For example, Dow Chemical developed a negative reputation because of its production of napalm, a chemical agent harmful to the environment and used in the Vietnam War. Recruitment of scientists on college campuses proved difficult. By highlighting products beneficial to the environment, Dow was able to recruit and retain the chemists it needed—a resource vital to its competitiveness in the industry (Bernardin, 2010). I-O psychologists can help organizations attract desirable recruits by emphasizing the importance of environmental sustainability in recruitment and selection programs.

Focusing on justice and rights also has implications for the design of performance management systems. Employees who are treated fairly help improve financial performance (Orlitzky, Schmidt, & Rynes, 2003). Companies in the "100 Best Companies" have significantly higher financial performance compared with industry competitors, and their employees have more positive attitudes toward work. Positive employee attitudes remain an intangible yet enduring asset and can be a source of sustained competitive advantage (Fulmer, Gerhard, & Scott, 2003). Promoting justice includes the concepts of environmental sustainability, community well-being, transparent accountability, legal and honest operations, global citizenship, and the rights of employees, suppliers, competitors and customers (Fenwick & Bierema, 2008).

The next section further develops an operational (supply chain) perspective to expand on five exemplars of social responsibility and sustainability. The descriptions are positioned as extremes for demonstration purposes (see Table 9.1).

TABLE 9.1

Social Responsibility and Sustainability

Socially Irresponsible and Unsustainable Supply Chains	Socially Responsible and Sustainable Supply Chains
Focus only on economic self-interest and short-term profit—people and the environment viewed as commodities; stakeholders' rights violated; neglecting employees and the environment through harmful business practices.	*Focus on justice, employee rights, sustainability and long-term investment*—policies and practices that take equity, reciprocity, and impartiality into consideration; intangible assets can be a source of advantage.
Zero inventory—employees and the environment represent inventory or stock that can be reduced to minimum levels.	*Time-phased investment*—employees and the environment represent capacity to be built up and developed.
Performance measured solely on conventional, short-term business metrics to the neglect of value and sustainability.	*Performance measures based on value and sustainability, and improving profit margins over the long term.*
Resource acquisition and development—lack of strategic development of resources to full potential over the long term.	*Flexibility through postponement*—strategic development of people and environmental resources to potential.
Free-riding—benefiting from the actions and efforts of others without sharing costs; using "heavy-handed" tactics assuming partners are easily replaced and expendable.	*Supply chain surplus*—distribution of both information (*traceability*) and profit gains (*transparency*) to all partners; results are superior to acting in isolated self-interest.
Bullwhip effect—each link responds to immediate demands of supplier or customer to the neglect of the chain as a system; creates volatility through insufficient coordination and communication.	*Building sustainable business by attending to issues of people, planet, profit*—social and environmental consciousness; proactive incentives for compliance with national/international standards that protect the environment.

RESOURCES SHOULD BE POSITIONED AS *TIME-PHASED INVESTMENTS* RATHER THAN *ZERO INVENTORY*

Zero inventory refers to the reduction of inventory or stock to minimal levels as a cost-saving measure (Heizer & Render, 2008). Initiatives such as zero inventory, just-in-time, and lean production address logistical problems of long lead times and high transportation costs associated with globalization (Levy, 1997). However, the earthquakes in Japan in 2011 provide an example of a critical weak point for industries (in this case, automotive and electronics) that rely on zero inventory models (Hookway & Poon, 2011).

Zero inventory approaches have been applied to human resources positing that employees be brought onboard on an as-needed basis (Cappelli, 2008a). But treating employees as a stockpile of inventory is inherently flawed. Specifically with regard to environmental issues, employee knowledge is critical for timely identification and response (Fugate, Stank, & Mentzer, 2009). In this regard, employees should more accurately be considered as agents of change in environmental sustainability and not just repositories of knowledge. In the field of environmental management, it is employee tacit knowledge—knowledge acquired through direct experience at work—that helps organizations to identify pollution source, manage emergency situations, and develop preventive solutions (Boiral, 2002, 2009).

Both human and environmental resources must be considered as part of a long-term investment strategy in that these resources represent capacity to be built up. In operational terms, employee contributions are *time-phased*, since they develop over time. As such, it is optimal to view these resources as investments rather than as costs (Cascio, 2000). Organizations cannot expect employees to contribute to environmental sustainability efforts that create value unless they themselves are treated as investments (Hart & Milstein, 2003).

FOCUS ON *PERFORMANCE MEASURES BASED ON VALUE AND SUSTAINABILITY,* RATHER THAN SOLE USE OF *CONVENTIONAL BUSINESS METRICS*

One challenge for I-O psychologists is to design metrics that go beyond conventional business performance metrics, such as return on investment

(ROI) and profit, and measure progress toward green goals. Perform-ance management systems can be used to help communicate and support management initiatives for green targets, goals, and responsibilities. Well-designed measurement and reward systems that reinforce an organiza-tional culture for sustainability and behavioral outcomes are needed but linking non-economic organizational goals to employees' incentives and behaviors remains difficult (Hervani, Helms, & Sarkis, 2005; Pagell & Wu, 2009).

Designers of management systems can make use of the U.S. Depart-ment of Labor job descriptions in the O*NET system (Dierdorff, Norton, Gregory, Rivkin, & Lewis, this book, discuss in detail O*NET and green jobs). The O*NET system describes the knowledge, skills, abilities, and other characteristics needed for "green economy" industries, defined as: "economic activity related to reducing the use of fossil fuels, decreasing pollution and greenhouse gas emissions, increasing the efficiency of energy usage, recycling materials, and developing and adopting renewable sources of energy" (Dierdorff et al., 2009).

Further definition and refinement of new performance measures for green economy jobs are needed and provide an opportunity for I-O psychologists.

Procter & Gamble (P&G) regularly operates offsite design workshops for employees from research and development (R&D), market research, and purchasing, using design methods such as visualization and proto-typing to solve problems (Wong, 2009). These innovative workshops are facilitated by volunteer employees around the world and last as long as a week. P&G tracks and measures the performance of the design-thinking inspired ideas and products that are created in this effort.

A management focus on environmental sustainability can impact employee attitudes and behaviors in a positive way. The New Belgium Brewing Company uses an energy-efficient brewing process with innova-tive, eco-friendly technology. Employees voted to forfeit their bonuses so that the company could invest in a wind turbine. This helped New Belgium reduce carbon dioxide emissions and made it the first fully wind-powered brewery (Sekerka & Stimel, 2011; also, see Pandey, Rupp, & Thornton, this book).

FOCUS ON THE CREATION OF *FLEXIBILITY THROUGH POSTPONEMENT*

Related, the operational concept of *flexibility through postponement* refers to delay of final product configuration as late in the production process as possible (Van Hoek, 2001). This suggests that organizations benefit when resources are developed to their full potential over the long term. Long-term development of employees is important because it can help them learn functions outside their own departments—one of the key factors in the portability of knowledge and continuous learning (Kerr, 2009). Managers gain understanding of how core value-adding processes are scattered across different departments and industries. Cross-trained employees are better able to adapt to uncertainty. High-potential trainees rotate through various assignments after a period of job rotation.

But industries that require that employees pay the costs for their own training assume that employees are the sole beneficiaries of their development (Cappelli, 2008b). This downplays the benefits of the skilled employee. Talent management involves the development of multiple career paths and talent pools; companies engaging in high-performance work systems clearly gain the most benefit from these practices (Heinen & O'Neill, 2004). Cost-based commoditization of human capital is questionable from a social responsibility standpoint and likely to be detrimental over the long term.

The Brazilian company SEMCO exemplifies flexibility through postponement using an employee development approach with a concern for the environment, innovative and diverse products, increased profits, motivated employees, and low turnover (Semler, 2004, 2006). Board membership is open to any employee and seats are filled on a first-come basis. Employees select their own training and rotate to jobs that fit their interest. The company culture values open communication, constructive dissent, and democracy.

FOCUS ON DEVELOPING A *SUPPLY CHAIN SURPLUS* RATHER THAN A *FREE RIDE*

Free-riding takes advantage of the efforts and resources of other organizations in the supply chain without sharing in the costs. Traditional purchasing strategy suggests that organizations use "heavy-handed" tactics with suppliers because they are easily replaced (Kraljic, 1983). In contrast, the operational concept of *supply chain surplus* refers to sharing the profit that remains after subtracting costs incurred in the production and delivery of products or services. Ideally, profit is distributed to supply chain partners via transfer prices. To maximize surplus, partners coordinate efforts to achieve results superior to that of each partner acting in isolation.

Supply chain surplus is related to sustainability and can be further understood through the practices of traceability and transparency. *Traceability* refers to the practice of sharing information among supply chain partners about materials (e.g., the presence of toxins, solvents, etc. used by a supplier) that meet industry standards for minimizing environmental risk (Pagell & Wu, 2009). The concept of *transparency* refers to the flow of money (profitability) through the entire supply chain with an explicit goal of ensuring that each organization makes enough of a profit to do more than just subsist. In essence, *traceability* is concerned with how things are made throughout the chain while *transparency* is concerned with keeping profits flowing through the entire chain (Pagell & Wu, 2009, p. 44). Ensuring continuity of the supply chain is a strategic practice that sustains the system by allowing each partner in the chain to reinvest, innovate, and grow (Pagell & Wu, 2009).

FOCUS ON *SUSTAINABILITY GOALS* RATHER TO COUNTERACT THE *BULLWHIP EFFECT*

The *bullwhip effect* occurs when organizations respond to the immediate demands of suppliers or customers to the neglect of a long-term systems approach (Lee, Padmanabhan, & Whang, 1997). Volatility in the bull whip creates insufficient coordination and communication between supply chain partners in the ordering and production of goods (Wu & Katok, 2006). The bullwhip can keep important stakeholders (such as employees and suppliers) out of the loop in terms of communication and coordination to the detriment of social and environmental sustainability goals. For example, Apple Computer maximized profits by micro-managing supply partners in China to keep costs as low as possible: "You can set all the rules you want, but they're meaningless if you don't give suppliers enough profit to treat workers well. If you squeeze margins, you're forcing them to cut safety" (former Apple executive).

Contrast this approach with the more sustainable, open communications approach at Hewlett-Packard: "Our suppliers are very open with us. They let us know when they are struggling to meet our expectations, and that influences our decisions (Zoe McMahon, Hewlett-Packard, Supply Chain Social and Environmental Responsibility Program) (Duhigg & Barboza, 2012).

The home furnishing retail chain IKEA has a long tradition of social and environmental consciousness concerning both cost and resource efficiency (Andersen & Skjoett-Larsen, 2009). IKEA requires its 1,500 suppliers from 55 countries to comply with national and international laws that protect the environment, employee working conditions, and child labor. The focus is on both internal (within the company) and external (outside of the company) supplier relationships. The internal dimension includes employee training and sharing of business experience among employee groups. The external dimension includes formal and informal training of key personnel at the supplier level, positive incentives for suppliers in terms of long-term contracts and the implementation of codes of conduct that includes regular auditing of suppliers' performance (Andersen & Skjoett-Larsen, 2009).

SUMMARY AND CONCLUSION

New opportunities for research, practice, and teaching in the area of social responsibility and environmental sustainability have emerged for I-O psychology. Initial public pressure for sustainability has focused on technical and physical aspects of the environment but has neglected the human and social environment—an area where I-O psychologists have expertise. Human resource professionals (including I-O psychologists) have been only marginally involved to any great extent (Fenwick & Bierema, 2008). Yet few organizations have the necessary skills to address social responsibilities using existing frameworks (Stolz & McLean, 2009). I-O psychologists have unique skills and abilities to contribute more directly to social responsibility and sustainability activities across industry supply chains.

The recent economic downturn has led to industry cost-cutting measures with the intent to drive profitability. Cost-cutting measures such as layoffs, reductions in compensation, reductions in benefits, and demands for increased productivity have a direct impact on employees. Reacting with a focus only on the short term can have unanticipated effects. Global concern for the environment will require thinking about people management at higher and broader levels to explore how behavior is connected across organizations and industries.

Without a sustainable, socially responsible strategy, green management is simply public relations. As discussed in this chapter, employees and supply chain partners can differentiate between business intentions and business action. Socially responsible and sustainable organizations reap benefits by attracting and retaining the best employees. The entire industry supply chain has an advantage since a longer term view includes fairness and justice for all stakeholders. This is all the more important in an economy in which environmental resources are depleted.

REFERENCES

Aguinis, H., & Glavas, A. (2012). What we know and don't know about corporate social responsibility: A review and research agenda. *Journal of Management, 38,* 932–968. doi: 10.1177/0149206311436079

Andersen, M., & Skjoett-Larsen, T. (2009). Corporate social responsibility in global supply chains. *Supply Chain Management: An International Journal, 14,* 2, 75–86.

Becker, W. S., Carbo, J. A. II, & Langella, I. M. (2010). Beyond self-interest: Integrating social responsibility and supply chain management with human resource development. *Human Resource Development Review, 9,* 2, 144–168.

Bernardin, H. J. (2010). *Human resource management: An experiential approach.* Boston, MA: McGraw-Hill Irwin.

Bielak, D., Bonini, S. M. J., & Oppenheim, J. M. (2007). CEOs on strategy and social issues. *The McKinsey Quarterly, 3,* 1–8.

Boiral, O. (2002). Tacit knowledge and environmental management. *Long Range Planning 35,* 291–317.

Boiral, O. (2009). Greening the corporation through organizational citizenship behaviors. *Journal of Business Ethics, 87,* 2, 221–236.

Bowen, H. R. (1953). *Social responsibilities of the businessman.* New York: Harper & Row.

Cappelli, P. (2008a). Talent management for the twenty-first century. *Harvard Business Review,* March, 74–81.

Cappelli, P. (2008b). *Talent on demand: Managing talent in an age of uncertainty.* Boston, MA: Harvard Business School Press.

Carroll, A. (1999). Corporate social responsibility: Evolution of a definitional construction. *Business and Society, 38,* 3, 268–295.

Carroll, A., & Shabana, K. M. (2010). The business case for corporate social responsibility: A review of concepts, research and practice. *International Journal of Management Reviews, 12*, 1, 85–105.

Cascio, W. F. (2000). *Costing human resources: The financial impact in organizations.* Cincinnati, OH: South-Western/Thompson Learning.

Dierdorff, E. C., Norton, J. J., Drewes, D. W., Kroustalis, C. M., Riukin, D., & Lewis, P. (2009). *Greening of the world of work: Implications for ONet-SOC and new and emerging occupations.* U.S. Department of Labor.

Duhigg, C., & Barboza, D. (2012). "In China, human costs are built into an iPad," *New York Times*, January 25.

Fenwick, T., & Bierema, L. (2008). Corporate social responsibility: Issues for human resource development professionals. *International Journal of Training and Development, 12*, 1, 24–35.

Fox, A. (2008). Get in the business of being green. *HR Magazine*, June, 45–50.

Fugate, B. S., Stank, T. P., & Mentzer, J. T. (2009). Linking improved knowledge management to operational and organizational performance. *Journal of Operations Management, 27*, 3, 247–264.

Fulmer, I. S., Gerhart, B., and Scott, K. S. (2003). Are the 100 best better? *Personnel Psychology, 56*, 965–993.

Hart, S. (2005). *Capitalism at the crossroads: The unlimited business opportunities in solving the world's most difficult problems.* Upper Saddle River, NJ: Prentice-Hall.

Hart, S. L., & Milstein, M. B. (2003). Creating sustainable value. *Academy of Management Executive, 17*, 56–67.

Heinen, J. S. & O'Neill, C. (2004). Managing talent to maximize performance. *Employment Relations Today*, Summer, *31*, 2, 67.

Heizer, J., & Render, B. (2008) *Operations management.* Upper Saddle River, NJ: Prentice-Hall.

Hervani, A. A., Helms, M. M., & Sarkis, J. (2005). Performance measurement for green supply chain management. *Benchmarking: An international journal, 12*, 4, 330–353.

Hookway, J., & Poon, A. (2011). Crisis tests supply chain's weak links. *The Wall Street Journal*, March 18.

Kerr, S. (2009). Some random thoughts on false dichotomies, common coffeepots, and the portability of knowledge. *The Industrial-Organizational Psychologist, 47*, 2, 11–24.

Kraljic, P. (1983). Purchasing must become supply management. *Harvard Business Review, 61*, 5, 109–117.

Lee, H. L., Padmanabhan, V., & Whang, S. (1997). The bullwhip effect in supply chains. *Sloan Management Review*, Spring, 93–102.

Lefkowitz, J. (2008). To prosper, organizational psychology should … expand the values of the organization to match the quality of its ethics. *Journal of Organizational Behavior, 29*, 4, 439–453.

Levy, D. L. (1997). Lean production in an international supply chain. *Sloan Management Review, 38*, 2, 94–102.

Lindgreen, A., Sen, S., Maon, F., & Vanhamme, J. (forthcoming 2013). *Sustainable value chain management: Analyzing, designing, implementing, and monitoring for social and environmental responsibility.* Surrey, UK: Gower.

Marcus, A. A., & Fremeth, A. R. (2009). Green management matters regardless. *Academy of Management Perspectives, 23*, 17–26.

Orlitzky, M., Schmidt, F. L., & Rynes, S. L. (2003). Corporate social and financial performance: A meta-analysis. *Organization Studies, 24*, 403–411.

Oskamp, S. (2000). A sustainable future for humanity? How can psychology help? *American Psychologist, 55,* 496–508.

Pagell, M., & Wu, Z. (2009). Building a more complete theory of sustainable supply chain management using case studies of 10 exemplars. *The Journal of Supply Chain Management, 45,* 2, 37–56.

Porter, M. E., & Kramer, M. R. (2006). Strategy and society: The link between competitive advantage and corporate social responsibility. *Harvard Business Review,* December, 78–92.

Sekerka, L. E., & Stimel, D. (2011). How durable is sustainable enterprise? Ecological sustainability meets the reality of tough economic times. *Business Horizons, 54,* 115–124.

Semler, R. (2004). *The seven-day weekend: Changing the way work works.* New York, NY: Warner Books.

Semler, R. (2006). Out of this world: Doing things the Semco way. *Global Business and Organizational Excellence,* July/August, 13–21.

Shrivastava, P., & Berger, S. (2010). Sustainability principles: A review and directions. *Organization Management Journal, 7,* 246–261.

Stolz, I. & McLean, G. N. (2009). Organizational skills for a corporate citizen: Policy analysis. *Human Resource Development Review, 8,* 2, 174–196.

"The World's Greenest Companies" (2011). *Newsweek,* October 16.

Treviño, L. K., & Nelson, K. A. (2010). *Managing business ethics: Straight talk about how to do it right* (4th Ed.). Hoboken, NJ: John Wiley and Sons.

Van Hoek, R. I. (2001). The rediscovery of postponement: A literature review and directions for research. *Journal of Operations Management, 19,* 2, 161–184.

Williams, D. (2002). Weaving ethics into corporate culture. *Communications World, 19,* 4, 38–39.

Wong, V. (2009). How business is adopting design thinking. *Bloomberg Business Week,* November 3.

World Commission on Environment and Development (1987). *Our common future.* New York, NY: Oxford University Press.

World Business Council for Sustainable Development (2005). *Driving success: Human resources and sustainable development.* Geneva, Switzerland: Author.

Wu, D. Y., & Katok, E. (2006). Learning, communication, and the bullwhip effect. *Journal of Operations Management, 24,* 839–850.

Zadek, S. (2004). The path to corporate responsibility. *Harvard Business Review, 82*(12), 125–132.

10

Motivating Behavior Change to Support Organizational Environmental Sustainability Goals

Cathy L. Z. DuBois, Marina N. Astakhova, and David A. DuBois

The current organizational context increasingly mandates adoption of sustainability strategies, as organizations respond to pressures created by declining availability of natural resources, increasing stakeholder expectations, and radical transparency of operations imposed by people and organizations who seek to hold organizations accountable for their impact on earth's ecology (Laszlo & Zhexembayeva, 2011). The notion of organizational success is also morphing from a profits-only perspective to a value-creation perspective (Porter & Kramer, 2011). Thus, the escalating need to embed sustainability thinking and action into the core of organizational identity has generated a fascinating array of organizational initiatives.

Organizations typically begin their environmental sustainability (ES) journey by addressing the "low-hanging fruit" of installing energy efficient heating/cooling/lighting systems that yield significant cost savings. Yet they soon find that ES can't be achieved through technology alone, for gleaning the efficiencies offered by technology is often dependent upon how people use it. As such, deep commitment to enduring ES requires changes from the people who are employed by and interact with the organization. For example, energy-efficient technology relies on employees setting controls with conservation in mind; recycling programs rely on employee use of recycling bins; pollution reduction efforts rely on employee innovation and engagement in ES. Thus, successful implementation of organizational ES strategies ultimately depends upon the collective array of behavior changes from individual employees. This chapter draws from systems, motivation, and diffusion of innovation theories to address how organizations can effectively encourage and support the array of behavior changes necessary to achieve their ES goals.

A SYSTEMS APPROACH TO ENVIRONMENTAL SUSTAINABILITY

A whole systems (Bertalanffy, 1968) perspective accommodates consideration of multiple stakeholder concerns and externalities, and is thereby useful when considering ES issues. A systems perspective also facilitates understanding of the organization as a whole and complex entity, with appreciation for how the various levels and areas of the organization function and interact. Implementing ES strategies requires considerable change that pervades the organizational system. Organizational change is difficult, as evidenced by the high rate of failure in change efforts (Beer, Eisenstat, & Spector, 1990). In fact, data suggest that one-third to two-thirds of organizational change initiatives fail (Beer & Nohria, 2000). In conjunction with a systems view of ES-related changes, an organizational learning perspective (Argyris & Schon, 1978) provides an appreciation for an iterative approach to dealing with the complexity of change requirements and processes. ES change is thus a complex process that evolves over time.

We highlight three systems elements necessary to provide a firm foundation of support for the organizational change necessary to embed ES within an organization: strong executive support, provision of sufficient resources, and engaging employees at all levels to develop and implement a variety of initiatives to support desired changes. These elements work together in an interactive manner to reach throughout the organization to effect necessary change.

Executive Support

Executive officer commitment leads our list of requirements, for executive support clears the path for the other two elements. Lueneberger and Goleman (2010) emphasize that executives need to understand how sustainability can fundamentally alter their business and how it differs from other corporate initiatives. Indeed, the early and exemplary organizational ES initiatives were driven by the personal conviction of the CEO, such as Ray Anderson at Interface Global (2011) and Chuck Fowler at Fairmount Minerals (2011). Because the CEO has the whole systems view of the organization, the CEO is ideally positioned to design the guiding ideas (Senge, 2006) of the ES strategy (see Barrett & Niekerk, this book, for an Intel CEO's perspective on ES strategy). Yet the idea to embark upon an ES journey need not originate with the CEO, for the CEO can be inspired to initiate sustainability strategy by a range of stakeholders, including investors, employees, customers, and external entities such as governments and non-governmental organizations (NGOs). For example, Ray Anderson's employees brought ES to his attention, called for him to articulate his environmental vision, and provided him with reading material; what he learned in the process of articulating his vision transformed his thinking and approach to doing business. Ideally the whole executive team will embrace the notion that ES strategies can actually create value for the organization and make a strong commitment to action. Senge (2006) makes the case that "Without effective local line leaders, new ideas—no matter how compelling—do not get translated into action, and the intentions behind change initiatives from the top can be easily thwarted" (p. 319). Indeed, to ensure support among senior executives, Sherwin-Williams's CEO, Christopher Connor, initiated the organization's ES focus at their annual strategy retreat (DuBois, 2012). Because executives provide emotional leadership for the organization, they can inspire employee choice to join in and give the change efforts their all. Further, employees look to executives for clear articulation of the business case for ES specific to their organization; they also scrutinize the actions of executives to ensure that they walk their talk.

Provision of Sufficient Resources

Executives signal their support for organizational strategies and change efforts through the allocation of key resources to support goal accomplishment: financial/budgetary, position power, and expertise. These are symbolic means through which they communicate their priorities (Pfeffer, 1981). Absent this set of resources, organization-wide process and behavior changes are difficult to accomplish. For example, one visible means through which executives show support for ES strategies is to hire a sustainability manager to bring increased awareness to organizationally relevant ES issues. However, if the sustainability manager has no budget or position power, their presence becomes merely a token nod to ES. This individual can initiate and manage ES projects, but lacks resources and power to produce the paradigm shift required to fully embed ES within the organization. Such partial or token organizational ES efforts reflect "bolted-on sustainability" (Laszlo & Zhexembayeva, 2011), where the organization's approach to sustainability is project-based as opposed to embedded within overall strategy. While bolted-on ES efforts are better than none, they carry the risk of being labeled "greenwashing" when perceived by stakeholders as merely token efforts to create a "green" image, as opposed to a substantive and transformative ES strategy. Such negative perceptions can impede much-needed employee buy-in and engagement with organizational ES efforts.

Engaging Employees in ES Initiatives

The third element necessary for embedding ES is the involvement of all levels of employees in designing and implementing ES solutions. Successful change efforts permeate the entire organizational system. Roberts and Kleiner (2006) identified four kinds of system thinking that can facilitate employee involvement in and understanding of organizational change efforts: open systems (seeing the world through flows and constraints), social systems (seeing the world through human interaction), process systems (seeing the world through information flow), and living systems (seeing the world through the interaction of its self-creating entities). Engaging employees in discussions about relevant ES issues for the organizational subsystems within which they work, and getting them to think about how their subsystems relate to other subsystems, as well as to the larger organizational system, can be a powerful means to reach employees and draw them into the ES change efforts. Such discussions give rise to ES-related innovations that fuel not only organizational ES progress but also employee engagement. Further, recent evidence (BlessingWhite, 2011) has demonstrated that employee engagement drives business results, such as profitability, earnings per share, quality and customer loyalty.

In sum, these three systems elements—executive leadership, sufficient resources, and employee engagement—work hand in hand to enact changes required to implement ES strategies. Upon this firm foundation, organizational leaders and members can design and implement initiatives to effectively embed sustainability in the thinking and behavior of all employees. We turn now to ways in which to reach the hearts and minds of employees.

IMPACTING MINDS AND HEARTS OF EMPLOYEES: GETTING EMPLOYEES TO "OWN" SUSTAINABILITY

Organizational change is best viewed as a learning endeavor (Argyris & Schon, 1978), one that requires learning from the CEO level to the lowest paid employee. When approaching ES-related organizational change from a learning organization perspective, a consideration of desired learning outcomes is relevant. Kraiger, Ford, and Salas (1993) presented learning as a function of changes in cognitive, skill-based, and affective states. Thus, here we consider each of these learning outcomes from the perspective of employees coming to "own" ES-related change: a *cognitive component*, through which the employee understands the risks that current actions of the organization and its employees pose to the environment, and the rationale upon which the organization's ES strategy is established; a *skill-based component*, through which the employee applies information regarding modification of actions that create negative environmental consequences; and an *affective component*, through which employee attitudes about ES-related changes and their motivation to initiate new behaviors is forged. These three learning outcomes are interrelated, and can interact in ways that can facilitate or hinder the adoption of behavior changes needed to support an organization's ES strategy (also see Werner, this book, for a discussion of fundamental assumptions and processes for developing internalized behavior). For example, employee A might find motivation in learning that organizational efforts can mitigate environmental damage, and eagerly seek information on how to change behavior. Employee B, who does not believe that humans contribute to climate change, might have a negative emotional reaction to learning about the organization's sustainability initiative and thereby resist information related to ES behavior change. As such, engaging employees in ES behavior extends beyond providing information to employees; dealing with their emotions is also necessary.

Because emotions can hinder acceptance of change efforts and the notion of climate change is an emotion-laden issue, focusing employee attention away from the distal issue of climate change can be a wise choice. The Sherwin-Williams company chose to focus on making the business case to employees rather than tying the rationale for their ES strategy to global warming (DuBois, 2012). However, their website and sustainability reporting also include information on their efforts to reduce greenhouse gas emissions, for their greenhouse gas metrics help stakeholders to see how ES initiatives can create efficiency, value, and competitive advantage. Framing current pollution and excess waste issues as proximal community issues can help employees grasp what needs to be done, as well as providing an emotional basis for change. For example, if an organization pollutes a local stream or lake in which employees fish, use of cleaning up this relevant body of water as an example through which to frame the organization's ES change efforts can engender positive emotions from employees, for it helps them view ES change as a means to improve their quality of life. Experienced sustainability consultants suggest that employees not be asked to connect the dots they can't connect; doing so creates cognitive and emotional distance or frustration. Few employees will object to cleaner air and water, or lower landfill usage, particularly when it impacts them personally.

Organizational communications and training sessions are typical means through which an organization's adoption of ES strategy is shared with employees. For example, management at KLM developed an awareness-raising course and scheduled a regular staff information day to familiarize employees with new technical solutions and programs developed to enable cleaner production techniques and improved worker health and safety. Because line managers play a key role in facilitating transfer of such training, as well as in helping employees understand the organizational rationale underlying the ES strategy, ensuring managerial alignment with ES strategy is critical to achieving successful change (DuBois, DuBois, & Astakhova, 2011). As noted earlier, when managers work with the human resource management (HRM) function to develop and implement systems to reinforce an ES culture—such as recruiting new employees who value ES, training current employees, and incorporating ES goals into performance management—they help to create horizontal alignment among HRM systems to support behavior change. Their day-in, day-out support for ES reinforces organizational strategy and provides employees with the assistance and encouragement they need to make changes.

Employee behavior change can also be facilitated by choice architecture (Thaler & Sunstein, 2008), through which behavior is shaped by making the sustainable choice the most convenient choice. For example, locating recycling bins in offices and limiting waste receptacles to central areas to which employees need to walk has been found to increase recycling significantly (Brothers, Krantz, & McClannahan, 1994). Thus, structuring the sustainable choice facilitates the process of automatizing desired behaviors. Involving employees in identifying myriad ways through which choice architecture can be applied in their work setting provides a creative means through which employees can engage in the change process, because it harnesses their buy-in for behavior change. Simple modifications in workstation set-up, processes, and equipment use can cumulatively result in significant efficiencies, which create positive feedback for employees.

Employee engagement in ES efforts builds a case that addresses what's in it for employees. Organizational communications that clarify the business case for ES address the organization level. But without bridging to employee interests, behavior change will likely be limited to compliance with new policies and procedures. We suggest that participative engagement in creating new social norms and ways of thinking about sustainability over time can transform an initially extrinsic organizational focus to an internal identity where employees understand deeply and personally care about ES. Self-determination theory provides a useful explanation of how this transformation might work.

SUSTAINED CHOICES: THE JOURNEY FROM EXTRINSIC TO INTRINSIC MOTIVATION

The extent and consistency of environmentally-friendly behavior among employees reflect the degree to which employees "own" a personal commitment to ES. Greater ownership leads to the sustained choice of ES behavior in situations that present a range of behavioral options. Behavioral choice is a complex cognitive phenomenon that is influenced by self-determination. Self-determination theory (Deci & Ryan, 1985; Gagné & Deci, 2005) posits a self-determination continuum that ranges from amotivation, which is wholly lacking in self-determination, to intrinsic motivation, which is invariantly self-determined. Between amotivation and intrinsic motivation, along this descriptive continuum, are four types of extrinsic motivation. These include compliance, introjection, identification, and integration, with compliance being the most controlled (i.e., least self-determined) type of extrinsic motivation, and integration being the most self-determined.

ES behavior change can be facilitated by organizational efforts to ignite employees' intrinsic motivation to behave in an environmentally-friendly manner. For example, an employee's ES journey might begin at the level of amotivation, accelerate through the four extrinsic motivation states and arrive at the level of intrinsically driven ES behavior. Regardless of the employee's initial motivation state, the success of individual motivation transformation over time can be significantly impacted by well-coordinated organizational actions to increase the extent to which employee ES behavior is self-determined. Each of the motivational states posited by self-determination theory is now explained, with corresponding suggestions for how organizations might encourage employees at each motivational state to move to the next, more self-determined state in order to strengthen employee commitment to organizational ES behavior.

Amotivation

Amotivation is a state lacking in intention to act. From an expectancy theory (Vroom, 1964) perspective, amotivation can result from expectations that the intended action will most likely not be successful or that it will fail to lead to the promised outcome, or from perceiving no value in the outcome. A significant challenge at the outset of an organizational ES change initiative is to minimize the number of employees who lack any motivation to support or participate in the change initiative. Just as expectancy theory can be used to explain why amotivation occurs, it can also provide insight regarding how an organization might move an employee from an amotivated state to an extrinsically motivated state. For example, if the employee believes that their individual actions will not meaningfully impact the desired outcome, training that employs example metrics demonstrating how individual actions create a cumulative impact might move the employee from an amotivated state to an extrinsically motivated state. Perhaps the greatest challenge would be posed by employees who do not believe that human activity contributes meaningfully to climate change, and therefore lack values for the outcome of environmental gains. These employees might view organizational ES efforts as much ado about nothing. A constructive approach in this case might be to shift the focus of the outcome from mitigating climate change to the business rationale, highlighting cost savings, increased efficiencies, and expanded market share. Winning employees over in this manner might nudge them to a state of extrinsic motivation, but additional work will be required to get them to a more self-determined state of extrinsic motivation.

Extrinsic Motivation

Compliance

At the compliance stage, individuals typically perceive externally regulated behavior as controlled and their actions have an external perceived locus of causality (Deci & Ryan, 1985). Being highly contingent upon external factors (rewards and/or punishment), this motivation state is highly impersonal and is characterized by short-term impact. Yet, as a starting point for ES efforts, compliance with ES policy and reporting creates an initial basis for employee ES behavior change. For example, a rule of not depositing trash in office recycling bins seems simple enough, but those employees who do not yet buy into the organization's ES effort might deposit trash when no one is looking. Thus, with rules comes the challenge of rule enforcement. Rules align the behaviors of "non-believers" and "true-believers" by uniformly targeting and reinforcing the desired ES behavior. However, because employees can resent excessive rules and organizations can't specify every behavior they seek, relying on compliance is highly limited in effectiveness. A connection to something within the employee, such as pride, is necessary to gain progress toward more self-determined behavior change.

Introjection

Introjected regulation of an individual's behavior involves taking in a regulation but not fully accepting it as one's own. At this stage, behaviors are performed to avoid guilt or anxiety, or to attain ego enhancement such as pride (Deci & Ryan, 1985). For individuals at the introjected motivation state, organizations might include employee reinforcement to instill pride in their contributions to organizational ES goal accomplishment. For example, Norm Thompson Outfitters' CEO promoted a clear ES vision for the organization, which helped to enhance the importance of the ES initiative in the eyes of employees and instill employees' pride in their own actions (Smith & Brown, 2003). ES was integrated into everyday performance goals and metrics in a manner that made employees' ES actions visible, which increased employee pride in their own performance. Yet at this stage of extrinsic motivation the employee still lacks personal value for ES; such personal value begins to emerge in the next stage toward self-determination.

Identification

Identification is a more autonomous, or self-determined, form of extrinsic motivation, which reflects conscious value for a behavior even in situations when the behavior might not be intrinsically appealing. Individuals with identification-regulated motivation will be driven by subjective norms about the ES behavior or will perceive value in behaviors that are socially important. Because personal moral obligation and moral intensity factors are generally viewed as essential drivers for ES behaviors (Flannery & May, 2000), the organization might benefit from facilitating the creation of ES-related social norms by its employees. The results of Flannery and May's (2000) study of organizations within the U.S. metal finishing industry indicated that intentions to perform ES behaviors were positively associated with employee assessment of support from important others. As such, "social approval" may be used to reinforce employee ES behaviors. This might be particularly effective among those employees with identification-regulated motivation, who might experience a collective bonding with regard to ES behavior. Cialdini, Reno, and Kallgren (1990) found that both descriptive and injunctive social norms impacted littering behavior; participants increased and decreased their littering according to the social norms made salient. Their research clarifies the significance of organizational efforts to shape the social norms surrounding desired behaviors. As a note of caution, if the organization allows employees to set norms that conflict with ES, such norms could impede sustainability strategy implementation. Thus, organizational leaders would be wise to monitor the creation and presence of ES social norms. Motivation at the identification stage is still heavily guided with reference to others; the shift toward internal reference begins with the integration stage of extrinsic motivation.

Integration

Integration occurs when identified behavior regulations are fully assimilated into the self; that is, they have become congruent with one's other values and needs. Integration closely resembles intrinsic motivation, although integration-regulated behaviors are still considered extrinsic because they are undertaken to attain separable outcomes rather than for their inherent enjoyment. The range of behaviors that can be assimilated to the self expands over time as cognitive capacities and ego development grow (Loevinger & Blasi, 1991). Thus, organizations aiming at ES might benefit from further developing employee ES-related knowledge, skills, and abilities, creating opportunities for ES innovation that enhance employees' pride in their own performance, or making ES a vehicle for employee social interaction. For example, the use of social networking may facilitate an increased exchange of ES knowledge, ideas, and decisions, which, in turn, will further strengthen employees' integration-regulated motivation. The Sherwin-Williams Company uses technology-driven communication to connect employees worldwide to share their eco-innovations (DuBois, 2012). Employees bond across cultures, trying to outdo one another in creating wins for the planet; their social connections fuel their individual passion for ES. Such behavior is highly effective for the organization. Yet there remains one more step in self-determined behavior—acting without regard to others or the organization, but for one's own belief in the significance of ES.

Intrinsic Motivation

The construct of intrinsic motivation describes one's natural inclination toward assimilation, mastery, spontaneous interest, and exploration, and represents a principal source of enjoyment and vitality throughout life (Ryan & Deci, 2000). Thus, positive emotions are connected with acting in accord with personal values. With intrinsic motivation being naturally present in those individuals who are the "true believers" in ES, the organization need only sustain this motivational state in these employees. As such, organizations can benefit from removing roadblocks to employee ES innovation. Simply providing a setting that facilitates intrinsically driven employee ES behavior that pushes the boundaries can forge new ways to optimize ES goals. Laszlo and Zhexembayeva (2011) highlight the importance of radical innovation to support embedded sustainability. Intrinsically motivated employees have the capacity and drive to truly think outside the box and challenge existing process and product norms to create a more sustainable future.

An over-determined environment rife with micromanagement, rigid procedures, and pressured evaluations is likely to constrain intrinsically motivated employees, who might resent an externally focused locus of causality. Such a person-environment fit mismatch could result in diminished intrinsic motivation (Ryan & Deci, 2000) and increase the risk of turnover among those employees who can most powerfully fuel an organization's ES efforts. Intrinsically motivated employees respond positively to acknowledgment of their convictions and opportunities for choice and self-direction; these fuel their sense of autonomy, which further enhances their intrinsic motivation (Deci & Ryan, 1985).

THE JOURNEY FROM AMOTIVATION TO INTRINSIC MOTIVATION

Empowering employees on their journey towards self-determined ES behavior is an effective means to propagate ES behavior throughout the organization. Organizational actions can create "a bandwagon effect" (Bansal, 2002, p. 130), initiating change in the mindsets of employees throughout the organization. In a similar manner, ES behaviors in one domain can spill over into other domains. For example, the goodwill generated from recycling can lead to new initiatives proposed by employees, such as ways in which energy can be better managed. Self-determination connects to personal values and emotions; organizations can leverage emotions to inspire further ES commitment among employees. Positive psychology highlights how individuals strive for a more fulfilling existence (Seligman, 1994). A central premise of positive psychology is that individuals can be happy in suboptimal situations, and can recognize situational limitations yet still work productively to improve their situation (Seligman & Csikszentmihalyi, 2000). These positively focused employees have the capacity to inspire others to join them in pursuing organizations' ES goals. Their presence is especially needed when organizations initiate their ES strategy, particularly if an organization's current practices create significantly negative ES impacts and accordingly daunting ES goals. Environments that cultivate positive emotions in employees, even those who don't accept the basis of the need for ES-related change, will be more open to ES innovations (Arnaud & Sekerka, 2010).

Xerox builds on positive emotion by bringing fun into ES through initiatives, such as their Earth Day event. In fact, a joyful perspective pervades their ES culture. As a result, people throughout the organization are more likely to turn off lights and computers when they leave the office, recycle their coffee cups, and consider environmental impacts in product design and marketing. Ashforth Pacific, Inc. was successful in engaging employees through an initial set of optional but fun opportunities, such as their "cookies for trash can trade." Employees were given cookies to motivate them to give up the trash cans in their individual offices, which eliminated the use of 9,000 trash can liners annually and increased employee recycling. Employees felt good about participation, rather than frustrated at the elimination of a convenience. The Wyland Foundation turned Earth Day into Earth Month, during which they publicly acknowledged each day an Earth Month Hero K-12 teacher who was a positive role model for their community. Such initiatives communicate positive messages that build employee awareness and demonstrate to customers and investors the importance of ES to the organization.

Empowering employees as well as bringing positive emotion to ES strategy can be used to develop and sustain employee intrinsic motivation for ES. Table 10.1 summarizes the earlier discussion. It lists the levels of self-

TABLE 10.1

Connecting Self-Determination Motivational States With Diffusion Groups

Motivational State	General Characteristics	Recycling Example	Rogers' Diffusion Group	Percentage
Amotivation	No action or unattached action	Don't bother to recycle	Laggards	16%
Extrinsic: Compliance	Externally regulated action	Recycle only when monitored	Late majority	34%
Extrinsic: Introjection	Act to avoid guilt or gain pride	Recycle to please your boss		
Extrinsic: Identification	Consciously value action	Recycle to do the right thing	Early majority	34%
Extrinsic: Integration	Value congruent action	Recycle to have positive impact	Early adopters	13.5%
Intrinsic	Act from natural inclination	Recycle spontaneously, habit	Innovators	2.5%

Note. Table 10.1 is based upon self-determination theory (Deci & Ryan, 1985) and diffusion of innovation theory (Rogers, 2003).

determination in conjunction with corresponding employee characteristics and an example of how recycling behavior might play out at each level. For example, amotivated employees might not bother to recycle, compliant employees will recycle when monitored, identified employees might recycle to please their boss, introjected employees might recycle to do the right thing, identified employees might recycle to have a positive impact, and intrinsically motivated employees will recycle because it's who they are and what they do—they simply can't not recycle; in fact, they will take recyclables home if they can't recycle them at work. The last two columns in Table 10.1 pertain to Rogers' categories of innovation diffusion (2003), and connect diffusion categories to states of self-regulation.

DIFFUSION OF ES BEHAVIOR CHANGE

Rogers' diffusion of innovation theory (2003) provides a useful way to understand how ES behavior change can propagate through an organization in response to organizational efforts to facilitate ES behavior. Rogers proposed five groups within a diffusion framework: innovators, early adopters, early majority, late majority, and laggards. Rogers' categories overlap meaningfully with Deci and Ryan's (1985) stages of self-determination, as noted in Table 10.1. In explaining diffusion, we work from the bottom to the top of the table, for organizations look to those who are most self-determined, the innovators, to lead organizational ES efforts.

The innovators (leading 2.5%) represent the leading edge of "true believers," those employees who have a passion for ES that manifests within their personal life. These employees are intrinsically motivated to pursue ES in everything they do. Thus, they carry their passion into the work setting, often igniting an interest in ES by others in the organization, enthusiastically pioneer innovation, take leadership roles in ES efforts, and serve as role models for other employees. Because innovators are intrinsically motivated, providing these individuals with opportunities for creativity, challenge, and self-direction will help sustain their engagement in pioneering a succession of environmental sustainability initiatives. Upon articulation of their ES strategy, the Sherwin-Williams Company engaged this set of employees in a task force that rolled out the ES initiative to the organization (DuBois, 2012). This not only energized these employees but also created early successes for the organization. Innovators frequently serve as opinion leaders who can persuade others to adopt new ways by providing evaluative information (Rogers, 2003). These individuals can play the role of gatekeepers in the flow of new ideas in the organization. An understanding of the characteristics of such individuals can assist managers in targeting innovation implementation appropriately. For example, as innovators often bear the burden of initial mistakes (Lozano, 2006), organizational support and encouragement is needed to prevent discouragement.

The next group to join the innovators is the early adopters, who comprise the adjacent 13.5%. Early adopters build upon the successes of the innovators. They admire the innovators and aspire to emulate them. Operating from a platform of integrated extrinsic motivation (Deci & Ryan, 1985), they value the importance of ES behavior, and they feed upon the social networking opportunities to connect with the innovators and other early adopters. They are looked upon by potential adopters, waiting in the wings, as reference individuals. They are speeding agents who may quicken the pace of the diffusion of ES initiatives. Like the innovators, early adopters thrive in an autonomous work environment where they can perceive their own importance and impact in driving the ES initiative. Because the early adopters thrive on connections and recognition, organizations benefit from promoting and rewarding these employees as champions of change, which also inspires successive groups of employees to join the initiatives (Montgomery, Bartram, & Elimelech, 2009).

This next wave comprises the early majority, the adjacent 34% who are willing to adopt new ideas more than the average organizational member. Through their numbers, they provide a significant increase in interconnectedness in the organizational system's interpersonal networks. From a self-determination perspective (Deci & Ryan, 1985), these individuals operate from a state of identified extrinsic motivation; they recognize the potential value in ES, and are inspired by the opportunity to validate social norms and bond with important others in the cause of ES. As with the early adopters, recognition and validation are important; thus an attractive reward system may serve as an effective driving mechanism for this group. These employees are likely to be active contributors to focus group and task force opportunities, though they are more likely to be group members than leaders. They possess sufficient value for ES to be inspired to innovate, yet they are also willing to go along with prescribed norms for needed ES actions. As such, they don't need the same sense of autonomy, for they are less driven from within by the mission of ES. Still, their expanded numbers and enforcement of organizational ES norms and values will be highly visible, and will serve to motivate the next group of onlooking employees to actively engage in organizational ES initiatives.

Following the full engagement of the early majority a tipping point will be reached, for at this point fully half of the organization's employees have engaged in the ES change efforts; at this point, the late majority will follow (34%). The late majority represents a mix of employees at the introjection and compliance stages of self-determination (Deci & Ryan, 1985). Because these employees do not personally value ES or find it important, their engagement in ES is limited to what can be obtained through compliance with external forces, such as guilt, pressure, rules, reinforcement, and punishment. Clearly this represents lack of full engagement, and these employees are not likely to go above and beyond expected norms to support ES efforts. For these employees, ES behavior change will be strengthened by compelling social norms and clearly specified performance expectations, for actual pressure from peers and superiors can motivate this group. As such, greater transparency of organizational policies and expectations is required to engage this group in ES behavior change. The "green flagging" innovation strategy adopted by Phillips assures that sustainability is placed on the radar of every company member due to its explicit objectives and clear vision (Arnold & Hockerts, 2011).

Finally, the laggards will hold out the longest and bring up the rear (16%). These are the amotivated (Deci & Ryan, 1985) employees who tend to be suspicious about both the ES notion and the change agents promoting it. They perceive their resistance to the ES change efforts as rational, and they have a strong bias to retain the status quo. Trust is sufficiently low that these employees might not even respond to rules, social pressure, or clear performance expectations—and when they do respond they do so begrudgingly. Should this group be perceived as a drag on the organization, and their performance fall seriously below expectations, they might need to be terminated and replaced by new employees who respect the organization's new direction.

Rogers' theory illustrates that, given the right start by the right people, increasing employee engagement can be self-propagating, providing that the organization maintains the appropriate conditions. Because innovation plays such an important role in creating organizational ES wins, the role of the HR function working in tandem with line management is critical to the development and implementation of employee systems and culture that feed innovation. Line managers will be challenged to provide autonomy and facilitate dialogue to support innovation. As such, the process of embedding ES into the DNA of an organization requires an organizational transformation that will evolve over a period of years, throughout which mindful attention, design work, and adjustment are required.

HUMAN RESOURCE SYSTEMS AND ENGAGEMENT

Because ES strategy implementation relies on employees, the HRM function is ideally positioned to play a prominent role in ES change efforts (DuBois & DuBois, 2012). The HRM function is involved in work design and interfaces with all employees, and can be a key partner in designing, developing, and implementing an array of systems to engage employees in ES. ES change impacts the full range of transformational, traditional, and transactional HRM functional areas (Lepak, Bartol, & Erhardt, 2005). For example, creating an organizational culture that values sustainability can require a paradigm shift in how employees perceive the organization and its interaction with a range of stakeholders. Sustainability leadership from all ranks of managers requires training and performance management to ensure that managers are on board with how sustainability can create organizational value, rather than view it as simply a source of added cost. When sustainability is integrated into recruiting, selection, and orientation processes, new employees enter their jobs knowing that sustainability is important and how they can play a role in creating it (also see Willness & Jones, this book, and Andrews, Klein, Forsman, & Sachau, this book, for a discussion of HR practices and ES). Ongoing training and performance management systems highlight continuous learning to support sustainability efforts, and pave the way for employees to design and implement eco-innovations. When employees are held accountable and rewarded for meeting sustainability targets, they produce expected results.

Clearly, both vertical alignment and horizontal strategic alignment of HRM systems with organizational strategy are needed to create coherence among the many interwoven HRM systems required to support ES strategy implementation. Indeed, HRM policy/strategy is one of the five factors that influence effective implementation of employee engagement strategies, as identified by BlessingWhite (2011). Further, the need for HRM to work with line managers on ES change implementation is evident, for line managers implement the systems the HRM function designs (DuBois et al. 2011). These managers are "squeezed between organizational mandates and the people on the front lines," and therefore "work in the vortex where employee engagement happens" (BlessingWhite, 2011, p. 24). As such, line managers are positioned to have significant influence on the day-to-day work experiences of employees. It is up to them to use HR systems in a manner that generates what they were designed to create. A partnership between HRM and line managers is needed to "unfreeze" restraining forces that may hinder ES-related organizational changes, and activate the essential components of employee engagement: employee learning, adaptability, and flexibility (Weick & Quinn, 1999).

Excellent models of how the HRM function can provide strong leadership to engage employees in ES transformation have been identified and documented. For example, EcoVision at the Sherwin-Williams Company has been led jointly by the Senior Vice President of HRM and the Senior Vice President of Operations Excellence Initiatives (DuBois, 2012). The whole systems perspective inherent in sustainability thinking reinforces the need for both vertical and horizontal alignment of HRM systems (Schuler & Jackson, 1987) intended to align employee thinking and behavior with organizational ES strategy. Sustainability poses the challenge of taking this a step further, to applying design thinking to create fully integrated HRM systems to support ES. Charettes are used in many fields to bring together a variety of stakeholders who collaborate creatively to design a system that best meets the varying needs represented in the group. Further, integrated system design addresses the intersections of systems to facilitate consistency and flow.

The examples that follow illustrate innovative actions taken by organizational leaders and employees to implement ES strategy. In many cases, these activities and systems reflect innovative ideas and collaborations. Although they fall short of integrated system design, they represent steps in the right direction that have yielded meaningful results on many levels.

THE PAYOFF: ORGANIZATIONAL "WINS" BY SUCCESSFUL COMPANIES

The articulation of ES strategy creates value for the firm (Laszlo, 2003) that extends well beyond increased efficiencies and decreased harm to the environment. Effective ES strategy implementation has a powerful impact on customer satisfaction and loyalty. For example, Starbucks Coffee Company's successful ES initiatives not only positively impacted customer satisfaction and loyalty, but also fueled stable organizational growth. Starbucks partnered with the Environmental Defense Fund to develop a more environmentally-responsible coffee cup and promote reusable cups; it purchases only organic, shade-grown, and fair-trade coffee. In local communities in the Pacific Northwest, Starbucks has reached outside the company to contribute to the development of recreational parks and to undertake initiatives that extend beyond the boundaries of ES to encompass a commitment to social sustainability. As a result, Starbucks scored the top rating for customer satisfaction among the U.S. largest limited-service restaurant chains in the 2008 American Customer Satisfaction Index (http://news.starbucks.com/article_display.cfm?article_id=45).

The processes required to implement sustainability provide a fertile ground for innovation and employee engagement, highly valuable organizational by-products sometimes unsuspectingly unleashed by ES strategy. Executives, when talking about successful ES efforts, will often elaborate on how their ES initiatives inspire innovation and engagement among their employees. Examples of employee-driven eco-innovations abound, both with regard to organizational processes and products. At the Allentown, Pennsylvania, Lucent Technologies manufacturing facility, employees developed a microchip cleaning process to replace a hazardous volatile organic compound with water. This action mitigated both employee safety/health and organizational pollution risks, as well as eliminating the cost of purchasing the compound (Ramus, Steger, & Winter, 1996). A team at the Neste Oil Company's research laboratory in Finland designed a renewable diesel fuel that is the world's cleanest diesel fuel and can be used in all diesel engines (Neste Oil, 2011).

Best Global Green Brands for 2011 ranks 3M as number two on its list of "greenest" brands based on public perception of a brand's environmental performance and the brand's actual performance based on publicly available information. Jean Sweeney, 3M Vice President of Environmental, Health and Safety Operations recognizes the importance of innovation for fueling the company's ES progress: "Innovation is a way of life at 3M, and this is a great way to align our culture with a continued commitment to reduce impact on the environment and underline the connection between 3M values and sustainability." 3M implemented their Pollution Prevention

Pays (3P) program in 1975, which has resulted in thousands of employee innovation projects, prevented the generation of billions of pounds of pollution, and collectively saved hundreds of millions in organizational costs. This spirit of innovation is ingrained in 3M culture, as reflected in the allowance for engineers to spend 15% of their work time pursuing projects of their own interest. 3M also involves stakeholders both locally and globally. Each local 3M site develops a custom plan to solicit feedback from various stakeholders, and the company then uses shareholders' feedback in shaping sustainability strategies. Further, their volunteer program emphasizes education and community partnerships, and many of their programs are inspired and created by employees themselves.

To create an engaging, thriving workplace, Fairmount Minerals sets management priorities for safety, health, and wellness, as well as community engagement. Feelings of personal attachment are generated among employees through their active participation in sustainability initiatives both at work and in the community. One example is innovation assemblies, organized by the company's innovation center, during which employees educate one another and community members on the ES-related operational impacts of the firm. Further, the employee Sustainable Development Advisory Committee oversees a variety of volunteer-based teams that lead important projects involving land restoration, recycling, energy conservation, and water filtration, to name a few. Every Fairmount Minerals QUEST site team participates in an environmental education project to enhance awareness of biodiversity impacts. Teams engage in such activities as building barn swallow bird boxes, creating a native plant educational exhibit, creating a pollinator garden, partnering with a local nursery to plant native grasses, and conducting a town planting project. These personally engaging opportunities nurture positive emotions and value for ES among employees, thereby supporting the development of self-determined ES behavior.

These examples of embedding ES into the very fiber of organizational culture reflect how organizational practices can deepen the value created not just for the organization but also for the employees, whose work lives are enriched with increased empowerment and personal development made available through organizational ES changes and associated opportunities. These practices also spill over into ES behaviors that generalize to employees' personal lives, compounding the positive planetary benefits. Clearly ES strategy can be a win-win endeavor.

206 • *Cathy L. Z. DuBois, Marina N. Astakhova, et al.*

REFERENCES

Argyris, C., & Schon, D. A. (1978). *Organizational learning: A theory of action perspective.* Reading, MA: Addison-Wesley.

Arnaud, A., & Sekerka, L. E. (2010). Positively ethical: The establishment of innovation in support of sustainability. *International Journal of Sustainable Strategic Management, 2*(2), 121–137.

Arnold, M. G., & Hockerts, K. (2011). The greening Dutchman: Philips' process of green-flagging to drive sustainable innovations. *Business Strategy and the Environment, 20,* 394–407.

Bansal, P. (2002). The corporate challenges of sustainable development. *The Academy of Management Executive (1993–2005), 16*(2), 122–131.

Beer, M., Eisenstat, R., & Spector, B. (1990). Why change programs don't produce change. *Harvard Business Review, 68*(6), 158–166.

Beer, M., & Nohria, N. (2000). Cracking the code of change. *Harvard Business Review,* May–June, 133–141.

Bertalanffy, L. (1968). *General system theory: Foundations, developments, applications.* New York, NY: Braziller.

BlessingWhite. (2011). *Employee engagement report.* Retrieved September 16, 2011, from http://www.blessingwhite.com/EEE__report.asp

Brothers, K. J., Krantz, P. J., & McClannahan, L. E. (1994). Office paper recycling: A function of container proximity. *Journal of Applied Behavior Analysis, 27*(1), 153–160.

Cialdini, R. B., Reno, R. R., & Kallgren, C. A. (1990). A focus theory of normative conduct: Recycling the concept of norms to reduce littering in public places. *Journal of Personality and Social Psychology, 58,* 1015–1026.

Deci, E. L., & Ryan, R. M. (1985). The general causality orientations scale: Self-determination in personality. *Journal of Research in Personality, 19,* 109–134.

DuBois, C. L. Z. (2012). EcoVision at Sherwin-Williams: Leadership at all levels. In S. Jackson, D. Ones, & S. Dilchert (Eds.), *Managing human resources for environmental sustainability.* A SIOP Professional Practice Series book. San Francisco, CA: Jossey-Bass.

DuBois, C. L. Z., & DuBois, D. A. (2012). Strategic HRM as social design for environmental sustainability in organizations. *Human Resource Management, 51*(6), 799–826.

DuBois, C. L. Z., DuBois, D. A., & Astakhova, M. (2011, June). *Sustainability diffusion through the HR-line manager partnership.* Proceedings of the Ashridge International Research Conference, 'The Sustainability Challenge: Organisational Change and Transformational Vision', Ashridge Business School.

Flannery, B. L., & May, D. R. (2000). Environmental ethical decision-making in the U.S. metal-finishing industry. *Academy of Management Journal, 43,* 642–662.

Gagné, M., & Deci, E. L. (2005). Self-determination theory and work motivation. *Journal of Organizational Behavior, 26,* 331–362.

Interface Global (2011). *Our sustainability journey – mission zero.* Retrieved November 20, 2011, from http://www.interfaceglobal.com/Sustainability/Interface-Story.aspx

Kraiger, L., Ford, J. K., & Salas, E. (1993). Application of cognitive, skill-based, and affective theories of learning outcomes to new methods of training evaluation. *Journal of Applied Psychology, 78,* 311–328.

Laszlo, C. (2003). *The sustainable company: How to create lasting value through social and environmental performance.* Washington, DC: Island Press.

Laszlo, C., & Zhexembayeva, N. (2011). *Embedded sustainability: The next big competitive advantage.* Sheffield, UK: Greenleaf Publishing.

Lepak, D. P., Bartol, K. M., & Erhardt, N. L. (2005). A contingency framework for the delivery of HR practices. *Human Resource Management Review, 15*, 139–159.

Loevinger, J., & Blasi, A. (1991). Development of the self as subject. In J. Strauss & G. R. Goethals (Eds.), *The self: Interdisciplinary approaches* (pp. 150–167). New York, NY: Springer-Verlag.

Lozano, R. (2006). Incorporation and institutionalization of SD into universities: Breaking through barriers to change. *Journal of Cleaner Production, 14* (9–11), 787–796.

Lueneburger, C., & Goleman, D. (2010). The change leadership sustainability demands. *Sloan Management Review, 51*(4), 49–55.

Montgomery, M. A., Bartram, J., & Elimelech, M. (2009). Increasing functional sustainability of water and sanitation supplies in rural sub-Saharan Africa. *Environmental Engineering Science, 26*(5), 1017–1023.

Neste Oil (2011). Innovations for combating climate change. Retrieved January 17, 2013, from http://www.nesteoil.com/default.asp?path=1,41,11991,12243

Pfeffer, J. (1981). Management as symbolic action: The creation and maintenance of organizational paradigms. In L. L. Cummings and B. Staw (Eds.), *Research in Organizational Behavior, 3*, 1–15. London: JAI Press.

Porter, M. E., & Kramer, M. R. (2011). The big idea: Creating shared value. *Harvard Business Review, 89*(1/2), 62–77.

Ramus, C., Steger, U., & Winter, M. (1996). Environmental protection can give a competitive edge. *Perspectives for Managers.* Lausanne, Switzerland: IMD International.

Roberts, C. & Kleiner, A. (2006). Five kinds of systems thinking. In P. Senge, A. Kleiner, C. Roberts, R. Ross, G. Roth, & B. Smith (Eds.), *The Dance of Change.* New York, NY: Currency/Random House.

Rogers, E. (2003). Diffusion of Innovations (1st/5th ed.). New York, NY: Free Press, Simon & Schuster.

Ryan, R. M., & Deci, E. L. (2000). Self-determination theory and the facilitation of intrinsic motivation, social development, and well-being. *American Psychologist, 55*, 68–78.

Schuler, R. S., & Jackson, S. E. (1987). Linking competitive strategies with human resource management practices. *Academy of Management Executive, 1*, 207–219.

Seligman, M. (1994). *What you can change and what you can't.* New York, NY: Knopf.

Seligman, M. E. P., & Csikszentmihalyi, M. (2000). Positive psychology: An introduction. *American Psychologist, 55*, 5–14.

Senge, P. (2006). *The fifth discipline: The art and practice of the learning organization.* New York, NY: Currency/Random House.

Smith, D., & Brown, M. S. (2003). Sustainability and corporate evolution: Integrating vision and tools at Norm Thompson Outfitters. *Journal of Organizational Excellence, 22*(4), 3–14.

Thaler, R., & Sunstein, C. R, (2008). *Nudge: Improving decisions about health, wealth, and happiness.* New Haven, CT: Yale University Press.

Vroom, V. H. (1964). *Work and motivation.* New York, NY: Wiley.

Weick. K. E., & Quinn, R. E. (1999). Organizational change and development. In J. T. Spence, J. M. Darley, & D. I. Foss (Eds.), *Annual review of psychology, 50*, 361–386. Palo Alto, CA: Annual Reviews.

11

Designing Interventions That Encourage Permanent Changes in Behavior

Carol M. Werner

Imagine your organization's leadership asks employees to adopt environmentally sustainable practices as permanent, internally motivated changes in behavior. There are many ways of approaching this challenge, including simply requiring the new behaviors or using an incentive program in which costs are covered by the savings. However, neither mandates nor incentives are likely to achieve your goal of autonomous, long-term change. This chapter describes psychological strategies designed to induce sustainable change, especially because the new behaviors are enjoyable, integral to the self, and/or automatic.

Four broad principles underlie the behavior change proposals in this chapter. The first principle is to treat change as a process rather than a one-time fix (Campbell, 1973). Start with clear goals and an effective intervention, then continually evaluate the program and modify it as needed. In some cases, unexpected physical barriers need to be removed; in other cases, people need to hear a new persuasive message or figure out new ways of keeping the task fresh. Be alert and respond to waning effectiveness. Most of all, avoid the impulse to assume that people don't want to change. Instead, identify weaknesses in the program and make improvements. For example, our campus dining area once decided students did not want to recycle because no one was using the new recycling bins. We analyzed the situation and concluded that patrons wanted to recycle but had not noticed the tiny signs. Large signs—visible across the room—turned the original failure into a gratifying success (Werner, Rhodes, & Partain, 1998).

The second broad principle is that behavior is always embedded in a physical environment that can facilitate or thwart change. Always evaluate the physical environment and make sure that it supports and does not impede the new behavior. Behavior should be as easy and convenient as possible, such as providing centrally located recycling bins and signs (Holland, Aarts, & Langendam, 2006), choosing recycling bins that are larger and closer than garbage cans, designing environments in which walking and biking are easier than driving (Staunton, Hubsmith, & Kallin, 2003), and so on. If you cannot remove physical barriers, it is important to use persuasion or normative pressures so that people overcome the barrier, such as acknowledging inconvenience as a way to reduce complaints and increase recycling (Werner, Stoll, Birch, & White, 2002). In sum, behavior change begins by reducing physical barriers so desired behaviors can be easier, more efficient, and more pleasant.

The third broad principle is to change the social environment. Use leadership and public praise to create a milieu of enthusiasm for the new pro-environmental behaviors. Ignore naysayers, move your program forward, and increase the visibility and voices of respected employees who support the change. Decades of research and anecdotes on social pressure show it is very difficult to be a deviant when others are performing new, socially valued behaviors.

The final general principle is to avoid using incentives to influence behavior. Incentives can include paying everyone for participating or it might mean using competitions and challenges to reward people who change the most. Incentive- and challenge-based interventions appear effective on the surface; however, they rarely yield sustained change: once the incentive or competition ends, the behavior change usually ends as well. When the behavior is already intrinsically motivated, there is an additional potential danger. The external challenge can replace the original internal motivation, and, when the program ends, the behavior ends as well. It might be counterintuitive that externally oriented programs reduce internal motivations. However, this is a well-established problem, referred to as the "overjustification effect" or the "undermining effect of reward" (Deci & Ryan, 2000; Lepper & Greene, 1978).

TWO-STEP MODEL FOR DURABLE PRO-ENVIRONMENTAL BEHAVIOR CHANGE

How does one create new behaviors that ultimately become permanent because they are internally motivated, whether attitude-driven, intrinsically motivated and/or habit-based? This chapter focuses on how interventions encourage individuals to become determined to change their behavior and then how this determination evolves over time into permanent behavior change (also see DuBois, Astakhova, & DuBois, this book, for a systems approach to behavior change). A simplified view of this evolution is provided in Table 11.1, which proposes the 2-step process for changing environmental behaviors. Step 1 (Column 1) reflects inducement for people to change using the listed interventions. This sets in motion Step 2 (Column 2), psychological changes that make the new behavior manageable and personally desirable and help sustain behavior. In essence, the model proposes that, once people are determined to switch to a new behavior, they need to figure out how to remember, organize, and experience the activities so they can maintain the behavior. Ultimately, with supportive physical and social environments, the behavior is maintained by habit or by cognitive or affective reminders.

Step 1: Inducing New Attitudes and Behaviors

Persuasion and Strong Attitudes

Definitions of environmental attitudes emphasize evaluation: "Attitudes are favorable and unfavorable evaluations of environmental issues and behaviors" (adapted from Fazio, 1995). Attitudes are good predictors of behavior, especially when (1) the attitude is "strong," (2) the attitude and behavior are measured at the same level of specificity, and (3) the physical and social environments support the behavior. The first principle, attitude strength, is a complex concept. Strong attitudes are not necessarily extreme, rather they are "well formed," which means they come to mind easily (called "accessible"), are held with certainty, pertain to important issues, are central to one's self-concept, and reflect central values. Such attitudes are more likely to persist over time, resist counterpersuasion, and—because they are readily accessible from memory—predict behavior (Fazio, 1995; Petty, Haugtvedt, & Smith, 1995). Accessibility is particularly important because, simply put, attitudes that do not come to mind are not available to guide behavior. You might want to try a new restaurant (a favorable behavioral intention), but, if that attitude is not strong and accessible, you will not remember your intention to go there. This is illustrated by a study that measured attitudes towards an envi-

TABLE 11.1

Fundamental Assumptions and Processes for Developing Internalized Behavior

Assumptions:
Treat change as a process; evaluate and change intervention or context as needed.
Physical environment must support new behavior.
Social milieu must support new behavior.
Avoid using incentives or challenges because they are short-term.

Intervention Strategies	Internal Supports for Behavior Development
Result: Individual is Determined to Change	**Result: Internally Motivated and Remembered Behavior**
End result of intervention: Person committed to behavior change. Person has strong attitude or strong goal directedness. Person is determined to change.	
Intervention	**Internal Mechanisms Form and Are Maintained**
Persuasion	**Learning Processes/Habit Formation**
Logical arguments that individual is motivated to think about and capable of appreciating. Arguments address abstract reasons as well as specific behaviors.	Practicing the behavior. Incorporating it into existing cognitive script; development of new script. Creating a habit so that behavior occurs automatically when goal is activated in familiar context.
Social Normative Information	**Motivational Processes. Transform the Task to be Interesting, Fun, and/or Worthwhile.**
Belief that significant others accept the persuasive message. Belief that significant others admire those who engage in behavior.	Psychologically transform behavior to be enjoyable, worthwhile, important.
Commitment and Implementation Intentions	**Self-concept Processes**
Voluntary, public, active, and effortful promise to engage in new behavior. Commitments that are specific about time, place, social milieu, and behavior.	"I am the kind of person who …" Pride in accomplishment. Behavior described as "meaningful" "worthwhile" "important." Belief in approbation of significant others. People feel good for doing behavior and experience regret or other negative affect when they fail to do the behaviour.

ronmental organization and measured the strength of those attitudes by tapping four characteristics of strong attitudes (certainty, importance, self-descriptiveness, and values relevance). Participants then returned to the laboratory to complete the study, after which they were invited to contribute money to the same environmental organization. Results confirmed that—independent of favorability—strong attitudes predicted making a donation but weak attitudes did not (Holland, Verplanken, & Knippenberg, 2002).

The second principle is that level of specificity distinguishes general environmental attitudes from specific attitudes towards particular behaviors. A general measure of "environmental concern" does not predict recycling (or other pro-environmental behaviors) as well as a measure of "attitude towards recycling." More specificity yields even better prediction: Asking about *behavioral intentions* to recycle predicts actual behavior better than asking about attitudes towards recycling (Ajzen, Albarracin, & Hornik, 2007). The implication is that persuasive messages should focus on specific behaviors as well as abstract reasons for engaging in them.

Finally, attitude-behavior relations are often weakened by the context, such as when an individual is reluctant to disagree with a superior in public but would disagree in private, or when a person favors walking to work but lives many miles from the office. When the attitude is strong, levels of specificity are in synchrony, and physical and social environments are supportive, attitude-behavior relationships are robust (Petty et al., 1995).

How does one construct and present persuasive messages so that they result in changed attitudes that can guide behavior? Decide on what behaviors to change and make those the focus of the message. Explain specific desired behaviors and reasons for needing to change.

Attitude formation and change is neither simple nor quick, but putting together an effective message is worth it because the change can be permanent. Furthermore, an ineffective message might result in no change or might actually boomerang, leaving the individual not only unpersuaded but actually negative about the proposed behavior.

Persuasion occurs when people think about and favorably "elaborate" the ideas in a message. During elaboration, the individual thinks about and evaluates message details and also adds his or her own ideas, either positive or negative. Indeed, years of research show that people do not remember details of the persuasive message. They remember their own thoughts about the message, and it is these thoughts that influence subsequent behavior (Petty & Cacioppo, 1986). Positive elaboration increases the favorability of the final attitude whereas negative elaboration or "counterarguing" leads to rejection of the message and an unfavorable final attitude. This process of evaluating and elaborating on arguments is a key memory process that helps create strong attitudes. The more an individual thinks about the ideas (message content and personal reactions), the more interconnected in memory they become, the more the information and evaluations solidify as a strong attitude, and the more likely it is that the attitude is accessible enough to guide behavior (Petty et al., 1995). In sum, creating persuasive messages requires using cogent arguments about specific behaviors and inducing the target audience to pay attention to and "elaborate" the message.

Thus, an important part of the persuader's task is to help people build strong attitudes by using cogent reasons that stand up to careful examination and cannot be dismissed out of hand (Petty & Cacioppo, 1986). Most cogent arguments are fact-based and are drawn from credible sources. A successful "turn off lights as you leave the room" program used several cogent reasons in its persuasive message (e.g., leaving lights on would waste energy and money; Werner, Cook, Colby, & Lim, 2012). When students already had pro-recycling attitudes, the argument that recycling was "important" was adequate to convince them to increase their recycling (Werner et al., 2002). Identifying cogent arguments for persuasive messages takes some effort, including careful pilot testing (Petty & Cacioppo, 1986). The process is generally adequate to develop a message that moves people to be determined to change their behavior.

Given the importance of elaboration, a critical question is "How do interventions induce people to really think about and mull over a persuasive message so that it becomes a strong accessible attitude leaving people determined to change their behavior?" Inducing people to examine a message is usually done by convincing them that the issue is relevant to them, such as showing how they and their families will be affected by a new policy. The more people are concerned about possible outcomes, the more they will closely examine the message (Crano, 1995; Petty & Cacioppo, 1986). Researchers have identified a number of additional ways of increasing attention to and elaboration of a message, including stating the message as a rhetorical question ("Why should you recycle?";

Petty, Cacioppo, & Heesacker, 1981); attributing the message to multiple but very different sources to give a sense of general endorsement (Harkins & Petty, 1987); using group discussion to create interest in the topic (Werner, Sansone, & Brown, 2008); and using validation as part of the message (e.g., validating complaints while encouraging change; Werner et al., 2002). Most of these techniques could be used by organizations to increase cognitive elaboration of messages whether the message is delivered in a group meeting or simply printed on reminder signs at the place where the behavior occurs.

In summary, decades of research show that when people are given cogent reasons for changing their attitudes, and are induced to "elaborate" or think deeply about those reasons, their attitudes are changed. With enough favorable elaboration of multiple cogent reasons, people develop "strong" attitudes, attitudes that persist, resist counterpersuasion, come easily to mind, and actively guide behavior. In essence, strong, well-developed pro-environmental attitudes leave individuals determined to change their behaviors and able to talk themselves into changing.

Social Pressures and Social Support for Change

Another mechanism for changing behavior is social influence, or how much support one perceives among family, friends, colleagues, and the broader society. The importance of social motivation as part of everyday behaviors and behavior change has been widely acknowledged in psychology and includes examination of concepts such as conformity, pluralistic ignorance, and injunctive and descriptive norms (for reviews, see Cialdini & Goldstein, 2004; Prislin & Wood, 2005; Schultz, Tabanico, & Rendón, 2008). Conformity and social influence research show that naive participants do change their public behaviors in order to fit into a group, group members do exert deliberate conformity pressure on deviants, and individuals are often aware of their feelings of discomfort when they deviate from their friends (Cialdini & Trost, 1998). This "normative social influence" has two forms, "descriptive" and "injunctive," and research shows that people are more influenced by seeing or hearing about others' behaviors ("descriptive norms") than by being given instructions for appropriate behaviors ("injunctive" or "prescriptive norms"). Indeed, using a negative descriptive message in persuasion—"look at how bad other people have been"—can actually be counterproductive (Cialdini, 2003).

Viewers remember and copy the descriptive norm that other people have misbehaved; they ignore the injunctive message that people should not misbehave. For the strongest normative influence, messages should both exhort behavior change and show people engaged in the desired behavior. A word of caution: if people become aware that they are complying more than others, they can backslide. This can be avoided by recognizing and praising their strong performance at the same time the normative information is provided (Schultz, Nolan, Cialdini, Goldstein, & Griskevicius, 2007).

Despite research showing favorable responses to normative information, if asked directly, people—especially those in individualistic societies like the United States—generally deny they are influenced by others. To demonstrate this in a compelling way, Nolan, Schultz, Cialdini, Goldstein, and Griskevicius (2008) conducted a two-step study. Participants first denied that knowledge about others' behaviors could influence how much energy they saved. But when they learned their neighbors were conserving energy, they reduced their own energy use. Indeed, this group saved more energy than participants who received other persuasive messages.

Combining Persuasion with Social Normative Information

Werner and colleagues developed an intervention called "Guided Group Discussion" (Werner et al., 2008; Werner & Stanley, 2011) that combines Petty and Cacioppo's (1986) ideas about cognitive processing and persuasion with Lewin's (1952) ideas about group conformity pressures. The purpose of these interventions was to encourage people to use non-toxic home and yard care products instead of the harsher toxic chemical products. The structure and content of the meetings were carefully developed to capitalize on both persuasion and conformity literatures. For example, in accord with the persuasion literature, the messages included cogent reasons for behavior change as well as strategies for increasing message elaboration (Werner et al., 2008). In accord with Lewin's admonition to embed persuasion in a relevant social group, the information was presented to groups of friends and colleagues who were encouraged to share their favorable opinions. These active discussions were successful in creating long-term attitudes and behavior change (Werner et al., 2008; Werner & Stanley, 2011).

Commitment, Implementation Intentions and Attitude/ Behavior Change

Promises to change, such as simple commitments and more involved "implementation intentions" have been very popular and successful ways of inducing behavior change (Cialdini, 2009; Lokhorst, Werner, Staats, & van Dijk 2011). Commitments and implementation intentions are similar in practice, but are described as having different underlying psychological processes. Making a commitment may lead one to sustain behavior out of a desire to maintain positive self-regard. Making implementation intentions emphasizes cognitive skills, the salience of personal goals, memory processes, and the development of habits. To highlight these different psychological processes, commitments, and implementation intentions are discussed separately.

Commitment. A widely used technique for inducing long-term change is to invite people to make a commitment to change their behavior. Cialdini (2009) described commitment making as one of the most effective behavior change interventions. He specified four characteristics that would increase commitment's effectiveness and durability: Commitments need to be (1) freely chosen, (2) public, (3) active, and (4) effortful. (1) Commitment has to be voluntary or made with minimal external pressure so that people own and accept responsibility for keeping their commitment. (2) Commitment should be public so that people would be embarrassed to fail or change their minds. (3) Making the commitment should be active, such as writing a name or statement rather than just checking a box or casually agreeing. Active commitment takes more thought, is more memorable, and may cue the individual that he or she really wanted to make the commitment. If the desired behavior is difficult, commitment can begin with a simpler behavior that is escalated to the larger behavior the communicator really desires. (4) Finally, the act of committing should incur some effort so that people increase their evaluation of the goal. Cialdini's literature review included few environmental behaviors; however, he did provide empirical support for each technique, suggesting they would also strengthen commitment for environmental behaviors. In particular, assuring that commitments are voluntary is extremely important because of the extensive research showing that, when people choose to commit, their self-concepts may change, supporting long-term change (Burger & Caldwell, 2003).

Commitment making for environmental behaviors has been popular because research shows it is effective both immediately and over time. A meta-analysis of environmental commitment making showed that commitment was consistently better than control conditions at effecting change both during the commitment period and after, when people believed they had been released from their commitments (Lokhorst et al., 2011). A more challenging question is whether commitment is more effective than other behavior change interventions (e.g., receiving success feedback, using data to track one's own success, receiving tokens for participating). The meta-analysis found the commitment was better than other treatments in the long term, a week or more after the program ended. Thus, after people had been released from their commitments or knew their interventions had ended, those who had made commitments sustained their new behavior more than did participants in the other treatments (Lokhorst et al., 2011).

Implementation intentions. Commitment making has been changed and strengthened with innovative "implementation intentions," which are commitments for specific behaviors in specific contexts. The goal is to create memory structures that are activated by the context, thereby increasing the likelihood that the individual will fulfill the intended commitment. The term "implementation intention" is designed to underscore that this is not an ordinary commitment (Gollwitzer & Sheeran, 2006). Individuals make "if-then" commitments so that when the relevant circumstances occur (i.e., the "if") the individual remembers to engage in the behavior. Implementation intentions usually specify particular goals, the time, physical setting, social group and purpose, and how the individual will engage in behaviors that help him reach his goal. Although environmental researchers have been slow to adopt implementation intentions (except see Bamberg, 2000, on transportation, and Holland et al., 2006, on recycling), it has been quite popular in health behavior change where a host of studies testify to its effectiveness (e.g., see meta-analysis, Gollwitzer & Sheeran, 2006), including behavior change sustained for one month (Prestwich, Perugini, & Hurling, 2010), two months (Holland et al., 2006), and two years (Stadler, Oettingen, & Gollwitzer, 2010). Implementation intentions enable people to want to change, and to remember that goal when the behavior opportunity occurs.

Being Determined to Change

The change strategies of persuasion, social pressure, and commitment/ implementation intentions are essential in Step 1 for three reasons. First, as just described, they have independent effects on the durability of attitude and behavior change. Persuasion, commitment/implementation intentions and social pressure can make people determined to change and can help them remember to do the new behavior. Second, these interventions can be combined for potentially stronger effects. Guided group discussion uses both persuasion and normative pressure (Werner et al., 2008), and research that combines implementation intentions with persuasion yields a stronger impact (Milne, Orbell, & Sheeran, 2002). Coupling interventions is a promising way to create pro-environmental attitudes that are reliable predictors of pro-environmental behaviors. Third, as explored next, the determination created by persuasion, commitment/implementation intentions and social pressures activates additional psychological processes that add further support to long-term change.

Step 2: Developing Internal Supports for New Behavior

When people are determined to succeed at a new behavior (have a strong attitude about doing the behavior, remind themselves why, and/or feel committed to engage in the behavior), they can use a variety of strategies for maintaining that behavior. The next section examines three very powerful psychological processes that support long-term change: (1) people can do the new behavior until it becomes automatic, and part of a routine, script, or habit (e.g., Bower, 2000; Fazio, 1995; Schank & Abelson, 1977; Wood & Neal, 2007); (2) people can come to look forward to the behavior; they can motivate themselves by making the behavior interesting, fun, or worthwhile (Sansone, Weir, Harpster, & Morgan, 1992); and (3) people can make the new behavior a part of their desired self-concept (Higgins, 1987).

It is possible that any of the three behavior change interventions (persuasion, social influence, and commitment/implementation intentions) could activate any of these three processes. However, some researchers have coupled these interventions with particular processes. Persuasion is typically associated with learning and motivation (Petty & Cacioppo, 1986); commitment has been linked with increased salience of self-concepts that emphasize consistency and reliability (Cialdini, 2009); implementation intentions have been associated with learning and the automaticity of habits; and social influence has emphasized concerns about social approval (Cialdini, 2003). In this chapter, in order to allow for the possibility that each intervention could activate any of these psychological processes, the processes are described independent of any particular intervention. Each section picks up at the point where the individual has become determined to succeed at a new behavior.

Learning: Procedural Knowledge, Mental "Scripts" and Habits

The section on attitude change noted the importance of including specific behaviors in any persuasive message. This section explores how knowledge becomes habitual, supporting long-term change.

Procedural knowledge. Whether people are determined to change because of persuasion, commitment, or social concerns, the individual needs to know what behavioral opportunities are available and how to act on them. Behavior change interventions need to include clear procedural information such as specific details about where, when, and how to enact new behaviors. For simple behaviors, changing the environment to increase convenience can sometimes be sufficient. In a recycling study, providing a recycling center was as successful as more complex interventions (Holland et al., 2006). Complicated behaviors—such as sorting instructions for multiple types of recycling—require more detailed instructions, including posted reminders (e.g., lists of acceptable recyclables) where the behavior occurs. Consider the complexity of learning to use public transportation systems: initially, people don't know how to use transit schedules, purchase tickets, or use the system (where to stand, how to open doors, etc.). Informal discussions with university students indicated that a common barrier to trying transit was lack of familiarity and a fear of looking foolish and inept in public. To reduce this barrier, both the university and the local transit system now post videos online showing the how-to's of transit use. Although procedural knowledge does not guarantee behavior change (Schultz, 2002), if an intervention has motivated people to change, they cannot be successful without clear instructions for the new behavior (and supportive social and physical environments). In sum, interventions must include ways of giving people the information they need.

Mental scripts and habits. Procedural knowledge is important, but if people don't remember to engage in the behavior, that knowledge is of little use. Considerable research has explored the cognitive structures and situational supports that enable complex behavioral routines to unfold regularly and even automatically. Early research showed that people had mental "scripts" or familiar sequences of events that facilitated everyday activities. For example, successful recyclers are those who develop an orderly set of behaviors and arrange their homes to support this sequence (Hormuth, Katzenstein, Bruch, & Ringenberger, 1993; Werner & Makela, 1998). Behavior change interventions can take advantage of an existing "mental script" and insert the new behavior into that ongoing sequence. Such script-enhancement is easily done with recycling, where people begin with a "throw-it-away" script and walk to the garbage can. This script can be interrupted and retrained with signs on garbage cans that stop the disposal process and redirect the person to the recycling bin (Werner, et al., 1998; Werner et al., 2002).

Being able to capitalize on a script requires a good understanding of why people behave as they do. In one case, we analyzed the "social ecology" of newspaper use and realized students did not recycle because that defeated the accepted practice of leaving newspapers for others to read. Recycling signs on walls and garbage cans were designed to support the "sharing" script, but then changed the script by encouraging students to recycle late in the afternoon, when papers were not likely to be read and were ready for recycling (Werner, Byerly, White, & Kieffer, 2004). In another case, we posted signs to teach people to turn off lights as they exited restrooms, but had little success with signs around the light switch. We were only successful when we thought about the script for exiting and realized the "lights out" signs needed to be where people would be looking as they exited (in this case, the bolt for unlocking the door, but in other settings, the door handle).

Habits have memory structures that are similar to those of scripts (linked sequences of events), except they tend to be more specifically linked to particular goals (Gollwitzer & Sheeran, 2006) or settings (Wood & Neal, 2007), and, because habits occur frequently, they may unfold more automatically. Many studies show that habitual behaviors are more accessible and more easily activated (Aarts & Dijksterhuis, 2000a, 2000b; Aarts, Dijksterhuis, & Midden, 1999; Webb & Sheeran, 2008).

This automaticity is a two-edged sword: it supports desired behaviors, but can also make undesirable behaviors resistant to change. Literature on habits addresses both sides of the issue: "How can new behaviors become habits?" and "How do we break old habits and create new ones around new pro-environmental behaviors?" Implementation intention researchers have focused on helping people develop new habits rather than breaking old ones. The strategy is to ask people to make formal commitments and especially to ask them to specify where, when, and how they will undertake the new behavior (Gollwitzer & Sheeran, 2006). Several studies using similar methodologies show that commitment alone is not as effective as commitments made while imagining the setting and circumstances around a desired new behavior (Aarts et al., 1999).

Well-entrenched habits can be difficult to change, which raises the question of whether it is easier to start from scratch and create a new habit, or to weaken an existing habit. Research suggests it is easier to create a new habit than to suppress an old one, even though it can be difficult to establish a new habit. Tobias (2009) remarked on the lack of consistent findings about the number of repetitions required to establish a new habit, but agreed it would be easier to establish a new habit than to change an existing one.

Other research asked which was a more successful strategy for behavior change: deliberately thinking about and suppressing an unwanted response, or just ignoring the unwanted response and focusing on creating the new cognition-behavior link. These results also supported creating a new association instead of worrying about the existing link. Indeed, when participants were instructed to actively suppress an existing link, the attention given to suppression actually helped to maintain the strength of the unwanted response (Danner, Aarts, & de Vries, 2007). Other research suggested that bad habits and good new behaviors can coexist, especially early on, when one is attempting to change a behavior (Verplanken & Faes, 1999). These authors made the point that people should persist in their efforts to change, even in the face of backsliding. There are benefits from the new behavior even if done infrequently, and new habits can be built, albeit slowly, through repeatedly performing the new behavior.

A final suggestion is to acknowledge that habits are activated and supported by circumstances, and may weaken when those circumstances change (Neal, Wood, & Quinn, 2006; Wood & Neal, 2007). In particular, research shows that habits are more easily changed in new contexts (Wood, Tam, & Witt, 2005). For example, when people relocate, they may find it easier to become a transit user because their car-driving habits are not fully developed in the new setting (Bamberg, 2006; Davidov, 2007).

One theme of this chapter is that behavior is difficult to change and often multiple forces are needed in order to effect permanent change. Consistent with this view, recent theorizing and research on undoing habitual responses advocates multifaceted interventions (Verplanken & Wood,

2006; Wood & Neal, 2007), including strengthening attitudes, making commitments and implementation intentions, changing the physical environment, and so on. A particularly useful framework suggests different strategies for changing behavior versus maintaining behavior (Rothman, Sheeran, & Wood, 2009).

Intrinsically Motivated Behavior: Making It Interesting, Fun, and/or Worthwhile

A frequent theme in environmental writings is that humans need to consume less in order to protect the environment. To some, this means that people should be willing to make sacrifices, be uncomfortable, and avoid the many conveniences of the modern world. For example, in the case of commuting via mass transit, the reduced consumption model assumes that people do not enjoy using transit, but persuade themselves to do so (e.g., transit saves money; transit protects the environment by reducing emissions of greenhouse gases and other toxics). Knowing one is doing the right thing should make up for the presumed unpleasantness of using transit. In a prescient article, De Young (1996) cautioned against this tack, because it made the new behaviors sound so unpleasant that no one would try them, no matter how much they wanted to help the environment. He suggested that people needed to focus on the intrinsic benefits of their environmental behaviors, such as the competency of successfully changing their behaviors (see De Young, this book, for further discussion on meaningful actions as a means to ES behavior).

Sansone and colleagues (Sansone et al., 1992) also said that people cannot maintain unpleasant behaviors that they force themselves to do. If people cannot figure out how to psychologically transform activities to make them more enjoyable, people will simply stop doing the behavior. Thus, we cannot force ourselves to put up with unpleasant experiences for a greater good, but we can find ways of changing how we do tasks so that they become genuinely enjoyable or worth doing. If people are determined to succeed with a new but boring behavior, they will figure out how to make the behavior more pleasant or meaningful. This is a fascinating insight, and Sansone and colleagues conducted several studies showing that—when people were highly motivated to succeed at a task—they actively transformed boring tasks into interesting activities (Sansone et al., 1992).

Sansone et al. suggested several transforming strategies people might employ to make tasks more intrinsically interesting. First, like De Young, they noted that people could focus on aspects of a task that were challenging so that success made them feel competent. Second, they cited studies of how people could use other aspects of the physical environment to maintain their interest. For example, transit users might manipulate or engage the environment by watching other passengers, enjoying the passing scenery, or studying the route to learn more about their community. Third, they suggested adding variety to how a repetitive task is done. This might entail taking a different walking route to transit, or taking different bus routes on different days of the week. Finally, Sansone and colleagues suggested changing the definition of the task so that the entire activity has a different meaning. For example, one reason transit has become so popular in Salt Lake City is because many riders think of the journey not as a boring commute but instead as "found time." They write reports, do background reading, study for exams and in other ways make their transit trips productive time. Others use the commute for texting, socializing with other riders, pleasure reading, making business and personal calls, and even doing crafts.

Empirical research supports and extends these ideas. Brown, Werner, and Kim (2003) used Sansone and colleagues' ideas to guide their analysis of students who made a successful switch from driving alone to using a new light rail line for commuting. They found that successful transit users reported using more interest-enhancing strategies than automobile users. The idea of creating interest provides a useful contrast to traditional cost-reward models that emphasize the inconvenience of public transport while ignoring the personal benefits that people can create (Everett & Watson, 1987). Additional support comes from a study of recycling that found that people with the most favorable pro-recycling attitudes and most sustained behaviors were most likely to psychologically transform the task so that it was more interesting and fun, or simply more personally meaningful (Werner & Makela, 1998).

Allowing participants to choose their strategies was probably an important aspect of this research because it is consistent with the theme that autonomy is fundamental to intrinsic motivation (Deci & Ryan, 2000). In sum, this set of studies shows that, when people are determined to be successful, they can psychologically transform their environmental activities so that they want to do them. This has distinct advantages compared with expecting people to suffer in order to protect the environment.

Self-Concept and Behavior

Positive self-concepts are one of the most powerful drivers of behavior. Simply put, most people like to think well of themselves. Sometimes positive regard comes from the approbations of friends and coworkers, and sometimes it comes from meeting internal values of how one should behave. We feel good when our behaviors are consistent with our goals, and we can experience disappointment and other negative affect if we fail to live up to our own standards or to others' standards for us (Higgins, 1987). Self-concepts have been of particular interest in the commitment literature where researchers have been interested in the relation between making a commitment and changes in self-concepts that are consistent with the commitment. For example, research showed that people changed their self-descriptions (responses to personality scales) to be more consistent with a voluntary behavioral commitment (Burger & Caldwell, 2003).

Cialdini (2009) suggested that a desire for self-consistency is one mechanism by which commitments lead to long-term change. People have been socialized to be responsible members of society and "keep their word." In Cialdini's particular example, a researcher asked people to commit to conserving energy for several months and told them their names would appear in a local newspaper as "public spirited fuel-conserving citizens" if they tried to reduce their energy use (Pallak, Cook, & Sullivan, 1980). Towards the end of the time period, the researchers apologized to participants and said they would not be able to publish their names after all. Although some might expect these participants to respond negatively to this change in plans, they did not and instead continued conserving energy long beyond their original commitment. They conserved more energy than the control group that had been given the same instructions for conserving but had made their commitment privately, without the promise of public recognition.

Cialdini (2009) suggested that as soon as these residents made their voluntary commitment, they began generating personal reasons for conserving energy. And when they lost their original reason for conserving (i.e., gaining social recognition), they had an even stronger need to justify their behavior with even more personal reasons for conserving. As they engaged in their behaviors, they became more committed to conservation and generated even more reasons for conserving. Cialdini hypothesized that eventually participants began to describe themselves as "conservation minded" to fit the description ascribed by the experimenters. Cialdini proposed that the change in their self-concept was a major contributor to their durable behavior.

Change That Is Internally Motivated

In summary, there are multiple ways in which behaviors can become internally driven. This section focused on three of these: memory processes can create scripts and habits; deliberate efforts to make a task interesting and worthwhile can transform how we do them and how we think of them; and we can change our self-concepts so that we take pride in the new behaviors and maintain them in order to maintain self-esteem.

SUMMARY AND CONCLUSION

The model proposed in this chapter is both simple and complex. As Table 11.1 shows, people go through two steps to achieve permanent changes in behavior. In the first stage (Table 11.1, Column 1), they go through an experience that leaves them determined to change their behavior. They are persuaded, they make a voluntary commitment/implementation intention, or they change because they want to fit in and to be admired. If they are truly determined to change at the end of this experience, they begin to undergo internal processes that enable them to maintain their new behavior (Table 11.1, Column 2). One process is that people develop memory structures so that, eventually, the new behavior is a habit. If this occurs, people no longer need to think about doing the behavior, it simply unfolds automatically. A second process that might occur when people are determined to maintain the new behavior is that they actively transform the task to make it interesting or fun. In this case, people look forward to doing the behavior, actively enjoy it, and no longer think of it as a burden. The third and final process is creation of a more positive self-concept, when a person thinks of the behavior as worthwhile or laudatory, feels good for his or her environmental behaviors, and perceives approbation from others.

It is useful to speculate how these psychological states and their related behaviors become permanent. In the case of habits, the behavior is based in memory and, as long as the precipitating events remain in place, the behavior is likely to continue. In the case of intrinsically motivated behavior, people simply enjoy the behavior. If this enjoyment wanes, but their determination is strong, they can cycle through the transformation processes and find additional ways of making the behavior interesting or fun. Finally, in the case of self-concept, people maintain the behavior through their own sense of doing the right thing and they can surround themselves with people who agree and support them.

For clarity and simplicity, the chapter considered one intervention at a time. Given the difficulty of effecting permanent changes in behavior, it makes sense to develop behavior change programs that use multiple interventions. Indeed, some researchers have used interventions in combination to good effect, such as combining implementation intentions with persuasion (Milne et al., 2002), adding normative influence to persuasion (Werner et al., 2008), and using texted memory aids to enhance implementation intentions (Prestwich et al., 2010).

Behavior is influenced by multiple factors, both inside the individual and in the physical, social, and policy environments. Organizations have considerable control over employees, and can insist on behavior change. But that would be an external motivator and the behavior would end when that external pressure was withdrawn. It is important to create an environment that supports internally motivated changes. This chapter has emphasized three strategies for creating internally motivated, self-sustaining interventions. It is hoped that organizations can adapt these strategies to their particular goals and circumstances, and adapt them in ways that create long-term change.

REFERENCES

Aarts, H., & Dijksterhuis, A. (2000a). The automatic activation of goal directed behavior: The case of travel habit. *Journal of Environmental Psychology, 20*, 75–82.

Aarts, H., & Dijksterhuis, A. (2000b). Habits as knowledge structures: Automaticity in goal directed behavior. *Journal of Personality and Social Psychology, 78*, 53–63.

Aarts, H., Dijksterhuis, A., & Midden, C. (1999). To plan or not to plan? Goal achievement or interrupting the performance of mundane behaviors. *European Journal of Social Psychology, 29*, 971–979.

Ajzen, I., Albarracin, D., & Hornik, R. (2007). *Prediction and change of health behavior: Applying the reasoned action approach.* Mahwah, NJ: Lawrence Erlbaum Associates.

Bamberg, S. (2000). The promotion of new behavior by forming an implementation intention. Results of a field-experiment in the domain travel mode choice. *Journal of Applied Social Psychology, 30*, 1903–1922.

Bamberg, S. (2006). Is residential relocation a good opportunity to change people's travel behavior? Results from a theory-driven intervention study. *Environment and Behavior, 38*, 820–840.

Bower, G. H. (2000). A brief history of memory research. In E. Tulving & F. I. M. Craik (Eds.), *The Oxford handbook of memory* (pp. 3–22). New York, NY: Oxford University Press.

Brown, B. B., Werner, C. M., & Kim, N. (2003). Personal and contextual factors supporting the switch to transit use: Evaluating a natural transit intervention. *Analyses of Social Issues and Public Policy, 3*, 139–160.

Burger, J. M., & Caldwell, D. F. (2003). The effects of monetary incentives and labeling on the foot-in-the-door effect: Evidence for a self-perception process. *Basic and Applied Social Psychology, 25*, 235–241.

Campbell, D. T. (1973). Reforms as experiments. In L. Rosen & R. H. West (Eds.), *A reader for research methods* (pp. 279–312). New York, NY: Random House.

Cialdini, R. B. (2003). Crafting normative messages to protect the environment. *Current Directions in Psychological Science, 12*(4), 105–109.

Cialdini, R. B. (2009). *Influence: Science and practice* (5th ed.). Boston, MA: Pearson.

Cialdini, R. B., & Goldstein, N.J. (2004). Social influence: Compliance and conformity. *Annual Review of Psychology, 55*, 591–622.

Cialdini, R. B., & Trost, M. R. (1998). Influence: Social norms, conformity, and compliance. In D. T. Gilbert, S. T. Fiske, & G. Lindzey (Eds.), *Handbook of social psychology* (4th ed., pp. 151–192). Boston. MA: McGraw-Hill.

Crano, W. D. (1995). Attitude strength and vested interest. In R. E. Petty & J. A. Krosnick (Eds.), *Attitude strength: Antecedents and consequences* (pp. 131–158). Mahwah, NJ: Lawrence Erlbaum Associates.

Danner, U. N., Aarts, H., & de Vries, N. K. (2007). Habit formation and multiple means to goal attainment: Repeated retrieval of target means causes inhibited access to competitors. *Personality and Social Psychology Bulletin, 33*, 1367–1379.

Davidov, E. (2007). Explaining habits in a new context: The case of travel-mode choice. *Rationality and Society, 19*, 315–334.

Deci, E. L., & Ryan, R. M. (2000). The "what" and "why" of goal pursuits: Human needs and the self-determination of behavior. *Psychological Inquiry, 11*, 227–268.

De Young, R. (1996). Some psychological aspects of reduced consumption behaviors: The role of intrinsic satisfaction and competence motivation. *Environment and Behavior, 28*, 358–409.

Everett, P. E., & Watson, B. G. (1987). Psychological contributions to transportation. In D. Stokols & I. Altman (Eds.), *Handbook of environmental psychology* (Vol. 2, pp. 987–1008). New York, NY: John Wiley and Sons.

Fazio, R. H. (1995). Attitudes as object-evaluation associations: Determinants, consequences, and correlates of attitude accessibility. In R. E. Petty & J. A. Krosnick (Eds.), *Attitude strength: Antecedents and consequences* (pp. 247–282). Mahwah, NJ: Lawrence Erlbaum Associates.

Gollwitzer, P. M., & Sheeran, P. (2006). Implementation intentions and goal achievement: A meta-analysis of effects and processes. In M. P. Zanna (Ed.), *Advances in experimental social psychology* (Vol. 38, pp. 69–119). San Diego, CA: Elsevier.

Harkins, S. G., & Petty, R. E. (1987). Information utility in the multiple source effects. *Journal of Personality and Social Psychology, 52*, 260–268.

Higgins, E. T. (1987). Self-discrepancy: A theory relating self and affect. *Psychological Review, 94*, 319–340.

Holland, R. W., Aarts, H., & Langendam, D. (2006). Breaking and creating habits on the working floor: A field-experiment on the power of implementation intentions. *Journal of Experimental Social Psychology, 42,* 776–783.

Holland, R. W., Verplanken, B., & van Knippenberg, A. (2002). On the nature of attitude-behavior relations: The strong guide, the weak follow. *European Journal of Social Psychology, 32,* 869–876.

Hormuth, S. E., Katzenstein, H., Bruch, B., & Ringenberger, B. (1993). Psychological studies on garbage avoidance and recycling. In J. Urbina-Soria, P. Ortega-Andeane, & R. Bechtel (Eds.), *Healthy environments: Proceedings of EDRA 21* (pp. 321–325). Oklahoma City, OK: Environmental Design Research Association (EDRA).

Lepper, M. R., & Greene, D. (1978). *The hidden costs of rewards: New perspectives on the psychology of human motivation.* Hillsdale, NJ: Lawrence Erlbaum Associates.

Lewin, K. (1952). Group decision and social change. In G. E. Swanson, et al. Rev. Ed. Editorial Committee: Guy E. Swanson, Theodore M. Newcomb and Eugene L. Hartley, Co-chairmen [and Others] (Eds.), *Readings in social psychology* (pp. 459–473). New York, NY: Holt.

Lokhorst, A. M., Werner, C. M., Staats, H., & van Dijk, E. (2011). Commitment and behavior change: A meta-analysis and critical review of commitment-making strategies in environmental research. *Environment and Behavior.* doi: 10.1177/0013916511411477

Milne, S., Orbell, S., & Sheeran, P. (2002). Combining motivational and volitional interventions to promote exercise and participation: Protection motivation theory and implementation intentions. *British Journal of Health Psychology, 7,* 163–184.

Neal, D. T., Wood, W., & Quinn, J. M. (2006). Habits – a repeat performance. *Current Directions in Psychological Science, 15,* 198–202.

Nolan, J. M., Schultz, P. W., Cialdini, R. B., Goldstein, N. J., & Griskevicius V. (2008). Normative social influence is underdetected. *Personality and Social Psychology Bulletin, 34,* 913–923.

Pallak, M. S., Cook, D. A., & Sullivan, J. J. (1980). Commitment and energy conservation. *Applied Social Psychology Annual, 1,* 235–253.

Petty, R. E., & Cacioppo, J. T. (1986).*Communication and persuasion: Central and peripheral routes to persuasion.* New York, NY: Springer-Verlag.

Petty, R. E., Cacioppo, J. T., & Heesacker, M. (1981). Effects of rhetorical questions onpersuasion: A cognitive response analysis. *Journal of Personality and Social Psychology, 40,* 432–440.

Petty, R. E., Haugtvedt, C. P., & Smith, S. M. (1995). Elaboration as a determinant of attitude strength: Creating attitudes that are persistent, resistant, and predictive of behavior. In R. E. Petty & J. A. Krosnick (Eds.), *Attitude strength: Antecedents and consequences* (pp. 93–130). Mahwah, NJ: Lawrence Erlbaum Associates

Prestwich A., Perugini, M., & Hurling, R. (2010). Can implementation intentions and text messages promote brisk walking? A randomized trial. *Health Psychology, 29,* 40–49.

Prislin, R., & Wood, W. (2005). Social influence in attitudes and attitude change. In D. Albarracín, B. T. Johnson, & M. P. Zanna (Eds.), *The handbook of attitudes* (pp. 671–706). Mahwah, NJ: Lawrence Erlbaum Associates.

Rothman, A. J., Sheeran, P., & Wood, W. (2009). Reflective and automatic processes in the initiation and maintenance of dietary change. *Annals of Behavioral Medicine, 38*(Suppl 1), S4–S17.

Sansone, C., Weir, C., Harpster, L., & Morgan, C. (1992). Once a boring task, always a boring task? Interest as a self-regulatory mechanism. *Journal of Personality and Social Psychology, 63*, 379–390.

Schank, R. C., & Abelson, R. P. (1977). *Scripts, plans, goals, and understanding*. Hillsdale, NJ: Erlbaum.

Schultz, W. (2002). Knowledge, information and household recycling: Examining the knowledge-deficit model. In T. Dietz & P. Stern (Eds.), *New tools for environmental protection: Education, information and voluntary measures* (pp. 67–82). Washington, DC: National Academy of Sciences.

Schultz, P. W., Nolan, J. M., Cialdini, R. B., Goldstein, N. J., & Griskevicius, V. (2007).The constructive, destructive, and reconstructive power of social norms. *Psychological Science, 18*, 429–434.

Schultz, P. W., Tabanico, J., & Rendón, T. (2008). Normative beliefs as agents of influence: Basic process and real-world applications. In W. D. Crano & R. Prislin (Eds.), *Attitudes and persuasion* (pp. 385–409). New York, NY: Psychology Press.

Stadler, G., Oettingen, G., & Gollwitzer, P. M. (2010). Intervention effects of information and self-regulation on eating fruits and vegetables over two years. *Health Psychology, 29*, 274–283.

Staunton, C. E., Hubsmith, D., & Kallin, W. (2003). Promoting safe walking and biking to school: The Marin County success story. *American Journal of Public Health, 93*, 1431–1433.

Tobias, R. (2009). Changing behavior by memory aids: A social psychological model of prospective memory and habit development tested with dynamic field data. *Psychological Review, 116*, 408–438.

Verplanken, B., & Faes, S. (1999). Good intentions, bad habits, and effects of forming implementation intentions on healthy eating. *European Journal of Social Psychology, 29*, 591–604.

Verplanken, B., & Wood, W. (2006). Interventions to break and create consumer habits. *Journal of Public Policy and Marketing, 25*, 90–103.

Webb, T. L., & Sheeran, P. (2008). Mechanisms of implementation intention effects: The goal of intentions, self-efficacy and accessibility of plan components. *British Journal of Social Psychology, 47*, 373–395.

Werner, C. M., Byerly, S., White, P. H., & Kieffer, M. (2004). Validation, persuasion and recycling: Capitalizing on the social ecology of newspaper use. *Basic and Applied Social Psychology, 26*, 183–198.

Werner, C. M., Cook, S., Colby, J., & Lim, H. (2012). "Lights out" in university classrooms: Brief group discussion can change behavior. *Journal of Environmental Psychology, 32*, 418–426.

Werner, C. M., & Makela, E. (1998). Motivations and behaviors that support recycling. *Journal of Environmental Psychology, 18*, 373–386.

Werner, C. M., Rhodes, M. U., & Partain, K. K. (1998). Designing effective instructional signs with schema theory: Case studies of polystyrene recycling. *Environment and Behavior, 30*, 709–735.

Werner, C. M., Sansone, C., & Brown, B. B. (2008). Guided group discussion and attitude change: The roles of normative and informational influence. *Journal of Environmental Psychology, 28*, 27–41.

Werner, C. M., & Stanley, C. P. (2011). Guided group discussion and the reported use of toxic products: The persuasiveness of hearing others' views. *Journal of Environmental Psychology, 31*, 289–300.

Werner, C. M., Stoll, R., Birch P., & White, P. H. (2002). Clinical validation and cognitive elaboration: Signs that encourage sustained recycling. *Basic and Applied Social Psychology, 24*, 185–204.

Wood, W., & Neal, D. T. (2007). A new look at habits and the habit-goal interface. *Psychological Review, 114*, 843–863.

Wood, W., Tam, L., & Witt, M. G. (2005). Changing circumstances, disrupting habits. *Journal of Personality and Social Psychology, 88*, 918–933.

12

Corporate Environmental Sustainability and Employee Recruitment: Leveraging "Green" Business Practices to Attract Talent

Chelsea R. Willness and David A. Jones

CHAPTER OVERVIEW

> ... an environmental lens is not just a nice strategy tool or a feel-good digression from the real work of a company. It's an essential element of business strategy in the modern world ... Smart companies seize competitive advantage through strategic management of environmental challenges.
>
> —Esty and Winston (2009, p. 3)

As described in by Pandey, Rupp, and Thornton (this book), corporate environmental sustainability is an important part of corporate social responsibility (CSR).[1] There is increasing pressure for companies to fulfill social goals beyond simply generating profits (Aguilera, Rupp, Williams, & Ganapathi, 2007; Aguinis, 2011) as more and more stakeholders now expect companies to conduct their business in a socially responsible manner (Chiu & Sharfman; 2011; Yoon, Gürhan-Canli, & Schwarz, 2006), including being environmentally sustainable. Corporate environmental sustainability refers to organizational practices intended to minimize an organization's impact on the natural environment, such as promoting internal or external environmental awareness campaigns, "greening" of the supply chain, and other efforts to reduce waste and conserve energy at and outside of work. Like other researchers who use the term *corporate social performance* to refer to an organization's commitment to principles, policies, and practices relating to social responsibility more broadly (Wood, 1991), we use *corporate environmental performance* (CEP) to refer to the extent to which an organization engages in practices that constitute environmental sustainability. Meta-analytic evidence suggests there is a business case for CEP, in that it is positively related to firm-level indicators of financial performance (Orlitzky, Schmidt, & Rynes, 2003). However, much less is known about how this occurs, in terms of the intervening factors or processes that link "planet" and "profit" (e.g., Aguinis & Glavas, 2012).

Recently, scholars have begun to examine how one stakeholder group—potential employees—might respond to companies' CEP. Human resources are among organizations' most valuable assets and can be a source of competitive advantage, and successful recruitment strategies enhance the utility of later human resource management practices like selection, training, and retention (Cable & Turban, 2001). In this chapter, we will describe studies on how environmentally-friendly business practices affect recruitment outcomes (e.g., Aiman-Smith, Bauer, & Cable, 2001; Backhaus, Stone, & Heiner, 2002; Greening & Turban, 2000). We will also present recent research that illuminates some of the reasons *why* CEP is attractive to some job seekers. We'll also explore several areas where more research is needed. In particular, we focus on a future research agenda to understand how job seekers find out about companies' CEP and the impact of information source credibility on recruitment outcomes. Lastly, we'll offer practical suggestions for leveraging CEP during recruitment.

ARE JOB SEEKERS ATTRACTED BY CEP?

The answer to this question appears to be "yes." Most recruitment studies have focused on corporate social performance more broadly, which comprises several domains in addition to environmental sustainability, such as attention to diversity, employee relations, and community involvement. Together, these studies suggest that companies known for social performance can attract more applicants (Aiman-Smith et al., 2001; Backhaus et al., 2002; Behrend, Baker, & Thompson, 2009; Greening & Turban, 2000; Luce, Barber, & Hillman, 2001; Schmidt Albinger & Freeman, 2000; Sen, Bhattacharya, & Korschun, 2006; Turban & Greening, 1997).

A few studies of employee recruitment have tested the effects of CEP more specifically, often in conjunction with other socially responsible business practices. For example, Aiman-Smith et al. (2001) conducted a study of graduating college students using a policy-capturing methodology. Their results showed that companies' ecological ratings had the strongest effects on attraction to organizations, followed by ratings of layoff policies. Greening and Turban (2000, pilot study) also used a policy-capturing approach and found that concern for the environment was related to student participants' ratings of organizational attractiveness, as well as the probability that they would accept a job offer with the company (they also found similar results for employee relations, treatment of women and minorities, and product quality).

In Bauer and Aiman-Smith's (1996) study, participants read a recruitment brochure about a fictitious company that was manipulated to be either ecologically oriented or not. Results showed that participants rated the company as more attractive when it was ecologically oriented. Backhaus et al. (2002) provided participants with numerical ratings on several dimensions of social responsibility for 50 companies from the Fortune 500 and found that information pertaining to the environment, community relations, and diversity had the strongest effects on organizational attractiveness. The causal effect of CEP on recruitment outcomes demonstrated in these experimental studies has also been corroborated by field research conducted among active job seekers (Jones, Willness, & Madey, 2010; Willness, Chapman, & Jones, 2011).

WHY ARE JOB SEEKERS ATTRACTED BY CEP?

As already shown, evidence is mounting that an organization's CEP is attractive to some job seekers. As such, CEP may ultimately increase selection system utility and, therefore, an organization's ability to hire top performers (Boudreau & Rynes, 1985). However, relatively little is known about *how* and *why* CEP may be effective for recruitment—indeed, Aguinis and Glavas (2012) observe an overall lack of individual-level research on CSR more broadly, as well as the need to examine the "underlying processes (i.e., mediating effects) and conditions under which (i.e., moderating effects) CSR leads to specific outcomes" (p. 3). So far, few studies have directly tested mechanisms that may explain this relationship, but there have been some promising findings suggesting at least three reasons why job seekers are attracted by CEP in particular. We argue that these mechanisms, which we soon describe, can be understood within the rubric of signaling theory (e.g., Rynes, 1991): because job seekers typically have little information about recruiting organizations upon which to base their job choice decisions, they make inferences based on signals from whatever information they do possess.

Signals From CEP and Perceived Value Fit

One mechanism examined in previous research is the value fit aspect of person-organization (P-O) fit (e.g., Kristof-Brown, Zimmerman, & Johnson, 2005). CEP sends signals about an organization's pro-environmental values, and job seekers who personally value the natural environment will find green companies attractive because they perceive a strong value fit with the organization. In recruitment studies on corporate social performance more broadly, several researchers have grounded their hypotheses in the P-O fit literature (e.g., Backhaus et al., 2002; Behrend et al., 2009; Turban & Greening, 1997). For instance, Greening and Turban (2000, p. 255) wrote, "Prospective applicants who have value systems that regard corporate social performance as an important endeavor will be more attracted to socially responsible firms than applicants without such values."

A few studies include explicit tests of a value fit mechanism to explain the attractiveness of CEP. Bauer and Aiman-Smith (1996) found that participants had stronger job pursuit intentions and rated a company as more attractive when it was ecologically oriented. However, there was mixed support in their study for the value fit mechanism: the effect of green practices on job pursuit intentions was stronger among participants with a pro-environmental stance, but no support was found for the hypothesis that individuals with stronger ecological orientations would be especially attracted to an ecologically-friendly company. Two other studies likewise failed to find support for the value fit mechanism (Behrend et al., 2009; Greening & Turban, 2000), although support was found in another study in which the relationship between an organization's overall image for social responsibility and organizational attractiveness was stronger among respondents who had greater environmental sensitivity (Tsai & Yang, 2010).

In our research, we have also found mixed support for the value fit mechanism. In a field study, we asked active job seekers to respond to survey items about an organization they identified as a desirable employment choice, and the results did not support the hypothesized interaction between individual and organizational environmental values in predicting attraction and job pursuit intentions (Willness, Jones, & Chapman, 2009). We did, however, find support for the value fit mechanism in another field study. We collected data from job seekers attending career fairs who provided ratings of a recruiting organization in which they were interested (Jones et al., 2010). Results showed that a direct measure of perceived value fit mediated the relationship between a company's green business practices and organizational attractiveness, including when CEP was measured via job seekers' perceptions of CEP or measured via the degree of CEP content in the organizations' recruitment materials. In an experimental study (Jones, Willness, & MacNeil, 2009), we asked participants to review the web pages of three companies, including a target company whose pages contained a manipulation such that some participants read about the organization's CEP, others read about the organization's community involvement, and the remainder did not read about any socially or environmentally responsible practices. Results showed that individuals had more favorable attitudes toward the target company and overwhelmingly ranked it as their top choice when its web pages contained information about its CEP than when it did not. We also found that perceived value fit mediated the relationship between pro-environmental attitudes and organizational attractiveness among individuals who read about a company's CEP. These findings support the notion that some job seekers are attracted to green organizations because they want to work in places they perceive as having similar values to their own. While this value fit mechanism passes the "common sense test," the evidence for it has been mixed. What explains this equivocal support?

The mixed support for the value fit mechanism may stem in part from a measurement choice. Unlike prior studies that failed to find support for the value fit mechanism for CEP (Backhaus et al., 2002; Bauer & Aiman-Smith, 1996; Behrend et al., 2009; Greening & Turban, 2000; Willness et al., 2009), in the Jones et al. (2010) study in which support was found, we did not attempt to measure specific personal values relating to the environment. Instead, we asked job seekers directly about the fit between their values and those of the organization. This direct measure of value fit allowed people to conceptualize value fit however they wished, including ways that could differ from the values that researchers assume to be most important. For instance, perhaps some job seekers perceive a good value fit with an organization that is high on CEP, but rather than this fit being due to job seekers' pro-environmental values, it is instead due to job seekers valuing the organization's attentiveness to external stakeholders.

Another potential reason for the equivocal support for the value fit mechanism is that a positive organizational reputation for CEP may be so universally appealing that it is attractive to job seekers for reasons that are largely independent from their environmental values. For instance, Greening and Turban (2000) suggest that even individuals who do not hold strong pro-environmental values may still evaluate an eco-friendly company positively. Similarly, Highhouse, Thornbury, and Little (2007) suggest that people may be motivated to work for green organizations due to value expressive concerns—in other words, job seekers may be attracted to a company's CEP because affiliation with an environmentally-friendly organization would allow them to express socially approved values, regardless of their own personal values. It is also conceivable that the findings for the value fit mechanism may be attributable in part to the "in vogue" nature of expressing concern for the environment, which introduces construct contamination in the measurement of environmental values; indeed, research has shown that these measures are particularly susceptible to response distortion (Ewert & Galloway, 2009).

Although research is needed to understand the reasons for this mixed support, the evidence warrants additional study of the value fit mechanism. Support for this mechanism has been found in the context of an organization's CEP (Jones et al., 2009; Tsai & Yang, 2010), including one field study in which CEP was operationalized in two ways (Jones et al., 2010).

Signals From CEP and Expected Employee Treatment

Recruitment scholars have suggested that potential applicants use information about a company's social and environmental performance as a signal upon which to base inferences about working conditions, which affects organizational attractiveness (Greening & Turban, 2000; Turban & Greening, 1997). Beyond the recruitment literature, other theory suggests that social responsibility can signal that an organization cares that people are treated in a just manner (Rupp, Ganapathi, Aguilera, & Williams, 2006; Pandey, Rupp & Thornton, this book). As such, we contend that job seekers infer an organization's prosocial orientation (i.e., that it is a caring organization) from its CEP, which leads to expectations of favorable employee treatment. Support for this expected treatment mechanism has been found in two of our studies. In Jones et al. (2009), we found that participants who read about a company's CEP had stronger expectations for favorable employee treatment, compared with individuals who read about the same company without information about its green practices, and that the effects of CEP information on organizational attractiveness were mediated by expected employee treatment (but only when a particularly strong mediated effect through anticipated pride was removed from the model).

In the Jones et al. (2010) field study of career fair attendees, we found that expected employee treatment mediated the relationship between job seekers' perceptions of an organization's CEP and its attractiveness as an employer, but the mediated effect for community involvement was relatively stronger. This difference was expected because community involvement pertains more directly to an organization's concern for people, which presumably sends a strong signal that the organization is also concerned for the well-being of its own people—its employees. Research is needed to test whether inferences about expected treatment follow from signals sent by CEP when the CEP conveys the organization's general moral standing. Favorable employee treatment, especially fair treatment, is inherently tied to moral concerns (Folger, 2001); thus, job seekers may form expectations about employee treatment upon learning about any morally laden information about an organization, including information about its CEP.

Signals From CEP and Anticipated Pride

Research suggests that another reason green practices foster attraction is because they provide signals about an organization's reputation and prestige, which leads some job seekers to anticipate feeling a sense of pride from being affiliated with that organization. This mechanism is grounded in the principles of social identity theories: people derive part of their identities through their employer (Dutton & Dukerich, 1991), and because positive self-images are desirable, individuals tend to identify more strongly with an organization when they believe other people view the organization as prestigious (Mael & Ashforth, 1992).

Several researchers have used social identity theories to explain why job seekers are attracted by CSR, but they did not test this mechanism explicitly (e.g., Backhaus et al., 2002; Greening & Turban, 2000; Turban & Greening, 1997). In one exception, Behrend et al. (2009) found that an environmental message on a website was associated with student participants' job pursuit intentions through its effect on perceived prestige. We have found support for the role of a prestigious organizational reputation and anticipated pride in three of our studies. In Jones et al. (2009), we found that the effect of the presence versus absence of CEP information on a website on organizational attractiveness was mediated by anticipated pride from organizational membership. In a study of 240 job seekers (Willness et al., 2011),[2] we found that perceived organizational prestige fully mediated the relationships between job seekers' perceptions of CEP with organizational attractiveness and job pursuit intentions. In Jones et al. (2010), we tested the organizational prestige signal among job seekers who attended career fairs and found that the relationship between organizational attractiveness and perceived CEP was mediated by job seekers' judgments of organizational prestige.

CEP AND RECRUITMENT: A RESEARCH AGENDA

> … future research needs to refocus on basic research in order to develop conceptual tools and theoretical mechanisms that explain changing organizational behavior from a broader societal perspective.
>
> —Lee (2008, p. 53)

We echo Lee's (2008) call for further research to inform how organizational practices can be designed in a manner that contributes to broader societal goals. To this end, we have discussed elsewhere several methodological issues and considerations for the study of socially and environmentally responsible business practices in the context of recruitment (Jones & Willness, forthcoming 2013). Additional research that offers insight into the effects of CEP on recruitment outcomes will better enable industrial-organizational (I-O) researchers and practitioners to assist organizations that wish to leverage their green practices for recruiting, thereby improving the return on those investments. This, in turn, should encourage and enhance companies' interest in continuing to invest in CEP, which ultimately can lead to social good and a healthier planet. In recent years, we have witnessed increasing scholarly attention given to how CEP impacts recruitment outcomes, but there are still many unanswered questions. For example, as outlined earlier, recent research has uncovered three signal-based mechanisms for explaining the CEP-recruitment relationship, but further research is necessary to examine additional signals that job seekers might infer from organizations' CEP (e.g., about the organization's financial standing, compensation levels, or the kinds of people who work there). In the next sections, we highlight several gaps in current knowledge about CEP and recruitment to inform a future research agenda.

How Do Job Seekers Acquire Information About an Organization's CEP?

In prior studies, researchers have communicated CEP information to experimental participants through company websites (Behrend et al., 2009; Jones et al., 2009) and recruitment brochures (Bauer & Aiman-Smith, 1996). Also plausible is that job seekers learn about CEP through recruiters, word of mouth, media articles, rankings of "greener" companies, and via the organization's advertising campaigns. However, other than evidence showing that recruitment materials are a source of CEP information (Jones et al., 2010), no other studies have tested whether job seekers use these or other sources for CEP information.

There is some evidence that people generally have low awareness of companies' socially responsible practices (Bhattacharya & Sen, 2004). For instance, Bhattacharya, Sen, and Korschun (2008) found that only 37% of employees surveyed were aware of their *own* company's social responsibility initiatives; in another study, these authors showed that external stakeholders' awareness was even lower, such that only 17% of respondents indicated any knowledge of a widely publicized social responsibility initiative undertaken by a well-known Fortune 500 firm (Sen et al., 2006). Thus, one fruitful avenue for future research would be examining the process through which job seekers, and other stakeholders, come to know about an organization's CEP—what catches their attention, when is the CEP information memorable or distinctive, and when is it perceived to be credible and believable?

Research has also shown that how deeply people process recruitment messages affects recruitment outcomes—argument quality matters most when messages are deeply processed, whereas "peripheral" characteristics of a message, such as its layout and use of symbols, are persuasive when processed with less scrutiny (Jones, Shultz, & Chapman, 2006). CEP information obtained from some sources may be processed quite carefully, such as when job seekers learn about it during an employment interview or from close friends, whereas CEP information from other sources may be processed relatively automatically and less critically, such as CEP information in marketing messages directed toward consumers.

What Affects the Credibility of CEP Information?

Stakeholders' perceptions of organizational legitimacy and the credibility of CEP information can be affected by the source of the information about a firm's socially and environmentally responsible practices (Groza, Pronschinske, & Walker, 2011). For instance, messages about the firm's CEP delivered from the organization's own public relations department may be seen as particularly self-serving, and even suspicious, leading people to question the credibility of the claim (Groza et al., 2011; Yoon et al., 2006), compared with hearing about the organization's CEP initiatives from some third party—in other words, a source that is external to the firm, such as the media or one's peers. In fact, when it comes to environmental issues, one study found that only about 8% of Americans saw business leaders as a credible information source, and even fewer felt that organizations were taking sufficient steps toward environmental protection (Dold, 1991).

Thus far, there has been very little research exploring source credibility issues in the recruiting literature with respect to CEP; however, scholars have highlighted the importance of information source credibility during recruitment more generally, noting that there are indeed differences in perceived credibility depending on the recruitment source (Fisher, Ilgen, & Hoyer, 1979). For example, past research demonstrates that trustworthiness, expertise, and the absence of personal gain are all related to how credible and believable—and ultimately how persuasive—a recruitment message is perceived to be (Breaugh & Starke, 2000; Cable & Turban, 2001; Pornpitakpan, 2004). For these reasons, and especially the role of attributed personal gain in credibility judgments, it is perhaps understandable why business leaders might be viewed as relatively poor sources of information about environmental issues, as described earlier. In contrast to this information source, Van Hoye and Lievens (2007) found that positive word of mouth, especially when it comes from close friends as opposed to other acquaintances, enhanced the credibility of recruitment advertising and organizational attractiveness. This same study also showed that negative, rather than positive, word of mouth about potential employers had a much greater impact on attractiveness. This finding is consistent with other research showing that negatively valenced information is typically more diagnostic and, thus, given greater weighting in judgments compared with positive information (Trope & Bassok, 1982).

Van Hoye and Lievens (2007) describe another important consideration: internal sources of information (like recruiters, or the company's own website) are sources within the organization's control. Organizations can largely dictate the content and presentation of that information, but external information sources such as word of mouth or media are outside the organization's control. Theory and research suggest that companies should attempt to build a positive CEP image through information provided by external sources (Cable & Turban, 2001; Groza et al., 2011), and pay close attention to organizational activities that have the greatest potential impact on word of mouth, such as campus recruiting or internships (Van Hoye & Lievens, 2007).

Despite the presumed appeal to organizations of utilizing external sources of CEP information, they should not discount the benefits of internal information sources. Walker, Feild, Giles, Armenakis, and Berneerth (2009) found that participants' perceptions of information credibility and organizational attractiveness were higher when they viewed employee testimonials about an organization's culture on its website, compared with when employee testimonials were not available. Walker et al. (2009) also found that credibility and attractiveness were higher when the testimonial was presented via video rather than text, concluding that media-richness does make a difference (see also Cable & Yu, 2006). Thus, organizations might show potential employees video footage and testimonials from employees who are actively involved in promoting the organization's green practices. Given that the vast majority of Fortune 500 firms include information about socially and environmentally responsible practices on their websites (e.g., Whitehouse, 2006), these findings offer a practical way to enhance the credibility of internally developed CEP information.

Researchers should examine whether the findings discussed in this section hold with respect to CEP information in particular, as well as continuing to investigate other factors that might affect how CEP information is perceived.[3] For instance, research on realistic job previews (e.g., Breaugh, 1992) suggests that providing a mix of both positive and negative information—a more balanced and accurate account—can increase the perceived trustworthiness of the source. The accuracy of job seekers' perceptions of CEP is also important, as un-met expectations have been associated with negative post-hire outcomes like voluntary turnover (Premack & Wanous, 1985). This has yet to be tested with respect to CEP and recruitment. Also, as mentioned earlier, we still know little about whether and how stakeholders become aware of organizations' CEP, making this an important question for future research because judging the credibility of CEP claims only becomes an issue if one is aware of the CEP information in the first place. As Cable and Turban (2001, p. 119) argue, "job seekers' employer knowledge is a primary source of a firm's recruitment success or failure," and knowledge of CEP may be an important key to recruitment success for organizations that leverage it.

The Hazards of "Greenwashing": Can CEP Be Perceived Negatively?

A cursory review of business Web sites reveals an astounding array of assertions about green management, some of them truly astonishing given that the businesses making them (consider for instance, Exxon-Mobil) have less than totally clean histories.
—Marcus and Fremeth (2009, p. 17)

Organizations' claims of pursuing the "triple bottom line" (simultaneously considering economic, social, and environmental goals) may be met with skepticism by stakeholders, especially in light of the numerous reasons why organizations may profess to have such goals, ranging from addressing public and media scrutiny to improving trust in the organizations' stakeholder relationships (Aguinis, 2011). In a recruitment context, the timing and strategic integration of CEP, as well as the perceived motivations for engaging in green business practices or environmental initiatives, might also impact job seekers' impressions of organizational attractiveness and other recruitment outcomes. For instance, some scholars have examined proactive versus reactive approaches to corporate environmental sustainability. Proactive CEP strategies are environmentally-oriented initiatives that the company engages in or supports prior to the occurrence of negative incidents involving the firm. In contrast, reactive CEP would occur after the fact as a way of attempting to mitigate the negative fallout or repair company image resulting from some socially irresponsible company action (Du, Bhattacharya, & Sen, 2007; Groza et al., 2011; Wagner, Lutz, & Weitz, 2009). The proactive approach likely engenders stronger trust and facilitates attributions of the credibility of CEP information among job seekers.

Consumer behavior studies on corporate social performance more broadly have used attribution theories, which outline how people ascribe underlying motives for others' behavior in order to understand cause and effect, to explain how individuals respond to companies' proactive versus reactive CEP. For instance, research demonstrates that proactive strategies are perceived to be more values-driven, and thus more altruistic, which elicits more favorable company evaluations (e.g., Becker-Olsen, Cudmore, & Hill, 2006; Ellen, Mohr, & Webb, 2006). However, reactive strategies are typically viewed negatively by consumers (Groza et al., 2011) and can even damage a company's previously positive image (Ricks, 2005). Furthermore, Ellen et al. (2006) propose different types of attributions that consumers ascribe to companies' social responsibility motives, including *values-driven* (e.g., owners and employees truly care about the cause), *stakeholder-driven* (e.g., customers, suppliers, stockholders, or employees expect certain practices), *egoistic* (e.g., to gain positive publicity), and *strategic-driven* (e.g., to promote customer retention or profits). They found that people's reactions to corporate social performance were more complex than originally thought, and different attributions resulted in different consequences for the firm. In general, values-driven and strategic-driven attributions resulted in positive perceptions of the company, while egoistic and stakeholder-driven motives were perceived more negatively.

Other consumer behavior studies have similarly shown that when consumers become suspicious or skeptical of a company's motives for social or environmental initiatives, it can activate negative attributions (Yoon et al., 2006) and greater elaborative processing about the company's social responsibility claims (White & Willness, 2009), leading to negative company and product evaluations. There has been little exploration of these factors in the recruiting literature, and future research examining different CEP strategies could offer important insights into applicant attraction and job choice.

Another phenomenon that has received surprisingly little research attention, despite potentially negative outcomes for recruiting organizations, is stakeholders' perceptions of "greenwashing": when a company provides misleading or disingenuous information about its environmental products, services, or overall business practices (e.g., TerraChoice, 2010). Some advertising researchers have observed that individuals are exposed to an overwhelming number of green claims on a daily basis, making it difficult to separate fact from fiction (e.g., Manrai, Manrai, Lascu, & Ryans, 1997). Indeed, in their study of over 5,000 products in Canada and the United States, TerraChoice(2010) found that the number of green products increased 73% in a single year between 2009 and 2010; of those green product claims, 95% were found to reflect some degree of greenwashing. Marketing studies have found, perhaps not surprisingly, that consumers can become suspicious of such claims and engage in message discounting, and may evaluate the company and its products negatively as a result (Manrai et al., 1997), but there has been no such investigation in a recruiting context to date.

Additional Questions

Past research has concluded that because CEP can positively impact job applicant attraction and other recruitment outcomes, organizations can gain a competitive advantage in recruiting talent (e.g., Greening & Turban, 2000). But what happens if several—or perhaps all—companies in a given industry begin promoting their CEP and it becomes par for the course? As Bhattacharya et al. (2008, p. 41) point out, "what was once ancillary to business practice is quickly becoming an essential element of corporate strategy." This highlights the fact that little, if any, research has explored the potential boundary conditions of the CEP-recruitment relationship, such as whether and the extent to which CEP innovations offer a distinctive and inimitable source of competitive advantage. Other fruitful avenues for future research include examining *who* is attracted by CEP—does CEP attract not just more applicants, but better applicants?—and how CEP information might affect recruitment outcomes when it is obtained during later recruitment stages (see Jones & Willness, forthcoming 2013, for a discussion of these issues).

GREEN RECRUITMENT IN PRACTICE

The research and theory reviewed in this chapter have several practical implications for organizations' recruiting strategies. We noted earlier that awareness of CEP and other socially responsible business practices is typically low, so an organization may gain competitive advantage by actively seeking out opportunities to increase stakeholders' knowledge of its CEP. In this way, the recruitment process provides an excellent venue for building awareness and reputational capital. Recruiters could highlight the organization's CEP via several media including on the organization's website; in job postings, recruitment posters, and handouts; and during conversations at job fairs, site visits, and employment interviews.

When communicating about CEP, recruiters can leverage the three signal-based mechanisms to increase the organization's return on its investments in green business practices. Pertaining to perceived value fit, recruiters could discuss the organization's environmental values and practices with job seekers, and advertise the company's CEP in order to attract applicants for whom there is a good fit. With respect to inferences about expectations for favorable employee treatment, recruiters and recruitment materials could provide information that makes this signal-based mechanism explicit for potential job applicants; for instance, "we care about how we treat the planet and we care about how we treat our people." To leverage the anticipated pride mechanism, organizations could also highlight the prestige of the firm that is associated with awards or other recognition for their CEP.

More broadly, the findings regarding signal-based mechanisms suggest that job seekers may get more information from CEP than meets the eye. Recruiters, managers, and marketers should be cognizant of the fact that job seekers—and potentially other stakeholders—appear to make numerous inferences about a company based on its CEP, beyond the face-value knowledge of its pro-environmental practices. Fortunately, it appears these inferences often have positive consequences, such as increased organizational attractiveness. However, recruiters should be mindful to ensure authenticity and accuracy when communicating about CEP in order to avoid the deleterious consequences that likely follow from skepticism about the credibility of CEP information, suspicions of greenwashing, and newly hired employees' unmet expectations.

Recruiters should recognize that internal versus external sources of CEP information may be perceived differently by job seekers, particularly in terms of its credibility and the underlying motives job seekers attribute to the organization's environmental practices. Credibility may be enhanced through communicating CEP through external sources, such as third-party recognition or word of mouth, and perhaps through the use of some internal sources like employee testimonials and live exposure to the organization's green practices in action during site visits. Credibility might also be enhanced by providing an honest assessment of "areas of opportunity" in conjunction with specific goals to demonstrate the organization's commitment to continuous improvement in its pursuit of sustainable business practices.

The credibility of CEP information is likely enhanced when an organization can demonstrate a proactive approach to CEP by embedding pro-environmental considerations and policies throughout its production and distribution of goods and services. An obvious starting point is the organization's core human resource management practices, including recruitment and selection, which should reflect a commitment to environmental sustainability (Jackson, Renwick, Jabbour, & Muller-Camen, 2011). Also important is to demonstrate support and commitment to CEP from all managers—from managers on the front lines to the senior leadership team—through visible statements and testimonials, because managerial support for CEP has been shown to "trickle down" to employees (Ramus & Steger, 2000). Commitment from management and embedding environmental considerations into core business practices also demonstrates that the organization's CEP is values-driven and strategic-driven—this not only leads to more favorable responses to the organization's CEP, but also shows that the organization "walks the walk." To the extent that recruiting organizations can communicate their CEP in a manner that is both credible and enticing to potential applicants, organizations will benefit from their enhanced ability to attract talent, and the natural environment will benefit from increasingly sustainable business practices.

NOTES

1. Although we use the term "corporate" for greater consistency with the existing literature, we note that the research and recommendations presented in this chapter apply to all types of organizations (for- and non-profit, cooperatives, sole proprietorships, etc.; see Aguinis, 2011, for a more detailed discussion of "organizational responsibility").

2. These participants were part of a larger study, portions of which were presented in Willness et al. (2009).
3. We refer the reader to Pornpitakpan's (2004) comprehensive review of the influence of source credibility, and the variables that may moderate message credibility and persuasiveness. Much of this research has been conducted in a marketing and consumer behavior context, but there are parallels between this context and a recruiting context (see Cable & Turban, 2001).

REFERENCES

Aguilera, R. V., Rupp, D. E., Williams, C. A., & Ganapathi, J. (2007). Putting the S back in corporate social responsibility: A multilevel theory of social change in organizations. *Academy of Management Review, 32,* 836–863.

Aguinis, H. (2011). Organizational responsibility: Doing good and doing well. In S. Zedeck (Ed.), *APA handbook of industrial and organizational psychology* (*Vol. 3,* pp. 855–879). Washington, DC: American Psychological Association (APA).

Aguinis, H., & Glavas, A. (2012). What we know and don't know about corporate social responsibility: A review and research agenda. *Journal of Management, 38,* 932–968.

Aiman-Smith, L., Bauer, T. N., & Cable, D. M. (2001). Are you attracted? Do you intend to pursue? A recruiting policy-capturing study. *Journal of Business and Psychology, 16,* 219–237.

Backhaus, K. B., Stone, B. A., & Heiner, K. A. (2002). Exploring the relationship between corporate social performance and employer attractiveness. *Business and Society, 41,* 292–318.

Bauer, T. N., & Aiman-Smith, L. (1996). Green career choices: The influences of ecological stance on recruiting. *Journal of Business and Psychology, 10,* 445–458.

Becker-Olsen, K. L., Cudmore, B. A., & Hill, R. P. (2006). The impact of perceived Corporate Social Responsibility on consumer behavior. *Journal of Business Research, 59,* 46–53.

Behrend, T. S., Baker, B. A., & Thompson, L. F. (2009). Effects of pro-environmental recruiting messages: The role of organizational reputation. *Journal of Business and Psychology, 24,* 341–350.

Bhattacharya, C. B., & Sen, S. (2004). Doing better at doing good: When, why, and how consumers respond to corporate social initiatives. *California Management Review, 47,* 9–24.

Bhattacharya, C. B., Sen, S., & Korschun, D. (2008). Using Corporate Social Responsibility to win the war for talent. *MIT Sloan Management Review,* Winter, 37–44.

Boudreau, J. W., & Rynes, S. L. (1985). Role of recruitment in staffing utility analysis. *Journal of Applied Psychology, 70,* 354–366.

Breaugh, J. A. (1992). *Recruitment: Science and practice.* Boston, MA: PWS-Kent.

Breaugh, J. A., & Starke, M. (2000). Research on employee recruitment: So many studies, so many remaining questions. *Journal of Management, 26,* 405–434.

Cable, D. M., & Turban, D. B. (2001). Establishing the dimensions, sources, and value of job seekers' employer knowledge during recruitment. In G. R. Ferris (Ed.), *Research in personnel and human resources management* (*Vol. 20,* pp. 115–163). New York, NY: Elsevier.

Cable, D. M., & Yu, T. K. Y. (2006). Managing job seekers' organizational image beliefs:

The role of media richness and media credibility. *Journal of Applied Psychology, 91,* 828–840.

Chiu, S. C., & Sharfman, M. (2011). Legitimacy, visibility, and the antecedents of Corporate Social Performance: An investigation of the instrumental perspective. *Journal of Management, 37,* 1558–1585.

Dold, C. A. (1991). Green marketing: Hold down the noise. *Advertising Age, 62, Green Marketing Special Report, 62,* GR 7 and GR 13.

Du, S., Bhattacharya, C. B., & Sen, S. (2007). Reaping relational rewards from Corporate Social Responsibility: The role of competitive positioning. *International Journal of Research in Marketing, 24,* 224–241.

Dutton, J. E., & Dukerich, J. M. (1991). Keeping an eye on the mirror: The role of image and identity in organizational adaptation. *Academy of Management Journal, 34,* 517–554.

Ellen, P. S., Webb, D. J., & Mohr, L. A. (2006). Building corporate associations: Consumer attributions for corporate socially responsible programs. *Journal of the Academy of Marketing Science, 34,* 147–157.

Esty, D. C., & Winston, A. S. (2009). *Green to gold: How smart companies use environmental strategy to innovate, create value, and build competitive advantage.* Hoboken, NJ: Wiley.

Ewert, A., & Galloway, G. (2009). Socially desirable responding in an environmental context: Development of a domain specific scale. *Environmental Education Research, 15,* 55–70.

Fisher, C. D., Ilgen, D. R., & Hoyer, W. D. (1979). Source credibility, information favorability, and job offer acceptance. *Academy of Management Journal, 22,* 94–103.

Folger, R. (2001). Fairness as deonance. In S. W. Gilliland, D. D. Steiner, & D. P. Skarlicki (Eds.), *Research in social issues in management (Vol. 1,* 3–33). New York, NY: Information Age.

Greening, D. W., & Turban, D. B. (2000). Corporate Social Performance as a competitive advantage in attracting a quality workforce. *Business and Society, 39,* 254–280.

Groza, M. D., Pronschinske, M. R., & Walker, M. (2011). Perceived organizational motives and consumer responses to proactive and reactive CSR. *Journal of Business Ethics, 102,* 639–652.

Highhouse, S., Thornbury, E. E., & Little, I. S. (2007). Social-identity functions of attraction to organizations. *Organizational Behavior and Human Decision Processes, 103,* 134–146.

Jackson, S. E., Renwick, D. W. S., Jabbour, C. J. C., & Muller-Camen, M. (2011). State-of-the-art and future directions for green human resource management: Introduction to the special issue. *Zeitschrift für Personalforschung (German Journal of Research in Human Resource Management), 25,* 99–116.

Jones, D. A., Shultz, J. W., & Chapman, D. S. (2006). Recruiting through job advertisements: The effects of cognitive elaboration on decision making. *International Journal of Selection and Assessment, 14,* 167–179.

Jones, D. A., & Willness, C. R. (forthcoming 2013). Corporate social performance, organizational reputation, and recruitment. In K. Y. T. Yu & D. Cable (Eds.), *The Oxford handbook of recruitment.* Oxford University Press.

Jones, D. A., Willness, C. R., & MacNeil, S. (2009). Corporate social responsibility and recruitment: Person-organization fit and signaling mechanisms. In G. T. Solomon (Ed.), *Proceedings of the 69th Annual Meeting of the Academy of Management,* ISSN 1543–8643. Descriptions of study results are based on an updated and full version of this paper obtained October 20, 2012.

Jones, D. A., Willness, C. R., & Madey, S. (2010). Why are job seekers attracted to socially responsible companies? Testing underlying mechanisms. In L. A. Toombs (Ed.), *Proceedings of the 70th Annual Meeting of the Academy of Management (CD)*, ISSN 1543–8643. Descriptions of study results are based on an updated and full version of this paper obtained October 20, 2012.

Kristof-Brown, A. L., Zimmerman, R. D., & Johnson, E. C. (2005). Consequences of individuals' fit at work: A meta-analysis of person-job, person-organization, person-group, and person-supervisor fit. *Personnel Psychology, 58*, 281–342.

Lee, M. D. P. (2008). A review of the theories of corporate social responsibility: Its evolutionary path and the road ahead. *International Journal of Management Reviews, 10*, 53–73.

Luce, R. A., Barber, A. E., & Hillman, A. J. (2001). Good deeds and misdeeds: A mediated model of the effect of corporate social performance on organizational attractiveness. *Business and Society, 40*, 397–415.

Mael, F. A., & Ashforth, B. E. (1992). Alumni and their alma mater: A partial test of the reformulated model of organizational identification. *Journal of Organizational Behavior, 13*, 103–123.

Manrai, L. A., Manrai, A. K., Lascu, D. N., & Ryans, J. K., Jr. (1997). How green-claim strength and country disposition affect product evaluation and company image. *Psychology and Marketing, 14*, 511–537.

Marcus, A. A., & Fremeth, A. R. (2009). Green management matters regardless. *Academy of Management Perspectives*, August, 17–26.

Orlitzky, M., Schmidt, F. L., & Rynes, S. L. (2003). Corporate social and financial performance: A meta-analysis. *Organization Studies, 24*, 403–441.

Pornpitakpan, C. (2004). The persuasiveness of source credibility: A critical review of five decades' evidence. *Journal of Applied Social Psychology, 34*, 243–281.

Premack, S. L., & Wanous, J. P. (1985). A meta-analysis of realistic job preview experiments. *Journal of Applied Psychology, 70*, 706–719.

Ramus, C. A., & Steger, U. (2000). The roles of supervisory support behaviors and environmental policy in employee "ecoinitiatives" at leading-edge European companies. *Academy of Management Journal, 43*, 605–626.

Ricks, J. M., Jr. (2005). An assessment of strategic corporate philanthropy on perceptions of brand equity variables. *Journal of Consumer Marketing, 22*, 121–134.

Rupp, D. E., Ganapathi, J., Aquilera, R. V., & Williams, C. A. (2006). Employee reactions to corporate social responsibility: An organizational justice framework. *Journal of Organizational Behavior, 27*, 537–543.

Rynes, S. L. (1991). Recruitment, job choice, and post-hire consequences: A call for new research directions. In M. D. Dunnette & L. M. Hough (Eds.), *Handbook of Industrial and Organizational Psychology* (2nd ed., Vol. 2, pp. 399–444). Palo Alto, CA: Consulting Psychologists Press.

Schmidt Albinger, H., & Freeman, S. J. (2000). Corporate social performance and attractiveness as an employer to different job seeking populations. *Journal of Business Ethics, 28*, 243–253.

Sen, S., Bhattacharya, C. B., & Korschun, D. (2006). The role of corporate social responsibility in strengthening multiple stakeholder relationships: A field experiment. *Journal of the Academy of Marketing Science, 34*, 158–166.

TerraChoice (2010). *The sins of greenwashing: Home and family edition 2010*. Retrieved December 29, 2012 from http://terrachoice.com/learn/reports

Trope, Y., & Bassok, M. (1982). Confirmatory and diagnosing strategies in information gathering. *Journal of Personality and Social Psychology, 43,* 22–24.

Tsai, W. C., & Yang, I. W. F. (2010). Does image matter to different job applicants? The influences of corporate image and applicant individual differences on organizational attractiveness. *International Journal of Selection and Assessment, 18,* 48–63.

Turban, D. B., & Greening, D. W. (1997). Corporate social performance and organizational attractiveness. *Academy of Management Journal, 40,* 658–672.

Van Hoye, G., & Lievens, F. (2007). Social influences on organizational attractiveness: Investigating if and when word of mouth matters. *Journal of Applied Social Psychology, 37,* 2024–2047.

Wagner, T., Lutz, R. J., & Weitz, B. A. (2009). Corporate hypocrisy: Overcoming the threat of inconsistent Corporate Social Responsibility perceptions. *Journal of Marketing, 73,* 77–91.

Walker, H. J., Feild, H. S., Giles, W. F., Armenakis, A. A., & Bernerth, J. B. (2009). Displaying employee testimonials on recruitment web sites: Effects of communication media, employee race, and job seeker race on organizational attraction and information credibility. *Journal of Applied Psychology, 94,* 1354–1364.

White, K., & Willness, C. R. (2009). Consumer reactions to the decreased usage message: The role of elaborative processing. *Journal of Consumer Psychology, 19,* 73–87.

Whitehouse, L. (2006). Corporate social responsibility: Views from the frontline. *Journal of Business Ethics, 63,* 279–296.

Willness, C. R., Chapman, D. S., & Jones, D. A. (2011, April). *Green business practices: Doing good and looking good.* Presented at the 26th Annual Conference of the Society for Industrial and Organizational Psychology (SIOP), Chicago, IL.

Willness, C. R., Jones, D. A., & Chapman, D. S. (2009, April). *Attracting applicants through corporate social responsibility: A real world test.* Presented at the 24th Annual Meeting of the Society for Industrial and Organizational Psychology, New Orleans, LA.

Wood, D. J. (1991). Corporate social performance revisited. *Academy of Management Review, 16,* 691–718.

Yoon, Y., Gürhan-Canli, Z., & Schwarz, N. (2006). The effect of corporate social responsibility activities on companies with bad reputations. *Journal of Consumer Psychology, 16,* 377

13

Sustainable Business: A Fortune 500 Corporate Perspective

Craig R. Barrett and Gary Niekerk

Inventions such as the printing press, automobile, and computer have radically altered the way people live, work, and connect to each other. The computer and related technologies such as the internet are all built on a foundation of ubiquitous, inexpensive, and ever-powerful semi-conductors. For over 40 years, Intel Corporation has been inventing and building the devices and technologies that are fueling an ongoing digital revolution.

Intel is the world's largest semiconductor chip maker, based on revenue (IC Insights, 2011). Intel develops advanced integrated digital technology, primarily integrated circuits, for industries such as computing, communications, and industrial control. Integrated circuits are semiconductor chips etched with interconnected electronic switches. The majority of Intel's revenue is derived from the design and manufacture of semiconductor chips for personal computers and servers.

Intel has one of the most recognizable brands in the world with an estimated brand value of over $35 billion (Interbrand, 2011). Intel has received wide recognition and acclaim for its technology prowess, innovations, and contribution to business around the world (White House, 2011); however, what may not be as widely known is Intel's leadership in environmental sustainability. Intel was named in the 2012 list of the "Global 100 Most Sustainable Corporations in the World" for the eighth consecutive year and was ranked in the top 20 on the international list (Corporate Knights, 2012). Similarly, in the United States, Intel was ranked #5 in the 2010 *Newsweek* magazine's "500 Greenest Companies in America." Intel has been included in the well-respected Dow Jones Sustainability Indexes (DSJI) for 13 consecutive years, and was ranked #8 in the 2010 Global 1000 Sustainable Performance Leaders (Dow Jones Indexes, 2011).

Intel has been the largest voluntary purchaser of renewable energy credits in the United States since 2008, and in 2011 it purchased more than 2.5 billion kilowatt-hours of renewable energy certificates, generated from wind, solar, geothermal, low impact hydro, and biomass sources—which were all Green-e certified (U.S. Environmental Protection Agency, 2012). Intel's purchase has the equivalent environmental impact of taking more than 340,000 passenger cars off the road each year, or avoiding the amount of electricity needed to power more than 215,000 average American homes annually (Intel, 2009a).

From its earliest days, Intel has been integrating environmental sustainability into the company's culture and business practices. This chapter will explore the cultural, organizational, and business factors driving Intel's success in the area of environmental sustainability. From its "design for the environment" program, which drives environmental improvements into each new manufacturing and technology process, to its efforts to create energy-efficient technologies and solutions to address the world's most pressing environmental challenges, Intel has been successful in making the company, its products, and the world more sustainable.

INTEL CORPORATION

It all started in 1968 when Gordon E. Moore, famous for "Moore's Law" (defined in the next paragraph) and Robert Noyce, co-inventor of the integrated circuit, founded a company called Intel. The name was derived from combining the words "integrated" and "electronics." From its modest beginning, Intel Corporation has developed into a technology titan that has significantly contributed to society through the development of innovative technologies, positive economic impacts, and its commitment to being a leader in corporate sustainability. Today, Intel is the largest semiconductor manufacturer in the world (IC Insights, 2011), and a prolific inventor of technologies as measured by being in the top five of American companies in patents received (1,255 patents) in 2011 (IFI CLAIMS Patent Services, 2012). Intel has more than 100,000 employees operating in over 50 countries and revenues from the fiscal year 2011 were over $50 billion.

MOORE'S LAW

In 1965, Gordon Moore published an article that contained his observation that the number of transistors on a semiconductor chip would double roughly every two years, and that this innovation was critically needed to drive the industry forward and meet the demands of future technologies (Moore, 1965). This visionary supposition, which later became known as "Moore's Law" has been a driving force in the semiconductor industry for over 45 years. Moore's Law has resulted in extraordinary achievements in semiconductor development where today a small hand-held consumer device can contain more computation power than what required rooms full of computers only a few decades ago. Relentlessly pursuing Moore's Law has created both challenges and opportunities for sustainability at Intel.

It should be noted that Intel co-founder Gordon Moore continues to promote environmental causes in his retirement. Gordon Moore retired from Intel in 2001, and in that same year the Gordon and Betty Moore Foundation pledged $261 million to Conservation International to identify and protect concentrations of biodiversity around the globe. At that time, it was reported as the largest gift ever to a private environmental organization (Marosi, 2001).

SUSTAINABILITY INSIDE INTEL

Building and designing the world's most sophisticated products in an environmentally-sustainable manner is a formidable task. Semiconductor manufacturing or fabrication is a complex process consisting of hundreds of individual steps many of which can be chemically intensive. Making semiconductors is complex and expensive, and doing it with a mind towards sustainability requires Intel to consider environmental impacts throughout all phases of the product development or life cycle. For example, Intel performs an environmental analysis when selecting a new site or designing a new building. It establishes environmental performance goals for manufacturing tools and process technologies, and sets specific energy-efficiency goals for new products.

Intel believes that you cannot separate the health of your business from the health of your manufacturing facility, and business has a fundamental responsibility to consider the long-term consequences of its activities on the environment. Furthermore, a strategy of sustainability creates long-term shareholder value by managing risks, driving operational efficiency, enhancing the corporation's brand and creating new potential sources of revenue.

Intel's formula for excellence in environmental sustainability is built around three main ideas: (1) sustainability in its most basic terms is simply good business, (2) to achieve success, companies need to integrate sustainability into their existing management systems, tools, and culture; and (3) the relentless pursuit of Moore's law—which in itself is a pursuit of ever greater efficiency—can drive greater environmental performance.

Moore's Law enables Intel to both increase the use of sustainability principles into the design of new products and sell technology solutions that can play a vital role in making the world more sustainable. Moore's Law has transformed the modern transistor into one of the world's most effective tools for environmental sustainability.

INTEGRATING SUSTAINABILITY INTO THE BUSINESS

Intel's vision, as published in its most recent corporate responsibility report, is to "create and extend computing technology to connect and enrich the lives of every person on earth." Intel further states that one of its four strategic focus areas is, "Care for our people and the planet, and inspire the next generation" (Intel, 2011). A commitment to sustainability from the highest levels in the company is a critical ingredient to success.

Intel has specific requirements around the oversight of sustainability codified into the charter of the Board's Corporate Governance and Nominating Committee. The charter states that the committee shall "review and report to the Board on a periodic basis with regards to matters of corporate responsibility and sustainability performance, including potential long and short term trends and impacts to our business of environmental, social, and governance issues." (Intel, 2010, p. 1).

Intel's Code of Conduct guides the ethical behavior of its employees, officers, non-employee directors, and suppliers, and it serves as a cornerstone of Intel's culture. The Code's business principles and guidelines seek to promote honest and ethical conduct, deter wrongdoing, and support compliance with applicable laws and regulation. Sustainability expectations are also embedded into the Intel Code of Conduct (Intel, 2012), which states, "we [Intel] demonstrate respect for people and the planet and ask all our employees to consider the short and long-term impacts to the environment and the community when they make business decisions" (p. 2). The Code further requires employees and contractors to "conserve natural resources" and reduce and minimize the "environmental impact of our manufacturing technologies" (p. 4). All Intel employees are expected to complete training on the Code of Conduct when they join the company and annually thereafter. The Code is available in 13 languages, and training sessions incorporate real case scenarios.

In addition to the Code of Conduct, Intel maintains a separate Environmental Health and Safety policy, which is approved and signed by the CEO. This policy outlines Intel's environmental philosophy in greater detail and discusses its commitment to "integrating design for the environment" into their operations and products. The policy states that Intel is committed to resources conservation and achieving it through "innovative processes and continuous improvement," and that Intel subscribes to the environmental hierarchy of "reducing, reusing, and recycling." The policy further states that Intel will design and manufacture products that are "safe, and energy efficient" and they will work to "minimize impact to the environment" from their products and operations.

Andy Grove, Intel's legendary CEO and former *Time* magazine "Man of the Year" (Isaacson, 1997) was known for often stating during his years at Intel that, "If you can't measure it, you can't improve it." Grove's philosophy about the value of measurement and indicators has been applied to improving sustainability performance at Intel. Since 2008, Intel has linked a portion of every employee's variable compensation (the employee bonus)—from frontline employees to the CEO—to the achievement of specific environmental sustainability targets. The sustainability targets are focused on carbon emission reductions from Intel's operations and energy-efficiency goals for new products. While the environmental component represents a small portion of the overall Employee Bonus (EB) calculation, the EB helps focus employees on the importance of achieving Intel's environmental objectives. Linking compensation to sustainability goals for all employees is a fairly unusual practice in corporate America today.

EMPLOYEE ENGAGEMENT

In addition to the employee bonus, Intel seeks to motivate and reward employees for integrating sustainability into their daily work through employee recognition programs. One of these programs is the Intel Environmental Excellence Awards. Since 2000, Intel has presented these awards to employees who have helped Intel reduce its environmental footprint. In 2010, 62 individuals and teams from around the world were nominated for this prestigious internal award. Their projects covered a broad range of sustainability issues, from efforts to promote recycling and waste reduction to lowering the environmental impact of Intel's products and educating community members on sustainability topics. Contributors to the winning projects received monetary awards and trophies. The 11 winning teams in 2010 involved projects such as achieving LEED (Leadership in Energy and Environmental Design) certification for a 14-year-old building in Malaysia, using rain water in cooling towers in India, improving Intel's internal data center efficiency, and eliminating sulfuric acid from a fluoride treatment process in manufacturing.

The projects submitted for the Environmental Excellence Awards not only have a positive environmental impact, but many of these projects have a positive return on investment (ROI) and save Intel money. The estimated cost savings from all of the winning projects in 2010 totaled $136 million (Intel, 2011). One environmental impact/cost savings example comes from Intel's facility in Leixlip, Ireland, where employees were able to reduce the number of filter changes needed on scanner tools used in the Fab (a semiconductor fabrication factory), saving some 350,000 gallons of water per year, along with over $500,000 related to waste reduction and improved productivity.

In addition to the more formal employee reward and recognition programs targeted at sustainability, Intel supports and encourages employee-initiated grassroots efforts. One of the more prominent is the Intel Employee Sustainability Network (IESN). ISEN is a chartered employee group that was started by employees in 2004. This group provides employee networking, volunteering, and educational opportunities that align with Intel's corporate efforts on sustainability.

Intel's "Sustainability in Action Grant" program is another effort designed to encourage and support employee enthusiasm for sustainability. This program encourages any Intel employee with an innovative idea around sustainability to apply for a grant to fund their effort. Employees are encouraged to include external stakeholders in their projects and seek projects that address local or community environmental needs. In 2010, Intel provided a total of $100,000 in funding for 13 employee projects. One of these projects was an innovative proof-of-concept model that captured and utilized Intel's boiler emissions to grow algae, which could then be converted into biofuel. The project lead for this initiative was an attorney working in Intel's legal department in Chandler, Arizona. The employee read about research being conducted at Arizona State University (Hermann & Williams, 2010) to turn algae into biofuels. The Intel attorney and his team members submitted the idea and received funding for a prototype project to grow algae utilizing carbon dioxide emissions from Intel's factory. The project was successful in growing algae and now the team is working on next steps. This example highlights that innovative ideas can come from anywhere in the corporation and companies should leverage what may be their most sustainable resource—the innovation, enthusiasm, and ideas of their employees (see DuBois, Astakhova, & DuBois, this book, for detailed discussion on the importance of including employees of all levels in environmental sustainability initiatives).

VALUE THROUGH SUSTAINABILITY

Intel believes that focusing on sustainability creates and preserves long-term value for stockholders, customers, employees, and the greater community. There are many ways in which environmental sustainability can have a positive impact on a company's business and revenue. Companies with successful sustainability programs are more attractive to potential employees, thereby helping attract and retain the best talent. Being perceived by consumers as a sustainable or "green" company can enhance your reputation and brand—and can make you more attractive to investments from social responsible investors. Intel benefits from all of these areas, but historically the most measured and identifiable business value to Intel from its sustainability initiatives are centered on its manufacturing operations. Looking towards the future, designing new products and services to address the world's environmental challenges does offer Intel significant opportunity.

LICENSE TO OPERATE

Intel's financial success is directly tied to its ability to follow Moore's Law, which requires Intel to produce faster and ever more powerful semiconductors on a regular cadence. Semiconductors are built in massive, billion dollar factories called Fabs. A modern Fab has close to a million square feet of space and is among the most technically advanced manufacturing facilities in the world. Intel fabricates semiconductors or "chips" from silicon wafers. A modern microprocessor semiconductor chip can contain billions of transistors or switches. Each transistor acts as an on/off switch, controlling the flow of electricity through the chip to send, receive, and process information almost instantaneously.

Building a state-of-the-art semiconductor Fab requires a large capital investment of between $3 and $5 billion; Intel reported its capital spending for 2012 at $11.03 billion and estimates 2013 capital spending to be $13 billion (http://www.intc.com)—mainly for expanding or constructing additional Fab capacity. Fabs are constructed with multiple floors, with the silicon chips fabricated in a special area of the Fab, called a cleanroom. Because dust particles (often invisible to the human eye) can interfere with extremely small circuitry on a chip, cleanroom air must be "ultra clean." Air in the cleanroom is constantly filtered and re-circulated, entering through the ceiling and exiting through perforated floor tiles so that a cubic foot of air contains near zero dust particles greater than 0.5 micron (millionth of a meter). Maintaining an environment that is nearly particle free requires sophisticated engineering systems and controls that are expensive to install, operate, and maintain.

Fabs are expensive to build so once a decision is made to invest in the construction of a Fab, there are large business incentives to construct it as quickly as possible, thereby minimizing the time from construction to when the Fab is actually producing semiconductors. Modern Fabs are complex industrial operations that require sophisticated mechanical systems for managing air flow and cooling systems, chemicals, waste collection and treatment systems, scrubbers and abatement systems for cleaning air emissions. Many of these industrial systems require an assortment of permits and licenses to construct and operate. These permits come from local, state, and federal regulatory and/or governmental agencies. These governmental bodies have the ability to significantly impact the schedule and overall costs of a project. This is where the phrase "license to operate" becomes relevant—it's an axiom that maintains that businesses are granted a license to operate from the greater community in which it does business. This license can be a formal permit given by a governmental body or it can be an implied license, meaning the communities in which you operate can ultimately decide whether your business should be allowed to continue in their community. This same theory can be applied to governments, as we saw in the Arab Spring where long-standing heads of state were eventually overthrown by the citizens—who essentially "revoked," through protests and demonstrations, the existing government's "license to operate."

Intel believes that operating Fabs with superior environmental performance and striving to be a role model for corporate citizenship not only protects the environment but also protects the company's license to operate. Maintaining a positive reputation as a good corporate citizen, being transparent and working with external stakeholders, maintaining good environmental performance and minimizing negative environmental impacts (major chemical spills, environmental fines, etc.) enables Intel to build new Fabs with the strong support of the local community. One example of this is at Intel's large industrial complex in Chandler, Arizona.

In 2005, Intel announced its plan to construct a new Fab (designated Fab 32) that would manufacture 300 millimeter sized semiconductor wafers (approximately 12 inches in diameter) at its existing campus in Chandler, Arizona. The Intel wafer manufacturing campus is located in an upscale master-planned community in the City of Chandler called "Ocotillo" (named after a plant that grows in the Southwest desert). Family income levels living in the same zip code as the Intel facility are among the highest in Arizona (Zip Atlas, n.d.). Fab 32 was to begin production of leading-edge microprocessors in the second half of 2007 and the cost of the investment was reported as $3 billion. Fab 32 was an enormous construction project utilizing thousands of contractors, and it required 19,000 tons of steel, 568 miles of wiring, 75 miles of conduit and 86,000 cubic yards of concrete (Intel, 2007). Furthermore, once the Fab was operating, it would use significant amounts of chemicals, water, and energy to manufacture its state-of-the-art semiconductors. This was clearly a massive construction project, with a significant environmental footprint, and it was enthusiastically supported by the local community and the State of Arizona.[1] Because of this community support, Intel was able to quickly obtain permits to construct, build, and operate this new factory with almost no opposition from the community.

Around the time Intel was announcing its plans to build a major semi-conductor factory, the Wal-Mart Corporation announced its plans to build a new supercenter grocery store in the same community of Ocotillo, and only a few miles from the proposed Intel factory. Unlike the favorable community reaction received by Intel for its new Fab, the Wal-Mart supercenter grocery store was met with stiff opposition from residents in Ocotillo, who did not want this facility constructed in their town, and made requests to city officials to not allow the construction.

As reported in the local newspaper, "Chandler has not been friendly to Wal-Mart, as residents fight to preserve their higher-end neighborhoods. Ocotillo residents carried on a six-year battle to successfully stop a Wal-Mart Supercenter and then a smaller Wal-Mart Neighborhood Market" (Beard, 2004). After the public opposition, Wal-Mart decided to move the proposed store to another location in Chandler; essentially Wal-Mart lost their license to operate in Ocotillo. The public opposition and challenges faced by Wal-Mart in building its store were not necessarily related to environmental sustainability issues; however, it does demonstrate that companies do exist under a "license to operate" and if the community and its residents do not support the enterprise it can have a difficult time being built or continuing its operations.

Intel clearly understands the criticality of this when considering the capital investment of billions of dollars in new Fabs. The fact that it was able to quickly build an industrial mega-factory and Wal-Mart had challenges constructing a large grocery store clearly demonstrates the power and potential impact of a company's license to operate.

The license to operate concept is not unique to Intel or the United States. Examples can be found in other regions of the world, and even in the unlikely place of China, a place not typically known for its community activism. In 2011, "tens of thousands" of community members protested over a chemical spill from a factory in Dalian, China. The outpouring of community outrage caused the local authorities to promise to shut down and relocate the chemical plant to another location (Jiangtao, 2011). Intel too operates a multi-billion dollar Fab in Dalian, China; however, unlike the factory just mentioned, Intel enjoyed a favorable relationship with the community. Its operations in China have received numerous recognitions and accolades for their work in corporate responsibility and sustainability. Intel is currently working on an environmental transparency web-based project at its facility in Dalian, China, that will give unprecedented transparency to the local community and the world on its environmental impacts at that location. The project "went live' as scheduled in 2012 (http://203.193.101.38/dalian).

Intel's positive reputation as a leading corporate citizen played a significant role in their favorable treatment by the community in Arizona and in other locations. Intel believes its performance in the area of environmental sustainability contributes significantly to its overall reputation. Minimizing negative impacts to the environment and preventing major environmental excursions play a critical role in protecting the company's license to operate.

RISK MANAGEMENT

As discussed, Fabs are expensive and complex to build and operate; consequently, these complexities create inherent risks in the operation of a Fab, and many of these risks can be tied to sustainability. Semiconductor Fabs require significant amounts of resources such as energy and water to operate. Like many manufacturing processes, water is a key requirement for making semiconductors, and Intel reported using over 8 billion gallons of water in 2010 (Intel, 2011).

Intel requires a predictable water supply in terms of availability, quality, and costs. If the availability of water becomes constrained for a Fab, this could greatly impact production; likewise, if the water quality changes, this could adversely impact a Fab because semiconductor manufacturing requires the use of "ultra-pure water." Water coming into an Intel operation normally contains micro-contaminants. These microscopic "contaminants" are not a health concern for humans drinking the water, but they can potentially interfere with the electrical and chemical properties of the semiconductor processes so they must be removed. The incoming water goes through specialized process steps that produce ultra-pure water—this very clean water is used to rinse the surface of silicon wafers as they go through the semiconductor manufacturing process. Using ultra-pure water increases a Fab's overall water consumption; however, Intel has improved the efficiency of these systems and the overall water processing systems at their sites. Intel estimates that it takes less than 10 gallons of water to make a state-of-the-art microprocessor—which is less water than it takes for a typical shower (Brady, 2010).

Water management at Intel is further complicated by the fact that many of its sites are located in water stressed-regions of the world such as Arizona, New Mexico, Israel, and Northern China. If the communities where Intel operates do not have enough water for their needs, or they perceive that Intel is not using water in a responsible manner, this can have a negative impact on the operations. An example of this happened recently to the Coca-Cola Company at one of its facilities in India. Coca-Cola was embroiled in a highly publicized controversy related to community perceptions of its water use and ground water contamination. The company was asked by a leading environmental research group to consider shutting down a bottling plant located there, because they believed the plant was depleting scarce water supplies (Gentleman, 2008). Coca-Cola had strong evidence and data to support that it was not impacting local water suppliers but public perception can be very difficult to manage. While Coke continues to deny any wrongdoing (Hills & Welford, 2005), it was reported by the Indian Resource Center that bottling plants were shut down due to public opposition (India Resource Centre (2008).

In 2009, Northstar Asset Management filed a shareholder resolution requesting Intel to recognize and implement a comprehensive Human Right to Water policy (Intel, 2009b). The resolution went to a vote and received only about 5% of the favorable vote. Intel continued to speak with Northstar Asset Management and the following year Intel published a public water management policy that further clarified its strategy around water. Intel is one of only a few companies in the United States that has a separate public policy on water.

Intel has a vested interest in effectively managing the water-related risks at its Fab locations—which includes comprehending their business needs as well as those of the local communities. Since 1998, Intel has invested more than $100 million in water conservation programs and saved nearly 40 billion gallons of water at its operations (Intel, 2011).

OPERATIONAL FLEXIBILITY

The relentless pursuit of Moore's Law requires Intel on average to implement a new semiconductor manufacturing process technology every 18 months to 2 years. Each new generation of process technology can require a Fab to replace 25% of its manufacturing tools. Over a 6-year period, a typical Intel Fab would introduce multiple generations of technology; make hundreds of process chemical changes; and install multiple new equipment types. This pace of change is substantially different from that of a typical chemical plant where the average process at a chemical plant may last up to 15 years, and the plant itself up to 75 years (Boyd, Krupnick, & Mazurek, 1998). Fab managers need the operational flexibility to quickly make process changes without delays or uncertainties resulting from extended permit reviews.

Intel's Fabs use various types of chemicals in the fabrication of semiconductors. These chemicals can volatilize and be emitted to the atmosphere, which can trigger regulations under the U.S. Clean Air Act; consequently, Intel (as well as any other company) needs to obtain air permits governing the use and control of these air emissions. Intel was concerned that the federal permit program governing air emissions contained agency review processes that were overly complex and burdensome; and this process was not compatible with a manufacturing operation that needed to be agile. Consequently, Intel needed an option to reduce the potential time impact and uncertainty from ongoing permit reviews triggered by process changes.

To achieve the speed and flexibility Intel desired, it decided to design, build, and operate all of its worldwide Fabs under a regulatory permit designation known as "minor source" by the U.S. Environmental Protection Agency (EPA). If Intel maintained its emissions below a threshold set by the EPA, it would be classified as a "minor source," thereby enabling greater flexibility and less risk of delays from permit reviews during upgrades and changes in manufacturing tools. Furthermore, there was a significant benefit to the environment because maintaining a minor source permit level would result in considerably less air pollution from Intel's operations.

To achieve minor source designation was a Herculean task for a company of Intel's size and it was further complicated by Intel's growth rate, which was double digit. In response to this challenge, Intel created a "design for environment" process—a collaborative approach among the environmental department, research and development (R&D), engineering, and manufacturing. The overarching goal of this approach was to integrate environmental performance into each step of the R&D process. Environmental goals were established at the onset of technology development, with specific emissions targets for each wafer manufactured (a standard unit of production in the semiconductor industry). Environmental process goals were held to the same level of criticality as other manufacturing goals, and correspondingly had the same level of scientific and engineering resources applied to achieving them.

Intel established a quarterly review process to understand the direction of its environmental goals and to drive accountability. This review was attended by Intel executives including the leader of Intel's technology and manufacturing organization. Performance indicators for water, chemical and solid waste, air emissions (hazardous air pollutants [HAPs], volatile organic compounds [VOCs], green house gases, etc.), and energy were established for each technology generation. With the minor source air emissions strategy in place, Intel was able to achieve its operational flexibility goals while improving environmental performance.

The combination of permit flexibility and integrated environmental design has driven exceptional results. During the period from 2001 to 2010, Intel's revenues grew by over 60%; however, in that same time period, Intel reduced its absolute worldwide emissions of HAPs by 27% and VOCs by 20%. These results are amazing given the increase in total manufacturing output by the company during this period, and given that these emission reductions are in absolute terms. If you normalized these air emission reductions to production or revenues, the percentage decreases would be even greater.

MOORE'S LAW APPLIED TO SUSTAINABILITY

Moore's Law, which predicts that the number of transistors on a semiconductor chip will double roughly every two years, creates both challenges and opportunities related to environmental sustainability. Making computer chips with smaller feature sizes allows more computing capacity to be produced on each chip in each factory. Fewer factories require fewer resources for construction and less energy and natural resources to operate. Additionally, each new process generation allows for opportunities to make sustainability improvements to the process chemistry and manufacturing tools. The power of Moore's Law applied to sustainability can be seen in Table 13.1.

TABLE 13.1

Moore's Law—Sustainability Challenges and Opportunities

Sustainability Challenges	Sustainability Opportunities
The constructions of new and more expensive Fabs are required on a frequent basis to keep up with Moore's Law, requiring massive outlays of capital. (Note: today's modern Fabs cost between $4 billion and $5 billion.)	New Fabs allow the opportunity to install state-of-the-art environmental abatement systems and control technologies. These controls are expensive to add post-construction; however, if designed into the process, they represent a relatively small percentage of the overall Fab capital costs.
New equipment and process technology tools are required every few years. Other semiconductor companies are reluctant to pursue this expensive path and there are significant technical challenges.	Sustainability improvements can be integrated into each new process generation and tool design, thereby greatly increasing the "sustainability efficiency" of each new tool set and process.
Efficiencies are necessary to increasing circuit density, which requires more circuits per chip (smaller feature sizes). This is technically very challenging as you are pushing the limits of physics. Traditionally, Moore's law requires moving to smaller feature sizes, which are measured in nanometer.	If designed correctly, higher density chips can increase the computation power per watt (energy used to power the computing device), thereby greatly increasing energy efficiency (González, 2011). Intel estimates that to produce the same computing power at the current 32 nanometer feature size would have required four times as many factories from the previous not too distant (65 nanometer feature size). Fewer factories require fewer resources for construction and less energy and natural resources to operate.
Semiconductors are fabricated on a silicon wafer. Larger wafer sizes would be needed to improve throughput and reduce costs. (Note: Intel has moved most of its production from 200 mm sized silicon wafers to 300 mm wafers.)	Larger sized wafers can contain more chips per wafer. There are potential resource efficiencies to be gained from moving in this direction. When a larger sized wafer is rinsed with water, you use less water on average per/chip than when you rinse a smaller sized wafer.

TACKLING CLIMATE CHANGE THROUGH MANUFACTURING

Intel's "design for the environment" program, which was instituted to create more operational flexibility, also greatly enhanced the company's ability to address other significant environmental challenges, such as water consumption, waste generation, and global climate change. Intel's scope one climate-change footprint resulted primarily from the use of perfluoro-compounds (PFCs) in manufacturing. PFCs are chemicals commonly used in semiconductor manufacturing to etch circuitry onto silicon wafers and for cleaning critical tools; unfortunately, one of the negative characteristics of PFCs is their potential high impact on global warming.

Utilizing the established design for the environmental process, Intel set process technology goals for the reduction of PFC emissions and, in 1996, Intel and other U.S. semiconductor manufacturers entered into a voluntary agreement with the EPA to reduce emissions of PFC materials used in semiconductor manufacturing. The agreement later expanded into a worldwide semiconductor industry agreement to reduce PFC emissions 10% below 1995 levels by 2010, representing what was believed to be the world's first voluntary industry greenhouse gas (GHG) reduction commitment. In 2010, Intel met this goal, reducing PFC emissions by 45% in absolute terms and over 80% on a per chip basis.

TACKLING CLIMATE CHANGE THROUGH PRODUCT DESIGN

Transistors are the building blocks of the electronics industry, so the creation of more energy-efficient transistors leads to more energy-efficient computers. With each new generation of process technology, Intel can fit more transistors onto an Intel chip, while also reducing the energy required to power them. Over the past 30 years, Intel has reduced the amount of energy consumed per transistor by a factor of approximately one million. Intel estimates that a billion PCs and servers will be installed between 2007 and 2014. These billion recently added computers, utilizing Intel technology, will consume 50% less energy and deliver 17 times the compute capacity of the first billion PCs and servers that were installed between 1980 and 2007.

Each new generation of processors brings important benefits for consumers and the environment. Intel estimates that the conversion to its energy-efficient Intel Core micro architecture saved up to 26 terawatt-hours of electricity between 2006 and 2009, compared with the technology it replaced. That is equivalent to eliminating the CO_2 emissions associated with the annual electricity use of more than 2 million U.S. homes. Replacing 15 five-year-old servers with Intel's latest server would cut annual energy costs by 95%.

TECHNOLOGY FOR THE ENVIRONMENT

Many segments of industry are undergoing a transformation based on information technology that can achieve improved levels of energy and environmental efficiency. Electricity grids, homes, buildings, water systems, transportation, agriculture, etc. are becoming "smart." These systems are incorporating information technology that measures (senses), models (analyzes), and manages (controls) these systems. Technology will increasingly provide consumers with information and insight about their environmental impact that empowers them to make smarter decisions and choices.

In 2008, the Climate Group and Global Sustainability Initiative published a report that concluded that better use of information technologies has the potential to reduce worldwide GHG emissions by 7.8 gigatons by the year 2020. This savings represents 15% of global GHG emissions and in economic terms translates into saving nearly $950 billion in costs (Climate Group, 2008). Information technology has the ability to transform industries and have a positive impact on the environment.

In a study examining the climate change implications of different music delivery methods, researchers compared an album published on a compact disc (CD), and shipped to a traditional retail outlet, to an album downloaded and used digitally; and an album downloaded and burned to a CD. The researchers concluded that buying digital music reduces the energy and CO_2 emissions of delivering the music by between 40% and 80% compared with traditional CD distribution methods (Weber, Koomey & Matthews, 2009).

Consider the sustainability implications of digital technology on photography—and the positive impacts these changes can have on the environment. Before the advent of digital photography, a typical amateur film photographer would drive to a store and purchase film (which was manufactured with significant amounts of energy and chemicals such as plastics, silver salts, etc.). The photographer would take their photos and then typically drive to a store to have the film and negatives processed (a chemically intensive process) and the photos printed. Later the photo enthusiast would drive back to the store to retrieve the printed photos, and they would discard those that were of poor quality (out of focus or over/under exposed), often a significant portion of the overall photos taken. Once they had identified and printed their favorite photos, they would typically put these in an album or frame, or mail them to a friend or relative. Often, after reviewing the photo negatives, consumers would have additional photos printed, which would duplicate many of these steps.

With today's digital photography, a photo is taken and stored as a digital image on a memory card in the camera. Consumers can instantly see the results without the need to drive somewhere and print the negatives or film, and they can easily delete unwanted photos. Photos can be shared nearly instantaneously over the internet without the need to print, and all of these steps can occur in a manner of minutes compared with developing print film, which would have taken several days or weeks. While the authors have not done a detailed life-cycle analysis between traditional film photography and digital photography, as in the case with digital music, it seems intuitive that digital technologies can significantly reduce the amount of materials and natural resources needed through dematerialization; and have a net-positive impact on the environment compared with the technologies they are replacing.

While the digital revolution, built on the foundation of Moore's Law, may enable innovative solutions to today's most pressing environmental challenges, the transition to a digital world and economy can be disruptive. Some companies will successfully navigate these changes while others will struggle to adapt to the speed and magnitude of the changes. As in the case of digital photography when, after 131 years of continuous business, Eastman Kodak, the pioneer of traditional film, filed for bankruptcy protection in early 2012 (De Le Merced, 2012).

These examples, digital music and photography, which demonstrate the positive impact of technology on sustainability, are both consumer related; however, there are numerous industrial applications in areas such as logistics, building management, and industrial systems where technology applications are having a positive impact on the environment. "Smart" controllers and sensors are being integrated with information technology capabilities to greatly reduce GHG emissions and increase efficiency. One example is in the area of motor systems; these are devices that convert electricity into mechanical power. Smart motor systems have the ability to adjust their power usage to a required output, usually through variable speed drives. Technology can make ubiquitous devices, such as compressors, pumps, conveyor belts, and elevators, much more efficient. It is estimated that carbon emissions could be reduced 970 metric ton of carbon dioxide equivalent by 2020 through the use of smart motor systems and industrial process optimization (Climate Group, 2008).

CONCLUSION

Intel's path towards environmental sustainability is based on a pragmatic approach—that sustainability is simply good business. Intel believes that to achieve significant results it needs to treat sustainability as it does other critical business functions. Intel realized early on that there were significant competitive advantages to integrating and designing sustainability into its technology development and manufacturing processes. These advantages have allowed Intel to design and build semiconductor fabrication plants with unprecedented speed and agility. Today its global network of semiconductor Fabs are considered one of its foremost competitive assets.

Achieving aggressive sustainability goals while growing at a rapid pace is a formidable challenge. Intel determined that, in order to achieve its goals, it would need to integrate sustainability into the culture and management systems of the company. It included sustainability into the charter of the Board of Directors, and environmental performance targets were tied to the bonuses of all employees. Programs were created to increase employee engagement around sustainability and tap into employees' creativity and enthusiasm. Strategic, long-range environmental goals were established by a cross-functional executive management committee and specific environmental process technology goals for air emissions, water, energy, waste, etc. were established for each new process technology. Moore's Law offered numerous challenges but there were related sustainability benefits that Intel leveraged in its operations. Additionally, Moore's Law is creating opportunities for the application of information technologies to address the world's most pressing sustainability challenges. Intel sees opportunities for smarter homes and systems that will enable more efficient use and management of our natural resources.

In 1995, Intel's then Chairman, Dr. Gordon Moore, published a letter in the company's first environmental report. In that letter, Dr. Moore stated that Intel's commitment to the environment is "an integral part of our success as a corporation," that "it is no longer enough to just produce a profit," and that Intel needs to "reduce its burden on the environment and become an asset to the communities in which we live and work." While these statements are not as famous as "Moore's Law," they are still relevant to Intel's business, and serve as a guidepost on Intel's continuing journey towards sustainability.

NOTE

1. Intel's latest addition to that same manufacturing site, Fab 42, received a highly publicized visit from current President Barack Obama in February 2012.

REFERENCES

Beard, B. (2004, October 19). Wal-Mart battles raging on. *Arizona Republic*. Retrieved January 17, 2013, from http://pqasb.pqarchiver.com/azcentral/access/1801448191. html?FMT=ABS&FMTS=ABS:FT&type=current&date=Oct+19%2C+2004& author=Betty+Beard&pub=Arizona+Republic&edition=&startpage=1&des c=WAL-MART+BATTLES+RAGING+ON

Boyd, J., Krupnick, A. J. & Mazurek, J. (1998, January). Intel's XL permit: A framework for evaluation, discussion paper 98–11. Resources for the future. Retrieved December 29, 2012, http://www.rff.org/rff/Documents/RFF-DP-98-11.pdf

Brady, T. (2010, March 17). *A water policy*. Message posted to http://blogs.intel. com/csr/2010/03/a_water_policy

Climate Group, (2008). *Smart 2020: Enabling the low carbon economy in the information age*. A report on behalf of the Global eSustainability Initiative. Retrieved January 17, 2013, from http://gesi.org/files/Reports/Smart%202020%20report%20in%20English.pdf

Corporate Knights (2012, January 25). *Global 100 Most Sustainable Corporations Announced in Davos*. Media release. Retrieved December 29, 2012, from http://www.corporate-knights.com/sites/default/files/Global100Release_Final_Jan25(1).pdf

De Le Merced, M. J. (2012, January 19). Eastman Kodak files for bankruptcy. *The New York Times*. Retrieved December 29, 2012, from http://dealbook.nytimes. com/2012/01/19/eastman-kodak-files-for-bankruptcy

Dow Jones Indexes (2011, September 8). *Dow Jones Indexes and Sam Announce the 2011 Results of the Dow Jones Sustainability Indexes Annual Review*. Retrieved December 28, 2012, from http://press.djindexes.com/index.php/dow-jones-indexes-and-sam-announce-the-2011-results-of-the-dow-jones-sustainability-indexes-annual-review

Gentleman, A. (2008, January 16). *Coca-Cola urged to close an Indian plant to save water*. *The New York Times*. Retrieved December 29, 2012, from http://www.

nytimes.com/2008/01/16/business/16coke.html?_r=0&adxnnl=1&adxnnlx=
1356807662-f3OYzCo83F7xIXgTzDSfKQ

González, A. (2011, January 24–26). *Proceedings from Moore's law implications on energy reduction.* Paper presented at High Performance and Embedded Architectures and Compilers, Heraklion, Crete, Greece.

Hermann, W., &Williams, H. (2010, August 27). Arizona set to become center for algae-based, biofuel industry. *Arizona Republic.* Retrieved December 29, 2012, from http://www.azcentral.com/arizonarepublic/news/articles/2010/08/27/20100827arizona-bio-fuel-industry-research.html

Hills, J. & Welford, R. (2005). Coca-Cola and water in India. *Corporate Social Responsibility and Environmental Management, 12,* 168–177.

IC Insights (2011, December 19). *Tracking the Top 10 Semiconductor Sales Leaders Over 26 Years.* Research bulletin. *IC Insights.* Retrieved December 28, 2012, from www.icin-sights.com/data/articles/documents/359.pdf

IFI CLAIMS Patent Services (2012, January. 10). *IFI Announces Top Global Companies Ranked By 2011 U.S. Patents.* Press Release. Retrieved at http://ificlaims.com/index.php?page=news&type=view&id=ifi-announces-top&wide_print=1&max=1000

India Resource Centre (2008) *Community welcomes decision, company cites "Unbearable" financial losses.* Retrieved January 19, 2013, from http://www.indiaresource.org/news/2008/1051.html

Intel (2007, October 25). *Fab 32: Intel's first high-volume 45nm factory opens its doors.* Fact sheet. Retrieved December 29, 2012, from http://www.intel.com/pressroom/kits/manufacturing/Fab32/AZFactsheet_FNL.pdf

Intel (2009a). *Intel climate change policy.* Retrieved January 17, 2013, from http://www.intel.com/content/www/us/en/corporate-responsibility/environment-climate-change-policy-harper.html

Intel (2009b, March 23). *Proposal 7: Human right to water.* Proxy statement. Retrieved December 29, 2012, from http://www.intc.com/intelproxy2009/statement/index.html

Intel (2010). *Charter of the Corporate Governance and Nominating Committee, as approved March 18, 2010.* Retrieved December 29, 2012, from http://www.intc.com/corp_docs.cfm

Intel (2011, May). *2010 Corporate Responsibility Report.* Retrieved January 12, 2013, from http://www.intel.com/content/www/us/en/corporate-responsibility/2010-corporate-responsibility-report-overview.html

Intel (2012, January). *Intel Code of Conduct.* Retrieved January 17, 2013, from http://www.intel.com/content/www/us/en/corporate-responsibility/governance-and-ethics.html

Interbrand (2011, October 4). *Top Global Brands Report 2011.* Retrieved December 29, 2012, from http://www.interbrand.com/en/best-global-brands/2012/Best-Global-Brands-2012-Brand-View.aspx

Isaacson, W. (1997, December 29). Andrew Grove: Man of the year. *Time Magazine, 150,* 27.

Jiangtao, S. (2011, August 16) Dalian protest 'won't be the last'. *South China Morning Post.* Retrieved 29 December 2012 from http://www.scmp.com/article/976293/dalian-protest-wont-be-last

Marosi, R. (2001, December 10). Millions given to activist cause. *Los Angeles Times.* Retrieved December 29, 2012, from http://articles.latimes.com/2001/dec/10/local/me-13429

Moore, G. (1965). Cramming more components onto integrated circuits, *Electronics, 38*(8).

Newsweek (2010). *500 Greenest Companies in America.* Retrieved 19 January, 2013, from http://www.thedailybeast.com/newsweek/features/2012/newsweek-green-rankings.html

U.S. Environmental Protection Agency (2012, January 5). *National Top 50.* Green Power Partnership, Retrieved January17, 2013, from http://www.epa.gov/greenpower/toplists/top50.htm

Weber, L. W., Koomey, J. G., and Matthews, H. S. (2009, August 17). *The energy and climate change impacts of different music delivery methods.* Lawrence Berkeley National Laboratory and Stanford University. Retrieved December 29, 2012, from http://download.intel.com/pressroom/pdf/cdsvsdownloadsrelease.pdf

White House. (2011, February 18). *Remarks by the President on winning the future in Hillsboro, Oregon.* Office of the Press Secretary. Retrieved December 28, 2012, from http://www.whitehouse.gov/the-press-office/2011/02/18/remarks-president-winning-future-hillsboro-oregon

Zip Atlas (n.d.). Zip Codes with the Highest Median Household Income in Arizona. Retrieved December 28, 2012, from http://zipatlas.com/us/az/zip-code-comparison/median-household-income.htm

Part 4

I-O Psychology and Environmental Sustainability for Tomorrow's Workforce

14

It Takes a World to Sustain a World: International Organizations' Contributions to Achieving Corporate Environmental Sustainability

Walter Reichman, Mary O'Neill Berry, Sean Cruse, and Megan C. Lytle

Environmental responsibility and sustainability require the cooperation and commitment of corporations, governments, and organizations that span the world. This chapter will describe the efforts of major international organizations to promote corporate environmental sustainability. The international organizations include the United Nations (UN) and four of its international affiliates, the United Nations Environment Program (UNEP), the United Nations University (UNU), the United Nations Global Compact, and the International Labour Organization (ILO).

These international organizations are limited in their ability to directly affect corporate behavior. The way they are able to collectively influence corporations is by conducting research, bringing information to corporate leaders, enlisting the agreement of nations to enforce standards on corporations, and becoming a "bully pulpit" to influence the attitudes of leaders who are either members or owe allegiance to organizations. The expectation is that these leaders will influence the attitudes and behaviors of others so that they will, in turn, affect those with the power to impact corporate activities across the globe.

Corporate environmental sustainability (CES) can also be considered a part of corporate social responsibility (CSR). A major feature of CSR is the task of serving multiple corporate stakeholders, such as investors, employees, customers, suppliers, and the community. It is the serving of the community, in particular, that leads to an emphasis on environmental sustainability, although an argument can be made that the environmental sustainability of corporations is increasingly in the interest of other multiple stakeholder groups. There is a link between environmental sustainability and corporate vitality as well as sustainability. You cannot have one without the other.

UNITED NATIONS

The UN is one of our best hopes for resolving the issues that may destroy our world. We must not confuse our world with our planet. Our planet is said to be 4.6 billion years old and has endured a variety of catastrophes and thrived. The danger to our world from our own hands started with the Industrial Revolution. Our planet will survive but will our world? The UN has the unbelievably difficult mission of bringing nations together to end conflict, end poverty, and enhance social, economic, and environmental development based on the principles of justice, human dignity, and well-being of people. This difficult mission can only be carried out by a complex, multi-faceted organization.

The UN was founded in 1945 at the end of World War II by 51 nations; with a current membership of 193 nations, it has become one of the most complex worldwide organizations (United Nations, 2013). Its main bodies are the General Assembly, the Security Council, the Economic and Social Council (ECOSOC), the Trusteeship Council, the International Court of Justice, and a Secretariat to manage the entire organization. Aside from these main bodies, the UN has a hierarchy of committees, boards, and working groups. One such entity is the United Nations Environment Programme (UNEP), which was established in 1972 as a governing council; it is headed by the environment secretariat (United Nations Environment Programme, 2003).

The council of UNEP (n.d.) was developed following the 1972 Conference on the Human Environment held in Stockholm, Sweden, and is concerned with issues that threaten the sustainability of our world (United Nations Environment Programme, 2003), such as climate change; resource depletion; ecosystem deterioration; disasters leading to conflict; and harmful chemicals as well as other substances that cross borders. Under the direction of UNEP, UN agencies conduct or oversee research on all of these concerns, communicate the results of this research, develop programs to mitigate the negative effects of misuse and abuse in these areas, develop governance protocols to institute regulations to protect these areas, develop international conferences and treaties to promote abiding by the governance structure, and provide direct aid to nations to help them to institute effective governance over these issues (United Nations Environment Programme, 2003). However, the impact of these efforts has not been what we might have hoped for.

Since the development of UNEP, there has been minimal adherence to the recommendations made at the 1972 meeting in Stockholm; thus, the Division of Environmental Law and Conventions was established in 1999 and has since developed a *Manual on Compliance with an Enforcement of Multilateral Environmental Agreements (MEAs)* and Guidelines on Compliance with and Enforcement of MEAs (United Nations Environment Programme, undated, a.). In 1992, the UN Conference on Environment and Development, the Earth Summit, was held in Rio de Janeiro and led to the expansion of the recommendations of 1972 into Principles (United Nations Environment Programme, undated, b). This chapter addresses some of the Principles and will focus on the most controversial one, Principle 16, which states that those responsible for major pollution should bear the cost of reducing pollution (Economic and Social Council, 2001). The Rio conference also established the Commission on Sustainable Development (CSD), which has become the major UN organization dealing with environmental sustainability (United Nations Environment Programme, n.d.).

Rio+20, held in June 2012, sought three objectives: (1) secure renewed political commitment to sustainable development, (2) assess the progress and implementation gaps in meeting already agreed commitments, and (3) address new and emerging challenges (UN Conference on Sustainable Development, 2011). Business, as a provider of sustainable solutions, has an essential role to play in advancing this agenda. Responsible business actions based upon universal principles can underpin economies with values essential for driving sustainable and inclusive growth. Practical solutions towards global sustainability must be widely mobilized.

On behalf of the private sector, the Global Compact has outlined objectives of Rio+20 related to the contribution of business to sustainability. These objectives include the following:

a. The intensification of the business contribution to global sustainability issues through responsible corporate practices that are based on the ten principles (see Figure 14.1).

The UN Global Compact asks companies to embrace, support and enact, within their sphere of influence, a set of core values in the areas of human rights, labour standards, the environment and anti-corruption:

HUMAN RIGHTS

- Principle 1: Businesses should support and respect the protection of internationally proclaimed human rights; and
- Principle 2: make sure that they are not complicit in human rights abuses.

LABOUR

- Principle 3: Businesses should uphold the freedom of association and the effective recognition of the right to collective bargaining;
- Principle 4: the elimination of all forms of forced and compulsory labour;
- Principle 5: the effective abolition of child labour; and
- Principle 6: the elimination of discrimination in respect of employment and occupation.

ENVIRONMENT

- Principle 7: Businesses should support a precautionary approach to environmental challenges;
- Principle 8: undertake initiatives to promote greater environmental responsibility; and
- Principle 9: encourage the development and diffusion of environmentally friendly technologies.

ANTI-CORRUPTION

- Principle 10: Businesses should work against corruption in all its forms, including extortion and bribery.

FIGURE 14.1
UN Global Compact.
© United Nations Global Compact

b. Demonstrating the proven ability of business to strategically address and provide practical solutions to global challenges, and making a clear case for businesses everywhere to comprehensively embed principles into their strategies, operations, and throughout their supply chain.

c. To reach an agreement at all government levels—national, city, community—on the need to prioritize sustainability and develop incentives to accelerate the transformation towards low-carbon and sustainable economies and societies.

d. To mobilize greater collaboration among business and industry— and in partnership with key actors including government, multilateral organizations, and civil society—to identify and scale up the most promising technologies and solutions towards sustainability, particularly related to climate change, energy, water, and food (UN Global Compact, 2012).

Another UN affiliate that plays a crucial role in regard to environmental sustainability is the United Nations University (UNU), which was established in 1973 as an international community of scholars who generate and share knowledge and strengthen capacities to promote human security and development with an emphasis on the needs of developing countries. The UNU was designed to be an academic institution within the UN to promote and conduct applied research to further the goals of the UN. The UN charter guarantees their independence in the selection of topics and dissemination of results. This has resulted in objective research that is accepted with confidence in its integrity by the intellectual and political community. Their strategic plans for 2009–2012 call for continuing their focus on research and teaching on issues of sustainability. Their method of research is to integrate natural sciences, social sciences, humanities, and engineering, as opposed to research in each discipline with limited cooperation among them.

UNU is voluntarily funded and seeks to collaborate with other UN agencies such as the ILO and Global Compact, and with leading industries around the world. Since the UNU is dependent on private support, this is an ideal opportunity for corporations to contribute to the continuation of sustainability research from an independent organization. In addition, it would be beneficial to conduct more psychological research at UNU. The attitudes and behaviors that go along with sustainability are not completely understood and could be an opportunity for psychologists to contribute to environmental sustainability within the UN.

The following sections draw heavily on the contributions of both UNEP and UNU to various aspects of environmental sustainability: climate change, resource depletion, ecosystem deterioration, and disasters and conflicts.

Climate Change

There are very few scientists (but too many politicians) who dispute the 1988 report of the Intergovernmental Panel on Climate Change (IPCC), in which participants reported that the release of carbon into the air is causing climate change (Boykoff & Boykoff, 2007), and stated that unless this process is reversed we will reach the "tipping point" after which nothing we do will reverse the process. It is also generally documented that the most vulnerable people in our world will suffer the most from climate change (Pettengell, Sharma, & Bailey, 2009). The UN efforts to prevent us from reaching this point include calling for a number of worldwide conferences and preparing agreements to reduce the amount of carbon released and to take measures to control the level of climate change. While the UN can disseminate information and provide recommendations, it cannot compel a nation to sign an agreement, follow an approved agreement, or prevent nations from abrogating an agreement after they have signed it. The independent nations that are members of the UN cannot be compelled to do anything they do not believe is in their best interest. At best the UN can act as a "bully pulpit," which means that, based on its political neutrality, confidence in its science, and its respect as an independent body, its influence can persuade nations and individuals to follow its pronouncements.

One of the major impediments to climate control is deciding which nations should shoulder the burden of controlling the emissions that affect climate. The UN Framework Convention on Climate Change, among other international accords, has resulted in different sets of standards for developed and developing countries in regard to their greenhouse emissions (Parker & Blodgett, 2010). According to Lang (1999), at the heart of this issue is the CSD's Principle 16, from the Rio Declaration, which states that the "polluter must pay," or that the developed countries are responsible for the world being in the state that it is in, climatically speaking (Division for Sustainable Development, 1997). Therefore, developed nations should bear the brunt of dealing with the problems they have wrought. Emerging market nations, such as China, India, Brazil, Mexico, Indonesia, South Korea, Iran, and South Africa, and the developing nations agree: they maintain that they should not have to curb carbon emissions or do many of the things necessary to prevent reaching the tipping point until they have reached the level of economic and social prosperity of developed countries (Parker & Blodgett, 2010). They are not responsible for causing the problem and therefore they should not have to be responsible for solving it. The developed countries maintain that it is a universal problem and there cannot be social and economic development without all countries utilizing resources so as to ameliorate the problems of climate change. According to Parker and Blodgett, in 2005, China had the highest levels of carbon emissions, accounting for 19% of the world's CO_2, whereas the United States was responsible for 18% and the eight countries with the highest levels accounted for 58% of the world's emissions.

The developers of the Division for Sustainable Development's Agenda 21 (1992) made a number of suggestions for industries, one being for businesses to include in their pricing of goods and services the environmental costs of production, use, and disposing of waste. They also recommended that business should be encouraged to report annually on their interaction with the environment and their use of energy and natural resources, and also to report on the implementation of codes of conduct promoting best environmental practices (Division of Sustainable Development, 1992). The authors of Agenda 21 also called for developing a culture of "stewardship" in managing and utilizing natural resources by entrepreneurs (Division of Sustainable Development, 1992). They recommended an increase in input into policies and proclamations from representatives of business, and for increased research on how small enterprises in developing countries can grow and prosper while protecting the environment. Every national budget allocates several million US dollars (USD) to these endeavors and there have been reports of successful cooperation between UN agencies and private enterprise in taking action to curb pollution.

In a 2009 UNU policy briefing, David, Huang, Soete, and van Zon, stated that research cannot conclude with complete certainty that there is a threshold of irreversibility on climate change, and certainly cannot determine the critical greenhouse gas concentration that will lead to irreversible climate change. They warn against the all too human temptation to wait and see. The risk of passing that point of no return is too big a risk to take. David et al. suggested adapting the mini-max precautionary principle of responding to the worst-case scenario. This policy also strongly suggests that adapting to climate change will be insurmountable. We should at least stabilize green house emissions at the current level in the hope that "there is enough surplus environmental absorption capacity to handle the emissions" (David et al., 1992, p. 2). The UNU suggest that two ways of dealing with the issue are a carbon tax and public funding to stimulate new technology.

The May–June 2011 issue of the *American Psychologist* dealt with psychology's contribution to understanding and addressing global climate change, and articles were written by members of the American Psychological Association (APA) Taskforce on the Interface between Psychology and Global Climate Change. The topics included (a) the human causes and consequences of climate change; and (b) the links between climate change and cognitive, affective, emotional, interpersonal, and organizational responses to climate change. The articles generally supported the principles and research provided by the UN, the UNU, the Global Compact, and the ILO. From a psychological perspective, Reser and Swim (2011), Gifford (2011), and Stern (2011), among others, emphasized the emotional price paid by people experiencing the effects of climate change. One of the articles (Reser & Swim, 2011) dealt with the psychological processes that influence adaptation to and coping with climate change. It has been suggested that focusing on adaptation is not sufficient to the process of climate control because it is not proactive in dealing with the problem, thereby allowing it to occur. These psychologists support the conclusions of David et al. (2009).

Gifford (2011) reported on the barriers to action and listed among them the mistrust of science, limited knowledge, and ideology. The important recommendation made by Gifford was that psychologists must work with other scientists, technical experts, and policy makers to help overcome these barriers. He did not, however, specify a process for overcoming them. Stern (2011) carried this idea further by suggesting that psychologists cannot bring about change by direct application of psychological concepts but must integrate psychological knowledge and methods with knowledge from other fields of science and technology. Further, Weber and Stern (2011) came the closest to bringing business into this process by recommending that the "leadership elite" of massive corporations must become publicly engaged and the public media must be involved to bring about change.

Resource Depletion

UNEP is the leading global environmental authority for preserving the earth's rich, diverse natural resources. Its research has shown how sustainable development of natural resources can help reduce poverty and improve the livelihood of millions. For example, UNEP (2010d) has joined with the United Nations Development Program (UNDP) to provide 22 countries with technical and financial support to develop their natural resources in ways that sustain these resources for the future. Researchers at UNEP (2010e, p. 2) have concluded that "economic growth and social development cannot be sustained with our current consumption and production patterns. Globally we are extracting more resources to produce goods and services than our planet can replenish." At the same time, an increasingly growing share of the world's population is struggling to meet basic necessities. It has been concluded that building green economies is required (United Nations Environment Programme, 2010f). In such economies, environmental harm is taken into consideration in developing and instituting procedures that lead to economic growth. In order to simultaneously meet the world's demands while moving towards a green economy, there needs to be more focus on designing and implementing low-impact environmental procedures, products, and services, coupled with resource efficiency.

According to the council of UNEP (2010f), resource efficiency "means reducing total environmental impact of production and consumption of goods and services, from raw material extraction to final use and disposition" (p. 2). Achieving these goals requires (a) investigating how resources are extracted, processed, consumed, and disposed of; (b) finding more efficient methods; (c) promoting investment opportunities in creating these efficiencies by developing networks of industry partnerships that will help businesses adopt resource-efficient technologies; and (d) enhancing products and services in developing markets. These networks must also stimulate demand for resource-efficient goods and services. They must develop market and consumer incentives to promote sustainable life styles and values as well as to promote public and private sector cooperation, finance innovation and entrepreneurs, and the business case for resource efficiency. UNEP (2010f) representatives have worked in partnership with financial institutions to create incentives to support more resource-efficient practices in regard to water, biomass, and energy. The program is working on alternative business models in building and construction industries, agriculture, food industries, and manufacturing. The possibilities for innovation and creativity in business are enormous.

Once again, however, since UNEP does not have enforcement power, it must work through governments, international associations, and networks of businesses to accomplish these goals. The credibility of the UN will play a large role in its success on these issues. To that end, UNEP (2010f) collaborates with media and communication networks to make its point. They also work with advertisers to promote changes in consumer behavior, develop responsible advertising practices, and conduct events around sustainable consumption with a focus on youth. They have allocated 2.8 million USD to supporting entrepreneurial innovations, 1.2 million USD to mobilizing financial investments, and 2.6 million USD to developing global partnerships for sustainable development (United Nations Environment Programme, 2010f).

While psychologists may not have the power to influence governments, Campbell and Campbell (2005) suggested that industrial-organizational (I-O) psychologists can work with organizations to promote sustainable practices. Specifically, psychologists could help modify hiring, training, employee appraisal, and management practices to facilitate CES by using the International Organization for Standardization (ISO)'s Strategic Plan 2011–2015, which includes suggestions for environmental sustainability (Campbell & Campbell, 2005; International Organization for Standardization, n.d.).

Ecosystem Deterioration and Innovation

In 2005, the UN Millennium Ecosystem Assessment that was completed by UNEP and contributors concluded that 15 out of 24 ecosystems were being debased by unsustainable utilization (United Nations Environment Programme, 2010c). They found that the decline disproportionately affects the most disadvantaged and vulnerable people in the world. These individuals are dependent on agriculture, fishing, and forest resources for a living and they live in areas where water is in short supply. UNEP (2010c) began a program, which is ongoing, to (a) raise awareness of the role of ecosystems services and biodiversity in building a sustainable world; (b) restore or manage ecosystems by providing nutrients for agriculture, water retention, restoring lakes, and protecting and growing new forests; (c) promote ecosystem sustainability in the national planning process of countries; and (d) collaborate with financial institutions to develop methods of integrating ecosystems services into their business and national strategies. UNEP has allocated almost a million USD to further this endeavor. Based on the empirical findings that human consumption of resources has lead to the extinction of animals, loss of non-renewable resources, and permanent damage to our environment, Campbell and Campbell (2005) have suggested that I-O psychologists take notice of the ecosystem deterioration and consider how they could address these concerns. For instance, these authors suggest that, at a minimum, psychologists could advocate for CES practices.

The UNU has researched a number of innovative procedures for sustaining ecosystems. A UNU 2010 policy brief (Duraiappah, Takeuchi, & Scherkenbach, 2011) described a Japanese project studying the interaction among humans, territorial-aquatic ecosystems and marine coastal ecosystems. They studied the changes over the past 50 years and projected further change into 2050, taking account of various drivers of change such as climate change, technology, and socio-behavioral responses. They found that the rate of biodiversity loss was most rapid in the past five years than at any time in history. Their studies indicated that the most effective response to degradation to date has been in passing laws against such actions along with the greater involvement of citizens and non-governmental agencies. Duraiappah et al. recommended economic incentives for preservation of land and the creation of governmental institutions to manage both private and public lands. A recent suggestion emanating from UNU is that this procedure be used in helping Japan recover from the recent earthquake and tsunami (Duraiappah et al, 2011).

Liang (2011) described a biodiversity system used in the Yunnan Province in China that could be a model for the rest of the world. It is a system that has been in existence for a multitude of generations and the Yunnan people have harnessed the products and services of the ecosystem they inhabit by dividing the land into specific functions and being certain that the land is used to maintain productivity. In addition, they have developed myths to support their behavior of sustainability. For example, one good reason to preserve forests is that their deities reside there. The study of the Yunnan people in China so impressed UNU that their Institute for Sustainability and Peace has begun studying "traditional" knowledge on forest and watershed protection, and crop diversity, as a means of reducing climate change. UNU suggests that we have a lot to learn especially from those who have survived for generations as partners with nature and the environment.

A UNU working paper (Arundel & Kemp, 2009) takes on the difficult task of developing procedures for evaluating the much-needed environmentally-motivated innovations. They suggest that all products, processes, or organizational innovation with environmental benefits be included in the measurement process. In addition, the following measures of eco-innovation were recommended: input measures (the cost and effort of development), intermediate output (patents, publications), direct output measures (the number of innovations), and indirect impact measures (change in efficiency and productivity and the value of the product or service divided by its environmental impact).

Disasters and Conflicts

Natural and manmade disasters take a drastic toll on the environment. Since 2000, more than 35 major conflicts and approximately 2,500 natural disasters have damaged infrastructure, forced populations to relocate, and endangered ecosystems as well as the individuals who depend on them (United Nations Environment Programme, 2010b). The 2011 earthquake and tsunami in Japan as well as the earthquakes in Chile and Haiti are recent examples of natural disasters that caused ecological damage that had to be repaired by UN agencies as well as by private, public, religious, and charitable organizations.

According to a UNU document written by Zissener (2011), climate change is influencing the frequency and intensity of natural catastrophes. Seventy-five percent of recent economic loss is due to climate-related hazards of flood, drought, and storms, and there has been an increase in geophysical disasters such as earthquakes and tsunamis. Ninety-five percent of deaths from natural disasters in the past quarter century occurred in developing countries. For instance, the melting of glaciers in the Arctic is causing water shortages in some parts of the world; the increase in ocean levels is causing people to leave their island homes (e.g., the island of Tuvalu in the Pacific), and become refugees seeking an acceptable place to live (Harris & Roach, 2009). As ecological damage continues, it is expected that there will be an increase in "climate refugees" (Harris & Roach, 2009). Further, dealing with the effects of natural disasters costs these countries additional money and further setbacks in their development as well as increasing their poverty. There has been an increase in environmental disasters since the 1950s; the annual average direct loss from environmental disasters increased from 3.9 billion to 40 billion USD by 1990 (Intergovernmental Panel on Climate Change, 2001). Hurricane Katrina cost the states of Louisiana, Alabama, and Mississippi alone 80 billion USD (Harris & Roach, 2009). Environmental disasters are most likely to occur where poor people live and they bear a disproportionate burden of the direct damage (Renaud, Bogardi, Dun, & Warner, 2008). Therefore, Zissener (2011) suggests acting ahead of a disaster to prepare for it and mitigate its effects. The suggestions include mapping and avoiding high-risk zones, building hazard-resistant structures, developing buffers such as forests, early warning systems, and insurance.

Conflicts among and within nations also account for damage to the environment that must be repaired and the dislocation of people as they flee from violence and death, becoming refugees. It is within the purview of the UN to prevent both natural and manmade disasters, reduce the likelihood of conflict, and resolve conflict when it occurs. The damage done to the environment will on its own cause disasters and conflict. As natural resources, water, useful land, forest products, animals, and fish become scarcer in various parts of the world, there will be greater competition for these resources, thus creating an increase in conflict over access and ownership. With these disasters and conflicts, there will be a toll on human life, health and well-being.

Disasters can also have enormous commercial impact such as the recent damage done to businesses along the Gulf coast as a result of the BP oil rig explosion in 2011. In addition, war within and between countries can ruin economies. Conflict between nations has a profound effect on the economies resulting in the destruction of business and infrastructure as well as the diversion of workers to military activities. Therefore, it is good business for companies to do everything possible to reduce the likelihood of disasters by investing in and protecting the environment and ecosystems as a part of their business plans and activities. They must also ensure they do no harm to the environment as they conduct their business—for example, by avoiding pollution of waterway and ground, caring for hazardous waste, controlling dangerous emissions, and taking safety precautions for employees, customers, and the general public.

Companies must also act responsibly with regard to conflicts and not exploit them as a means of increasing profits. CSR is essential for the survival of our world. In addition, psychological organizations such as the New Zealand Psychological Society have examined the role psychologists can play in natural disaster management (O'Driscoll, Carr, & Forsyth, 2007). For instance, Carr (2008) has utilized I-O psychology to research disasters, in order to apply his findings in improving readiness plans, training first responders, and developing recovery plans.

UNITED NATIONS GLOBAL COMPACT

The UN Global Compact is a strategic policy initiative for businesses that are committed to aligning their operations and strategies with ten universally accepted principles in the areas of human rights, labor rights, environment, and anti-corruption (United Nations Global Compact, 2011a). By doing so, business, as a primary driver of globalization, can help ensure that markets, commerce, technology, and finance advance in ways that benefit economies and societies everywhere, thus demonstrating successful CES. Launched in 2000, the Global Compact stands as the office within the UN with the exclusive mandate to engage with the private sector. Businesses that endorse the Global Compact commit to two complementary objectives (United Nations Global Compact, 2011a): (1) to mainstream the ten principles in business activities around the world; and (2) to catalyze actions in support of broader UN goals, including the Millennium Development Goals (MDGs).

With these objectives in mind, the Global Compact has shaped an initiative that provides collaborative solutions to the most fundamental challenges to sustainability facing both business and society. The initiative seeks to combine the best properties of the UN, such as moral authority and convening power, with the private sector's solution-finding strengths, and the expertise and capacities of a range of key stakeholders. The Global Compact is global and local; private and public; voluntary yet accountable.

The local presence of the Global Compact is fostered via its extensive Local Network system. Participants come together voluntarily to advance the Global Compact and its principles at the local level by creating Local Networks. Today, there are over 97 established and emerging Global Compact Local Networks (GCLNs), (United Nations Global Compact, 2011b). GCLNs have diverse operational structures and systems, yet all operate with the mission to advance the Global Compact principles in business. The multistakeholder GCLNs serve an essential role in rooting the Global Compact within different national contexts—and their distinct economic, cultural, and linguistic needs. GCLNs provide an important base for jump-starting business action and awareness on the ground.

In the space of environmental stewardship, the Global Compact has developed and endorsed a number of key initiatives to support businesses and other stakeholders in their efforts to address sustainability in their strategies and operations. The following are among these key initiatives.

Caring for Climate

"Caring for Climate" is a voluntary and complementary action platform for Global Compact participants who seek to demonstrate leadership on the issue of climate change (United Nations Global Compact, 2010a). It provides a framework for business leaders to advance practical solutions and help shape public policy as well as public attitudes. Chief executive officers who support the initiative are prepared to set goals, to develop and expand strategies and practices, and to publicly disclose emissions.

Caring for Climate, co-convened with the UNEP, is a commitment to action by business and a call to governments, incorporating transparency (United Nations Global Compact, 2010a). It offers an interface for business and governments at the global level, with the potential of rapidly becoming the leading platform for pragmatic business solutions—transcending national interests and responding to the global nature of the issues at stake. Moreover, the broad geographical spread of its supporters, involving both leading actors from developed and emerging economies, reinforces the novel nature of this engagement platform.

In 2011, Caring for Climate launched a multistakeholder working group to specifically address the linkages between climate change and the MDGs. The working group seeks to enhance the understanding of ways in which businesses can find strategic solutions throughout their operations and value chains to address the impacts of climate change on poverty and development (United Nations Global Compact, 2010b).

CEO Water Mandate

The CEO Water Mandate is a public-private initiative designed to assist companies in the development, implementation, and disclosure of water sustainability policies and practices. The Mandate recognizes that the business sector, through the production of goods and services, impacts water resources—both directly and through supply chains. Endorsing CEOs acknowledge that in order to operate in a more sustainable manner, and contribute to the vision of the Global Compact and the realization of the MDGs, they have a responsibility to make water-resources management a priority, and to work with governments, UN agencies, non-governmental organizations, and other stakeholders to address the global water challenge (United Nations Global Compact, 2007).

As of 2011, the CEO Water Mandate is focusing on three priority areas: responsible business engagement with water policy and management, corporate water disclosure, and the human right to water (United Nations Global Compact, 2011c). In 2010, the UN General Assembly and Human Rights Council agreed to resolutions affirming the human right to water and sanitation (United Nations News Centre, 2010). CEO Water Mandate endorsers and other stakeholders alike have recognized that there is now a corporate responsibility to conduct business operations in a manner that respects the right to water and sanitation. However, endorsers have requested more clarity on what it specifically means for a company to act consistently with this right, and how to operationalize respect for the right to water (United Nations Global Compact and Pacific Institute, 2010).

Low Carbon Leaders

The Low-Carbon Leaders Project (LCLP) is a collaboration between the Global Compact and the World Wildlife Fund (WWF). The initiative is an open source, multi-media platform aimed at capturing and sharing transformative low-carbon solutions. To date, LCLP has issued 12 illustrative cases and toolkits for calculating the impacts of energy-efficient solutions; additionally, LCLP has collected nearly 60 low-carbon solutions estimated to help avoid over 10 million tonnes of CO_2 emissions (United Nations Global Compact and World Wildlife Fund, 2010). These solutions—submitted to a website and available for public review and rating—have the capacity to contribute to a broader shift in society, a shift to a focus on companies as solution providers and to a focus on transformative solutions.

Transformative Solution Leadership

Through the research of the LCLP, the Global Compact issued the report *Transformative Solution Leadership*, which presents a model for corporations to transform the way they strategize their business so as to make the reduction of emissions and sustainable development a central component of their business success. The model suggests that businesses start by setting their goals and then strategizing as to how the goals can be reached in a sustainable way. In the process of strategizing, they should look at their current business model and ask what changes would allow them to benefit from reduced carbon emissions and reduced use of natural resources. In this process, companies have to go beyond the focus on the way goods and services are being produced now and develop systems that will support sustainability as well as a low-carbon economy. As part of this process they will have to help customers understand what goods and services they should buy in order to achieve this desired economy (United Nations Global Compact and World Wildlife Fund, 2010).

Among the strategies suggested in this model that are applicable to all organizations is the use of "smart work." Smart work includes teleworking or working from home in order to reduce emissions from vehicles (for more on smart work and technology-enabled strategies, see Andrews, Klein, Forsman, & Sachau, this book). In addition, there are data that indicate an increase in productivity, greater retention, easier recruitment, and savings in use of paper and supplies due to increases in faxing, emailing, and scanning (United Nations Global Compact and World Wildlife Fund, 2010). There is also greater employee satisfaction resulting from flexible work schedules. Another strategy that seems to be gaining adherence is the replacement of travel to meetings and conferences with teleconferences of various sorts: "Travelling by plane to meetings and conferences makes up a significant part of many companies' internal carbon footprint, often 50 percent or more among non-manufacturing companies." (Low-Carbon Leaders Project, n.d., p. 2).

In addition, companies should be aware of the environmental costs of transportation of goods. For example, air transport and shipping account for a significant emission of CO_2 (ships emitted 1.1 billion tonnes of CO_2 in 2005 and airlines carry 30 million tonnes of freight each year) (United Nations Global Compact and World Wildlife Fund, 2010). The model suggests that all companies should review their infrastructure for shipping including ports, shipping, and storage. The authors believe this could save between 10% and 50% of CO_2 emissions. The model suggested is a roadmap for corporations seriously concerned with sustainable development (United Nations Global Compact and World Wildlife Fund, 2010). The principles these solutions illustrate can help unlock innovation and trigger the paradigm shift in society necessary to deliver the kind of reductions needed to avoid the dangers of climate change, while also helping to eradicate poverty.

WindMade

With the intention of connecting more directly with consumers, in 2011 the Global Compact partnered with The Global Wind Energy Council, WWF, the LEGO Group, Vestas Wind Systems, PricewaterhouseCoopers and Bloomberg to establish WindMade (WindMade, 2011). The WindMade initiative is a direct response to increasing consumer demand for sustainable products. It is dedicated to increasing corporate investments in wind power by informing consumers about companies' use of wind energy, and increasing demand for products that embrace this clean and renewable energy source. The WindMade label will provide qualifying companies the ability to effectively communicate to consumers a commitment to wind energy that differentiates their brand, and signals a strong commitment to renewable energy (Pfanner, 2011).

Embedding the tenets of CES within corporate strategies and operations will ultimately be essential for a business's long-term stability. The Global Compact has instituted the platforms described earlier to guide businesses on how they can advance environmental sustainability in their strategies and operations. For the value of these approaches to seep throughout communities and societies, policy makers as well as businesses and other stakeholders must in part move beyond a narrow technology focus and ask what the service provided by a company does, and what kind of lifestyle it promotes.

In the perspective of the Global Compact, the pieces are in place to move toward an era of sustainability. Corporate leaders increasingly see the business landscape though a lens where the world's challenges are in sharp focus. The Global Compact will continue to underscore how environmental, social, and governance issues affect the bottom line, and support companies to align strategies and operations accordingly. For a single business, sustainability practices are an essential element for protecting and building its long-term value. When undertaken by a critical mass, corporate responsibility and environmental sustainability can help deliver a more peaceful and prosperous future to all corners of our planet. As noted by Berry, Reichman, and Schein (2008) in an interview with Georg Kell, the Executive Director of the Global Compact, I-O psychologists could assist international organizations by disseminating information and working together on the aforementioned global concerns.

INTERNATIONAL LABOUR ORGANIZATION (ILO)

The ILO was founded in 1919 to create and supervise international labor standards. It became the first specialized agency of the UN in 1946, and is still actively functioning today (International Labour Organization, 2013a). The ILO functions in a unique manner in which representatives from government, employees, and companies work together to promote the concept of "decent work" for all. All decisions are made by consensus and the Director General of the ILO maintains that while it takes longer to reach agreement, when agreement is achieved it sticks and really works. "Decent work" is achieved by ensuring that there is (a) productive and secure opportunities for work, entrepreneurship, and investments; (b) respect for the rights of labor; (c) adequate income; (d) social protection; and (e) collective bargaining and dialogue between labor and management (International Labour Organization, 2013b).

As might be expected, representatives of the ILO are concerned with environmental sustainability from the point of view of jobs and employment. They have cooperated with UNEP to develop a relationship between employment and sustainability and as such are very involved in the promotion of organizations that will employ individuals to sustain and protect the environment (International Labour Organization, n.d.) Along with UNEP, the International Employer Organization, and the International Trade Union Confederation, ILO representatives have developed the concept of the "green job" or the "green collar job" (Mass, Moss, Hopkins, & Ross, 2010).

The Green Collar Job/The Green Economy

Green jobs or green collar jobs have been defined by UNEP (2008) as work that contributes substantially to preserving and restoring environmental quality, such as protecting ecosystems and biodiversity, reducing energy, water, and materials consumption through strategies to increase efficiency, decarbonizing the economy, and minimizing all forms of waste and pollution. (Please see Dierdorff, Norton, Gregory, Rivkin, and Lewis, this book, for an overview of the U.S. Department of Labor's initiative to identify and classify green jobs.) ILO representatives have been promoting investments in green enterprises so as to increase the number of new jobs in this industry, provide decent work for millions of people, and reduce the level of poverty. To this extent they have fostered cooperation among governments, entrepreneurs, investors, and labor (International Labour Organization, n.d.). UNEP (2008, p. 1) maintains that a green job "aims to preserve the environment for both present and future generations and to be more equitable and inclusive of all people and all countries." The ILO contributors perceive a movement to the "green" as a win-win for the economy and for economic development.

Researchers at the ILO (2013c) believe and have presented hard evidence that the world will arrive at a green economy, but the transition to it will be difficult. What is necessary is for government, labor, and management to guide the transition so it does as little harm as possible and the time lag is as short as possible, as some jobs become eliminated, some professions contract, new skills and abilities are required and new jobs multiply (International Labour Organization, 2011c). There is little doubt that the transition will be problematic and possibly painful. The challenge for the entrepreneurs and the workers is to demonstrate that the green workplace pays off in terms of greater productivity and greater profits. It will call for new competencies and new entrepreneurial skills, linking the protection of the environment with employment as opposed to seeing a conflict between them. It will also link the protection of the environment to the reduction of poverty through more job opportunities (International Labour Organization, 2011c). As an example of this linkage, the ILO reported a United States estimate that, for every billion dollars invested in a green recovery, 30,000 jobs would be created and up to 450 million USD per year would be saved on energy costs (Barbier, 2009). As would be expected, ILO representatives call for the new green economy to include investments into social dimensions such as education, health, social security, gender equality, and labor. The most vulnerable segments of society must be included in the green economy.

The optimism of the ILO for the future of the world is tempered by a realistic assessment of the problems in transitioning to the green economy. ILO representatives recognize that there will be individual losses along the way, that green will not be a pure color (there will be "shades of green" in the economy), and that not all green jobs will offer "decent work." Nevertheless, its view of the future is energizing and should be motivating to corporations and entrepreneurs all over the world. The ILO (2013a) tripartite approach to resolving issues and moving toward a sustainable environment calls for closer cooperation between business, government, and labor organizations as opposed to conflict and demonizing the motivation and goals of each.

CONCLUSIONS

The world is obviously facing a number of serious environmental crises that can alter life on our planet as we know it. We are facing climate changes and resource depletion that are likely to destroy our ability to maintain our land, our livelihood, our culture, as well as to incite conflict. International organizations have become the first responders in this crisis. The UN, through the policies and procedures developed by UNEP, and through the research and theories developed by UNU, are primary examples. Added to the UN, its affiliates, the ILO, and the Global Compact have also developed best practices to deal with these problems.

These great international organizations are instruments of change and I-O psychology can play a role in enabling these organizations to achieve their lofty goals. I-O psychology can also facilitate the relationships between these international organizations and the world theater in which they strive to accomplish their missions. Much remains to be done, but with I-O psychologists' support, direction, and influence, these international organizations can and will deliver the kind of CES so vital to our earth's, and humanity's, future.

REFERENCES

Arundel, A., & Kemp, R. (2009). *Measuring eco-innovation.* UNU-MERIT working paper #2009-017.

Barbier, E. B. (2009, April). *A global green new deal. Green Economy Initiative and Division of Technology, Industry and Economics of the UN Environment Programme UNEP-DTIE.* Retrieved December 28, 2012, from http://www.uwyo.edu/barbier/publications/a%20global%20green%20new%20deal-executive%20summery.pdf

Berry, M. O., Reichman, W., & Schein, V. E. (2008, April). The United Nations Global Compact needs I-O psychology participation. *The Industrial-Organizational Psychologist, 45*(4), 33–37.

Boykoff, M. T., & Boykoff, J. M. (2007). Climate change and journalistic norms: A case-study of US mass-media coverage. *Geoforum, 38,* 1190–1204.

Campbell, J. E., & Campbell, D. E. (2005, October). Eco-I-O psychology? Expanding our goals to include sustainability. *The Industrial-Organizational Psychologist, 43*(2), 23–28.

Carr, S. (2008, July). How can I-O psychology assist with the management of natural disasters and climate change. *The Industrial-Organizational Psychologist, 46,* 71–73.

David, P. A., Huang, C., Soete, L., & van Zon, A. (2009). Toward a global science and technology policy agenda for sustainable development. United Nations University, policy brief 4. Retrieved December 28, 2012, from http://www.merit.unu.edu/publications/pb/unu_pb_2009_4.pdf

Division for Sustainable Development. (1992). *Agenda 21, UNCED.* Retrieved January 17, 2013, from http://sustainabledevelopment.un.org/index.php?page=view&nr=23&type=400&menu=35

Division for Sustainable Development. (1997). *Resolution adopted by the General Assembly for the Programme for the Further Implementation of Agenda 21.* Retrieved January 17, 2013, from http://sustainabledevelopment.un.org/index.php?page=view&nr=319&type=111&menu=35

Duraiappah, A. K., Takeuchi, K., & Scherkenbach, C. (2011). *As Japan rebuilds, it should look to Satoyama and Satoumi for inspiration.* United Nations University. Retrieved December 28, 2012, from http://unu.edu/articles/global-change-sustainable-development/as-japan-rebuilds-it-should-look-to-satoyama-and-satoumi-for-inspiration

Economic and Social Council (ECOSOC) (2001). *Commission on sustainable development: Report on the ninth session (Supplemental No. 9).* Retrieved January 17, 2013, from http://sustainabledevelopment.un.org/index.php?menu=1118

Gifford, R. (2011). The dragons of inaction: Psychological barriers that limit climate change mitigation and adaptation. *American Psychologist, 66*(4), 290–302.

Harris, J. M., & Roach, B. (2009). *The economics of global climate change.* Global Development and Environment Institute, Tufts University. Retrieved December 28, 2012, from http://www.ase.tufts.edu/gdae/education_materials/modules/The_Economics_of_Global_Climate_Change.pdf

Intergovernmental Panel on Climate Change (2001). *Climate change 2001: Impacts, adaptation, and vulnerability.* Retrieved December 28, 2012, from http://www.grida.no/publications/other/ipcc_tar

International Labour Organization (2013a). *Origins and history.* Retrieved January 17, 2013, from http://www.ilo.org/global/about-the-ilo/history/lang--en/index.htm

International Labour Organization (2013b). *Decent work agenda.* Retrieved December 28, 2012, from http://www.ilo.org/global/about-the-ilo/decent-work-agenda/lang--en/index.htm

International Labour Organization (2013c). *Promoting decent work in a green economy.* Retrieved December 28, 2012, from http://www.ilo.org/employment/Whatwedo/Publications/WCMS_152065/lang--en/index.htm

International Labour Organization (n.d.). *Decent work and the Millennium Development Goals – MDG7.* Retrieved January 18, 2013, from http://www.ilo.org/pardev/development-cooperation/millennium-development-goals/lang--en/index.htm

International Organization for Standardization (ISO) (n.d.). *ISO strategic plan 2011–2015: Solutions to global challenges.* Retrieved January 17, 2013, from http://www.iso.org/iso/iso_strategic_plan_2011-2015.pdf

Lang, W. (1999). *UN-principles and international environmental law.* Retrieved December 28, 2012, from http://www.mpil.de/shared/data/pdf/pdfmpunyb/lang_3.pdf

Liang, L. (2011). *Biodiversity in China's Yunnan province*. United Nations University. Retrieved December 28, 2012, from http://unu.edu/articles/global-change-sustainable-development/biodiversity-in-chinas-yunnan-province

Low-Carbon Leaders Project (LCLP) (n.d.). *Smart meeting*. Retrieved January 17, 2013, from LCLP, Materials/reports, Transformative solution leadership: http://transformative-solutions.net

Mass, W., Moss, P., Hopkins, M., & Ross, M. (2010). *Skills for green jobs in the United States*. Retrieved December 28, 2012, from http://www.ilo.org/skills/pubs/WCMS_142470/lang--en/index.htm

O'Driscoll, M., Carr, S., & Forsyth, S. (2007, October). I-O psychology in Aotearoa, New Zealand: A world away? *The Industrial-Organizational Psychologist, 45*(2), 59–64.

Parker, L. & Blodgett, J. (2010, January). *Greenhouse gas emissions: Perspectives on the top 20 emitters and developed versus developing nations*. (Congressional Research Service RL32721). Retrieved January 17, 2013, from http://www.google.com/url?sa=t&rct=j&q=&esrc=s&source=web&cd=1&ved=0CDQQFjAA&url=http%3A%2F%2Fop.bna.com%2Fhl.nsf%2Fid%2Fthyd-7zhq46%2F%24File%2FCRS%2520-%2520Comparing%2520GHG%2520Emissions.pdf&ei=IiDnUIy3HPPG0AHSh4CQAg&usg=AFQjCNGyx9Id6_em1asM7d5kQd5nylqGHw&bvm=bv.1355534169,d.dmQ

Pettengell, C., Sharma, A., & Bailey, R. (2009, September). *Beyond aid: Ensuring adaptation to climate change works for the poor*. Retrieved January 17, 2013, from Oxfam International, http://www.preventionweb.net/english/professional/publications/v.php?id=11158

Pfanner, E. (2011, January 29). Group wants "WindMade" to join other feel-good labels. *The New York Times*, Retrieved December 28, 2012, from http://query.nytimes.com/gst/fullpage.html?res=9B01E1DE1030F93AA15752C0A9679D8B63

Renaud, F., Bogardi, J. J., Dun, O., & Warner, K. (2008, September). *Environmental degradation and migration*. Retrieved December 28, 2012, from http://www.berlin-institut.org/online-handbookdemography/environmental-migration.html

Reser, J. P. & Swim, J. K. (2011). Adapting to and coping with the threat and impacts of climate change. *American Psychologist, 66*(4), 277–289.

Stern, P. C. (2011). Contributions of psychology to limiting climate change. *American Psychologist, 66*(4), 303–314. Retrieved January 17, 2013, from http://www.unmillenniumproject.org/documents/131302_wssd_report_reissued.pdf

United Nations (2013). *UN at a glance*. Retrieved December 28, 2012, from http://www.un.org/en/aboutun/index.shtml

United Nations Conference on Sustainable Development (2011). *About Rio+20*. Retrieved December 28, 2012, from http://www.uncsd2012.org/rio20/index.php?menu=17

United Nations Environment Programme (2003). *About UNEP: The organization*. Retrieved December 28, 2012, from http://www.unep.org/Documents.Multilingual/Default.asp?DocumentID=43

United Nations Environment Programme (2008). *UNEP Background paper on green jobs*. Retrieved January 17, 2013, from http://ebookbrowse.com/green-jobs-background-paper-18-01-08-pdf-d371103575

United Nations Environment Programme (2010a). *UNEP six priority areas factsheets – Climate change*. Retrieved December 28, 2012, from http://www.unep.org/publications/contents/title_search.asp?search=priority+areas&image.x=0&image.y=0

United Nations Environment Programme (2010b). *UNEP six priority areas factsheets – Disasters and conflicts*. Retrieved December 28, 2012, from http://www.unep.org/publications/contents/title_search.asp?search=priority+areas&image.x=0&image.y=0

United Nations Environment Programme (2010c). *UNEP six priority areas factsheets –Ecosystem management.* Retrieved December 28, 2012, from http://www.unep.org/publications/contents/title_search.asp?search=priority+areas&image.x=0&image.y=0

United Nations Environment Programme (2010d). *UNEP six priority areas factsheets –Environmental governance.* Retrieved December 28, 2012, from http://www.unep.org/publications/contents/title_search.asp?search=priority+areas&I mage.x=0&image.y=0

United Nations Environment Programme (2010e). *UNEP six priority areas factsheets – Resource efficiency.* Retrieved December 28, 2012, from http://www.unep.org/publications/contents/title_search.asp?search=priority+areas&image.x=0&image.y=0

United Nations Environment Programme (undated, a) *About DELC.* Retrieved December 29, 2012, from http://www.unep.org/delc/AboutDELC/tabid/54412/Default.aspx

United Nations Environment Programme (undated, b). *UNEP: Organization profile.* Retrieved December 28, 2012, from http://www.unep.org/PDF/UNEPOrganizationProfile.pdf

United Nations Global Compact (2010a). *Caring for climate: The business leadership platform.* Retrieved December 28, 2012, from http://www.unglobalcompact.org/docs/news_events/8.1/caring_for_climate.pdf

United Nations Global Compact (2010b). *Caring for climate working group on climate change and development.* Retrieved December 28, 2012, from http://www.unglobalcompact.org/docs/issues_doc/Environment/climate/Caring_for_Climate_Working_Group_Climate_and_Development.pdf

United Nations Global Compact (2011). *The CEO water mandate: An initiative by business leaders in partnership with the international community.* Retrieved December 28, 2012, from http://www.unglobalcompact.org/docs/news_events/8.1/Ceo_water_mandate.pdf

United Nations Global Compact (2011a). *Corporate sustainability in the world economy.* Retrieved December 28, 2012, from http://www.unglobalcompact.org/docs/news_events/8.1/GC_brochure_FINAL.pdf

United Nations Global Compact (2011b). *Global Compact local networks.* Retrieved December 28, 2012, from http://www.unglobalcompact.org/docs/networks_around_world_doc/LN_Brochure.pdf

United Nations Global Compact (2011c). *UN Global Compact CEO water mandate: Overview of priority areas in 2011 and 2012.* Retrieved December 28, 2012, from http://www.unglobalcompact.org/docs/issues_doc/Environment/ceo_water_mandate/Mandate_Workstreams.pdf

United Nations Global Compact (2012). *About Rio+20.* Retrieved December 28, 2012, from http://www.unglobalcompact.org/NewsAndEvents/rio_2012/about_rio_2012.html

United Nations Global Compact and Pacific Institute (2010). *The human right to water: Emerging corporate practice and stakeholder expectations.* Retrieved December 28, 2012, from http://www.unglobalcompact.org/docs/issues_doc/Environment/ceo_water_mandate/Water_Mandate_Human_Rights_White_Paper.pdf

United Nations Global Compact and World Wildlife Fund (2010). *Transformative solution leadership: 12 illustrative transformative low-carbon solutions.* Retrieved December 28, 2012, from http://www.unglobalcompact.org/docs/issues_doc/Environment/climate/LCLP_Transformative_Solutions.pdf

United Nations News Centre (2010). *General Assembly declares access to clean water and sanitation is a human right.* Retrieved December 28, 2012, from http://www.un.org/apps/news/story.asp?NewsID=35456&Cr=SANITATION

United Nations University (n.d.). *United Nations University Strategic plan 2009–2012: Towards sustainable solutions for global problems.* Retrieved December 28, 2012, from

Weber, E. U., & Stern, P. C. (2011). Public understanding of climate change in the United States. *American Psychologist, 66*(4), 315–328.

WindMade (2011). WindMade website. Retrieved from http://www.windmade.org

Zissener, M. (2011). *Solutions for those at risk in climate disasters.* United Nations University. Retrieved December 28, 2012, from http://unu.edu/articles/global-change-sustainable-development/solutions-for-those-at-risk-in-climate-disasters

15

Combining I-O Psychology and Technology for an Environmentally Sustainable World

Tara S. Behrend and Lori Foster Thompson

Technology lies at the heart of the green economy (Dierdorff, Norton, Gregory, Rivkin, & Lewis, this book). Trends in pollution, climate change, and the increasing scarcity of natural resources have heightened concern for the environment, prompting new technological solutions and innovations across the globe (Strietska-Ilina, Hofmann, Durán Haro, & Jeon, 2011). Implications for the world of work abound, providing opportunities for industrial and organizational (I-O) psychology research and practice to contribute to environmental sustainability.

Green technologies span a wide range of products, services, and processes that lower performance costs, reduce or eliminate negative ecological impact, and promote the productive and responsible use of natural resources (Henton, Melville, Grose, & Maor, 2008). Clean energy innovations provide one example of what can be considered green technology. These innovations produce heat, electricity, and transportation fuel through the use of sun, water, wind, and plant matter (Dierdorff et al., 2009). In 2006 alone, renewable energy and energy efficiency technologies generated 8.5 million new jobs in the United States (Bezdek, 2007).

Information and communication technology (ICT) provides another example of innovation with implications for the environment. ICT is an umbrella term referring to tools and systems (e.g., computers, mobile phones, the internet, social media) used in combination with procedures and processes that facilitate communication and assist in capturing, processing, and transmitting information electronically (Ahmad, Ibrahim, & Oye, 2011; Ssewanyana, 2007). Green ICT can be defined as "ICT which, as a result of usage, produce(s) comparatively low levels of carbon emissions while having the potential to exponentially reduce emissions in other areas by catalyzing technological, institutional and behavioral change" (Fernando & Okuda, 2009, p. 6). ICT is believed to be both an enabler as well as a driver of sustainable solutions to today's environmental problems (International Chamber of Commerce, 2010).

No matter how innovative it may be, technology alone does not guarantee results. In order to advance progress toward green goals and initiatives, the development, implementation, and application of technology needs to be managed carefully and strategically. I-O psychology can play an important role in this endeavor—for example, by contributing to the development of online work and occupational analysis information systems designed to identify the skills needed for occupations that are created or redefined by green technologies (Dierdorff et al., this book).

With a particular emphasis on ICT, this chapter describes a variety of opportunities for I-O psychology to interface with technological innovation in service of environmental sustainability. We begin with a consideration of social media, especially as a means to connect I-O psychologists, organizations, employees, and customers who share interests in working toward environmental sustainability. Afterwards, we discuss how I-O psychology can help employers and workers successfully implement, manage, and engage in a host of virtual, "green ICT" work practices, such as e-learning and telework. Under the right circumstances, such practices can favorably impact the environment. Expertise within the domain of I-O psychology can contribute to their effectiveness, acceptance, and sustained usage. Lastly, this chapter concludes by discussing the need to focus research and practice at the intersection of I-O psychology, ICT, and environmental sustainability on impoverished regions of the world.

SOCIAL NETWORKS

ICT offers a mechanism to connect global networks of organizational stakeholders and I-O psychologists with prosocial aims. Social networking and online communities can be particularly useful in this regard. Networking services are internet-based platforms or websites that connect users sharing similar interests. Online communities, an extension of this idea, are group-focused sites that allow members to communicate with one another directly or in groups. A wide range of social networking services exists, and their use is becoming increasingly popular. According to the Pew Research Foundation, 47% of adults used online social networking sites in 2010, an increase from 37% in 2008 (Lenhart, Purcell, Smith, & Zickuhr, 2010). Popular online communities and social networks vary with respect to their focus and intended audience; for example, LinkedIn has a professional theme. Twitter, another popular networking service, is used by individuals and organizations to directly communicate, to organize for an event or cause, and for publicity or customer service communication. Several distinct sustainability goals can be met with the use of social networks such as these. Below, we include several examples of how organizations can take advantage of these tools.

Social Network Use #1: *Communicate with customers and stakeholders.* Organizations can use social networks to communicate with customers about green practices and strategic initiatives. For example, the City of Berkeley has used this approach to generate interest in its wide-ranging corporate environmental sustainability (CES) initiatives (Presidio Graduate School, 2011). Many companies have begun to set up their own Facebook and Twitter pages in order to communicate efficiently with interested customers and stakeholders as well. Bortree (2011), in a survey of organizational public relations practitioners, found that organizations are interested in communicating to the public about recycling and energy reduction initiatives, though most relied on web and intranet sites, internal newsletters, and speeches more than social networks (e.g., Twitter, blogs). At the same time, the organizations surveyed indicated a desire to reach customers, activists, and shareholders, indicating a mismatch between their desired objectives and the means used. This suggests that organizations may be able to better reach their communication goals by using social networking tools more extensively.

Social Network Use #2: *Find resources and connect with peers.* Organizations can use services such as Twitter to search for others who are tackling similar problems or have ideas using keywords: for example, search for "corporate sustainability" or "telecommuting." This technology can also be used to connect people who are interested in various initiatives occurring through social networks.

Social Network Use #3: *Establish norms.* By issuing updates and statements relating to green practices, organizations can establish a clear set of norms and cultural values surrounding environmental sustainability practices. For example, Lehrer and Vasudev (2011) used a workplace social network to promote energy-saving behaviors by encouraging people to post updates about their own behaviors and monitor their peers' behavior. This capitalizes on the benefits of social influence for effecting positive behavior changes.

Despite these opportunities, organizations should also be aware of the potential limitations and challenges of using social networks. The ease of communication can create problems if messages are not considered carefully before being made public. All employees need to have a shared understanding of the appropriate use of the network. Support for the network can be increased if employees are given the opportunity to participate in the design and implementation of the program. In general, concerns regarding the effective implementation of social media will be of increasing importance as "digital natives" (i.e., people who grew up with social media) join the workforce with expectations about easy and open digital collaboration with others (Landers & Goldberg, in press). Some I-O psychologists specialize in research and practice designed to help organizations and employees make effective use of social media (e.g., Digital Culture Consulting [http://www.digitalcultureconsulting.com]; Stoughton, Thompson, Meade, & Wilson, 2012). Thus, I-O psychology can facilitate social media's usefulness for green projects and initiatives.

DIGITAL/VIRTUAL WORK

ICT can also be a means through which employees and organizations accomplish sustainability goals directly. I-O psychology can aid in this effort. By way of analogy, consider GreenPlumbers®, a training program designed to teach plumbers about the environmental considerations of their work (Strietska-Ilina et al., 2011). This Australian program, which has recently expanded into New Zealand and North America, puts plumbers in a better position to advise clients and help them make green choices. Similarly, I-O psychologists are in a good position to help their clients make green choices. In the context of work organizations, such choices may entail virtual work practices.

Organizations are adopting new ways of using green ICTs to work, and this necessarily requires a period of adjustment on the part of workers and managers (Leung & Peterson, 2011). I-O psychology is poised to offer advice and guidance to ease this adjustment and provide tools to ensure that technology is used effectively. Here we highlight several such possibilities, though we acknowledge that as workplace technology continues to evolve at a rapid rate, so too will the ways in which I-O psychologists can support these efforts.

E-Learning/Development

Shifting learning experiences from classroom-style courses to individualized, computer-based courses can save resources by permitting people to learn anytime and anywhere, reducing travel and energy costs associated with a physical classroom. Many organizations are now using e-learning for these reasons, either as a supplement or replacement for in-person training. According to the American Society for Training and Development (2008), over one-third of training courses in 2008 were delivered electronically, either remotely or on-site. Frequently, environmental concerns are a primary reason for the adoption of e-learning. For example, the World Bank/International Finance Corporation uses e-learning as part of an overall strategy to become carbon neutral (Christopher & Hellman, 2011). The United Nations Institute for Training and Research (UNITAR) also emphasizes e-learning. According to Carlos Lopes, Executive Director of UNITAR:

> Enhancing the use of technology-supported learning, such as e-learning and video-conferencing, is an important dimension of our strategy to become carbon-neutral and can be an effective complement to traditional learning approaches, such as face-to-face training. UNITAR is committed to becoming carbon-neutral and...will monitor and prepare annual inventories of its greenhouse gas emissions, take systematic steps to reduce its emission per unit of training delivered, and offset remaining emissions by purchasing offsets under the UN-approved Clean Development Mechanism (http://www.greeningtheblue.org/what-the-un-is-doing/united-nations-institute-training-and-research-unitar).

E-learning has obvious appeal for its flexibility and efficiency, but these characteristics can also introduce difficulties. Given ultimate flexibility in where and when they learn, some learners may rush through material or skip important information (Brown, 2001; DeRouin, Fritsche, & Salas, 2005).

Put another way, learner control over training decisions such as pace and sequence of training materials is not always a good thing, and can encourage busy or distracted learners to take detrimental shortcuts. From existing research, we know that problems with e-learning can be minimized if learners are equipped to make good decisions and are motivated to do so. This implies that remote, self-paced e-learning should only be considered when trainees are motivated (e.g., recognize the connection between the training and their job duties) and are given sufficient time and support to complete the training without distractions. It is also important to ensure that trainees have sufficient computer skill and computer self-efficacy to succeed in the course (Brown, 2001; Welsh, Wanberg, Brown, & Simmering, 2003).

The importance of good design and evaluation practices should also be emphasized. Good web-based training is designed to be engaging without distracting; this means using interesting visuals and keeping modules short (Clark & Mayer, 2008; Noe, 2010). The content of courses should also be created according to sound learning principles. Trainees should be given opportunities to practice what they learn, and they should receive feedback on their progress. Through avatars and pedagogical agents, virtual coaches can be employed for this purpose. The inclusion of an animated character can reduce some of the felt isolation that occurs in many e-learning courses and can be a source of valuable feedback and guidance (Lee et al., 2007).

This discussion centers on "using technology to train workers," which is clearly important to the green economy. "Training workers to use technology" is another area of importance where I-O psychology can play a role. As technological innovations change the nature of and demand for various occupations (Dierdorff et al., this book), there will be a steady need to equip youth entering the labor market as well as mid- and late-career older workers with the skills required to use green technologies (Strietska-Ilina et al., 2011). Evidence-based guidelines for training older workers to use technology exist (e.g., Thompson & Mayhorn, 2012) and should be incorporated into learning programs where appropriate—for example, to speed reemployment into new, greener industries and occupations when older workers lose jobs in "brown" industries (Strietska-Ilina et al., 2011).

E-Recruitment and Selection

As with learning, moving the functions of recruitment and selection to the internet has environmental appeal, reducing paper usage and eliminating travel for applicants, recruiters, and interviewers. Attention to careful design and implementation can help reduce problems such as unfavorable applicant reactions, decision-making errors, or inadvertent dismissal of qualified applicants.

Recruitment

Nearly every organization of size promotes itself via the internet, in the form of a "careers" page on its website or through distributing information by other means such as jobs portals, job boards, or online applications (Stone, Lukaszewski, & Isenhour, 2005). However, just as small interactions with recruiters can have large effects on applicants (Rynes, Bretz, & Gerhart, 1991), so too can seemingly unimportant elements of an organization's web presence. A poorly designed or difficult to use website can lead applicants to form negative impressions of the organization as a whole (Braddy, Meade, & Kroustalis, 2008; Sinar, Reynolds, & Paquet, 2003). Moving recruitment online can be seen as inflexible or impersonal by applicants (Stone et al., 2005). Further, a poorly designed website leads to confusion on the part of applicants, who may end up applying for jobs they are unqualified for, or choosing not to apply based on some misinformation (Dineen, Ling, Ash, & DelVecchio, 2007). For instance, Cable and Yu (2006) found that face-to-face communication led to more accurate organizational image beliefs than traditional websites, and Badger, Kaminsky, and Behrend (2011) found that highly interactive websites were especially poor in communicating organizational culture information clearly.

On the other hand, a recruiting website, when designed well, can be used to promote attractive organizational values. For example, Walker, Feild, Giles, Armenakis, and Bernerth (2009) showed that the use of video testimonials led applicants to view the organization as more innovative and more attractive as a result. An organization's web presence can also be used to communicate directly to applicants about an organization's environmental sustainability values and goals. For example, Behrend, Baker, and Thompson (2009) showed that a simple message on an organizational careers site was effective in communicating organizational sustainability values, and that these values led applicants to view the organization as a more prestigious and desirable employer.

However, we caution that the increase in the sheer number of recruits/applicants attracted with online recruiting makes screening and selection processes all the more important. That is, a larger proportion of the applicant pool may be unqualified or a poor fit given the relative ease of applying for many jobs online (Dineen et al., 2007). Presenting clear information about minimum qualifications and job requirements in online postings can help somewhat with this problem, as can presenting applicants with personalized information about their likely fit with particular openings (Dineen et al., 2007).

Selection

The use of ICT for assessment and selection is increasingly popular (Tippins, 2011). It is possible to administer a wide range of personality, cognitive ability, or work sample tests online, eliminating travel for test administrators and candidates and reducing paper for record-keeping (see Andrews, Klein, Forsman, & Sachau, this book, for a discussion on the environmental impact of online selection systems). I-O researchers have helped with this transition, investigating the equivalence of assessments administered in paper and electronic formats. For the most part, these investigations have shown that online assessments are roughly equivalent to paper assessment for non-cognitive measures such as personality (e.g., Meade, Michels, & Lautenschlager, 2007; Richman, Kiesler, Weisband, & Drasgow, 1999). Conversely, cognitive measures, especially speeded tests, may diverge from their paper counterparts when moved to online formats (Reynolds & Dickter, 2010); however, some of these differences can be beneficial (e.g., more normally distributed data and better reliability in online situational judgment tests; Ployhart, Weekly, Holtz, & Kemp, 2003).

Online testing presents a number of challenges for I-O psychology research and practice. Primary among these challenges is the need to make sure that technology-enhanced tests only measure job-related constructs and no other factors; these other factors can include bias due to technology anxiety, hardware difficulties, cheating, or inadequate internet access. The use of unproctored internet testing, in particular, has raised concerns about test security and possible cheating (Naglieri et al., 2004). These concerns can be partially addressed, though not eliminated, with verification of scores at a later date; or a warning that scores will be subject to verification (Nye, Do, Drasgow, & Fine, 2008). In the United States, administering a test online also requires consideration of fairness based on access or accommodations specified by the Americans With Disabilities Act (1990), such as extra time or readable text (Tippins, 2009). It can be difficult to balance these concerns with the goals of providing a standardized and secure testing environment.

In addition to deploying internet versions of paper tests, new ways of assessment can be developed through ICT. For example, the U.S. Department of Homeland Security uses video-based assessment for selection (Cucina et al., 2011). In this assessment, applicants view taped scenes on a TV monitor in a testing room equipped with a video camera. The video depicts frequently encountered situations for the job in question. Applicants are instructed to respond to the scene in character as if they are involved in the situation, and their response is video-taped. This assessment has replaced an in-person oral interview, eliminating the need for assessors to travel in order to screen candidates. This process also allows for multiple raters to score each candidate. Given that the Department of Homeland Security screens 5,000–15,000 applicants each year using this assessment, the energy savings are substantial. This example reflects a growing trend in selection towards more efficiency, speed, and automation (Reynolds & Dickter, 2010; Reynolds & Weiner, 2009). We offer it as one example of highly vivid and interactive technologies being used in selection with some success. Though this type of simulation is gaining popularity, there is relatively little research regarding its effectiveness to date. I-O research can help to inform the use of high-fidelity assessments such as these.

Virtual Work/Telecommuting

Another potential way in which I-O and ICT can work together to support CES goals is in the domain of telecommuting. Telecommuting, or remote work, is defined as work that takes place anywhere other than an organization's primary office space; this can mean an employee's home, a satellite office, or a designated telework center (e.g., an office that is available for employees of various organizations to use on a rental or lease basis). Telecommuting may make up all or part of an employee's time. The key components of telework are the physical location away from the primary office, and the use of electronic tools for communicating with coworkers and accomplishing one's work. Telecommuting, remote work, and virtual work are currently increasing in popularity as ways to reduce commuting-related time and expense, and increase employee autonomy (Gajendran & Harrison, 2007; see Andrews et al., this book, for a full discussion on the environmental impact of telework). The U.S. Office of Personnel Management (OPM) emphasizes and encourages telework to reduce travel. According to their 2010 report to Congress, 113,946 Federal employees teleworked in 2009; an increase of 11,046 employees from 2008. The report notes that "President Obama, the Congress, and OPM have all encouraged Federal agencies to expand their use of telework to ensure continuity of operations; find targeted productivity improvements and reduce overhead, real estate, environmental, and transit costs" (U.S. Office of Personnel Management, 2011, p. 4). Environmental impact due to energy savings and CO_2 emissions is noted as an explicit goal of the government's telecommuting initiative.

Though telecommuting initiatives are very popular, virtual work has the potential to create problems for employees, including isolation from coworkers (Golden, 2008). Frequent telecommuters are at risk for deterioration of work relationships, which can have a number of adverse effects (Gajendran & Harrison, 2007). However, MacDuffie (2008) notes that while the mere presence of others and shared social contexts are good, many studies comparing collocated and distributed teams show no clear differences in group identity or satisfaction (e.g., Webster & Wong, 2008), suggesting that if virtual work is planned thoughtfully, it can be a positive experience. For telecommuters to be successful, they need clear structure and expectations about roles, norms, procedures, and expectations (Leung & Peterson, 2011). Remote workers also need access to the appropriate tools for conducting their work, which may add costs.

Additional factors should be taken into consideration when remote staff members work collaboratively in teams. New teams need more structure and support than ongoing teams when using digital media (Maruping & Agarwal, 2004). Digital aids should also be used for decision making and organization when teams work virtually. It has been generally assumed in the past that virtual teams are at a disadvantage compared with face-to-face teams. But, to the extent that they can take advantage of available support software, they may outperform face-to-face teams (e.g., on brainstorming tasks; Martins, Gilson, & Maynard, 2004). For example, databases and decision-making tools can help equalize participation and record or organize information (Carte & Chidambaram, 2004). Coovert & Thompson (2003) present an overall summary of the difficulties that can be faced by virtual teams, providing suggestions for how to improve a team's overall functioning. First, they recommend giving teams additional time to complete their work, because coordination is more difficult virtually. Second, they recommend that teams participate in informal kickoff meetings, where they can begin to discover similarities and form friendships that will help them in later collaboration. Third, they recommend building "awareness moments" into teamwork. This can reduce the sense of isolation that many virtual team members experience. Awareness moments can take the form of a shared real-time discussion board, instant messaging system, or another method of conveying the sense that others are present. Fourth, they recommend that teams participate in training to learn how to go about virtual teamwork and become familiar with the technology.

Building trust may be one of the most important activities in which virtual teams need to engage. Several studies have demonstrated the importance of trust (e.g., Hinds & Bailey, 2003; Naquin & Paulson, 2003; Wilson, Straus, & McEvily, 2006). Kirkman, Rosen, Tesluk, and Gibson (2006) showed that in high-tech teams trust was the critical factor in predicting performance as measured by customer satisfaction ratings. Specifically, teams who performed well in teamwork skills training (e.g., how to make a charter, goal setting) but had low trust had the worst customer ratings. Teams with high trust had higher ratings. Essentially, teams who did not trust one another had difficulty coordinating their efforts to complete tasks—they were unable to use the information they gained in training.

Paperless Offices/Cloud Computing

Emphasis on digital files, communication, and project management is the norm in many organizations. This can be taken one step further by storing files on central cloud servers, further reducing energy costs associated with local hardware. Many organizations are beginning to take advantage of inexpensive products that can accomplish this with ease. For example, American Airlines has recently begun a test to switch from paper flight documents to digital documents stored on tablet computers, and estimates this switch will save $1.2 million in fuel annually (*Washington Post*, 2011).

An extension of the paperless office is the use of remote servers for storage and distribution of documents and software, typically referred to as cloud computing. At the time of this writing, examples of commonly used cloud computing services include Google Docs, Dropbox, and Amazon's Cloud Drive. Cloud computing can save energy because central servers have the potential to be more energy efficient than many individual hard drives. According to the Carbon Disclosure Project, which tracks business-related climate change information, cloud computing is expected to lead large U.S. companies to save $12.3 billion on energy costs and cut out 85.7 million metric tons of carbon dioxide emissions annually by 2020 (Fehren-bacher, 2011).

Despite these benefits, several concerns become relevant when an organization moves documents and files online. Some individuals may feel that documents are less reliable online, and may wish to retain paper copies, negating any environmental benefits. Thus, ensuring that employees actually trust and adopt the tools provided is critical. In the case of cloud computing adoption, users must have confidence in their computing skills and they must perceive the tool as reliable (Behrend, London, Wiebe, & Johnson, 2010). Since any early technology failures or errors will significantly reduce the likelihood that employees trust cloud computing for storage of important documents, careful planning and testing are essential.

Monitoring, Feedback, and Tracking

Some organizations intensely focused on sustainability have moved to a "triple bottom line" paradigm, which sets environmental and social goals alongside financial ones (Lombardo, Schneider, & Koppes Bryan, in press; Marsden, 2000). This offers opportunity and challenge to I-O psychologists and business leaders interested in developing ways to assess environmental performance, not only at the organizational level, but at the individual level as well. Electronic monitoring could play a role.

Technology can be used to track employee behavior and deliver feedback regarding specific environmental goals or milestones, much in the same way that many organizations collect and report information about wellness initiatives (e.g., healthy eating and exercise campaigns). The electronic monitoring of employees at work has become commonplace. According to a 2007 American Management Association (AMA) survey, 66% of organizations monitor internet usage, 45% track keystrokes/content/time spent on the computer, and 43% monitor email. Though progress on CES goals has not been commonly included as part of the set of behaviors that is monitored or tracked, it could be. These goals may include, for example, using public transportation or walking/biking to work, conserving energy, recycling, and turning off printers and lights before leaving the office.

Froehlich, Findlater, and Landay (2010) point out that existing eco-feedback tools are rarely designed with an understanding of what motivates human behavior. Feedback and learning principles are important and can be used to design effective tools for delivering eco-feedback effectively. As one example, Van Houwlingen and Van Raaij (1989) used immediate electronic feedback to alter people's in-home energy use, showing that a combination of goal setting and daily electronic feedback caused a 12.3% reduction in home energy consumption. Similar principles could also work well for work-related energy use. However, if this type of feedback is to be successful in changing people's habits, it must be implemented with careful consideration of psychological factors. Electronic monitoring, CES related or otherwise, should be viewed as fair to be effective. Given that electronic monitoring can be pervasive, occur without awareness, and record virtually every action, especially on the computer, concerns over the privacy of personal information are growing (Alge, Ballinger, Tangirala, & Oakley, 2006). Stanton (2000) found that consistency, control, and justification are related to the fairness of a monitoring system. Perceived fairness, in turn, has been shown to positively relate to job performance and satisfaction (Alder & Ambrose, 2005; McNall & Roch, 2009).

Some monitoring systems are already being used experimentally to encourage employees to engage in sustainable behaviors. For example, Medland (2010) used a system designed to track individual employees' paper consumption and deliver regular feedback. It is important to note that this study showed that employees did not respond uniformly to the feedback; the author attributed these variable reactions to differing motivations and beliefs. These isolated findings bear further scrutiny, and more research is needed to determine how to best design CES monitoring systems that will be fair, accepted by employees, and effective.

Looking forward, another way that ICT and electronic monitoring can aid in CES initiatives is through the incorporation of social and gaming features into behavior change initiatives. Such systems could incorporate "carbon footprint calculators," which have been developed for computers and smartphones to enable people to gauge their consumption of resources such as paper, fuel, and power. This information could be shared with coworkers and form the basis of games or competitions that encourage environmentally-friendly behaviors.

Indeed, games have been discussed as a medium for increasing environmental awareness, employee motivation, and job skills (International Chamber of Commerce, 2010; Silverman, 2011).

One example of using games to develop job skills is provided by the U.S. government, which contracted with Raytheon to develop a game with an international detective theme, which was designed to teach users about decision-making skills (Cooney, 2011). Such "serious games" are also being used experimentally to train military personnel (Orvis, Horn, & Belanich, 2009) and medical professionals (e.g., Zero Hour: America's Medic; Virtual Heroes Inc.). Currently, serious games such as these are used predominantly for training purposes, but a similar logic might be used to incorporate gaming elements into CES goals. Employees can compete to reach recycling, transportation, or energy goals. They can receive points for meeting milestones. Social elements can be incorporated, such that teams can see each other's progress and compete. There is a great deal of potential in this arena, and research is needed to determine how to use serious games effectively to motivate behavior that will contribute to CES initiatives.

EXPANDING THE FOCUS TO IMPOVERISHED REGIONS

As discussed earlier, ICT can be a valuable mechanism for promoting environmental sustainability at and through work. Just as plumbers are being taught to help their clients make green choices, I-O psychologists can help organizations and workers do the same—for example, through education, science, and best practices pertaining to virtual collaboration, e-learning, and online recruitment. Travel substitutions (e.g., virtual meetings, online selection instruments) mean less traffic; if there is less traffic, there is less CO_2 (International Chamber of Commerce, 2010). Evidence-based recommendations that help turn virtual work practices into a business advantage thus have the potential to help workers, organizations, and the environment. To this end, Figure 15.1 offers some example principles, extracted from the literature, which can begin to guide organizations toward virtual work effectiveness.

Note, however, some unstated assumptions implied throughout this chapter—namely, that workers generally have access to broadband

Though the challenges of implementing technology may vary according to the purpose of the tool and its features, some general principles for the successful implementation of technology in the workplace are as follows.

- Good leadership is essential in reducing the uncertainty and ambiguity that comes with virtual work. Zaccaro and Bader (2003) note that trust building is an especially important skill for leaders of virtual workers.
- Successful technology adoption depends on a number of factors. Employees will be more willing to adopt new technologies if they have the skills to use them well; if the tools are perceived to be user-friendly; and, most importantly, if the tool serves a clear purpose and is seen as more useful than the low-tech alternative (Venkatesh & Bala, 2008; Venkatesh, Morris, Davis, & Davis, 2003).
- As more technology-delivered services become available, a greater burden will be placed on individual employees to exercise autonomy and self-regulation. That is, employees will be expected to seek out the tools they need and make decisions for their own learning and development. It is wise to assess whether individual workers have the skills and knowledge to do this effectively.
- In the other direction, as tailoring and customization become exponentially easier to accomplish, people's expectations for tailoring will increase as a result, meaning people will expect services that are customized to their needs.
- Remember that the most advanced or newest solution is not always the best one. Media differ in terms of how much they allow for the transmission of information (conveyance) and how much they allow people to come to agreement or disagreement (requiring give and take; convergence; Dennis, Fuller, & Valacich, 2008). Various tasks and functions will require technological tools that vary with regard to conveyance and convergence capabilities. For example, email is not the most appropriate tool for group discussion. A highly rich virtual world is similarly inappropriate for the communication of dense factual information. It is important to consider *task-technology fit* in this way before adopting technological tools for the purposes of meeting sustainability goals.

FIGURE 15.1
General principles for the use of technology in organizations.

internet, a computer, and electricity that can be depended upon. Although these assumptions arguably underlie much of the literature on virtual work and I-O psychology in general, they are not always valid. The vast majority of the world's population lives in developing countries (United Nations Development Programme, 2010). Such regions face a variety of resource constraints, some of which pertain to internet connectivity and access to modern energy services (United Nations Conference on Trade and Development, 2011a). Indeed, global disparities in access to, usage of, and motivation to use ICT have been at the heart of discussions of the so-called "digital divide" (United Nations, 2011; Van Dijk, 2006). See Reichman, Berry, Cruse, and Lytle (this book) for a review of international organizations that promote CES.

Even though they are the least responsible for climate change, developing countries are hit the hardest by its consequences (Strietska-Ilina et al., 2011). People whose livelihood depends on farming, fishing, and traditional crafts, for example, are at risk for extreme poverty when climate change deprives them of those sources of income. Interventions can help to build and channel talent among members of developing countries to fruitful, productive, and fulfilling ends. Such interventions could entail various aspects of I-O psychology, such as work and occupational analysis, job placement, training for green skills, and the design of programs to select and develop leadership and entrepreneurial competencies.

In short, we propose that I-O psychology's role in the CES sphere needs to expand to include a greater focus on developing countries. This suggestion is consistent with recent trends toward humanitarian work psychology (HWP), which can be defined as the synthesis of I-O psychology with deliberate and organized efforts to enhance human welfare (Gloss & Thompson, in press). To be effective, such a synthesis requires attention to other disciplines outside of I-O, as well as the perspectives and cultural nuances of workers and work in developing countries (Carr & Bandawe, 2011). The effect of local culture on core constructs such as work motivation, for example, needs to be identified and taken into account when conducting research and practice in developing countries (Franco, Bennett, Kanfer, & Stubblebine, 2004).

It is important to note that the call for I-O psychology's increased involvement in sustainable work practices in lower income regions of the world is by no means unrelated to this chapter's emphasis on ICT. In our view, I-O psychology's potential to contribute to sustainability efforts devoted to international development cannot be fully realized without a careful consideration of technology. ICT can be combined with I-O psychology in a variety of ways—for example, in the development and evaluation of computer-based training programs, virtual assessment centers, and online screening instruments to determine candidates' suitability for loans to support small and medium-sized enterprises—that are seen as important to international development (Carr, 2011). Another example entails combining social networking with research and best practices pertaining to virtual collaboration. Specifically, social networking tools can be used as a mechanism to turn global mobility into a source of "information gain" for impoverished regions of the world, by organizing and mobilizing off-shore diasporas—that is, groups of expatriates living abroad, such as those forced out of their country of origin due to political unrest, lack of resources, or fear of persecution. Through ICT, community members living abroad can collaborate with individuals in their country of origin, in some cases enabling developing countries to benefit from the "green" knowledge and skills that diaspora members gain after relocating to a more developed region of the world (Thompson & Atkins, 2010). I-O psychology research on virtual teamwork can contribute to the effectiveness of such efforts.

Clearly, the potential for ICT to contribute to the development of low-income countries is not a new idea. Indeed, an entire multidisciplinary field has coalesced around this notion. This field is commonly referred to as Information and Communication Technologies for Development (ICTD or ICT4D). Topic areas addressed by the field of ICTD include business (e.g., e-commerce, entrepreneurship, employment, industry, microfinance), empowerment (e.g., community development, citizen participation, social capital), and education (e.g., literacy and science). Issues pertaining to the environment are also addressed (Gomez, Baron, & Fiore-Silfvast, 2012). Many ICTD studies and interventions center on the use of mobile phones for work or business, as mobile phones have become the most prevalent ICT tool among the poor and are commonly being used for micro-enterprise initiatives in low-income countries (United Nations Conference on Trade and Development, 2011b). To illustrate, an example ICTD intervention could entail the development and evaluation of a phone-based short message service (SMS) system that connects entrepreneurs in low-income rural areas to mentors with expertise pertaining to environmental issues and green technologies. Such a system could be implemented following an instructional program on topics pertaining to the environment, in order to encourage and reinforce green business practices taught during training.

ICTD interventions with environmental aims would benefit from I-O psychology's involvement. For instance, research and best practices pertaining to training transfer, mentorship, mobile business practices, and virtual collaboration would be useful in designing and implementing the illustrative SMS-based mentorship system just described. To date, however, I-O psychology and ICTD have had little involvement with one another. As noted by Behrend, Gloss, and Thompson (in press), there is a need for increased cooperation between these two fields. Such collaboration offers promise for the environment as well as for disadvantaged communities and workers in impoverished regions of the world, thereby facilitating "a green and just transition, not just a green transition" to a low-carbon and green economy worldwide (Strietska-Ilina et al., 2011, p. 166).

REFERENCES

Ahmad, M. S., Ibrahim, I., & Oye, N. D. (2011). Role of information communication technology (ICT): Implications on unemployment and Nigerian GDP. *Journal of International Academic Research, 11*, 9–17.

Alder, G., & Ambrose, M. L. (2005). An examination of the effect of computerized performance monitoring feedback on monitoring fairness, performance, and satisfaction. *Organizational Behavior and Human Decision Processes, 97*(2), 161–177.

Alge, B. J., Ballinger, G. A., Tangirala, S., & Oakley, J. L. (2006). Information privacy in organizations: Empowering creative and extra-role performance. *Journal of Applied Psychology, 91*(1), 221–232.

American Management Association (AMA) (2007). *Electronic monitoring and surveillance survey*. New York, NY: Author. Retrieved January 1, 2013, from http://www.amanet. org/training/whitepapers/2007-Electronic-Monitoring-and-Surveillance-Survey-41.aspx

American Society for Training and Development (ASTD) (2008). *ASTD state of the industry report*. Alexandria, VA: Author.

Badger, J. M., Kaminsky, S., & Behrend, T. S. (2011, April). Employee recruitment in virtual worlds: Effects on information transfer. In R. L. Landers & T. S. Behrend (chairs), *Empirical evidence for emerging technology: MUVEs/virtual worlds in human resources*. Symposium presented to the 26th Annual Meeting of the Society for Industrial and Organizational Psychology, Chicago, IL.

Behrend, T. S., Baker, B. A., & Thompson, L. F. (2009). Effects of pro-environmental recruiting messages: The role of organizational reputation. *Journal of Business and Psychology, 24*, 341–350.

Behrend, T. S., Gloss, A. E., & Thompson, L. F. (in press). Global development through the psychology of workplace technology. In M. D. Coovert & L. F. Thompson (Eds.), *The psychology of workplace technology*. New York, NY: Routledge Academic.

Behrend, T. S., London, J. E., Wiebe, E. N., & Johnson, E. C. (2010). Cloud computing adoption and usage in community colleges. *Behaviour & Information Technology, 30*, 231–240.

Bezdek, R. (2007). *Renewable energy and energy efficiency: Economic drivers for the 21st century*. Boulder, CO: American Solar Energy Society. Retrieved January 1, 2013, from http://www.greenforall.org/resources/renewable-energy-and-energy-efficiency-economic.

Bortree, D. S. (2011). The state of environmental communication: A survey of PRSA members. *Public Relations Journal, 5,* 1–17.

Braddy, P. W., Meade, A. W., & Kroustalis, C. M. (2008). Online recruiting: The effects of organizational familiarity, website usability, and website attractiveness of viewers' impressions of organizations. *Computers in Human Behavior, 24,* 2992–3001.

Brown, K. G. (2001). Using computers to deliver training: Which employees learn and why? *Personnel Psychology, 54,* 271–296.

Cable, D. M., & Yu, K. Y. T. (2006). Managing job seekers' organizational image beliefs: The role of media richness and media credibility. *Journal of Applied Psychology, 91,* 828–840. doi: 10.1037/0021-9010.91.4.828

Carr, S. C. (2011). Enabling capacity in the "missing middle": Expanding roles for psychometric tests? *The Industrial-Organizational Psychologist, 48*(3), 97–100.

Carr, S. C., & Bandawe, C. R. (2011) Psychology applied to poverty. In P. R. Martin, F. M. Cheung, M. C. Knowles, M. Kyrios, J. B. Overmier, & J. M. Prieto (Eds.), *IAAP handbook of applied psychology* (pp. 639–662). Oxford, UK: Wiley-Blackwell.

Carte, T., & Chidambaram, L. (2004). A capabilities-based theory of technology deployment in diverse teams: Leapfrogging the pitfalls of diversity and leveraging its potential with collaborative technology. *Journal of the Association for Information Systems, 5,* 448–471.

Christopher, D., & Hellman, P. (2011, May). *Connecting talent champions to build global talent at the World Bank Group.* Presentation at the Annual Meeting of the American Society for Training and Development, Washington, DC.

Clark, R. C., & Mayer, R. E. (2008). *E-Learning and the science of instruction: Proven guidelines for consumers and designers of multimedia learning.* San Francisco, CA: Jossey-Bass.

Cooney, M. (2011, November 18). Raytheon gets $10.5m to develop "serious games." *Network World,* retrieved January 1, 2013, from http://www.networkworld. com/community/blog/raytheon-gets-105m-develop-serious-games

Coovert, M. D. & Thompson, L. F. (2001). *Computer-supported cooperative work: Issues and implications for workers, organizations, and human resource management.* Thousand Oaks, CA: Sage.

Cucina, J. M., Busciglio, H. H., Thomas, P. H., Callen, N. F., Walker, D. D., & Schoepfer, R. J. G. (2011). Video-based testing at US Customs and Border Protection. In S. Adler & N. T. Tippins (Eds.), *Technology-enhanced assessment of talent* (pp. 338–354). San Francisco, CA: Jossey-Bass.

Dennis, A. R., Fuller, R. M., & Valacich, J. S. (2008). Media, tasks, and communication processes: A theory of media synchronicity. *MIS Quarterly, 32,* 575–600.

DeRouin, R. E., Fritsche, B. A., & Salas, E. (2005). E-learning in organizations. *Journal of Management, 37*(5), 249–265.

Dierdorff, E. C., Norton, J. J., Drewes, D. W., Kroustalis, C. M., Rivkin, D., & Lewis, P. (2009). *Greening of the world of work: Implications for O*NET®-SOC and new and emerging occupations.* Raleigh, NC: National Center for O*NET Development.

Dineen, B. R., Ling, J., Ash, S. R., & DelVecchio, D. (2007). Aesthetic properties and message customization: Navigating the dark side of web recruitment. *Journal of Applied Psychology, 92,* 356–372.

Fehrenbacher, K. (2011, July). *Cloud computing could lead to billions in energy savings.* Retrieved January 1, 2013, from: http://www.nytimes.com/external/gigaom/2011/07/21/21gigaom-cloud-computing-could-lead-to-billions-in-energy-s-7485.html

Fernando, P., & Okuda, A. (2009). *Green ICT: A "cool" factor in the wake of multiple melt-*

downs. ESCAP technical paper. Retrieved 1 January, 2013, from http://www.unescap. org/idd/working%20papers/IDD_TP_09_10_of_WP_7_2_907.pdf

Franco, L. M., Bennett, S., Kanfer, R., & Stubblebine, P. (2004). Determinants and consequences of health worker motivation in hospitals in Jordan and Georgia. *Social Science & Medicine, 58,* 343–355.

Froehlich, J., Findlater, L., & Landay, J. (2010). *The design of eco-feedback technology.* Proceedings of the SIGCHI Conference on Human Factors in Computing Systems, 2010, 1999–2008.

Gajendran, R. S. & Harrison, D. A. 2007. The good, the bad, and the unknown about telecommuting: Meta-analysis of psychological mediators and individual consequences. *Journal of Applied Psychology, 92,* 1524–1541.

Gloss, A. E., & Thompson, L. F. (in press). I-O psychology without borders: The emergence of humanitarian work psychology. In J. B. Olson-Buchanan, L. L. Koppes Bryan, & L. F. Thompson (Eds.), *Using I-O psychology for the greater good: Helping those who help others.* New York, NY: Routledge Academic.

Golden, T. D. (2008). The impact of professional isolation on teleworker job performance and turnover intentions: Does time spent teleworking, interacting face-to-face, or having access to communication-enhancing technology matter? *Journal of Applied Psychology, 93*(6), 1412–1421.

Gomez, R., Baron, L. F., & Fiore-Silfvast, B. (2012). *The changing field of ICTD: Content analysis of research published in selected journals and conferences, 2000–2012.* Paper presented at the meeting of the International Conference on Information and Communications Technologies and Development (ICTD), Atlanta, GA.

Henton, D., Melville, J., Grose, T., & Maor, G. (2008). Clean technology and the green economy: Growing products, services, businesses, and jobs in California's value network – DRAFT. *Digest of Green Reports and Studies.* Retrieved January 1, 2013, from http://www.labormarketinfo.edd.ca.gov/contentpub/GreenDigest/Clean-Technology-and-the-Green-Economy.pdf

Hinds, P., & Bailey, D. (2003). Out of sight, out of sync: Understanding conflict in distributed teams. *Organization Science, 14,* 615–632.

International Chamber of Commerce (2010). ICTs and environmental sustainability. Paris, France. Retrieved January 1, 2013, from http://www.iccwbo.org/Advocacy-Codes-and-Rules/Document-centre/2010/ICTs-and-environmental-sustainability-Discussion-Paper

Kirkman, B. L., Rosen, B., Tesluk, P., & Gibson, C. (2006). Enhancing the transfer of computer-assisted training proficiency in geographically-distributed teams. *Journal of Applied Psychology, 91,* 706–716.

Landers, R. N. & Goldberg, A. S. (in press). Online social media in the workplace: A conversation with employees. In M. D. Coovert & L. F. Thompson (Eds.), *The psychology of workplace technology.* New York, NY: Routledge Academic.

Lee, J. R., Nass, C., Brave, S., Morishima, Y., Nakajima, H., & Yamada, R. (2007). The case for caring colearners: The effects of a computer-mediated colearner agent on trust and learning. *Journal of Communication, 57,* 183–204.

Lehrer, D., & Vasudev, J. (2011). Evaluating a social media application for sustainability in the workplace. *Proceedings of CHI11,* 2161–2166.

Lenhart, A., Purcell, K., Smith, A., & Zickuhr, K. (2010). *Social media use among teens and young adults.* Washington DC: Pew Research Center.

Leung, K., & Peterson, M. (2011). Managing a globally distributed workforce: Social and interpersonal issues. APA handbook of industrial and organizational psychology, Vol 3: Maintaining, expanding, and contracting the organization (pp. 771–805). Washington, DC: American Psychological Association. doi: 10.1037/12171-022

Lombardo, T., Schneider, S. K., & Koppes Bryan, L. L. (in press). Corporate leaders of sustainable organizations: Balancing profit, planet and people. In J. B. Olson-Buchanan, L. L. Koppes Bryan, & L. F. Thompson (Eds.), *Using I-O psychology for the greater good: Helping those who help others.* New York, NY: Routledge Academic.

MacDuffie, J. F. (2008). HRM and distributed work: Managing people across distances. In J. P. Walsh and A. P. Brief (Eds.), *The Academy of Management Annals* (pp. 549–615). New York, NY: Erlbaum.

Marsden, C. (2000). The new corporate citizenship of big business: Part of the solution to sustainability? *Business and Society Review, 105*, 9–25.

Martins, L. L., Gilson, L. L., & Maynard, M. T. (2004). Virtual teams: What do we know and where do we go from here? *Journal of Management, 30*, 805–835.

Maruping, L. M., & Agarwal, R. (2004). Managing team interpersonal processes through technology: A task-technology fit perspective. *Journal of Applied Psychology, 89*, 975–990.

McNall, L. A., & Roch, S. G. (2009). A social exchange model of employee reactions to electronic performance monitoring. *Human Performance, 22*(3), 204–224.

Meade, A. W., Michels, L. C., & Lautenschlager, G. J. (2007). Are internet and paper-and-pencil personality tests truly comparable? An experimental design measurement invariance study. *Organizational Research Methods, 10*, 322–345.

Medland, R. (2010). Curbing paper wastage using flavoured feedback. *Proceedings of OZCHI 2010: Design – Interaction – Participation*, 224–227.

Naglieri, J. A., Drasgow, F., Schmit, M., Handler, L., Prifitera, A., Margolis, A., & Velasquez, R. (2004). Psychological testing on the internet: New problems, old issues. *American Psychologist, 59*, 150–162.

Naquin, C., & Paulson, G. (2003). Online bargaining and interpersonal trust. *Journal of Applied Psychology, 88*, 113–120.

Noe, R. A. (2010). Employee training and development (5th ed.), Burr Ridge, IL: McGraw-Hill Irwin.

Nye, C. D., Do, B-R., Drasgow, F., & Fine, S. (2008). Two-step testing in employee selection: Is score inflation a problem? *International Journal of Selection and Assessment, 16*, 112–120.

Orvis, K. A., Horn, D. B., & Belanich, J. (2009). An examination of the role individual differences play in videogame-based training. *Military Psychology, 21*, 461–481.

Ployhart, R. E., Weekly, J. A., Holtz, B. C., & Kemp, C. (2003). Web-based and paper-and-pencil testing of applicants in a proctored setting: Are personality, biodata, and situational judgment tests comparable? *Personnel Psychology, 56*, 733–752.

Presidio Graduate School (2011, May 15). *Using social media to promote energy efficiency and sustainability programs in the City of Berkeley.* Retrieved January 1, 2013, from http://www.triplepundit.com/2011/05/social-media-promote-energy-efficiency-sustainability-programs-city-berkeley

Reynolds, D. H., & Dickter, D. (2010). Technology and employee selection. In N. T. Tippins and J. L. Farr (Eds.), *Handbook of employee selection* (pp. 171–194). New York, NY: Routledge.

Reynolds, D. H., & Weiner, J. A. (2009). *Online recruiting and selection: Innovations in talent acquisition.* Oxford, UK: John Wiley and Sons.

Richman, W. L., Kiesler, S., Weisband, S., & Drasgow, F. (1999). A meta-analytic study of social desirability distortion in computer-administered questionnaires, traditional questionnaires, and interviews. *Journal of Applied Psychology, 8,* 754–775.

Rynes, S. L., Bretz, R. D., Jr., & Gerhart, B. (1991). The importance of recruitment in job choice: A different way of looking. *Personnel Psychology, 44,* 487–521.

Silverman, R. E. (2011, October 10). Latest game theory: Mixing work and play. *The Wall Street Journal.* Retrieved January 1, 2013, from http://online.wsj.com/article/SB10001 424052970204294504576615371783795248.html

Sinar, E. F., Reynolds, D. H., & Paquet, S. L. (2003). Nothing but 'net? Corporate image and web-based testing. *International Journal of Selection and Assessment, 11,* 150–157.

Ssewanyana, J. K. (2007). ICT access and poverty in Uganda. *International Journal of Computing and ICT Research, 1*(2), 10–19.

Stanton, J. M. (2000). Reactions to employee performance monitoring: Framework, review, and research directions. *Human Performance, 13*(1), 85–113.

Stone, D. L., Lukaszewski, K. M., & Isenhour, L. C. (2005). E-recruiting: Online strategies for attracting talent. In H. G. Gueutal & D. L. Stone (Eds.), *The brave new world of eHR: Human resources management in the digital age* (pp. 22–53). San Francisco, CA: Jossey-Bass.

Stoughton, J. W., Thompson, L. F., Meade, A. W., & Wilson, M. A. (2012, April). *Reactions to using social networking websites in pre-employment screening.* Paper presented at the 27th annual meeting of the Society for Industrial and Organizational Psychology, San Diego, CA.

Strietska-Ilina, O., Hofmann, C., Durán Haro, M., & Jeon, S. (2011). Skills for green jobs: A global view. Geneva, Switzerland: International Labour Organization.

Thompson, L. F., & Atkins, S. G. (2010). Technology, mobility, and poverty reduction. In S. C. Carr (Ed.), *The psychology of global mobility* (pp. 301–322). New York, NY: Springer.

Thompson, L. F., & Mayhorn, C. B. (2012). Aging workers and technology. In J. W. Hedge & W. C. Borman (Eds.), *Oxford handbook of work and aging* (pp. 341–361). New York, NY: Oxford University Press.

Tippins, N. T. (2009). Internet alternatives to traditional proctored testing: Where are we now? *Industrial and Organizational Psychology, 2,* 2–10.

Tippins, N. T. (2011). Overview of technology-based assessments. In N. T. Tippins & S. Adler (Eds.), *Technology-enhanced assessment of talent.* San Francisco, CA: Jossey-Bass.

United Nations (2011). *The Millennium development goals report 2011.* Retrieved January 3, 2013, from http://www.un.org/millenniumgoals/11_MDG%20Report_EN.pdf

United Nations Conference on Trade and Development (UNCTAD) (2011a). *Technology and innovation report 2011: Powering development with renewable energy technologies.* New York, NY, and Geneva, Switzerland: Author. Retrieved January 1, 2013, from http://unctad.org/Sections/site_dir/docs/dtl_stat2011-11-29_en.pdf

United Nations Conference on Trade and Development (2011b). *Information economy report 2011: ICTs as an enabler for private sector development.* New York, NY, and Geneva, Switzerland. Retrieved January 1, 2013, from http://unctad. org/en/PublicationsLibrary/ier2011_en.pdf

United Nations Development Programme (2010). *Human development report 2010: The real wealth of nations: Pathways to human development.* Retrieved June 3, 2012, from http://hdr.undp.org/en/reports/global/hdr2010

U.S. Office of Personnel Management (OPM) (2011, February). *Status of telework in the federal government: Report to the congress.* Washington, DC: Author.

Van Dijk, J. A. G. M. (2006). Digital divide research, achievements and shortcomings. *Poetics, 34,* 221–235.

Van Houwlingen, J. H., & Van Raaij, W. (1989). The effect of goal-setting and daily electronic feedback on in-home energy use. *Journal of Consumer Research, 16,* 98–105.

Venkatesh, V., & Bala, H. (2008). Technology Acceptance Model 3 and a research agenda on interventions. *Decision Sciences, 39,* 273–315.

Venkatesh, V., Morris, M. G., Davis, F. D., and Davis, G. B. (2003). User acceptance of information technology: Toward a unified view. *MIS Quarterly, 27,* 425–478.

Walker, J. H., Feild, H. S., Giles, W. F., Armenakis, A. A., & Bernerth, J. B. (2009). Displaying employee testimonials on recruitment websites: Effects of communication media, employee race, and job seeker race on organizational attractiveness and information credibility. *Journal of Applied Psychology, 94,* 1354–1364.

Washington Post (2011). Test moves airlines toward paperless cockpits. Retrieved June 3, 2013, from http://www.washingtonpost.com/blogs/dr-gridlock/post/test-moves-airlines-toward-paperless-cockpits/2011/06/20/AGmHM2cH_blog.html

Webster, J., & Wong, W. (2008). Comparing traditional and virtual group forms: Identity, communication and trust in naturally occurring project teams. *The International Journal of Human Resource Management, 19,* 41–62.

Welsh, E. T., Wanberg, C. R., Brown, K. G., & Simmering M. J. (2003). E-learning: Emerging uses, empirical results, and future directions. *International Journal of Training and Development, 7*(4), 245–258.

Wilson, J. M., Straus, S. G., & McEvily, W. J. (2006). All in due time: The development of trust in computer-mediated and face-to-face groups. *Organizational Behavior and Human Decision Processes, 99,* 16–33.

Zaccaro, S., & Bader, P. (2003). E-leadership and the challenges of leading e-teams: Minimizing the bad and maximizing the good. *Organizational Dynamics, 31,* 377–387.

16

Protecting Green Consumers and Investors to Make Business Greener[1]

Kurt Strasser

Many companies seem determined to persuade us how green they are. Consider IBM, one of the most committed and most widely recognized companies. Its formal policy begins: "IBM is committed to environmental affairs leadership in all its business activities" (IBM, n.d.). It was the first major company to commit to a company-wide environmental management system, covering all its operations worldwide. Its policies include being an environmentally-responsible neighbor, conserving natural resources, using processes that do not adversely affect the environment, and sharing appropriate pollution prevention technology. And it has achieved real results while attaining substantial growth. For example, using the widely accepted Global Reporting Initiative standards, IBM has shown: 50% CO_2 emissions reductions between 1990 and 2009, recycling 76% of its non-hazardous waste in 2009, and reducing its emissions of PFCs in manufacturing by 48.8% from 1995 to 2009 (IBM, 2010). This is business environmentalism at its best, achieving results and going well beyond regulatory requirements.

Of course, not all the examples are so favorable. BP had worked very hard at burnishing its environmental reputation, claiming that their brand could be summed up by the words "beyond petroleum" (BP, 2011). These words now take on a richly ironic meaning about the company's recent oil spill problems, rather than its environmental commitment. Yet when weighed against what we now know to have been a reckless disregard of care and precaution in drilling operations, which were doubtless major contributors to the worst oil spill in U.S. history, the sincerity of BP's commitment to business environmentalism has been seriously undermined. However, even in this admittedly selective worst case, the fact that the company wished to appear green and continues to claim its environmental commitment is of note. The mantle of business environmentalism appears to have some value even when the reality of it has been called into serious question.

More generally, there is good news about business environmentalism to be found. For example, many of the world's largest banks have agreed, via the Equator Principles, to provide project financing only for large projects that demonstrate environmental responsibility (http://www.equator-principles.com). Our daily experience with consumer advertising provides an almost continuous exposure to business claims of greenness. Interestingly, the company actions behind these claims are virtually all voluntary efforts by the companies involved—voluntary in the sense that they are not undertaken in response to applicable government requirements (e.g., Esty & Winston, 2006; Hirsch, 2001). Why are companies doing this? Does it really result in meaningful improvement of environmental performance? What policies are being implemented to support these efforts, and what policies should be?

Voluntary environmental efforts have not always been so important, nor has their discussion always figured so prominently in company activity and environmental policy making. In the United States, the modern environmental protection era began with almost exclusive use of public regulation to control the worst environmental harms, and for most countries this continues to be the primary approach to environmental protection today. This regulation seeks to limit, for example, air pollution and toxic waste disposal to levels that protect human health and the environment, and the same regulatory approach prevails in our efforts to protect special natural resource areas such as wetlands. By making rules against the activities that cause these risks, and enforcing the rules as best we can, we seek to protect the planet's ecosystem for ourselves, for future generations, and for the sake of its own existence. This regulatory approach to environmental protection is familiar, well established, and well developed. In the nearly 40 years we have been seriously working on environmental protection in the United States, beginning in the early 1970s, this regulatory approach has given us many successes in the areas where we have tried to regulate. Certainly the air, the water, and the land are cleaner than they were, even though they are not as clean as they could and should be.

Of course, it does not feel as though we have made any progress at all; the environmental progress we have made to date is, in the press and the public mind, often overshadowed by new environmental threats and risks that we did not know of or consider when we started the modern era of environmental regulation. For example, consider climate change; it is surely our greatest environmental problem today, although it was largely unrecognized and unappreciated 40 years ago. Similarly, our contemporary concerns with unsustainable levels of resource use or the rapid pace of species extinction were not well recognized 40 years ago. For the most part, we did not tackle these problems with serious regulatory policy when we started trying to protect the environment. Our past success in tackling other environmental problems with good policy, partial though it is, should inspire some cautious hope that we can make progress on these newer issues as well.

When we address these issues, and continue to pursue progress on traditional regulatory matters, we will have to continue to expand our policy thinking beyond the traditional regulatory approaches. Beginning around 1990, many environmental policy thinkers began to consider that voluntary efforts should be added to the policy mix that had traditionally emphasized regulatory tools almost exclusively. This approach has been most highly developed in the Netherlands with the implementation of the system of industry covenants, although the idea of voluntary agreements with industry has now spread quite widely to many countries (Croci, 2005; Mazurkiewicz, 2005; Organisation for Economic Co-operation and Development, 1999, 2003; ten Brink, 2002). In the 1990s, the United States tried a number of voluntary programs under the general philosophy of "regulatory reinvention," (for an introduction, see U.S. Environmental Protection Agency, 1999) although the success of these programs has been much more mixed and many are no longer current. If the 1970s and 1980s were the classic period of environmental protection regulation, the period since the 1990s has been one of widespread experimentation with voluntary efforts by business, sometimes to supplement regulation and on occasion to replace it.

Much of today's business environmentalism has grown out of these programs. This chapter will first propose a policy for business environmentalism, one emphasizing information rather than programmatic controls. Next, it will discuss what companies are doing in their environmental programs and consider the empirical evidence of how successful these programs are in improving environmental performance. The programs are diverse and varied; perhaps unsurprisingly, so are the empirical results.

PROTECTING GREEN CONSUMERS AND INVESTORS: A POLICY FOR BUSINESS ENVIRONMENTALISM

In short, we need business environmentalism because we cannot regulate our way to sustainability. Today's environmental challenges, together with the increasing worldwide recognition of the need to shift toward more sustainable societies, will require that we enlist business initiative and commitment, beyond that required by regulation, to make progress. We need business to do things that regulation cannot effectively command (Strasser, 2011). Regulation provokes one kind of business response, but other, different kinds of business efforts will also be required. In addition to compliance with rules, we need innovation, cooperation, and continuous improvement that regulation cannot command; these must come from businesses themselves. Living sustainably on the planet and passing a livable ecosystem on to our children will require business, and everyone else, to do things that must be motivated, indeed inspired, by other social controls and influences, things which regulation usually cannot command. Regulation is a useful policy tool to control particular conduct that causes specific, identifiable harms, but its commands are not very effective to reduce resource use, or to pursue ongoing adaptive management of environmental impacts needed for continuous improvement and technological innovation. In pursuing environmental protection, regulation is workably effective at policing the floor, but it is a poor tool to inspire or require a reach for the ceiling. Yet sustainability requires that we do more than police the floor. We also need voluntary business efforts that are inspired by the lure of social norms, moved by the pull of market profits, and channeled by creative public policies. To get these, we need wise policy, based on well-designed voluntary and regulatory programs that are used in an effective policy mix. I reject the argument that the best policy is a choice between imperfect regulation and imperfect voluntary business programs; the best policy is a wise and effective mix of the best of both kinds of efforts.

In addition, we need a policy for business environmentalism because it is so prevalent, and indeed it is growing. The widespread adoption of business environmental programs requires a policy to structure it to promote better environmental performance, but also to protect green consumers, green investors, and green civil society from being mislead. This paper will argue that, if business provides information about its environmental programs and performance, we should require that information to be truthful and accurate. My argument is that we should not regulate the content of voluntary business environmental programs, but that we should regulate the accuracy of information about them aimed at both green investors and green consumers.

At the most general level, this is not a novel idea, for we now have substantial regulation of truthfulness of information to protect consumers and investors. While this current regulation potentially reaches these business environmentalism issues, for the most part it does so only obliquely and incompletely; the current regulatory systems for both kinds of information are fragmented and incomplete in their application to environmental issues. Yet the regulatory authority to reach further exists, for the most part, in the breadth of current law and regulation. What is needed is new policy to move regulators and others to so use the authority they have. The current weakness in policy is not really surprising; our regulatory regimes to protect both consumers and investors were established at a time when environmental concerns were not central to the policy agenda. However, times have changed, as has the policy agenda, and robust policy response is now needed.

One of the principal reasons business adopts environmental programs is the hope of companies to appeal to green consumers, green investors, and ultimately green civil society more generally. While the effort may be to appeal to parties to encourage specific transactions, such as particular consumer purchases or specific investment decisions, the appeal is often broader and less tied to specific transactions. Beyond seeking particular sales to consumers and investors, companies and industry groups want to be seen as responsible, productive, and contributing members of a greener and more sustainable society. Even a casual glance at the pervasive contemporary corporate image advertising shows that many companies are most concerned to present a green corporate image, one that goes beyond promoting specific products, specific services, or specific investments. For example, in 2008 the consulting firm KPMG surveyed the corporate responsibility reporting practices of the Global 250 (G250), the largest 250 companies in the world, and a companion survey of the largest 100 companies in each of the 22 jurisdictions (N100) conducted every three years. Through this survey (KPMG, 2008), they found that company reputation or brand enhancement was cited as an important reason for sustainability reporting by 55% of the largest 250 companies. Of course the positive image is an important contributor to a company's ability to appeal to consumers and investors, but its importance reaches further. Thus, many thoughtful business leaders refer to their "social license to operate" and note that the license is based on performance and perceptions, including products and financial returns, that ultimately reflect a broad commitment to responsible behavior throughout the entire organization (Howard-Grenville, Nash, & Coglianese, 2008). Voluntary environmental efforts are an important part of this corporate effort.

Should we regulate the voluntary environmental programs that are part of this image-building effort? One major concern is that regulating the content of the programs may well discourage company participation in them altogether, or steer participants toward an overly cautious approach, which could rob the programs of their company initiative and innovation discussed earlier. The fear is that regulation, in undercutting company initiative and innovation, would weaken or destroy this most potentially valuable social attribute of business environmentalism. By regulating voluntary programs, do we run the risk of taking away one of their greatest social contributions? This concern is well placed and must be carefully considered.

What I propose here is a different and more limited kind of regulation. We should avoid direct regulation of the content and operation of these voluntary programs, but instead we should require that companies that publicize their environmental efforts tell the truth in doing so. As part of this admittedly more limited public policy effort, we should also require that companies be able to substantiate the environmental commitments and performance claims they make. Beyond specific products and programs, companies that choose to present an overall image of good environmental performance should, again, be required to tell the truth and verify their claims. This approach, to regulate the accuracy of information about business environmentalism but not its content, is needed because the information is important.

Why regulate the information if not the program? Inaccurate, unregulated information about business environmentalism risks unjustified claims and deceived stakeholders. Information can change consumer behavior, investor behavior, and company behavior. The fact that companies engage in so much business environmentalism now is perhaps the best evidence that they think it is important to their operation in today's world. Information about their programs and efforts is the key to improved performance. If false and inaccurate information becomes the order of the day, then it will not spur real company change and it will fail to achieve improvement in environmental performance (for more information concerning this type of regulation, please refer to Magat & Viscusi, 1992; Menell, 1995; Sage, 1999; for an introduction and summary, please refer to Backer, 2008; Hess, 2007; Hirsch, 2010; Kysar, 2005; Shatz, 2008; Weil, Fung, Graham, & Fagotto, 2006). As I will now discuss, there is some empirical data supporting this concern about the claims of environmental worthiness of specific products.

When false and inaccurate information is common, real environmental performance is devalued by fake environmental performance, and the fake performance may well drive real performance from the market. First, fake environmentalism is doubtless cheaper than real environmentalism. In addition, information about fake environmentalism makes it even harder for information about real environmentalism to be credible and thus effective. In the worst case, the cost of finding out what is real and what is not simply overwhelms customers, investors, employees, and other stakeholders, and they stop responding to any information. In this unhappy scenario, business environmentalism becomes a chimera, without value, and the potential for motivating better business performance for the environment is lost completely.

In the policy proposed here, requiring that information be accurate comes into play only if a company chooses to publicize information about the environmental attributes of its products and its business. This approach, requiring accuracy if a company provides information, is a central concept in contemporary consumer protection regulation and it also figures prominently in the anti-fraud provisions of securities regulation in the United States and, to a degree, in Europe. This section will first consider whether, in both the United States and Europe, consumer protection regulation currently reaches information about business environmentalism to protect green consumers. Next it will discuss whether securities regulation currently reaches business environmentalism to protect information given to green investors. We will see that both of these regulatory systems provide only limited protection. Both consumer protection and securities regulation have traditionally shown only limited interest in reaching environmental information and claims, although this is beginning to change somewhat with each.

Policing the truthfulness of information about voluntary environmental programs and environmental performance is achievable and should be required. Beyond requiring truthfulness, should we go further and mandate information disclosure of the environmental implications of a company's products and business? This is the harder policy question, which this chapter will also discuss but not definitively answer. We will see that securities regulation is changing, requiring more information on climate change and potentially on other environmental issues as well.

Information for Green Consumers

Company claims about business environmentalism directed to green consumers have been subject to some but limited regulation, most of it focused on specific products rather than company-wide programs or image (see Strasser, 2011, for a detailed discussion of legal authorities). However, the recent non-binding Guidance in the European Union, together with the ongoing process of revising the Federal Trade Commission (FTC)'s Green Guides in the United States, show some much-needed movement toward greater protection in this area. Advertising aimed at green consumers should be regulated for accuracy and truthfulness; there is some recent empirical evidence that companies often make exaggerated or unjustified green claims for their products. For example, a survey conducted by TerraChoice in 2009 found that when very high standards were used to assess accuracy and transparency related to green products' claims, at least one aspect of 98% of the products were faulted as inaccurate (based on 40 big box stores, 4,996 green claims, 2,219 products). In fact, Lyon and Maxwell (2004) concluded that the empirical literature "has reached mixed conclusions regarding whether 'green consumerism' plays a significant role in influencing corporate environmental decisions" (p. 19). For the most part, in both the United States and the European Union, there is general regulation of advertising claims for specific products that could be applied to green claims as well. However, this author can find little record that this general body of law has in fact been so used.

In the United States, the FTC does have specific guides for green advertising of specific products (see Federal Trade Commission, 2006). The FTC, in negotiated consent decrees on specific matters, has applied these, although there are no contested cases reported, and overall enforcement has been limited during the history of the guides. Several U.S. states also have specific regulation of green advertising, although again this does not appear to have been an active area of enforcement. These are all directed to green advertising for specific products and none of these regulations has been applied to reach business environmental information intended to create a favorable green corporate image or persona, separate from sale of specific products. As a result, this regulation has had only limited use in controlling information about business environmentalism aimed at creating or burnishing a company-wide green image. While the general standards are broad and could be applied to reach such claims about business environmentalism, to date there has been no such application. In the European Union, the 2005 Commercial Practices Directive offers some potential and it is reinforced by the 2009 non-binding guidance, which has specific coverage of environmental claims (European Commission, 2009). The potential breadth of this regulation offers promise for greater protection in future implementation and enforcement.

Companies are increasingly using business environmentalism and the related publicity for this kind of promotion; many clearly must think this is an important factor for some consumers and perhaps other stakeholders as well. While our current regulatory tools are not well focused on company business environmentalism claims aimed at fostering a green corporate image—superior environmental performance and responsibility by the whole company—these company-wide claims are the ones most typical of business environmentalism programs. All consumers and other stakeholders should have accurate information on business environmentalism; additional regulatory controls are needed. The statutes authorizing regulatory controls are broad, but they have never been applied to reach company-wide claims of green management, operations and policy.

Doing so will require that we tackle an additional difficult question: what is the standard against which the claim is to be measured? A claim of business environmentalism is a claim to be a greener corporation in management, operations, and policy. The question is of a greener corporation, rather than an absolutely green one because the range of potential environmental impacts of any large company, its processes, and its products, is vast, and perfect performance is an ideal but not a realistic expectation. In addition, tradeoffs among different kinds of environmental impacts will have to be evaluated. How do we rate a company with clean operations that makes products that are not green in their use, such as high-mileage cars or coal to be burned in power plants? Where the business claim concerns particular products or particular operations, we can require accuracy and specificity. Yet a company's implicit or explicit claim to being a greener business because it has, for example, an environmental management system or issues a sustainability report is much harder to be made specific—for instance, greener than whom? On what criteria? Etc.

While we could simply abandon the effort because of this complexity, doing so would leave consumers and civil society vulnerable to deception, potentially devaluing accurate claims if widespread skepticism results. My proposal is that we avoid trying to articulate criteria for measuring a company-wide claim of greenness and focus instead on the company's business environmentalism claim being made. If the company claims to have an ISO-certified environmental management system, it must actually have one. If the company claims that better environmental performance results, then it must actually be able to substantiate that claim as well.

But what if it says nothing overt about environmental performance results? Is the claim to have a certified environmental management system, for example, an implicit claim of better environmental performance? If so, then the company or the certifying entity should be prepared to substantiate that claim. If it is not so prepared, then protecting the reasonable consumer requires that it disclaim the environmental performance claim expressly in order to avoid the implicit misrepresentation. More generally, companies claiming business environmentalism efforts must go beyond literal truth—having a certified environmental management system if that is what is claimed. The companies must either make explicit their implicit representation of better environmental performance, substantiating it themselves or through their certifiers, or they must disclaim the implicit representation. The European Union law as interpreted in its non-binding guidance clearly seems to require this; the revised FTC Green Guides in the United States should do so as well.

Presumably there is a role here for environmental regulators, as many commentators have proposed to the FTC (Avallone, 2006; Cavanaugh, 1998; Gibson, 2009; Woods, 2008). Environmental regulators may have much insight to offer about the substantiation that should be required for business environmental claims. Comparison to industry averages, to prior performance of this company, or to industry best practices all suggest themselves. Crafting such a set of criteria will be challenging, and necessary, but it should not be beyond the reach of sophisticated regulators. This is particularly true when we remember that what we seek is accuracy in the explicit and implicit claims companies choose to make to green consumers, not the single exclusive definition of corporate environmental virtue. Our regulations need not state a universal standard of good corporate environmental performance, and indeed, given the variety of business operations and environmental impacts, it would be impossible to do so. What our regulations should do is ensure accuracy in the explicit and implicit claims of environmental performance and practices that the company makes.

The extent of business environmentalism and the degree of its publicity that we all see today show that business thinks it is important to consumers and presumably to other stakeholders as well. If it is significant to them, then they deserve accurate information with which they can express their preferences, enabling companies that are better environmental performers to reap their deserved marketplace advantage. More is necessary to ensure the accuracy of information about business environmentalism. We need to prohibit misleading information about business environmentalism, whether it is aimed at sale of specific products or at creating a general image of company environmental performance, practice, and commitment. Expansive use of the current law has the potential to accomplish this, although our existing law has not been used in this way to date. If current law is not enough, or if existing regulators are unwilling to so aggressively use it, we should establish new law and regulatory mandates if necessary. Enforcement should be regular and energetic. Markets and broader social pressures provide incentives for companies to use business environmentalism to proclaim their green performance, practices, and commitment to burnish their green images; with regulation and enforcement of the claims, they will be encouraged to actually become greener as they pursue business environmentalism.

Information for Green Investors

Of course, there is a large, sophisticated, and well-developed body of law regulating financial and business information provided to investors. This section will consider how well that body of law reaches the company information aimed at green investors. Just as companies want to use business environmentalism to appeal to green consumers, they also increasingly want to use it to appeal to green investors as well. Consider the individual company sustainability reports now discussed. In these increasingly numerous and sophisticated reports, companies go to substantial lengths to review their environmental, social, and economic performance as well as their policies and commitment. This is an effort to provide information about the company and its operations that will cast it in a favorable light with investors, as well as with other constituencies. Much the same can be said of voluntary adoption of environmental performance standards and environmental management systems, also discussed here.

We need at least a working definition of who green investors are and the nature of their investment objectives. For our purposes, this group can be divided into two types. First are a group that I will call green "responsible investors," a subcategory of socially responsible investors who wish to invest in companies because they approve of the company's conduct, products, and services. These socially responsible investors often want to support companies that treat the environment well, treat their employees fairly and humanely, and make social and economic contributions to their communities. Traditional investment analysis has thought this group of green investors to be small with only a marginal impact, but this seems to be changing. In 2003, a social investment trade group estimated that 11% of all assets under professional management in the United States at the time, about $2 trillion of the $19.2 trillion total, were managed with reference to some social criteria (Social Investment Forum, 2003). A 2007 study confirmed this conclusion (Social Investment Forum, 2007). The breadth and diversity of available mutual funds and other social investment options further evidence a substantial demand for socially responsible investment.

The second group I will call green "financial investors." This group is interested in company environmental performance, and more broadly in company sustainability performance, for its financial implications more than for its social impact. These investors think that firms with better environmental performance, or with better sustainability performance more broadly, often also have better long-term financial performance (Florida & Davison, 2001). One interesting study of UK firms finds that better managed firms use less energy per unit of output, substituting capital and labor inputs for it (Bloom, Genakos, Martin, & Sadun, 2008). Of course, this view flies in the face of hard-boiled traditional investment wisdom, which says that restricting the potential investment opportunities in this way, or indeed in any systematic way, will reduce returns. Whether socially responsible investing raises or lowers financial returns is a large, extensive, and ongoing debate that this chapter will not attempt to referee or resolve (see Assadourian, 2006; Blazovich & Smith, 2008; Mercer, 2009; Orlitzky,

Schmidt, & Rynes, 2003; Rodgers, Choy, & Guiral, 2008; Social Investment Forum Foundation, 2009, for further discussion). For our purposes, it is sufficient to note that today the debate surfaces, indeed rages, often enough to make clear that company environmental performance information is an important matter to many green financial investors as well as to green responsible investors, and there is every reason to think that this group will grow over time.

What information do both groups of green investors want? Three broad categories of information are key. First, they want to know about the company's compliance with legal requirements, and the regulatory risks the company faces for the costs of achieving compliance, as well as the costs of sanctions for being out of compliance. For example, does the company face the prospect of fines and penalties, as well as the reputation damage, for past or continuing violations of environmental law in its operations? Is the company responsible for cleanup of past contamination at its facilities or that was otherwise caused by its other operations? Does the company anticipate substantial expense to comply with current regulations or to comply with anticipated future regulatory requirements? Environmental regulation is extensive today. Compliance is expensive, and violating regulations can be even more expensive as well as damaging to the company, ultimately hurting the company's financial performance. Investors quite reasonably want to know whether the company has existing regulatory liabilities or contingent risks of them, in order to be able to evaluate the company on both social and financial performance.

Yet, green investors are interested in much more than just the cost of current and likely future compliance with or violation of environmental law; they also want to know about the present and future business risks of the company's environmental performance, including the environmental performance of its products and its processes. For instance, the whole world is quite worried about global climate change from carbon dioxide and other contributing air emissions. There is a substantial and growing body of state regulation. Despite the current legislative deadlock, most observers expect there will eventually be extensive new national regulation in the United States as well as greatly increased regulation worldwide. While the cost of directly complying with this regulation will be a significant financial item for most companies, climate change will also pose other business risks: a company's performance in responding to global climate change will doubtlessly have a great impact on consumer preferences for its products and services. Consider that a company that makes most of its profits from vehicles that are highly polluting, for example, presents a substantial business risk of poor future performance from both a social and a financial perspective (e.g., Woodyard, 2010). Further, a company whose suppliers use very carbon intensive processes will almost surely see its costs increase over time, whether its own operations are carbon intensive or not.

In addition to climate change, water usage offers a second illustration of business risks from environmental performance. Many areas of the world are experiencing water shortages, and most expert opinion expects this problem to get worse (for recent discussions, see Brown, 2009, and Sachs, 2008). A company that uses water inefficiently, or one whose products or suppliers do so, runs a quite substantial business risk of poor financial performance, as well as poor social performance, in what will be an increasingly water constrained world. Green investors are most interested in knowing the business risks of the company's environmental performance, whether these are risks of changed regulation or changed market conditions, or both.

Environmental performance presents companies with business opportunities as well as business risks, and green investors want to know about this third area as well. Today's concern with global climate change, to return to this familiar example, leads to a worldwide demand for low carbon energy production technologies. Similarly, consumers will doubtless become more interested in products that use less energy, particularly less energy from carbon intensive sources. Some companies will be well positioned and able to invent and supply the products and services that will be brought forth by this new market demand; some will not. For example, while we have not historically considered automobile companies to be environmental champions, the anticipated market demand for electric vehicles has lead to major development efforts and advance product announcements from Ford, Hyundai, and BMW (Henry, 2010; Jin, 2010; LaMonica, 2010). Both green responsible investors and green financial investors will want to know about companies' potential to respond, and they will want to support those companies whose environmental business prospects are good.

These three general categories of company environmental information—environmental regulatory risks and compliance costs, environmental business risks, and environmental business opportunities—are the core categories of information green investors want. Many companies now supply a great deal of this information as part of their voluntary environmental programs discussed earlier. Is it regulated? Should it be? The current system for regulating investment information in the United States reaches the voluntary provision of this environmental business information, but it does so only indirectly, sporadically, and incompletely (Strasser, 2011). At the most general level, the regulatory goal is to police all voluntary disclosure of information to require that it be accurate and complete enough to avoid being misleading. However, the system has done a poor job of this with voluntarily provided environmental business information. To date, regulators have shown only limited enforcement interest in environmental information and much of the minimal enforcement that has taken place has come from private actions. After considering this regulation of information, which is voluntarily provided, this section will discuss the extent to which current U.S. regulatory systems require information for green investors, as well as the extent to which they could and should. Finally, it will consider regulation of information provided to green investors in the European Union.

In the United States, there is substantial regulation of voluntary disclosure of information aimed at investors. The subject is technical, and only a brief summary is possible here (Strasser, 2011). Taken together, the U.S. rules governing voluntary information disclosure for investors have substantial potential to be applied to voluntary corporate environmental programs. The rules are general and written broadly, without specific focus on environmental information, and they have seen only limited application to protect green investors to date. However, as companies are more active with voluntary programs, and investors are increasingly interested in environmental performance information, this is likely to change. Companies are making many more environmental disclosures as part of their business environmentalism efforts, and investors are increasingly interested in the information. For these reasons, the history of inattention will not likely continue.

Most of the large body of law dealing with information for investors is not concerned with voluntarily supplied information, but rather with information that companies are required to disclose to investors. Although companies are required to furnish a great deal of business and financial information, the law is not well developed to require environmental information. There are some limited requirements, but they are sufficiently qualified that companies that wish to avoid or minimize reporting under them have many options for doing so. Although there have been substantial calls for the Security and Exchange Commission (SEC) to adopt greater disclosure requirements for environmental performance, in the past the agency has largely resisted (Wallace, 2009; Wallace, 1993; Weil, Fung, Graham, & Fagotto, 2006; Williams, 1999). However, this is changing; the SEC has recently issued new guidance on reporting climate change business information, and the Environmental Protection Agency is now requiring large companies to report on their greenhouse gas emissions (Daily Environment Report, 2009; Security and Exchange Commission, 2010).

In sum, prior to these very recent positive developments, we have seen a consistent pattern in the U.S. legal requirements about providing environmental information for green consumers and green investors. The pattern is that, while the general rules and principles are broadly worded and could quite reasonably be read to require such information, there has been only limited application of these general rules and principles to any environmental information. Further, there are virtually no specific rules for information about voluntary business environmentalism. With both consumer protection and investor protection, there are broad general requirements that information that is supplied voluntarily must be accurate. While these general requirements are written broadly enough that they could be interpreted to cover environmental information, there has been only limited application of them to do so. With both consumer information and investor information, there is some but limited specific regulation of the content and accuracy of environmental information that the company does provide. Going beyond voluntarily supplied information, there is some but an even more limited requirement to supply environmental information for green investors, although very recent developments are encouraging. With all this information regulation, there is almost no specific provision for information about voluntary business environmentalism, although it is often, in fact, an important part of a company's effort to appeal to green consumers and green investors. A sophisticated policy for voluntary business environmentalism must require that information about it be accurate and sufficiently complete that it is not misleading. A robust policy would go further and set minimum standards requiring provision of environmental information.

However, a robust policy must be concerned with limits as well as requirements. A policy that supervises the accuracy of information on business environmentalism is well founded, for only then can green consumers and investors make good decisions about what the companies say they are doing. Yet, going further and commanding disclosure requires a more nuanced balance. As discussed earlier, the optimistic vision of voluntary business environmentalism is that it can call forth creativity and energy to attain environmental results that regulations are unlikely to be able to command. To preserve this possibility, at least for some companies, a wise policy must be concerned that it does not mandate too much. If companies are required to comment on business environmentalism, will their programs be shaped by this requirement, pushing them back toward their history of public relations greenwash rather than the optimistic vision of real substantive improvement? Certainly this would be a grave concern if companies were required to go further and implement these "voluntary" environmentalism programs. In the middle is a requirement that companies disclose their environmental impacts and effects. Here, the question is difficult; such a requirement provides green consumers and investors with needed information, but it also runs the risk of stifling the most creative and energetic aspects of the programs. On balance, disclosure should be required, but with concern that it not be so specific and demanding as to undercut the programs themselves. At the European Union level, there has been strong policy support for voluntary reporting of business environmental information for investors, but as yet no mandatory requirement of it. The Commission Recommendation of May 2001 on the Recognition, Measurement and Disclosure of Environmental Issues in the Annual Accounts and Annual Reports of Companies (2001/453/EC, 2001 O.J. [L 156] 33) recommended more consistent environmental information in annual reports, but it contained no binding legal requirement.

The policy discussion is continuing, and several member states now do require reporting of some environmental business information. In the European Union, the question of disclosure of business environmental information is developing rapidly, with much more conscious focus than in the United States, and in the context of a recently enacted harmonization plan for all financial information. The whole system is currently in a state of flux, with new developments coming quickly and more anticipated; this brief review must be taken as a snapshot of what is in fact a rapidly moving picture. In contrast to the United States, in the European Union, there appears to be real movement toward providing some supervision of information furnished to green investors. The harmonization directives are commanding action by the member states; the form of the action and the details on environmental issues are very much being worked out now, and a number of member states are requiring environmental information disclosure. The seeds of real reform have been planted but we must wait to see if the plants will bear fruit.

With better information for green consumers, investors, and civil society, companies' business environmentalism has the potential to use the power of markets and social norms to improve performance. Will it? A look at what companies do in their programs now, and the empirical environmental performance of those companies, offers a snapshot of the starting point for analysis.

BUSINESS ENVIRONMENTALISM: WHAT ARE COMPANIES DOING AND HOW IS IT WORKING?

Companies are doing many different things as business environmentalism, from voluntary sustainability reporting—the most voluntary efforts—to adopting private environmental performance standards that go beyond regulatory compliance, and adopting environmental management systems. After considering these, this section will conclude with a look at the least voluntary of these programs, negotiated compliance, with special emphasis here on the Dutch environmental covenants. Do companies with voluntary programs have better environmental performance? This question will be a central inquiry in the discussion of each of the four types of voluntary programs now discussed.

The types of voluntary programs are quite different from each other, and thus their environmental performance results may well be different as well, as the discussion in each section will show. In addition to reviewing each type of program, this section will focus on the extent to which there is systematic empirical evaluation of how much each program is associated with improved environmental performance by its participants. The emphasis is on systematic empirical evaluation of the entire program, although qualitative evaluations and survey data have been considered when they are the only material available, always recognizing their limitations. Two general conclusions emerge. These voluntary business programs have had a mixed environmental performance history, with some types associated with substantial environmental performance improvement, and others not. Second, our knowledge is quite thin in many places, and much more work is needed in many areas to provide a firmer basis for evaluation or policy making.

Companies and policymakers use a variety of voluntary environmental programs, with quite diverse results (Strasser, 2011). The most voluntary of these efforts, corporate sustainability reporting, is growing, such that the vast majority of large companies now do some kind of reporting (KPMG, 2008; n.d.). These reports often originated as largely public relations-oriented self-promotion, but they have evolved into serious, comprehensive efforts to study and evaluate a company's environmental and other sustainability impacts. There is progress on the problem of consistent reporting standards, with the Global Reporting Initiative's guidelines emerging as the de facto standard. While real and consistent auditing and monitoring have been weak spots, quite substantial progress has been made here, too. Today, sustainability reports that do not use reporting standards and auditing or other third party evaluation are simply not credible and likely to be self-impeaching and counterproductive.

The empirical evaluation of whether reporting companies have better environmental performance has been both limited and mixed, but recent studies do provide some direct and indirect support. A 2003 review of the empirical literature found that such reporting was not shown to be associated with better environmental performance (Berthelot, Cormier, & Magnan, 2003). However, a 2007 study of 191 U.S. companies in high polluting industries refined the analysis and did find that better performance was associated with better reporting (Clarkson, Li, Richardson, & Vasvari, 2007). While no one study is definitive, particularly in the face of conflicting evidence, it does offer support for the positive association. One further study offered indirect supporting evidence. Van Staden and Hooks (2007) looked at a group of 26 New Zealand firms, comparing the quality of environmental reporting to an unrelated measure of the firms' environmental "responsiveness." The latter had been separately determined by an independent survey of company management to evaluate the company's specific environmental management and performance efforts. Van Staden and Hooks concluded that the extent of disclosure was highly correlated with the degree of environmental responsiveness, and significantly correlated with the quality of the disclosure. In sum, while the empirical evidence is limited, it is beginning to support sustainability reporting as legitimate business environmentalism.

The second type of voluntary program considered here—adopting voluntary environmental performance standards by individual companies, trade associations, and government partnerships—suffers an even greater dearth of empirical evaluation. These standards usually require better environmental performance than that commanded by regulation, setting a goal to go "beyond compliance." The most visible and familiar kinds of performance standards programs are government sponsored ones, such as the well-known Performance Track program, which sought to identify and recognize corporate environmental leaders (Coglianese & Nash, 2008). Similar programs have been adopted by industry trade groups and individual companies.

While individual companies report improved performance, the empirical literature raises serious questions when one asks whether the participating companies as a group have better environmental performance than non-participants. Most of the studies in this area find that participation in these voluntary performance standards programs is not associated with better environmental performance (Koehler, 2007; Lyon & Maxwell, 2007; Strasser, 2011). As the programs mature, and more empirical study is done, these results may change. To date, the case for public recognition and support of these programs has simply not been made, although many of these programs are new and future evaluations may support more positive conclusions.

Environmental management systems, the third kind of voluntary program considered, present a different case for policymakers. These are special kinds of modern business management systems that are instituted to evaluate and document the company's environmental performance across a number of aspects, and then to continuously improve it. Environmental management systems typically include a top-level statement of company policy supporting environmental protection, typically a brief statement of aspirational goals articulated at a high level of generality. The environmental management systems then implement this commitment by setting up an internal system, first to evaluate a company's environmental impacts, and, second, to manage daily operations and long-term decisions to reduce them. The management effort is to extend from the top to the bottom, throughout the entire company hierarchy, and it is designed to be an ongoing process that aims at continuous evaluation and improvement. At each stage, the system plans and evaluates, then undertakes to implement the plans, and finally checks to evaluate progress before repeating the sequence using the "plan, do, check" structure so familiar in modern business management.

Here, there is substantial empirical support for the proposition that firms that implement these environmental management systems have measurably better environmental performance than firms that do not, and, for this reason, environmental management systems deserve public support (Andrews, Hutson, & Edwards, 2006; Koehler, 2007; Strasser, 2011). There are limits: management systems have not been shown to improve regulatory compliance, and they are not associated with fundamental technological innovation. However, with a clear recognition of what can and cannot be expected, support for development and implementation of environmental management systems is good environmental protection policy.

The fourth type of voluntary program considered here is negotiated compliance with regulatory requirements. For this type of program, the picture is mixed (Strasser, 2011). The Dutch covenants are the clearest success story; they are generally associated with meeting the agreed environmental targets and thereby improving environmental performance (for a collection of recent case studies drawn from worldwide examples of voluntary agreements, see Morgenstern & Pizer, 2007). Where these covenants or similar arrangements are possible, they should be supported. However, negotiating and implementing these covenants depend on a number of specific factors in the industry, as well as the regulatory context and the broader national legal culture; thus, their lessons must be limited to settings where the presence of these factors make success likely, such as the Netherlands, but not where they are not, such as the United States. This is made clearer by considering negotiated compliance under the United States' Project XL program. Here, the program's accomplishments were few, achieved only with great expense, delay, and effort, and the program has now been abandoned (Hirsch, 2001; Morgenstern & Pizer, 2007; Organisation for Economic Co-operation and Development, 2003). Even with the generally successful Dutch covenants, there is some concern that their success may be limited to achieving results consistent with or not far ahead of business as usual. Yet even these are positive results and should be respected. As with the other voluntary programs considered, they are not generally associated with substantial development of new technology.

The conclusion is complex. Some kinds of business environmentalism have been shown to be associated with better environmental performance by companies, others have not.

CONCLUSION

Business environmentalism is widespread, growing, and appears to be here to stay. It has the potential to make important contributions to environmental protection and the pursuit of sustainability in the performance of genuinely green organizations. Yet to make these contributions, and motive genuinely green behavior, green consumers, investors and civil society need good information about business programs and results. With accurate and credible information, they will harness the power of their respective markets and institutions to motivate better performance from green organizations. To this point, there is a lot of business environmental activity and a mixed record of environmental performance from it. With the right policy to support and channel it, business environmentalism has the potential do much more.

NOTE

1. This chapter draws upon the author's recent book, *Myths and realities of business environmentalism: Good works, good business or greenwash?* (Edward Elgar, 2011). A version of the chapter is forthcoming as an article in the Environmental Law Reporter®.

REFERENCES

Andrews R. N. L., Hutson A. M., & Edwards, D., Jr. (2006). Environmental management under pressure: How do mandates affect performance? In C. Coglianese & Nash J. (Eds.), *Leveraging the private sector: Management strategies for environmental performance.* Washington, DC: Resources for the Future Press.

Assadourian, E. (2006). The state of corporate responsibility and the environment. *Georgetown International Law Review, 18,* 573–578.

Avallone, L. (2006). Green marketing: The urgent need for federal regulation. *Penn State Environmental Law Review, 14,* 685–702.

Backer, L. C. (2008). From moral obligation to international law: Disclosure systems, markets and the regulation of multinational corporations. *Georgetown Journal of International Law, 39,* 591–593.

Berthelot, S., Cormier, D., & Magnan, M. (2003). Environmental disclosure research: Review and synthesis. *Journal of Accounting Literature, 22,* 1–44.

Blazovich, J., & Smith, L.M. (2008), *Ethical corporate citizenship: Does it pay?* Working paper. Retrieved January 2, 2013, from http://ssrn.com/abstract=1125067

Bloom N., Genakos, C., Martin, R., & Sadun, R. (2008). *Modern management: Good for the environment or just hot air?* National Bureau of Economic Research (NBER) working paper 14394. Retrieved January 2, 2013, from http://www.nber.org/papers/w14394. pdf

BP (2011). *Sustainability Review 2011*. Retrieved January 7, 2013, from http://www.bp.com/assets/bp_internet/globalbp/STAGING/global_assets/e_s_assets/e_s_assets_2010/downloads_pdfs/bp_sustainability_review_2011.pdf

Brown, L. R. (2009). Population pressure: Land and water (Chapter 2). In *Plan B 4.0: Mobilizing to save civilization*. New York, NY: W. W. Norton & Company.

Cavanaugh, K. C. (1998). Comment, it's a Lorax kind of market! But is it a Sneeches kind of solution?: A critical review of current laissez-faire environmental marketing regulation. *Villanova Environmental Law Journal, 9*, 133–135.

Clarkson, P., Li, Y., Richardson, G. D., & Vasvari, F. P. (2007). Revisiting the relations between environmental performance and environmental disclosure: An empirical analysis. *Accounting Organizations and Society, 33*, 303–327. doi: 10.1016/j.aos.2007.05.003

Coglianese, C., & Nash, J. (2008). *Government clubs: Theory and evidence from voluntary environmental programs*. Corporate Social Responsibility Initiative Working Paper No. 50. Cambridge, MA: John F. Kennedy School of Government, Harvard University.

Croci, E. (2005) (Ed.). *The handbook of environmental voluntary agreements: Design, implementation and evaluation issues*. Dordrecht, The Netherlands: Springer.

Daily Environment Report (2009, July 24). *Push for disclosure of environmental risks expected to lead to new SEC requirements*, 140 DEN B-l (BNA).

Esty, D. C., & Winston, A. S. (2006). *Green to gold: How smart companies use environmental strategy to innovate, create value, and build competitive advantage*. New Haven, CT: Yale University Press.

European Commission (2009, December). *Commission staff working document: Guidance on the implementation/application of Directive 2005/29/EC on unfair commercial practices*, Brussels 3 SEC 1666. Retrieved January 2, 2013, from http://ec.europa.eu/consumers/rights/docs/Guidance_UCP_Directive_en.pdf

Federal Trade Commission (2006) *Guides for the Use of Environmental Marketing Claims*, 16 C.F.R. §§ 260.1-260.17.

Florida, R., & Davison, D. (2001). Gaining from green management: Environmental management systems inside and outside the factory. *California Management Review, 43*, 64–85.

Gibson, D. (2009). Awash in green: A critical perspective on environmental advertising. *Tulane Environmental Law Journal, 22*, 423–440.

Henry, J. (2010, July). BMW follows electric car trend with its megacity vehicle, CBS News. Retrieved January 2, 2013, from http://www.bnet.com/blog/auto-business/bmw-follows-electric-car-trend-with-its-megacity-vehicle/1295

Hess, D. (2007). Social reporting and new governance regulation: The prospects of achieving corporate accountability through transparency. *Business Ethics Quarterly, 17*, 453–476.

Hirsch, D. (2001). Understanding Project XL: A comparative legal and policy analysis. In E. W. Orts and K. Deketelaere (Eds.), *Environmental contracts: Comparative approaches in regulatory innovation in the United States and Europe*. London, UK: Kluwer Law International.

Hirsch, D. (2010). Green business and the importance of reflexive law: What Michael Porter didn't say. *Administrative Law Review, 62*, 18–24.

Howard-Grenville, J., Nash, J., & Coglianese, C. (2008). Constructing the license to operate: Internal factors and their influence on corporate environmental decisions. *Law & Policy, 30,* 70–107.

IBM (2010). *IBM and the environment: 2009 annual report.* Retrieved July 26, 2010, from http://www.ibm.com/ibm/environment/annual

IBM (n.d.). *Responsibility at IBM.* Retrieved July 26, 2010, from http://www.ibm.com/ibm/responsibility/ibm_polities.shtml

Jin, H. (2010, September). *Hyundai unveils its first electric car.* Reuters. Retrieved from http://www.reuters.com/article/idUSTRE6880BG20100909

Koehler, D. A. (2007). The effectiveness of voluntary environmental programs – A policy at a crossroads? *Policy Studies Journal, 35*(4), 689–722.

KPMG (2008). *KPMG International Survey of Corporate Responsibility Reporting 2008.* Retrieved January 2, 2013, from http://www.kpmg.com/EU/en/Documents/KPMG_International_survey_Corporate_responsibility_Survey_Reporting_2008.pdf

KPMG (n.d.) *KPMG International Corporate Responsibility Reporting Survey 2011.* Retrieved January 2, 2013, from http://www.kpmg.com/global/en/issuesandinsights/articlespublications/corporate-responsibility/pages/default.aspx

Kysar, D. A. (2005). Sustainable development and private global governance. *Texas Law Review, 83,* 2109–2166.

LaMonica, M. (2010, March). *Ford taps Microsoft Hohm for electric-car charging.* CNET News. Retrieved January 2, 2013, from http://news.cnet.com/8301-11128_3-20001491-54.html

Lyon, T. P., & Maxwell, J. W. (2004). *Corporate environmentalism and public policy.* Cambridge, UK: Cambridge University Press.

Lyon, T. P., & Maxwell, J. W. (2007). Environmental public voluntary programs reconsidered. *Policy Studies Journal, 35,* 724–747.

Magat, W. A., & Viscusi, W. K. (1992). *Informational approaches to regulation.* Cambridge, MA: MIT Press.

Mazurkiewicz, P. A. (2005). Voluntary agreements for environmental policy: Effectiveness, efficiency and usage in policy mixes. In E. Croci (Ed.), *The handbook of environmental voluntary agreements: Design, implementation and evaluation issues.* Dordrecht, The Netherlands: Springer.

Menell, P. S. (1995). Structuring a market-oriented federal eco-information policy. *Maryland Law Review, 43,* 1435.

Mercer (2009, November) *Shedding light on responsible investment: Approaches, returns and impacts.* Retrieved January 1, 2013, from http://www.mercer.com/ri

Morgenstern, R. D., and Pizer, W. A. (eds.) (2007). *Reality check: The nature and performance of voluntary environmental programs in the United States, Europe, and Japan.* Washington, DC: Resources for the Future.

Organisation for Economic Co-Operation and Development (OECD) (2000). *Voluntary approaches for environmental policy: An assessment.* Paris, France: Author. doi: 10.1787/9789264180260-en

Organisation for Economic Co-operation and Development (2003). *Voluntary approaches for environmental policy: Effectiveness, efficiency and usage in policy mixes.* Paris, France: Author. doi: 10.1787/9789264101784-en

Orlitzky, M., Schmidt, F., & Rynes, S. (2003). Corporate social and financial performance: A meta-analysis. *Organizational Studies, 24,* 405–441.

Rodgers, W., Choy, H. L., & Guiral, A. (2008). *Do investors value a firm's commitment to social* activities? The moderating role of intangibles and the impact of the Sarbanes-Oxley Act* (working paper). Retrieved January 3, 2013, from http://ssrn.com/abstract=1311473

Sachs, J. D. (2008). Securing our water needs (Chapter 5). In *Common wealth: Economics for a crowded planet.* New York, NY: Penguin Group.

Sage, W. M. (1999). Regulating through information: Disclosure laws and American health care. *Columbia Law Review, 99*(7), 1701–1829.

Security and Exchange Commission (2010, February 8). *Commission guidance regarding disclosure related to climate change,* Release Nos. 33-9106, 34-61469; FR-82. Retrieved January 2, 2013, from http://www.sec.gov/rules/interp/2010/33-9106.pdf

Shatz, A. (2008). Regulating greenhouse gases by mandatory information disclosure. *Virginia Environmental Law Journal, 26,* 335–37.

Social Investment Forum (2003). *2003 Trends report: Report on responsible investing trends in the U.S. 2003.* Author. Retrieved January 2, 2013, from ussif.org/resources/research/documents/2003TrendsReport.pdf

Social Investment Forum (2007). *2007 Trends report executive summary: 2007 Report on Responsible Investing Trends in the United States.* Author. Retrieved January 2, 2013, from http://ussif.org/resources/research

Social Investment Forum Foundation (2009, December). *Investment consultants and responsible investing: Current practice and outlook in the United States.* Retrieved January 1, 2013, from http://ussif.org/documents/Investment_consultant.pdf

Strasser, K. (2011) *Myths and realities of business environmentalism: Good works, good business or greenwash?* Northampton, MA: Edward Elgar.

ten Brink, P. (2002). *Voluntary environmental agreements: Process, practice and future use.* Sheffield, UK: Greenleaf Publishing.

TerraChoice (2009). *The seven sins of greenwashing: Environmental claims in consumer markets.* Retrieved January 2, 2013, from http://sinsofgreenwashing.org/indexd49f.pdf

U.S. Environmental Protection Agency (1999, September). *Identification of evaluation criteria for EPA's reinvention programs, final report and recommendations of the reinvention criteria committee.* National Advisory Council for Environmental Policy and Technology (NACEPT) (SuDoc EP 1.2:IN 2/22).

Van Staden, C., & Hooks, J. (2007). A comprehensive comparison of corporate environmental reporting and responsiveness. *British Accounting Review, 39,* 197–210.

Wallace, P. (1993). Disclosure of environmental liabilities under the securities laws: The potential of securities-market-based incentives for pollution control. *Washington and Lee Law Review, 50,* 1093–1144.

Wallace, P. E. (2009). Climate change, corporate strategy, and corporate law duties. *Wake Forest Law Review, 44,* 767–775.

Weil, D., Fung, A., Graham, M., & Fagotto, E. (2006). The effectiveness of regulatory disclosure policies. *Journal of Policy Analysis and Management, 25,* 155–181.

Williams, C. (1999). The Securities and Exchange Commission and corporate social transparency. *Harvard Law Review, 112,* 1197–1311.

Woods, J. (2008). Of selling the environment—Buyer beware? An evaluation of the proposed FTC Green Guides revisions. *Loyola Consumer Law Review, 21,* 75–95.

Woodyard, C. (2010, February 25). GM ends talks to sell Hummer brand to Chinese buyer. *USA Today.* Retrieved January 3, 2013, from http://www.usatoday.com/money/autos/2010-02-24-gm-hummer_N.htm

17

O*NET's National Perspective on the Greening of the World of Work

Erich C. Dierdorff, Jennifer J. Norton,
Christina M. Gregory, David Rivkin,
and Phil M. Lewis

The past decade has indeed been marked with a heightened emphasis on all things "green," "clean," or "sustainable." This prevalence has led to a substantial body of literature spanning multiple disciplines (e.g., organizational behavior, labor economics, engineering, environmental science) and dedicated to myriad issues linked to "going green" such as corporate environmental sustainability, clean energy technology, and employment growth in green jobs. The general conclusion of this broad body of literature is that greening of the global economy, and the organizations operating within it, is clearly underway and that it is imperative for organizations to recognize and respond to the various demands associated with these changes. This literature further purports that engaging in green economy activities promises substantial positive contributions to the global environment, societies, organizations, and individuals.

As discussed throughout this book, industrial-organizational (I-O) psychology can and should play a key role in helping to realize these promises. Not only would such efforts be congruent with the overall mission of our field to enhance human well-being, and performance in organizational and work settings, but they would also be squarely within our domains of science and practice. The concern for going green or promoting sustainability essentially entails addressing a host of issues pertaining to identifying and creating more efficient, sustainable, or environmentally-friendly products, work processes, and work behaviors relevant to both organizations and occupations. Clearly, addressing these issues falls within several domains of I-O psychology such as leadership, organizational development and change, work design, training and development, and work and occupational analysis.

The scientific approach that typifies I-O psychology necessarily requires that any phenomenon of interest be clearly defined. In this sense, to realize the promises of a greener economy, it is vital to first understand what actually comprises the green economy as well as to discern the world of work consequences of activities associated with it. Put simply, clear and bounded definitions are essential to any discussion of clean technology, green jobs, or sustainable practices. This chapter provides examples of how a traditional domain of I-O psychology—occupational analysis—can meaningfully contribute to research and practice that seeks to promote a more sustainable and greener world of work.

Along these lines, the purpose of this chapter is to describe recent efforts sponsored by the U.S. Department of Labor to identify the major occupational consequences associated with the greening of the world of work. These efforts are central to national strategic workforce development, which is an important role of the Department of Labor's Occupational Information System (O*NET). Toward this end, we first define the green economy, describe the occupational consequences associated with the green economy, and outline the major sectors of the green economy. We next provide numerous examples from recent O*NET research to illustrate the impacts of the green economy on occupations. Finally, we end with a discussion of several key imperatives that must be addressed in order to meet the future demands of the green economy.

OCCUPATIONS AND THE GREEN ECONOMY

A thorough understanding of any job or occupation requires an understanding of the context in which these entities exist (Dierdorff, Rubin, & Morgeson, 2009). One way to conceptualize the broader context of work is through an economic lens—in the present case, what is referred to as the green economy. A review of the existing literature reveals a consensus regarding the scope of the green economy, which is described as encompassing activities related to reducing the use of fossil fuels, decreasing pollution and greenhouse gas emissions, increasing the efficiency of energy usage, recycling materials, and developing and adopting renewable energy sources (Dierdorff, Norton, et al., 2009; Global Insight, 2008; McCarthy, 2008).

At the heart of these green economy activities is technology. Technological innovations drive the many activities that comprise the green economy. For example, clean energy technologies use the sun, wind, water, and plant matter to produce electricity, heat, and transportation fuel. Green technologies also span a broad range of products, services, and processes that lower performance costs, reduce or eliminate negative ecological impact, and improve the responsible use of natural resources. Thus, understanding green technologies can help to depict the potential workforce implications of various green economy activities.

In relation to green economy activities and technologies, terms such as "green jobs" or "green collar jobs" are frequently used. Despite the prevalence of these terms in both the popular press and concerted research, many have pointed out that their variability and ambiguity have greatly limited these terms' utility and generalizability (Anderberg, 2008, Dierdorff, Norton, et al., 2009; Georgetown University Center on Education and the Workforce, 2010). Recent efforts, however, have added much-needed clarity around the notion of jobs or occupations linked to the green economy. Here, two definitional approaches have been undertaken. In the first, green jobs are defined via the output or consequences of the work. For instance, the U.S. Department of Labor Bureau of Labor Statistics (BLS) (2010) defines green occupations as either:

> Jobs in businesses that produce goods or provide services that benefit the environment or conserve natural resources. [Or] jobs in which workers' duties involve making their establishment's production processes more environmentally friendly or use fewer natural resources.

A second complementary definitional approach is to emphasize the consequences of the green economy for occupations themselves. This approach extends the notion of a green job or occupation beyond labeling (i.e., green as *adjective*) and encompasses the dynamic nature of job or occupational performance (i.e., greening as *verb*). A parallel can be seen in the shift away from an emphasis on "organization" to "organizing" in the general management literature in order to address the effects of contextual changes during the 1990s (e.g., flattening of firms, use of teams, project-based work). This conceptual shift to the occupational consequences of green economy activities and technologies leads to the concept of the "greening of occupations," where such greening refers to the extent to which green economy activities and technologies increase the demand for existing occupations, shape the work and worker requirements needed for occupational performance, or generate unique work and worker requirements (Dierdorff, Norton, et al., 2009). In the O*NET system, these differential consequences of green economy activities and technologies are delineated by three occupational categories now described.

1. *Green increased demand occupations.* The impact of green economy activities and technologies is an increase in the employment demand for an existing occupation. However, this impact does not entail significant changes in the occupation's work and worker requirements. The work context may change, but the tasks themselves do not.

2. *Green enhanced skills occupations.* The impact of green economy activities and technologies results in a significant change to the work and worker requirements of an existing O*NET occupation. This impact may or may not result in an increase in employment demand. The essential purposes of the occupation remain the same, but tasks, skills, knowledge, and external elements, such as credentials, have been altered.

3. *Green new and emerging occupations.* The impact of green economy activities and technologies is sufficient to create the need for unique work and worker requirements, which results in the generation of a new occupation relative to the O*NET taxonomy. This new occupation could be entirely novel or "born" from an existing occupation.

To reiterate, the major activities of the green economy include decreasing fossil fuel use and greenhouse gas emissions, increasing energy efficiency and recycling, and developing and adopting renewable energy sources. While useful for describing the general functions of the green economy at a broad level, more precise delineations are necessary for efficiently and effectively determining the potential consequences suggested by the three occupational greening categories. The current literature suggests numerous segments that pertain to the green economy (Chapple & Hutson, 2010; McCarthy, 2008; Muro, Rothwell, & Saha, 2011; Perry, 2008; Strietska-Ilina, Hofmann, Durán Haro, & Jeon, 2011; White & Walsh, 2008). Dierdorff and colleagues (2009, 2012) reviewed this literature and summarized these segments as 12 green economy sectors. These sectors are used in the O*NET system and are highlighted as follows.

1. *Renewable energy generation.* This sector covers activities related to developing and using energy sources such as solar, wind, geothermal, and biomass.

2. *Transportation.* This sector covers activities related to increasing efficiency and/or reducing the environmental impact of various modes of transportation including trucking, mass transit, and freight rail.

3. *Energy efficiency.* This sector covers activities related to increasing energy efficiency (broadly defined), making energy demand response more effective, constructing "smart grids," and so forth.

4. *Green construction.* This sector covers activities related to constructing new green buildings, retrofitting residential and commercial buildings, and installing other green construction technology.

5. *Energy trading.* This sector covers financial services related to buying and selling energy as an economic commodity, as well as carbon trading projects.

6. *Energy and carbon capture and storage.* This sector covers activities related to capturing and storing energy and/or carbon emissions, as well as technologies related to power plants using the integrated gasification combined cycle (IGCC) technique.

7. *Research, design, and consulting services.* This sector encompasses "indirect jobs" in the green economy, including energy consulting and related business services.

8. *Environment protection.* This sector covers activities related to environmental remediation, climate change adaptation, and ensuring or enhancing air quality.

9. *Agriculture and forestry.* This sector covers activities related to using natural pesticides, efficient land management or farming, and aquaculture.

10. *Manufacturing.* This sector covers activities related to industrial manufacturing of green technology as well as energy-efficient manufacturing processes.

11. *Recycling and waste reduction.* This sector covers activities related to solid waste and wastewater management, treatment, and reduction, as well as processing of recyclables.

12. *Governmental and regulatory administration.* This sector covers activities by public and private organizations associated with conservation and pollution prevention, regulation enforcement, and policy analysis and advocacy.

In summary, the concept of occupational greening describes three discrete forms of impact from green economy activities and technologies. Such occupational consequences range from increased labor demand to changes in the nature of the work itself. Further, the broader green economy can be depicted by 12 distinct but related sectors. Conceptualizing the green economy and its consequences for occupations in this way has led to several research efforts to update and extend the O*NET system with green economy information across each of the 12 sectors. Results from these efforts are described in the following section.

IDENTIFYING OCCUPATIONAL CONSEQUENCES

In recognition of the potential shifts in labor market supply and demand as well as changes to occupational performance requirements due to green economy activities and technologies, several O*NET-related research projects have been conducted. This research has primarily focused on identifying and designating the types of changes for occupations linked to green economy activities and technologies. Numerous books, reports, associations, websites, and webinars were researched to identify green occupations for the O*NET-SOC (Occupational Information Network-Standard Occupational Classification) taxonomy. As a result of the research, a total of 204 O*NET-SOC occupations were identified across the three greening categories described earlier. Specifically, 64 O*NET-SOC occupations were identified as "green increased demand" occupations, 62 O*NET-SOC occupations were identified as "green enhanced skills" occupations, and 78 O*NET-SOC occupations were identified as "green new and emerging" occupations. The following sections provide examples of these research efforts across each of the 12 green economy sectors. In a later section, a description of additional O*NET green research projects is presented. More in-depth procedural descriptions and research findings can be found by consulting O*NET OnLine (http://www.onetonline.org), the O*NET Resource Center (http://www.onetcenter.org), and Dierdorff et al. (2009; 2012). Campbell and Campbell (this book) also provide a comprehensive review of engineering occupations in particular and their role in the green economy.

Renewable Energy Generation

This sector is at the heart of most green economy discussions and research, and is central to the definitional approaches many federal agencies have taken in relation to green jobs, such as the BLS definition presented earlier. Government regulations, energy costs, climate change, and the depletion of natural resources are all factors driving growth and change in this sector. As of 2010, 37 states and the District of Columbia have enacted regulations ("renewable portfolio standards") that require a particular portion of electricity to be generated from renewable sources, a 64% increase from 24 states in 2008 (Energy Information Administration, 2010). Such renewable energy sources include wind, solar, geothermal, hydropower, biomass, and hydrogen (Perry, 2008; Pollin et al., 2008; Pollin & Wicks-Lim, 2008; White & Walsh, 2008). It has been estimated that total net renewable power generation accounts for approximately 11% of total domestic power generation (Energy Information Administration, 2011).

As seen in Table 17.1, not only are traditional occupations experiencing increased demand (e.g., power distributors and dispatchers), but many are also being changed by the sector as well (e.g., electrical engineers, geological sample test technicians, and mechanical engineers). In addition, renewable energy technologies being used have led to several new occupations (e.g., solar photovoltaic installers, wind turbine service technicians, geothermal production managers, biofuels processing technicians, hydroelectric plant technicians).

Transportation

Concerns about global warming, fuel shortages and rising costs, and a more general move toward sustainable transportation are examples of factors impacting this sector. A large proportion of the change occurring in this sector is attributed to increased production of renewable transportation fuels, such as ethanol and biodiesel, development and production of new vehicle engines, and re-engineered (eco-friendly) transportation systems (Global Insight, 2008). The U.S. Department of Energy provides numerous grants to support innovation in green transportation technology, recently offering $14.55 million along with matching private funds to total $29.3 million for alternative vehicle technologies (U.S. Department of Energy, 2008).

TABLE 17.1

Renewable Energy Generation Sector

O*NET-SOC Code	O*NET-SOC Title	Green Occupation Type
51-8012.00	Power Distributors and Dispatchers	Increased Demand
11-3071.02	Storage and Distribution Managers	Enhanced Skills
17-2051.00	Civil Engineers*	Enhanced Skills
17-2071.00	Electrical Engineers*	Enhanced Skills
17-2141.00	Mechanical Engineers*	Enhanced Skills
19-4041.02	Geological Sample Test Technicians*	Enhanced Skills
19-4051.01	Nuclear Equipment Operation Technicians	Enhanced Skills
47-2211.00	Sheet Metal Workers*	Enhanced Skills
47-5013.00	Service Unit Operators, Oil, Gas, and Mining*	Enhanced Skills
47-5041.00	Continuous Mining Machine Operators*	Enhanced Skills
49-9071.00	Maintenance and Repair Workers, General*	Enhanced Skills
51-4041.00	Machinists*	Enhanced Skills
51-8011.00	Nuclear Power Reactor Operators	Enhanced Skills
51-8013.00	Power Plant Operators*	Enhanced Skills
51-9012.00	Separating, Filtering, Clarifying, Precipitating, and Still Machine Setters, Operators, and Tenders*	Enhanced Skills
11-3051.02	Geothermal Production Managers	New & Emerging
11-3051.03	Biofuels Production Managers	New & Emerging
11-3051.04	Biomass Power Plant Managers	New & Emerging
11-3051.05	Methane/Landfill Gas Collection System Operators	New & Emerging
11-3051.06	Hydroelectric Production Managers	New & Emerging
11-9041.01	Biofuels/Biodiesel Technology and Product Development Managers	New & Emerging
11-9199.09	Wind Energy Operations Managers	New & Emerging
11-9199.10	Wind Energy Project Managers	New & Emerging
17-2199.10	Wind Energy Engineers	New & Emerging
17-2199.11	Solar Energy Systems Engineers	New & Emerging
41-4011.07	Solar Sales Representatives and Assessors	New & Emerging
47-1011.03	Solar Energy Installation Managers	New & Emerging
47-2231.00	Solar Photovoltaic Installers	New & Emerging
47-4099.02	Solar Thermal Installers and Technicians	New & Emerging
49-9081.00	Wind Turbine Service Technicians	New & Emerging
49-9099.01	Geothermal Technicians	New & Emerging
51-8099.01	Biofuels Processing Technicians	New & Emerging
51-8099.02	Methane/Landfill Gas Generation System Technicians	New & Emerging
51-8099.03	Biomass Plant Technicians	New & Emerging
51-8099.04	Hydroelectric Plant Technicians	New & Emerging

Note. * denotes occupations linked to multiple sectors.

Table 17.2 lists the O*NET-SOC occupations identified within this sector. The green transportation sector has increased the demand for several traditional occupations, such as railroad conductors, locomotive engineers, and bus drivers. In addition, existing occupations have experienced changes in the tasks and competencies that are required for occupational performance (e.g., automotive specialty technicians, transportation managers, and electronics engineers). Finally, several new and emerging occupations have been identified in this sector, including fuel cell engineers

TABLE 17.2

Transportation Sector

O*NET-SOC Code	O*NET-SOC Title	Green Occupation Type
43-5032.00	Dispatchers, except Police, Fire, and Ambulance	Increased Demand
47-4061.00	Rail-Track Laying and Maintenance Equipment Operators	Increased Demand
53-3021.00	Bus Drivers, Transit and Intercity	Increased Demand
53-4011.00	Locomotive Engineers	Increased Demand
53-4031.00	Railroad Conductors and Yardmasters	Increased Demand
53-7051.00	Industrial Truck and Tractor Operators*	Increased Demand
11-3071.01	Transportation Managers	Enhanced Skills
17-2011.00	Aerospace Engineers*	Enhanced Skills
17-2072.00	Electronics Engineers, except Computer*	Enhanced Skills
17-2141.00	Mechanical Engineers*	Enhanced Skills
43-5071.00	Shipping, Receiving, and Traffic Clerks*	Enhanced Skills
49-3023.02	Automotive Specialty Technicians	Enhanced Skills
49-3031.00	Bus and Truck Mechanics and Diesel Engine Specialists	Enhanced Skills
53-3032.00	Heavy and Tractor-Trailer Truck Drivers	Enhanced Skills
53-6051.07	Transportation Vehicle, Equipment and Systems Inspectors, except Aviation*	Enhanced Skills
11-3071.03	Logistics Managers*	New & Emerging
11-9199.04	Supply Chain Managers*	New & Emerging
13-1081.01	Logistics Engineers*	New & Emerging
13-1081.02	Logistics Analysts*	New & Emerging
17-2051.01	Transportation Engineers*	New & Emerging
17-2141.01	Fuel Cell Engineers*	New & Emerging
17-2141.02	Automotive Engineers*	New & Emerging
17-3027.01	Automotive Engineering Technicians	New & Emerging
17-3029.10	Fuel Cell Technicians	New & Emerging
19-3099.01	Transportation Planners*	New & Emerging
43-5011.01	Freight Forwarders	New & Emerging

Note. * denotes occupations linked to multiple sectors.

and technicians, automotive engineers and technicians, and transportation engineers and planners.

Energy Efficiency

This sector of the green economy includes activities related to increasing energy efficiency and making energy demand response more effective. Because this sector is closely related to numerous industries, it often defies clear delineation. For instance, most financial investment in this sector is within segments of larger industries such as vehicles, buildings, lighting, and appliances (Bezdek, 2007; Perry, 2008). A number of green technologies have been brought to bear in efforts to increase energy efficiency. For example, light-emitting diodes (LED) are a semiconductor technology whose application to general-purpose lighting holds the promise of significant energy savings, with currently available products three to four times more efficient than incandescent bulbs (Gereffi, Dubay, & Lowe, 2008; Hansen, 2009). The promotion of "smart electrical grids" is also significantly impacting change within this sector. Smart grids employ a number of more specific technologies to meet several criteria set out by the U.S. Department of Energy including self-healing, attack resistance, higher quality power, accommodating generation and storage options, promoting energy markets, and increasing overall efficiency (National Energy Technology Laboratory, 2007; Pike Research, 2011). Some traditional occupations, such as refrigeration mechanics and insulation workers, have experienced increased employment demand while others have experienced changes in performance requirements of the work (e.g., heating and air conditioning mechanics and installers, electrical engineers, and mechanical engineers). Three new and emerging occupations have also been identified in the energy- efficiency sector: energy auditors, energy engineers, and weatherization installers and technicians (see Table 17.3).

Green Construction

Design or construction firms undertake two-thirds of this sector's activities, with the remainder involved with the production and sales of green construction materials (Environmental Defense Fund, 2008; Global Insight, 2008). Government-sponsored initiatives have been central to promoting green construction. For example, efforts by the U.S. Environmental

TABLE 17.3

Energy Efficiency Sector

O*NET-SOC Code	O*NET-SOC Title	Green Occupation Type
47-2011.00	Boilermakers	Increased Demand
47-2131.00	Insulation Workers, Floor, Ceiling, and Wall	Increased Demand
49-9021.02	Refrigeration Mechanics and Installers	Increased Demand
49-9051.00	Electrical Power-Line Installers and Repairers	Increased Demand
51-8021.00	Stationary Engineers and Boiler Operators	Increased Demand
47-2011.00	Boilermakers	Increased Demand
47-2131.00	Insulation Workers, Floor, Ceiling, and Wall	Increased Demand
49-9021.02	Refrigeration Mechanics and Installers	Increased Demand
49-9051.00	Electrical Power-Line Installers and Repairers	Increased Demand
51-8021.00	Stationary Engineers and Boiler Operators	Increased Demand
11-1021.00	General and Operations Managers*	Enhanced Skills
13-1151.00	Training and Development Specialists*	Enhanced Skills
13-2051.00	Financial Analysts*	Enhanced Skills
17-2071.00	Electrical Engineers*	Enhanced Skills
17-2141.00	Mechanical Engineers*	Enhanced Skills
49-9021.01	Heating and Air Conditioning Mechanics and Installers*	Enhanced Skills
49-9071.00	Maintenance and Repair Workers, General*	Enhanced Skills
53-6051.07	Transportation Vehicle, Equipment and Systems Inspectors, except Aviation*	Enhanced Skills
13-1199.01	Energy Auditors*	New & Emerging
17-2199.03	Energy Engineers*	New & Emerging
47-4099.03	Weatherization Installers and Technicians	New & Emerging

Note. * denotes occupations linked to multiple sectors.

Protection Agency's Energy Star® buildings program and the U.S. Green Building Council's LEED™ rating system develop systems by which the energy and environmental performance of office buildings can be measured and compared to national norms, and LEED ratings for residential buildings have been introduced (Conway, 2005; Global Insight, 2008). Several green technologies are also influencing green construction activities. Many fall into "mechanical technologies" and include innovations such as on-site electricity generating equipment and blackwater recycling systems (Dierdorff, Drewes, Norton, & Hansen, 2005). Other new technologies include insulation materials, cement alternatives, modular housing, and architectural designs for thermal management (Weinerth, 2010).

As shown in Table 17.4, most of the occupational consequences of this sector fall on traditional occupations. For example, occupations such as

TABLE 17.4

Green Construction Sector

O*NET-SOC Code	O*NET-SOC Title	Green Occupation Type
17-3011.01	Architectural Drafters	Increased Demand
47-2011.00	Boilermakers*	Increased Demand
47-2031.01	Construction Carpenters	Increased Demand
47-2031.02	Rough Carpenters	Increased Demand
47-2051.00	Cement Masons and Concrete Finishers	Increased Demand
47-2073.00	Operating Engineers and Other Construction Equipment Operators	Increased Demand
47-2111.00	Electricians	Increased Demand
47-2131.00	Insulation Workers, Floor, Ceiling, and Wall*	Increased Demand
47-2221.00	Structural Iron and Steel Workers*	Increased Demand
47-3012.00	Helpers—Carpenters	Increased Demand
49-9021.02	Refrigeration Mechanics and Installers*	Increased Demand
49-9098.00	Helpers—Installation, Maintenance, and Repair Workers	Increased Demand
51-2041.00	Structural Metal Fabricators and Fitters*	Increased Demand
51-4121.06	Welders, Cutters, and Welder Fitters*	Increased Demand
51-4121.07	Solderers and Brazers*	Increased Demand
53-7051.00	Industrial Truck and Tractor Operators*	Increased Demand
53-7062.00	Laborers and Freight, Stock, and Material Movers, Hand*	Increased Demand
11-9021.00	Construction Managers*	Enhanced Skills
13-1151.00	Training and Development Specialists*	Enhanced Skills
13-2051.00	Financial Analysts*	Enhanced Skills
17-1011.00	Architects, except Landscape and Naval*	Enhanced Skills
17-1012.00	Landscape Architects*	Enhanced Skills
17-2051.00	Civil Engineers*	Enhanced Skills
17-2071.00	Electrical Engineers*	Enhanced Skills
17-2141.00	Mechanical Engineers*	Enhanced Skills
19-3051.00	Urban and Regional Planners*	Enhanced Skills
47-2061.00	Construction Laborers	Enhanced Skills
47-2152.01	Pipe Fitters and Steamfitters	Enhanced Skills
47-2152.02	Plumbers	Enhanced Skills
47-2181.00	Roofers	Enhanced Skills
47-2211.00	Sheet Metal Workers*	Enhanced Skills
47-4011.00	Construction and Building Inspectors*	Enhanced Skills
47-4041.00	Hazardous Materials Removal Workers*	Enhanced Skills
49-9021.01	Heating and Air Conditioning Mechanics and Installers*	Enhanced Skills
49-9071.00	Maintenance and Repair Workers, General*	Enhanced Skills
51-8013.00	Power Plant Operators*	Enhanced Skills
17-2199.03	Energy Engineers*	New & Emerging

Note. * denotes occupations linked to multiple sectors.

architectural drafters, electricians, construction carpenters, and structural iron and steel workers, have experienced increased employment due to activity in this sector. Occupations such as architects, civil engineers, and construction managers have been changed by the introduction of new task or skill requirements. Only a single green new and emerging occupation associated with green construction, which is also associated with the energy-efficiency sector, has been identified (i.e., energy engineer).

Energy Trading

At least part of the growth of this sector has stemmed from financial industry deregulation, which has led to the increase of trading electricity as a commodity, also known as "power marketing" or "energy marketing." Another significant portion of this sector is devoted to emission trading, frequently focused on carbon trading. In short, the carbon trading market has developed from caps or limits on the amount of carbon dioxide that can be emitted by a particular entity. Companies or other groups are granted emission permits and must hold an equivalent number of credits that represent the right to emit a specific amount of carbon dioxide. Because of the limiting caps, companies that need to increase their emission allowance need to purchase (trade) credits from other firms.

Table 17.5 lists the O*NET-SOC occupations identified within this sector. Energy marketing, power conservation, and emissions trading have implications for employment and new occupational growth in areas such as auditing, market analysis, and brokerage work. For example, occupations related to both financial analysis and emissions analysis are required for carbon trading. However, evidence suggests that occupational greening is likely to only occur for three new and emerging occupations: investment underwriters, securities and commodities traders, and energy brokers. The first

TABLE 17.5

Energy Trading

O*NET-SOC Code	O*NET-SOC Title	Green Occupation Type
13-2099.03	Investment Underwriters*	New & Emerging
41-3031.03	Securities and Commodities Traders*	New & Emerging
41-3099.01	Energy Brokers	New & Emerging

Note. * denotes occupations linked to multiple sectors.

two occupations are more generally associated with the financial services industry at large but are still tightly bound to the energy trading sector.

Energy and Carbon Capture and Storage

The primary force in this sector is the increase in coal-based power plants using IGCC techniques. The benefit of IGCC plants is that they use less water and emit fewer airborne sulfur oxides, nitrogen oxides, particulates, and mercury than conventional pulverized coal plants. IGCC plants still produce carbon dioxide but this greenhouse gas can be concentrated and removed prior to combustion (i.e., "carbon capture and storage"). Although IGCC technology is currently being implemented, most industry analysts agree that carbon capture and storage is farther behind in terms of development and especially use (Francis, Gordon, Hanniman, & Rhodes-Conway, 2007). Because much of the activity in this sector centers on research and development of technology rather than implementation and use (Wesoff, 2011), this sector overall is not likely to experience significant occupational greening in the immediate future. This is evident in only a single green enhanced skill occupation identified during O*NET research (i.e., 50-8031.00 Power Plant Operators).

Research, Design, and Consulting Services

This sector encompasses "indirect jobs" that support green economy activities such as energy consulting or research and other related business services. Although not directly related to green technology, these types of occupations have accounted for a significant portion of employment growth in the green economy. For example, it has been estimated that jobs in this sector have grown by 52% from 1990 to 2008 as compared to a 38% increase in direct jobs during the same time period (Global Insight, 2008).

Occupations in all three greening categories have been identified in this sector (see Table 17.6). Congruent with the prevalence of indirect jobs in this sector, much of the occupational impact is on traditional occupations and/or new occupations from related industries (e.g., biotechnology). For example, 11 green increased demand occupations and 23 green enhanced skills occupations have been identified during O*NET research. In addition, a large number of new and emerging occupations were linked to this sector (37 in total); however, all but one occupation were indirect and

TABLE 17.6

Research, Design, and Consulting Services

O*NET-SOC Code	O*NET-SOC Title	Green Occupation Type
115-1133.00	Software Developers, Systems Software	Increased Demand
17-2041.00	Chemical Engineers	Increased Demand
17-2111.01	Industrial Safety and Health Engineers*	Increased Demand
17-2112.00	Industrial Engineers	Increased Demand
19-2031.00	Chemists*	Increased Demand
19-2032.00	Materials Scientists*	Increased Demand
19-2043.00	Hydrologists*	Increased Demand
27-1021.00	Commercial and Industrial Designers*	Increased Demand
29-9011.00	Occupational Health and Safety Specialists*	Increased Demand
43-4051.00	Customer Service Representatives	Increased Demand
49-2094.00	Electrical and Electronics Repairers, Commercial and Industrial Equipment*	Increased Demand
11-2021.00	Marketing Managers	Enhanced Skills
11-9041.00	Architectural and Engineering Managers*	Enhanced Skills
13-1022.00	Wholesale and Retail Buyers, except Farm Products	Enhanced Skills
13-1151.00	Training and Development Specialists*	Enhanced Skills
13-2051.00	Financial Analysts*	Enhanced Skills
13-2052.00	Personal Financial Advisors	Enhanced Skills
17-1011.00	Architects, except Landscape and Naval*	Enhanced Skills
17-2011.00	Aerospace Engineers*	Enhanced Skills
17-2051.00	Civil Engineers*	Enhanced Skills
17-2071.00	Electrical Engineers*	Enhanced Skills
17-2072.00	Electronics Engineers, except Computer*	Enhanced Skills
17-2141.00	Mechanical Engineers*	Enhanced Skills
17-2161.00	Nuclear Engineers*	Enhanced Skills
19-2021.00	Atmospheric and Space Scientists*	Enhanced Skills
19-2042.00	Geoscientists, except Hydrologists and Geographers*	Enhanced Skills
19-3051.00	Urban and Regional Planners*	Enhanced Skills
19-4041.01	Geophysical Data Technicians	Enhanced Skills
19-4041.02	Geological Sample Test Technicians*	Enhanced Skills
23-1022.00	Arbitrators, Mediators, and Conciliators*	Enhanced Skills
27-3022.00	Reporters and Correspondents*	Enhanced Skills
27-3031.00	Public Relations Specialists*	Enhanced Skills
41-4011.00	Sales Representatives, Wholesale and Manufacturing, Technical and Scientific Products*	Enhanced Skills
43-5071.00	Shipping, Receiving, and Traffic Clerks*	Enhanced Skills
11-2011.01	Green Marketers	New & Emerging
11-3071.03	Logistics Managers*	New & Emerging
11-9199.04	Supply Chain Managers*	New & Emerging
13-1081.01	Logistics Engineers*	New & Emerging

13-1081.02	Logistics Analysts*	New & Emerging
13-2099.01	Financial Quantitative Analysts	New & Emerging
13-2099.02	Risk Management Specialists	New & Emerging
13-2099.03	Investment Underwriters*	New & Emerging
15-1199.04	Geospatial Information Scientists and Technologists	New & Emerging
15-1199.05	Geographic Information Systems Technicians	New & Emerging
17-2051.01	Transportation Engineers*	New & Emerging
17-2141.01	Fuel Cell Engineers*	New & Emerging
17-2141.02	Automotive Engineers*	New & Emerging
17-2199.01	Biochemical Engineers*	New & Emerging
17-2199.02	Validation Engineers*	New & Emerging
17-2199.03	Energy Engineers*	New & Emerging
17-2199.04	Manufacturing Engineers*	New & Emerging
17-2199.05	Mechatronics Engineers*	New & Emerging
17-2199.06	Microsystems Engineers*	New & Emerging
17-2199.07	Photonics Engineers*	New & Emerging
17-2199.08	Robotics Engineers*	New & Emerging
17-2199.09	Nanosystems Engineers*	New & Emerging
17-3024.01	Robotics Technicians*	New & Emerging
17-3029.02	Electrical Engineering Technologists*	New & Emerging
17-3029.03	Electromechanical Engineering Technologists*	New & Emerging
17-3029.04	Electronics Engineering Technologists*	New & Emerging
17-3029.05	Industrial Engineering Technologists*	New & Emerging
17-3029.06	Manufacturing Engineering Technologists*	New & Emerging
17-3029.07	Mechanical Engineering Technologists*	New & Emerging
17-3029.08	Photonics Technicians*	New & Emerging
17-3029.09	Manufacturing Production Technicians*	New & Emerging
17-3029.11	Nanotechnology Engineering Technologists*	New & Emerging
19-2099.01	Remote Sensing Scientists and Technologists	New & Emerging
19-3099.01	Transportation Planners*	New & Emerging
19-4099.03	Remote Sensing Technicians	New & Emerging
41-3031.03	Securities and Commodities Traders*	New & Emerging

Note. * denotes occupations linked to multiple sectors.

from other more specific industries (e.g., nanotechnology). The lone direct green new and emerging occupation for this sector is green marketers.

Environmental Protection

Environmental remediation, climate change adaptation, and ensuring or enhancing air quality are essential activities in this sector. Several new technologies are associated with these activities. For example, cattails have been successfully used to reduce water pollutants such as phosphorous (Casey, 2009a). In terms of contaminated soil remediation, rather than digging and removing the soil to landfills, new "bioremediation" processes have been employed, such as those using the cleaning power of bacteria (Casey, 2009b). Federal grant programs have sought to stimulate growth in this sector. For instance, the U.S. Environmental Protection Agency awarded over $2.2 million as part of their Small Business Innovation Research program in 2011 (Green Progress, 2011).

Table 17.7 shows examples of occupations from all three greening categories in this sector. Among the occupations experiencing employment growth are traditional occupations such as environmental scientists, natu-

TABLE 17.7

Environment Protection

O*NET-SOC Code	O*NET-SOC Title	Green Occupation Type
11-9121.00	Natural Sciences Managers	Increased Demand
19-1023.00	Zoologists and Wildlife Biologists	Increased Demand
19-2041.00	Environmental Scientists and Specialists, Including Health	Increased Demand
19-2043.00	Hydrologists*	Increased Demand
19-4093.00	Forest and Conservation Technicians	Increased Demand
25-9021.00	Farm and Home Management Advisors	Increased Demand
33-3031.00	Fish and Game Wardens	Increased Demand
45-1011.05	First-Line Supervisors of Logging Workers	Increased Demand
45-4011.00	Forest and Conservation Workers	Increased Demand
11-9021.00	Construction Managers*	Enhanced Skills
11-9041.00	Architectural and Engineering Managers*	Enhanced Skills
17-1012.00	Landscape Architects*	Enhanced Skills
17-2081.00	Environmental Engineers*	Enhanced Skills
17-3025.00	Environmental Engineering Technicians	Enhanced Skills
19-1013.00	Soil and Plant Scientists	Enhanced Skills
19-1031.01	Soil and Water Conservationists*	Enhanced Skills
19-2021.00	Atmospheric and Space Scientists*	Enhanced Skills
19-2042.00	Geoscientists, except Hydrologists and Geographers*	Enhanced Skills
19-4091.00	Environmental Science and Protection Technicians, Including Health	Enhanced Skills
27-3022.00	Reporters and Correspondents*	Enhanced Skills
27-3031.00	Public Relations Specialists*	Enhanced Skills
47-4041.00	Hazardous Materials Removal Workers*	Enhanced Skills
49-9071.00	Maintenance and Repair Workers, General*	Enhanced Skills

Note. * denotes occupations linked to multiple sectors.

ral sciences managers, forest and conservation workers, and hydrologists. Several occupations are also likely to experience changes in the tasks or skills required for occupational performance (e.g., environmental engineers, hazardous materials removal workers, atmospheric and space scientists, soil and water conservationists). Finally, seven new and emerging occupations have been identified, including brownfield redevelopment specialists and site managers, climate change analysts, environmental economists, environmental restoration planners, and industrial ecologists.

Agriculture and Forestry

Broadly speaking, many of this sector's activities are often referred to as "sustainable agriculture" (National Center for Appropriate Technology, 2011). Activities in this sector focus on using natural pesticides and more efficient land management or farming (Perry, 2008). Efficient land use and management have been facilitated by the application of geospatial technology. For example, "precision farming" uses geospatial data and information systems to plan, manage, and evaluate farming processes. Other technology includes measurement tools to more accurately assess levels of soil nutrients for more efficient application of fertilizers, as well as hydroponic and aeroponic farming systems (GreenTechnologyInvestments.com, 2011; Wesoff, 2010). Finally, there is some evidence that farming practices designed to reduce emissions not only achieve reductions in carbon emissions but also promote farm profitability (Organisation for Economic Co-operation and Development, 2010; Wreford, Moran, & Adger, 2010).

This sector has at least some consequences for all three categories of occupational greening (see Table 17.8). However, most of the occupational consequences relate to either increased employment demand or changes to the performance requirements of existing occupations (i.e., green increased demand occupations or green enhanced skills occupations). Precision agriculture technician is the only occupation to be identified thus far as a green new and emerging occupation in this sector.

Manufacturing

There are two broad facets of green economy activities in the manufacturing sector. The first is the manufacturing of "green" materials that are required by other sectors of the green economy (e.g., renewable energy and

TABLE 17.8

Agriculture and Forestry

O*NET-SOC Code	O*NET-SOC Title	Green Occupation Type
11-1021.00	General and Operations Managers*	Enhanced Skills
13-1021.00	Buyers and Purchasing Agents, Farm Products	Increased Demand
45-1011.07	First-Line Supervisors of Agricultural Crop and Horticultural Workers	Increased Demand
45-2011.00	Agricultural Inspectors*	Increased Demand
11-9013.02	Farm and Ranch Managers	Enhanced Skills
17-1012.00	Landscape Architects*	Enhanced Skills
19-4011.01	Agricultural Technicians	Enhanced Skills
19-4099.02	Precision Agriculture Technicians	New & Emerging

Note. * denotes occupations linked to multiple sectors.

construction). The second is the application of techniques and/or technologies to the manufacturing process. This latter category is highly related to previous sectors, such as energy efficiency and carbon capture. According to the Center for Green Manufacturing at the University of Alabama, the purpose of green manufacturing is "to prevent pollution and save energy through the discovery and development of new knowledge that reduces and/or eliminates the use or generation of hazardous substances in the design, manufacture, and application of chemical products or processes" (Center for Green Manufacturing, n.d.).

Occupations across all three occupational greening categories have been identified during O*NET research (see Table 17.9). A host of existing manufacturing occupations have been linked to this sector with increases in employment demand (e.g., industrial machinery mechanics, millwrights, solderers, and brazers) as well as changes in performance requirements (e.g., industrial engineering technicians, machinists, occupational health and safety technicians). In addition, 23 new and emerging occupations have been identified with activities in the green manufacturing sector. As evident from Table 17.9, most of these new and emerging occupations are engineering related (e.g., biochemical engineers, logistics engineers, photonics technicians).

Recycling and Waste Reduction

This sector includes municipal waste and recycling as well as wastewater treatment and management. Many firms within this sector typically

TABLE 17.9

Manufacturing

O*NET-SOC Code	O*NET-SOC Title	Green Occupation Type
11-3051.00	Industrial Production Managers	Increased Demand
17-2111.01	Industrial Safety and Health Engineers*	Increased Demand
17-3023.01	Electronics Engineering Technicians	Increased Demand
19-2031.00	Chemists*	Increased Demand
19-2032.00	Materials Scientists*	Increased Demand
19-4031.00	Chemical Technicians	Increased Demand
27-1021.00	Commercial and Industrial Designers*	Increased Demand
29-9011.00	Occupational Health and Safety Specialists*	Increased Demand
43-5061.00	Production, Planning, and Expediting Clerks	Increased Demand
47-2221.00	Structural Iron and Steel Workers*	Increased Demand
49-1011.00	First-Line Supervisors of Mechanics, Installers, and Repairers	Increased Demand
49-2094.00	Electrical and Electronics Repairers, Commercial and Industrial Equipment*	Increased Demand
49-9041.00	Industrial Machinery Mechanics	Increased Demand
49-9044.00	Millwrights	Increased Demand
51-1011.00	First-Line Supervisors of Production and Operating Workers	Increased Demand
51-2022.00	Electrical and Electronic Equipment Assemblers	Increased Demand
51-2031.00	Engine and Other Machine Assemblers	Increased Demand
51-2041.00	Structural Metal Fabricators and Fitters*	Increased Demand
51-2092.00	Team Assemblers	Increased Demand
51-4011.00	Computer-Controlled Machine Tool Operators, Metal and Plastic	Increased Demand
51-4031.00	Cutting, Punching, and Press Machine Setters, Operators, and Tenders, Metal and Plastic	Increased Demand
51-4032.00	Drilling and Boring Machine Tool Setters, Operators, and Tenders, Metal and Plastic	Increased Demand
51-4121.06	Welders, Cutters, and Welder Fitters*	Increased Demand
51-4121.07	Solderers and Brazers*	Increased Demand
51-8091.00	Chemical Plant and System Operators	Increased Demand
51-9011.00	Chemical Equipment Operators and Tenders	Increased Demand
51-9023.00	Mixing and Blending Machine Setters, Operators, and Tenders	Increased Demand
53-7062.00	Laborers and Freight, Stock, and Material Movers, Hand*	Increased Demand
17-3023.03	Electrical Engineering Technicians	Enhanced Skills
17-3024.00	Electro-Mechanical Technicians	Enhanced Skills
17-3026.00	Industrial Engineering Technicians	Enhanced Skills
29-9012.00	Occupational Health and Safety Technicians	Enhanced Skills
41-4011.00	Sales Representatives, Wholesale and Manufacturing, Technical and Scientific Products*	Enhanced Skills
43-5071.00	Shipping, Receiving, and Traffic Clerks*	Enhanced Skills

TABLE 17.9 (Continued)

O*NET-SOC Code	O*NET-SOC Title	Green Occupation Type
47-2211.00	Sheet Metal Workers*	Enhanced Skills
49-9071.00	Maintenance and Repair Workers, General*	Enhanced Skills
51-2011.00	Aircraft Structure, Surfaces, Rigging, and Systems Assemblers	Enhanced Skills
51-4041.00	Machinists*	Enhanced Skills
51-9012.00	Separating, Filtering, Clarifying, Precipitating, and Still Machine Setters, Operators, and Tenders*	Enhanced Skills
51-9061.00	Inspectors, Testers, Sorters, Samplers, and Weighers*	Enhanced Skills
11-3071.03	Logistics Managers*	New & Emerging
11-9199.04	Supply Chain Managers*	New & Emerging
13-1081.01	Logistics Engineers*	New & Emerging
13-1081.02	Logistics Analysts*	New & Emerging
17-2199.01	Biochemical Engineers*	New & Emerging
17-2199.02	Validation Engineers*	New & Emerging
17-2199.04	Manufacturing Engineers*	New & Emerging
17-2199.05	Mechatronics Engineers*	New & Emerging
17-2199.06	Microsystems Engineers*	New & Emerging
17-2199.07	Photonics Engineers*	New & Emerging
17-2199.08	Robotics Engineers*	New & Emerging
17-2199.09	Nanosystems Engineers*	New & Emerging
17-3024.01	Robotics Technicians*	New & Emerging
17-3029.02	Electrical Engineering Technologists*	New & Emerging
17-3029.03	Electromechanical Engineering Technologists*	New & Emerging
17-3029.04	Electronics Engineering Technologists*	New & Emerging
17-3029.05	Industrial Engineering Technologists*	New & Emerging
17-3029.06	Manufacturing Engineering Technologists*	New & Emerging
17-3029.07	Mechanical Engineering Technologists*	New & Emerging
17-3029.08	Photonics Technicians*	New & Emerging
17-3029.09	Manufacturing Production Technicians*	New & Emerging
17-3029.11	Nanotechnology Engineering Technologists*	New & Emerging
17-3029.12	Nanotechnology Engineering Technicians	New & Emerging

Note. * denotes occupations linked to multiple sectors.

specialize in designing and manufacturing water purification products. Other firms focus more heavily on managing recycling and/or waste treatment operations. This green sector has experienced significant growth in the past few years attributed to factors such as high prices for energy and metals, rising costs for natural resource extraction, and concerns over pollution (Prouty & Glover, 2011). Investments by state and local government programs to increase recycling also continue to increase activity in this sector. A recent trend in this sector is an increased focus on reducing "e-waste" generated by disposal of consumer electronics (e.g., computers, cell phones, televisions). For example, approximately 3.5 million tons of electronics were recycled in the United States in 2010 (Gerlat, 2011).

With respect to occupational greening, the substantial activity and growth in this sector has primarily resulted in enhancing the competencies of existing occupations or generating new occupations (see Table 17.10). For example, hazardous materials removal workers and refuse and recyclable material collectors are two green enhanced skills occupations that have been identified. In addition, recycling and reclamation workers and recycling coordinators are two green new and emerging occupations that have been designated during O*NET research.

Governmental and Regulatory Administration

Within public or governmental organizations, many of this sector's activities involve conservation and pollution prevention efforts and creation and enforcement of regulations. In addition, non-profit organizations are frequently involved with policy analysis and advocacy related to conservation, climate change, and other energy-related issues. Profit-oriented organizations, such as venture capitalists and private equity firms, are often engaged in financing small- and large-scale renewable energy projects and other green technology projects. The employment landscape of this sector has shown growth, with a 5.9% increase in jobs between 2003 and 2010 to a total of 141,890 jobs in 2010 (Muro et al., 2011). The increase in the activities related to this sector translates into a demand for both specialist-type occupations (e.g., testing specialists, researchers) and more general occupations related to regulation or administration (e.g., compliance managers, policy advisors). With regard to the greening of occupations,

TABLE 17.10

Recycling and Waste Reduction

O*NET-SOC Code	O*NET-SOC Title	Green Occupation Type
47-4041.00	Hazardous Materials Removal Workers*	Enhanced Skills
53-7081.00	Refuse and Recyclable Material Collectors	Enhanced Skills
51-9199.01	Recycling and Reclamation Workers	New & Emerging
53-1021.01	Recycling Coordinators	New & Emerging

Note. * denotes occupations linked to multiple sectors.

this sector has at least some consequences for all three occupational categories, but mostly for the enhanced skills and new and emerging categories (see Table 17.11). For example, a single occupation was identified as green increased demand, whereas nine occupations were found to be green enhanced skills (e.g., soil and water conservationists, environmental engineers) and seven occupations were identified as green new and emerging occupations (e.g., chief sustainability officers, compliance managers, sustainability specialists).

Active O*NET Research on the Green Economy

All 204 O*NET-SOC occupations identified across the three greening categories are undergoing data collection and/or data augmentation. Since their identification (see Dierdorff et al., 2009), 100% of the green increased demand occupations have been updated by new data collection from 2010 to 2011, 98% of green enhanced skills occupations have been fully updated

TABLE 17.11

Governmental and Regulatory Administration

O*NET-SOC Code	O*NET-SOC Title	Green Occupation Type
45-2011.00	Agricultural Inspectors*	Increased Demand
13-2051.00	Financial Analysts*	Enhanced Skills
17-2081.00	Environmental Engineers*	Enhanced Skills
17-2161.00	Nuclear Engineers*	Enhanced Skills
19-1031.01	Soil and Water Conservationists*	Enhanced Skills
19-3051.00	Urban and Regional Planners*	Enhanced Skills
23-1022.00	Arbitrators, Mediators, and Conciliators*	Enhanced Skills
47-4011.00	Construction and Building Inspectors*	Enhanced Skills
51-9061.00	Inspectors, Testers, Sorters, Samplers, and Weighers*	Enhanced Skills
53-6051.07	Transportation Vehicle, Equipment and Systems Inspectors, except Aviation*	Enhanced Skills
11-1011.03	Chief Sustainability Officers	New & Emerging
11-9199.01	Regulatory Affairs Managers	New & Emerging
11-9199.02	Compliance Managers	New & Emerging
13-1041.07	Regulatory Affairs Specialists	New & Emerging
13-1199.01	Energy Auditors*	New & Emerging
13-1199.05	Sustainability Specialists	New & Emerging
19-3099.01	Transportation Planners*	New & Emerging

Note. * denotes occupations linked to multiple sectors.

through data collection in 2011, and 35% of the green new and emerging occupations have been fully updated through data collection. The remaining 65% of green new and emerging occupations are awaiting the start of data collection and have received partial data updates (e.g., updated tasks) from 2009 to 2011.

Other recent research efforts include the O*NET Green Task Development Project (see http://www.onetcenter.org/reports/GreenTask.html), which was completed in 2010 to generate new task data for all green enhanced skills and green new and emerging occupations. Green increased demand occupations were not included in the green task development process because, by definition, the work context of these occupations may change, but the tasks themselves do not. A total of 140 green enhanced skills and green new and emerging occupations were included in the project. As a result of the task updating process, 1,371 green tasks were identified across these green economy occupations to be included in the O*NET database.

In addition to O*NET data collection efforts on green occupations and the identification of green tasks, an ongoing review of the green economy and compilation of related resources allows for quarterly updates to the *Greening of the World of Work: O*NET Project's Green Book of References* product (see http://www.onetcenter.org/reports/GreenRef.html). This resource contains a list of references identified through O*NET's research of the green economy, organized by green sector. The extensive research of the green economy has also been incorporated into numerous O*NET products and resources, including the O*NET Resource Center (http://www.onetcenter.org), O*NET OnLine (http://www.onetonline.org), the O*NET Academy (http://www.onetacademy.org), My Next Move (http://www.mynextmove.org), and My Next Move for Veterans (http://www.mynextmove.org/vets).

GREENING OF OCCUPATIONS AND STRATEGIC WORKFORCE DEVELOPMENT

Much has been written in the past few years about the challenges facing the green economy, both domestically and internationally. Forces such as inadequate fossil fuel supplies to meet ever-increasing global demand, concerns over linkages between greenhouse gas emissions and climate change, and how to continue promoting clean technology development and adoption during the recent economic recession present significant challenges to the green economy as a whole. Further still, the need for increased financial capital investment to promote technological innovation, consumer adoption, and industry stability have been documented across the various green sectors (Muro et al., 2011). These broader contextual forces have created several workforce development imperatives coinciding with the greening of the world of work that include responding to workforce restructuring, focusing financial and human capital investments, and identifying and building workforce capabilities.

RESPONDING TO WORKFORCE RESTRUCTURING

A recent report sponsored by the International Labour Organization (Strietska-Ilina et al., 2011) described broader workforce "restructuring" as the major consequence of the greening of the economy, and noted that such restructuring poses both benefits and drawbacks for employment and work itself. For instance, U.S. employment in extractive industries, fossil fuel energy generation, and emissions-intensive manufacturing is likely to remain flat or decrease due to intra-industry restructuring such as the introduction of sustainable production practices, energy and resource efficiency, clean coal, and carbon capture and storage. At the same time, significant employment gains are expected from restructuring in industries such as renewable energies, green building and retrofitting, and water and waste management. Coinciding with this restructuring are labor market shortages of human and intellectual capital, which further inhibit effective responses and adaptation by governments and work organizations. For example, evidence suggests that the paucity of skilled labor in the workforce at large also holds implications for human capital flow into occupations linked to the green economy (Martinez-Fernandez, Hinojosa, & Miranda, 2010). Moreover, green economy activities and technologies create additional demands for individuals with specialized skills and knowledge that are often in short supply in the current labor market (Apollo Alliance, 2010; Gregg, Beaulieu, & Durán, 2011; Strietska-Ilina et al., 2011). In short, organizations associated with green economy activities and technologies will be faced with continuing difficulties pertaining to recruiting and selecting individuals who possess the requisite competencies for successful performance.

Focusing Financial and Human Capital Investments

Another imperative relates to strategic workforce development. Taken collectively, current deficiencies of human capital to meet the evolving demands of green economy activities and technologies impede both national competitiveness and individual participation in green economy activities. Many have noted that the United States lags behind other industrialized nations in its overall investment and growth in green technologies (e.g., Muro et al., 2011). Still others have pointed out the criticality of developing career pathways to help individuals move into occupations linked to the green economy as well as creating national standards for workforce credentialing (Apollo Alliance, 2010; Urban Institute, 2011; White, Dresser, & Rogers, 2010; Zabin et al., 2011). Yet, financial investments influence workforce development insofar as they allow or sustain efforts to research, design, and implement training or educational programs that facilitate workforce competence and competitiveness.

One advantage of the occupational greening concept used in the O*NET system is that it facilitates the identification of areas in the U.S. workforce that may benefit most in terms of financial and intellectual capital investments. That is, a focus on the consequences of green economy activities and technologies allows efforts, such as those aimed at designing and conducting specialized training and education initiatives, to be better positioned for greater impact. For example, green new and emerging occupations are those most in need of such investments because they represent new roles that will require intellectual capital that may not yet exist. Similarly, but to a lesser extent, green enhanced skills occupations may require training investments to update skill sets to meet the newer duties and/or knowledge requirements resulting from green economy activities and green technologies.

Identifying and Building Workforce Capabilities

Also critical to workforce development is the creation of a domestic system that identifies the essential capabilities requisite to occupational roles within the green economy. Such capabilities should reflect human capabilities that are most malleable or trainable, such as key knowledge and skill requirements (Morgeson & Dierdorff, 2010). Although there have been efforts toward outlining the various capabilities associated with occupations tied to the green economy (e.g., Martinez-Fernandez, Hinojosa, & Miranda 2010; White et al., 2010), several key needs remain. First, there is a clear need for more concise definitions of what "green skills" are meant to entail. This would also include depicting the boundaries of such competencies by addressing the uniqueness of the knowledge and skill requirements (i.e., are the competencies new or are they manifesting in some unique fashion?). Second, there is a need for a systematic organization of competencies related to the greening of occupations. The approach most likely to be useful here is to generate a taxonomic depiction of the competencies required for occupations with a high probability of being changed by green economy activities and technologies. Such occupations would specifically include green enhanced skills and green new and emerging occupations. Lastly, any domestic effort at identifying key competencies for green economy occupations should strive to describe the linkages or crosswalks to existing national occupational information systems such as O*NET. This is especially important considering that research suggests some of the skills or knowledge required for occupations in the green economy are transferable to or from other more traditional "non-green" occupations (Gregg et al., 2011; Krumenauer & Johnson, 2011; White et al., 2010).

CONCLUSION

In this chapter we provided examples of how I-O psychology can contribute both conceptually and empirically to research and practice related to the green economy at large. A hallmark of the scientist-practitioner model underlying I-O psychology is the examination of work-related phenomena through a more rigorous lens. In the present case, we illustrated how occupation analysis provided valuable insight into the various implications of a greener or cleaner world of work and led to more concise and bounded descriptions of the differential occupational consequences associated with green economy activities and technologies. Evidence of the practical value of this approach can be seen in the successful integration of the occupational greening concept in the national O*NET system, its use in state labor market and information offices (e.g., Tennessee, Indiana, Michigan, Missouri, and Iowa), educational initiatives (e.g., Illinois Green Economy Network), and career counseling and assessments (e.g., the Strong Interest Inventory® and the ASVAB Career Exploration Program®).

Beyond the imperatives we discussed facing individuals and organizations linked to the green economy, other important challenges to be addressed by future research include examining connections between many of the concepts mentioned in other chapters of this book. For example, by definition occupations cut across organizations (Dierdorff & Morgeson, 2007) and thus a better understanding of the interplay between occupational greening and corporate (organization) environmental sustainability is needed. In addition, it would be important to examine how various sustainable or green work behaviors, such as those discussed by Ones and Dilchert (this book), manifest in different occupational greening categories that could serve to amplify or attenuate their impact. Yet despite the variety of challenges presented by the greening of the world of work, it is essential to recognize that a central theme is the manner with which people work and the occupations and organizations within which they work. This certainly entails human capital management systems and practices that encompass recruitment, selection, training and development, career planning, vocational counseling, and so forth. With this in mind, I-O psychology is not only relevant but also vital to addressing these future challenges.

REFERENCES

Anderberg, M. (2008). *Green collar workers and other mythical creatures.* Labor Market and Career Information Department, Texas Workforce Commission.

Apollo Alliance, (2010, January). *Mapping green career pathways: Job training infrastructure and opportunities in Ohio.* San Francisco, CA: Author.

Bezdek, R. (2007, November). *Renewable energy and energy efficiency: Economic drivers for the 21st century.* Management Information Services Inc. for the American Solar Energy Society.

Casey, T. (2009a, May 16). *Cattail army deployed to fight water pollution.* Clean Technica.

Casey, T. (2009b, December 17). *Got milk? Lactate helps clean polluted soil.* Clean Technica.

Center for Green Manufacturing (n.d.). *Mission statement.* Center for Green Manufacturing: Innovations in Green Chemistry. Retrieved January 17, 2013, from http://bama.ua.edu/~cgm

Chapple, K., & Hutson, M. (2010). *Innovating the green economy in California regions.* Berkeley, CA: Center for Community Innovation, University of California.

Conway, B. (2005). Office building. In *Whole building design guide.* Washington, DC: National Institute of Building Sciences.

Dierdorff, E., Drewes, D., Norton, J., & Hansen, M. (2005). *N&E industry report for construction: A description of the domain, its growth, and occupational implications.* Raleigh, NC: National Center for O*Net Development.

Dierdorff, E. C., & Morgeson, F. P. (2007). Consensus in work role requirements: The influence of discrete occupational context on role expectations. *Journal of Applied Psychology, 92,* 1228–1241.

Dierdorff, E., Norton, J., Drewes, D., Kroustalis, C., Rivkin, D., & Lewis, P. (2009). *Greening of the world of work: Implications for O*NET®-SOC and new and emerging occupations.* Raleigh, NC: National Center for O*Net Development.

Dierdorff, E., Norton, J., Gregory, C., Rivkin, D., & Lewis, P. (2012). *Greening of the world of work: Revisiting occupational consequences.* Raleigh, NC: National Center for O*Net Development.

Dierdorff, E. C., Rubin, R. S., & Morgeson, F. P. (2009). The milieu of managerial work: An integrative framework linking work context to role requirements. *Journal of Applied Psychology, 94,* 972–988.

Energy Information Administration (2010). *Renewable energy consumption and electricity preliminary statistics 2010.* Washington, DC: Author.

Energy Information Administration (2011, June). *Electric power monthly.* Washington, DC: Author.

Environmental Defense Fund (2008, September). *Green Jobs Guidebook.* Washington, DC: Author.

Francis, G., Gordon, K., Hanniman, K., & Rhodes-Conway, S. (2007, October). *IGCC with carbon capture and storage: Opportunities and challenges for labor.* Madison, WI: Center on Wisconsin Strategy, University of Wisconsin.

Georgetown University Center on Education and the Workforce (2010). *State of green: The definition and measurement of green jobs.* Washington, DC: Author.

Gereffi, G., Dubay, K., & Lowe, M. (2008, November). *Manufacturing climate solutions: Carbon reducing technologies and U.S. jobs.* Durham, NC: Center on Globalization, Governance & Competitiveness, Duke University.

Gerlat, A. (2011, October 5). Report: U.S. Electronics Recycling Industry Shows Significant Growth. *Waste Age.*

Global Insight (2008, October). *U.S. metro economies: Green jobs in U.S. metro areas.* Author.

Green Progress (2011, May 31). *EPA funds 10 small businesses to develop environmental technologies.* Author.

GreenTechnologyInvestments.com (2011, July). *Phototron (PHOT) is well-positioned in booming hydroponic industry.* Whitefish, MT: Author.

Gregg, C., Beaulieu, & J. Durán, M. (2011). *Comparative analysis of methods of identification of skill needs on the labour market in transition to the low carbon economy.* Geneva, Switzerland: International Labour Organisation.

Hansen, M. (2009). *Energy-efficient lighting lifecycle –White Paper: LED lighting: More energy-efficient than CFL?* Durham, NC: Cree.

Johnson, C., and Krumenauer, G. (2011, May 25). New survey counts jobs in natural resources. *Oregon Labor Market Information System.*

Martinez-Fernandez, C., Hinojosa C., & Miranda G. (2010) *Green jobs and skills: The local labour market implications of addressing climate change.* Organisation for Economic Cooperation and Development.

McCarthy, M. (2008, February). *Going from "blue collar" to "green collar" in work force development.* Sacramento, CA: State of California Employment Development Department.

Morgeson, F. P., & Dierdorff, E. C. (2010). Job and work analysis: From technique to theory. In S. Zedeck (Ed.), *APA handbook of industrial and organizational psychology* (Vol. 2, pp. 3–41). Washington, DC: APA.

Muro, M., Rothwell, J, & Saha, D. (2011, July 13). *Sizing the green economy: A national and regional jobs assessment.* Washington, DC: The Brookings Institution.

National Center for Appropriate Technology (2011). *What is sustainable agriculture?* Greensboro, NC: Author.

National Energy Technology Laboratory (2007). *A vision for the modern grid, US Department of Energy.* Morgantown, WV: Author.

Organisation for Economic Co-operation and Development (OECD) (2010). *Agricultural policies and rural development: A synthesis of recent OECD work.* Paris, France: Author.

Perry, F. N. (2008). California green innovation index, 2008 inaugural issue. Palo Alto, CA: Next 10.

Pike Research (2011). *Energy management.* Boulder, CO, and Washington, DC: Author.

Pollin, R., Garrett-Peltier, H., Heintz, J., & Scharber, H. (2008, September). *Green recovery: A program to create good jobs and start developing a low-carbon economy.* University of Massachusetts, Amherst.

Pollin, R., & Wicks-Lim, J. (2008, June). *Job opportunities for the green economy: A state-by-state picture of occupations that gain from green investments.* Political Economy Research Institute, University of Massachusetts, Amherst.

Prouty, E., & Glover, E. (2011, January). Big opportunity. *Recycling Today.*

Strietska-Ilina, O., Hofmann, C., Durán Haro, M., & Jeon, S. (2011). *Skills for green jobs: A global view.* Geneva, Switzerland: International Labour Organization.

Urban Institute (2011, July). *What to do about the new unemployment.* Washington, DC: Author.

U.S. Department of Energy (2008, December 3). *DOE announces up to $29.3 million in projects for research, development, and demonstration of alternative vehicle technologies.* Washington, DC: Author.

U.S. Department of Labor Bureau of Labor Statistics. (2010, September 21). *Federal register, 75*(182).

Weinerth, D. (2010, January 21). *The university's role in the green economy.* Innovating the green economy conference. Berkeley, CA: University of California.

Wesoff, E. (2010, March 25). *Green agriculture—The next hot investment sector?* Greentech Media.

Wesoff, E. (2011, August 29). *DOE pumps $41m into carbon capture research, $141m into new facility.* Greentech Media.

White, S., Dresser, L., & Rogers, J. (2010). *Greener skills: How credentials create value in the clean energy economy.* Madison, WI: Center on Wisconsin Strategy, University of Wisconsin.

White, S., & Walsh, J. (2008). *Greener pathways: Jobs and workforce development in the clean energy economy.* Madison, WI: Center on Wisconsin Strategy, University of Wisconsin.

Wreford, A., Moran, D., & Adger. N. (2010). *Climate change and agriculture: Impacts, adaptation and mitigation.* Paris, France: OECD.

Zabin C., Chapple, K., Avis, E., Halpern-Finnerty, J., et al. (2011). *California workforce education and training needs assessment: For energy efficiency, distributed generation, and demand response.* Donald Vial Center on Employment in the Green Economy, Berkeley, CA: University of California.

18

What Corporate Environmental Sustainability Can Do for Industrial-Organizational Psychology

Herman Aguinis and Ante Glavas

The premise for this edited volume is that industrial-organizational (I-O) psychology has much to contribute to corporate environmental sustainability (CES) research and practice (Klein & Huffman, this book). In fact, the book's title suggests that I-O psychology can serve as a driver for change regarding CES. We agree fully. In fact, each of the excellent chapters included in this book offers numerous suggestions in this regard.

Our chapter offers an alternative yet complementary perspective on the relationship between I-O psychology and CES. To paraphrase former U.S. President John F. Kennedy's famous inaugural address statement, in our chapter we ask not what I-O psychology can do for CES, but what CES can do for I-O psychology. More specifically, we argue that CES can help I-O psychology consider the role of context and "go macro," be more open and explicit about values, consider people at work in terms of long-term investments and partnerships, and reach out to other fields of inquiry as well as re-think traditional areas of research and practice. Overall, we believe that CES can help I-O psychology in important and meaningful ways particularly regarding the bridging of two troubling and often-lamented gaps in our field: the science-practice gap and the micro-macro gap.

First, regarding the science-practice gap, Cascio and Aguinis (2008) conducted a 45-year (1963 to 2007, inclusive) content analysis and review of published research in the two leading journals in I-O psychology: *Journal of Applied Psychology* (*JAP*) and *Personnel Psychology* (*PPsych*). Results based on a database including 5,780 articles published over almost half a century showed that, for the most part, I-O psychology research has not addressed important societal issues (e.g., human-capital trends). In cases when I-O psychology has addressed societal issues, it has done so modestly and mostly indirectly. For example, consider the topic of talent management. As noted by Cascio and Aguinis (2008), talent management encompasses the domains of recruitment, development, retention, human resource effectiveness, and organizational demographics. The record is decidedly mixed regarding the extent to which I-O psychology research has addressed these issues. Specifically, consider publication trends for the most recent period included in the review: 2003 to 2007. During this time, 1.53% of articles published in *JAP* addressed recruitment; 3.28% of *JAP* articles and 3.26% of *PPsych* articles addressed development; 1.75% of articles in *JAP* and none in *PPsych* addressed retention; no articles in either journal addressed human resource effectiveness (although there were some published methodological critiques of the body of literature that relates human resource activities to firm performance); finally, 0.44% of *JAP* articles and 0% of *PPsych* articles addressed demographic changes. In short, although talent management seems to be one of the most important recent human-capital trends (e.g., "The battle for brainpower," 2006), I-O psychology research does not seem to be paying much attention to it. In fact, based on these and other results, Cascio and Aguinis (2008) concluded that if:

> we extrapolate past emphases in published research to the next 10 years, we are confronted with one compelling conclusion, namely, that I-O psychology will not be out front in influencing the debate on issues that are (or will be) of broad organizational and societal appeal. (p. 1074)

In short, there is a gap between I-O psychology research and broader organizational and societal trends.

A second troubling gap is the micro-macro divide. I-O psychology research and practice focuses mostly on individual- and, to some extent, team-level phenomena. An examination of I-O psychology textbooks (e.g., Cascio & Aguinis, 2011) and compendia (e.g., Rogelberg, 2007; Zedeck, 2011) indicates that major topic headings include personnel selection, training, performance appraisal and management, individual differences, and job analysis and design. The vast majority of these topics address individual-level phenomena. For the most part, organization-, industry-, and society-level phenomena are not discussed in detail and do not play a major role.

The emphasis on micro- rather than macro-level phenomena is not surprising given I-O psychology's historical roots in differential psychology. However, in today's globalized and hypercompetitive business milieu driven by technological advancements, speed of communications, and flow of information, a sole emphasis on micro-level phenomena can mean that I-O psychology risks becoming irrelevant. As noted by Aguinis, Boyd, Pierce, and Short (2011), "practitioners who face day-to-day management challenges are interested in solving problems from all levels of analysis. For example, they are interested in performance issues at the organizational and individual levels of analysis" (p. 397). If the research produced by I-O psychology addresses only the individual level, then it is likely that the science-practice gap mentioned earlier will continue to widen.

CES is of great importance to organizations and society at large. Thus, I-O psychology research on CES is likely to be received with interest by stakeholders outside of the field, thereby improving I-O psychology's stature in terms of perceived relevance. When was the last time we have watched an individual on television discuss the latest I-O psychology knowledge or interventions and their implications for society? In contrast, we can foresee how I-O psychology research addressing CES has potential to be widely disseminated and, again, this can help bridge the much lamented science-practice gap in the field. Moreover, CES can help I-O psychology move beyond an almost exclusive emphasis on micro-level phenomena to a combination of micro- and macro-level phenomena. By its nature, CES has mostly been studied at the macro-level phenomenon (Aguinis & Glavas, 2012). However, individuals make decisions about CES, have values, attitudes, and beliefs about CES, and react to CES initiatives in various ways. So, CES can serve as a conduit for I-O psychology to consider both micro- and macro-level issues and thereby help narrow the micro-macro gap.

In the remainder of our chapter, we provide a more detailed description of illustrative domains and issues for which CES can make a contribution to I-O psychology. To do so, we rely on the many excellent ideas and data included in this volume's chapters. Before we proceed, we clarify that we define corporate social responsibility (CSR) following Aguinis (2011, p. 855) and also adopted by others (e.g., Aguinis & Glavas, 2012; Rupp, 2011) as "context-specific organizational actions and policies that take into account stakeholders' expectations and the triple bottom line of economic, social, and environmental performance." Thus, based on this definition, and consistent with its conceptualization in most of the chapters in this book, CES refers to the environmental performance aspect of CSR. In other words, CES consists of context-specific organizational actions and policies that take into account stakeholders' expectations specifically regarding environmental issues.

CES CAN HELP I-O PSYCHOLOGY CONSIDER THE ROLE OF CONTEXT AND "GO MACRO"

As noted earlier, I-O psychology is essentially a micro-level discipline. In other words, the majority of I-O psychology research and practice topics focus on phenomena at the individual and, less often, team level of analysis. On the other hand, CES is essentially a macro-level field of study and practice. CES refers to policies and actions by organizations. However, such policies and actions are influenced and implemented by actors at all levels of analysis (e.g., institutional, organizational, and individual). Accordingly, CES also subsumes the individual and team levels of analysis (Lindenberg & Steg, this book; Pandey, Rupp, & Thornton, this book).

CES can help I-O psychology consider the role of context and go macro because research and practice concerning CES will need to adopt a systems approach that involves individual, organizational, and societal-level variables (Andrews, Klein, Forsman, & Sachau, this book; DuBois, Astakhova, & DuBois, 2013; Ones & Dilchert, 2013). Much like Aguinis and Glavas (2012) concluded regarding CSR in general, an understanding of CES requires a consideration of actors and variables at multiple levels of analysis. For example, such systems and multi-level perspective include a consideration of organizational-level characteristics as well as pressure from external stakeholders (i.e., macro level) and individual motivation and goals (i.e., micro level). I-O psychology has a long and illustrious tradition in terms of the generation of knowledge regarding foundations of a field that are based on individual action and interactions, what is labeled *microfoundations* (e.g., Foss, 2011). CES can help I-O psychology place these microfoundations within a broader organizational and societal context.

Our proposed integration of micro- and macro-level actors and processes will not be easy given the traditional I-O psychology emphasis on the micro level. Thus, to achieve this integration, it is helpful to categorize CES into peripheral and embedded CES. *Peripheral CES* focuses on activities that are not integrated into the daily strategies and operations. Examples are volunteering and philanthropy. On the other hand, *embedded CES* refers to an integration into strategy and daily operations by using the firm's core competencies.

We model our distinction between peripheral and embedded CES after the notion of embedded sustainability recently put forward in the practitioner literature by Laszlo and Zhexembayeva (2011). Embedded CES can include building on the core competencies of the company in order to deliver sustainable products and services and is integrated into the daily operations and overall organizational culture (e.g., Bertels, Papania, & Papania, 2010). Examples of how firms build on their core competencies to embed CES are GE's ecoimagination program through which GE uses technology to provide environmentally-friendly products, and IBM's use of their information systems capabilities to help create smarter and greener cities through their Smarter Planet program. Stated differently, similar to how Aguinis (2011) proposed regarding CSR in general, CES is not viewed as separate from overall organizational strategy and daily operations; rather, "all policies and actions are affected throughout the entire organization and at all levels of analysis (i.e., individual, group, and organization)" (Aguinis, 2011, p. 865).

Viewing CES as peripheral or embedded is important in terms of what CES can do for I-O psychology for the following reasons. First, it is crucial for future research, especially research at the individual level of analysis—the "bread and butter" of I-O psychology. If CES is at the periphery and managed by only a few organizational members (e.g., sustainability officer or corporate foundation), then it is unlikely that micro-level research will make important contributions. However, if CES is embedded, then scholars can use current I-O psychology theories to conduct further research on how human capital systems may promote integration of CES into daily operations. Second, such a categorization allows future research to more precisely assess outcomes at the individual level of analysis. As the meaningfulness literature has put forward (e.g., Pratt & Ashforth, 2003), employee outcomes (e.g., identification, commitment, satisfaction) can vary depending on whether individuals find meaning in work (i.e., embedded in one's daily work). So, for example, our categorization can help I-O psychology understand when and why employees are likely to "own" sustainability (DuBois, Astakhova, & DuBois, this book) and the extent to which CES is likely to affect the effectiveness of human resource management practices such as recruiting (Willness & Jones, this book).

CES CAN HELP I-O PSYCHOLOGY BE MORE OPEN AND EXPLICIT ABOUT VALUES

In a comprehensive compendium of the field of I-O psychology, Rogelberg (2007, p. xxxv) noted that "...the goals of I/O psychology are to better understand and optimize the effectiveness, health, and well-being of both individuals and organizations." Likewise, the Society for Industrial and Organizational Psychology (SIOP) makes an explicit mention of values by noting that the field's mission "is to enhance human well-being and performance in organizational and work settings by promoting the science, practice, and teaching of I-O psychology" (Society for Industrial and Organizational Psychology, 2012). In other words, one of I-O psychology's very open and explicit goals is to help individuals, organizations, and society. This clear and explicit goal seems to collide with the goal of a silent majority of academics who advocate disinterest in practice in order to achieve scientific objectivity (Palmer, 2006). Such a detachment from values has been advocated so that research will "not be subverted to those of management, and that [I-O psychology researchers and practitioners] will not become mere servants of those in positions of power" (Cascio & Aguinis, 2008, p. 1074).

Tushman and O'Reilly (2007) argued that this self-imposed distancing from values, with the goal of achieving objectivity, reduces the quality of I-O psychology research, undermines the external validity of our theories, and reduces the overall relevance of the data used to test ideas. CES offers I-O psychology a different path: the possibility of making clear and open statements about values—values that I-O psychology researchers and practitioners hold but often may choose to not make public. As argued by Lowman (2013), it is better to discuss values and ethical standards in the open—and debate them—rather than hiding them or pretending they do not exist. For example, Intel's leadership believe, and openly proclaim, that "business has a fundamental responsibility to consider the long-term consequences of its activities on the environment" (Barrett & Niekerk, this book). An open discussion about values is needed because, acknowledged or not, they play an important role in how people make decisions. As noted by Swanson (1999), "values cannot be ignored and are part of the decision-making process whether managers realize it or not" (p. 507).

A discussion of values within the context of specific research and practice domains is not new to I-O psychology (Werner, this book). For example, consider the rationale for and use of test-score banding in personnel selection. Users and developers of personnel selection tools face a paradoxical situation: the use of cognitive abilities and other valid predictors of job performance leads to adverse impact (Aguinis & Smith, 2007). Thus, choosing predictors that maximize economic utility often leads to the exclusion of members of certain demographic groups. Pre-employment test-score banding has been proposed as a way to incorporate both utility and adverse impact considerations in the personnel selection process (Aguinis, 2004). Banding avoids the strict top-down selection strategy that typically leads to adverse impact and, instead, is based on the premise that (a) pre-employment measures are never perfectly valid, and (b) both predictors and criteria (i.e., measures of performance) are also never perfectly reliable (Aguinis, Cortina, & Goldberg, 1998). Thus, an observed difference in the scores of two job applicants may be the result of measurement error and less than perfect test validity instead of actual differences in the construct that is measured (e.g., general cognitive abilities). Consequently, if it cannot be determined with a reasonable amount of certainty that two applicants differ on the construct underlying a predictor, these two applicants are deemed statistically indistinguishable from one another and tie-breaking criteria may be used to choose one of them over the other. For example, assume that the computation of bands leads to the conclusion that pairs of applicants John-Susan and Peter-Ed have indistinguishable test scores. If a school of business is seeking to increase the number of female students in the program because women are severely underrepresented vis-à-vis the relevant population, Susan may be a preferred candidate over John. Similarly, if a police department is attempting to increase the ethnic diversity of its workforce, they may wish to choose Peter (African-American applicant) over Ed (Caucasian applicant).

Test-score banding has generated very strong and emotional reactions from the I-O psychology community. For example, Schmidt and Hunter (2004) argued that banding is internally logically contradictory and thus scientifically unacceptable. In their view, banding violates scientific and intellectual values and, therefore, its potential use presents selection specialists with the choice of embracing the "values of science" or "other important values." In contrast, Aguinis, Cortina, and Goldberg (2000) argued that, if two scores fall within the same band, they are considered statistically indistinguishable and secondary criteria (e.g., job experience, ethnicity) may be used in making a hiring decision—particularly if an organization places strategic importance on such "tie-breakers." In the end, as concluded by Murphy (2004), whether someone supports the use of banding is likely to reflect broader conflicts in interests, values, assumptions about human resource selection, and one's position regarding the tradeoff between efficiency and equity. In other words, "there is no question there is an issue of values here that should be directly addressed" (Barrett & Lueke, 2004, p. 95).

In sum, CES gives an opportunity to I-O psychology to discuss values openly and explicitly. What is a researcher's position regarding CES? Does a practitioner believe that CES is a necessary evil, or something that I-O psychology should support and encourage? Based on our earlier discussion, should CES be embedded or peripheral? More broadly, CES can help the field of I-O psychology be more open about values and belief systems in other areas such as diversity (e.g., what is the value of diversity for an organization, its stakeholders, and society?) and performance management (e.g., is it acceptable that pay-for-performance systems lead to large differences in pay across employees?). Given the nature of I-O psychology and SIOP's value-laden mission statement, an open and explicit discussion about values can be highly beneficial for the field.

CES CAN HELP I-O PSYCHOLOGY CONSIDER PEOPLE AT WORK IN TERMS OF SUSTAINABLE LONG-TERM INVESTMENTS AND PARTNERSHIPS

As noted earlier, a long-standing concern in the field is that I-O psychology researchers' and practitioners' interests and values may be subverted to those of management, thereby turning I-O psychology into a mere servant of those in positions of power (Baritz, 1960). To address this concern, CES can help I-O psychology think about organizational members in terms of long-term investments and partnerships. Consistent with SIOP's mission, I-O psychology researchers and practitioners can work towards the dual goal of enhancing individual well-being and organizational performance.

A highly influential theoretical model in management, and particularly strategic management, is the resource-based view (RBV) of the firm (Barney, Ketchen, & Wright, 2011). In a nutshell, the perspective is that firms that are able to acquire valuable resources that are neither perfectly imitable nor substitutable without great effort are likely to gain a competitive advantage. Human resources is an important component of RBV, which is consistent with a view held in the field of I-O psychology that people are a critical asset (Cascio & Aguinis, 2011).

Consider the perspective that CES can contribute to I-O psychology regarding the view of people as a source of a firm's competitive advantage. First, the "acquisition" of people should consider a future long-term and sustainable employee-employer relationship. Operationally speaking, this means that personnel selection procedures should focus not only on predicting individual job performance, which is the current focus of I-O psychology, but also a sustainable employee-employer relationship over time. For example, what will be the growth opportunities for a job applicant should she join the organization? What will be the possible career paths for the job applicant? Will there be leadership opportunities? What will be the opportunities to expand into other types of responsibilities? CES also allows for more overt integration of values into the entire human resource development process. CES has been found to signal to potential employees that an organization has deeper values than simply short-term profit maximization (Turban & Greening, 1997). In turn, such values have given companies a competitive advantage in recruiting. Moreover, embedding CES in the organization cannot be done without a shift of the organizational culture to one that embraces values of CES (e.g., caring for well-being of stakeholders and environment). As a result, succession planning would need to expand to consider the whole person. Currently, there is an overemphasis on pay and promotion. As Wrzesniewski (2003) puts forward in her model, employees have three major needs that should be met: job related (e.g., pay, job security), career related (e.g., pay equity, promotion, ability to apply skills to a job, feeling useful), and calling oriented (e.g., doing something to make the world a better place). It is the latter calling orientation that is often overlooked in I-O psychology research and practice.

Second, based on CES principles, training and development interventions should also be implemented within a broader perspective of long-term and sustainable employee-employer relationships. The traditional approach to training and development is to consider skills that are required for the current position (Aguinis & Kraiger, 2009). A consideration of sustainability means that an important component of training and development are the skills that will be needed for positions in the future.

Third, adopting a CES perspective suggests that performance management systems should also focus on a long-term and sustainable employee-employer relationship (Aguinis, 2013). The typical performance management approach in I-O psychology emphasizes performance appraisal—the measurement of job performance. Moreover, performance appraisal emphasizes past performance (Aguinis, Joo, & Gottfredson, 2011). In contrast, CES can help I-O psychology frame performance management such that it "takes into account both past and future performance. Personal developmental plans specify courses of action to be taken to improve performance. Achieving the goals stated in the developmental plan allows employees to keep abreast of changes in their field or profession" (Aguinis et al., p. 505). In addition, performance appraisal often emphasizes the successful implementation of tasks based on a job description that usually does not include macro-level issues. CES allows for an expansion of performance appraisal to also include contributions to broader organizational goals.

Finally, the view of people as resources is also reflected in the literature on the psychological contract, which refers to an unwritten agreement in which the employee and employer develop expectations about their mutual relationship (Rousseau, 1995). Downsizing, mergers, acquisitions, and other inter-firm transactions have led to a decrease in satisfaction, commitment, intentions to stay, and perceptions of an organization's trustworthiness, honesty, and concern for its employees (e.g., Osterman, 2009). CES can help I-O psychology think about long-term and sustainable employee-employer relationships (Becker, this book). Just as CES has been found to have a positive signaling effect to external stakeholders resulting in increased value-based congruence (Sen & Bhattacharya, 2001) and trust (Vlachos, Tsamakos, Vrechopoulus, & Avramidis, 2009), CES can have a signaling effect on internal stakeholders—employees. Firm involvement in CES can signal that the organization cares about more than just short-term profit maximization at all costs, that it cares about the well-being of stakeholders. As a result, employees might have more trust and faith in the firm, thus strengthening the psychological contract and reinforcing a long-term employee-employer relationship.

CES CAN HELP I-O PSYCHOLOGY REACH OUT TO OTHER FIELDS OF INQUIRY AND RE-THINK TRADITIONAL AREAS OF RESEARCH AND PRACTICE

The content analysis of the I-O psychology literature conducted by Cascio and Aguinis (2008) revealed that research in the field has remained fairly stable in terms of the relative attention devoted to various topics and research domains. CES can help I-O psychology research and practice reach out to other fields of inquiry such as engineering (Campbell & Campbell, this book), information and communication technology (Behrend & Foster Thompson, this book), and environmental studies (De Young, this book). Although research domains closer to engineering including human factors and ergonomics were popular early on, studies addressing these issues are now absent from *JAP* and *PPsych*.

In addition to reaching out to other fields, CES can help I-O psychology re-think traditional I-O psychology research domains such as job analysis and job design. Given trends toward a green economy, the nature of many occupations is changing. CES can help I-O psychology keep up the pace regarding these changes in the world of work (Dierdorff, Norton, Gregory, Rivkin, & Lewis, this book). In order to design work that leads to both high motivation and job satisfaction, I-O psychology researchers have explored the impact of characteristics such as skill variety, task identity, task significance, and autonomy (Humphrey, Nahrgang, & Morgeson, 2007). Although such an approach has led to great success "because the motivational approach is widely accepted, it appears that many in the fields of I-O psychology and management concluded it was a 'case closed' with respect to work design" (Humphrey et al., 2007, p. 1332). As a result, the literature on work design has remained focused on a narrow set of characteristics (Humphrey et al., 2007). CES provides I-O psychology with the opportunity to explore how work can be designed in a way that goes beyond skills, knowledge, and attitudes and taps into meaningfulness, deeply held values (e.g., caring for others), and purpose (e.g., feeling of contributing to a greater purpose). Employees are increasingly seeking to find greater fulfillment at work that goes beyond pay satisfaction and career advancement (Wrzesniewski, Dutton, & Debebe, 2003) and CES has become an avenue for finding meaning at work by addressing issues about which many people are truly passionate.

CONCLUSIONS

We began our chapter by asking the question of not only what I-O psychology can do for CES, but what CES can do for I-O psychology. Overall, CES can help I-O psychology address two important gaps: the science-practice gap and the micro-macro gap. First, CES can help I-O psychology researchers conduct studies that address issues of concern to society. Second, CES can help I-O psychology researchers and practitioners conceptualize individual behavior (micro-level variables) within the broader organizational and societal contexts (macro-level variables).

In our chapter, we made the points that CES can help I-O psychology bridge the science-practice and micro-macro gaps by focusing on several specific issues and domains. First, CES can help I-O psychology consider the role of context and "go macro." A conceptualization of CES as embedded, as opposed to peripheral, can guide I-O psychology research and practice towards the inclusion of higher level variables including the organizational and societal levels of analysis. Second, CES can help I-O psychology be more open and explicit about values. At its core, CES is about an explicit statement that sustainability is good and I-O psychology can benefit from a more explicit discussion of values and belief systems, which influence decision making whether individuals realize it or not. Third, CES can help I-O psychology consider people at work in terms of long-term investments and partnerships. Although I-O psychology does consider people to be a key organizational asset, the field could benefit from re-thinking employee-employer relationships on a more long-term and sustainable basis. Finally, CES can help I-O psychology reach out to other fields of inquiry as well as re-think traditional areas of research and practice. CES addresses issues that go beyond any specific field of study and, thus, can help I-O psychology build productive bridges with other disciplines such as engineering.

In closing, our chapter points to only a few specific I-O psychology domains and issues to which CES can make contributions. In addition to the points we addressed in our chapter, CES can also help I-O psychology become more global (Reichman, Berry, Cruse, & Lytle, this book) and make important contributions to the measurement of CES initiatives and their impact (Strasser, this book). We hope our chapter will serve as a catalyst in terms of future research and practice to establish further synergies between CES and I-O psychology.

REFERENCES

Aguinis, H. (Ed.) (2004). *Test-score banding in human resource selection: Legal, technical, and societal issues.* Westport, CT: Praeger.

Aguinis, H. (2011). Organizational responsibility: Doing good and doing well. In S. Zedeck (Ed.), *APA handbook of industrial and organizational psychology* (Vol. 3, pp. 855–879). Washington, DC: American Psychological Association.

Aguinis, H. (2013). *Performance management* (3rd ed.). Upper Saddle River, NJ: Pearson Prentice Hall.

Aguinis, H., Boyd, B. K., Pierce, C. A., & Short, J. C. (2011). Walking new avenues in management research methods and theories: Bridging micro and macro domains. *Journal of Management, 37*, 395–403.

Aguinis, H., Cortina, J. M., & Goldberg, E. (1998). A new procedure for computing equivalence bands in personnel selection. *Human Performance, 11*, 351–365.

Aguinis, H., Cortina, J. M., & Goldberg, E. (2000). A clarifying note on differences between the W.F. Cascio, J. Outzz, S. Zedeck, and I.L. Goldstein (1991) and H. Aguinis, J.M. Cortina, and E. Goldberg (1998) banding procedures. *Human Performance, 13*, 199–204.

Aguinis, H., & Glavas, A. (2012). What we know and don't know about corporate social responsibility: A review and research agenda. *Journal of Management, 38*, 932–968.

Aguinis, H., Joo, H., & Gottfredson, R. K. (2011). Why we hate performance management—and why we should love it. *Business Horizons, 54*, 503–507.

Aguinis, H., & Kraiger, K. (2009). Benefits of training and development for individuals and teams, organizations, and society. *Annual Review of Psychology, 60*, 451–474.

Aguinis, H., & Smith, M. A. (2007). Understanding the impact of test validity and bias on selection errors and adverse impact in human resource selection. *Personnel Psychology, 60*, 165–199.

Baritz, L. (1960). *The servants of power.* Middletown, CT: Wesleyan University Press.

Barney, J. B., Ketchen, D. J., & Wright, M. (2011). The future of resource-based theory: Revitalization or decline? *Journal of Management, 37*, 1299–1315.

Barrett, G. V., & Lueke, S. B. (2004). Legal and practical implications of banding for personnel selection. In H. Aguinis (Ed.), *Test-score banding in human resource selection: Legal, technical, and societal issues* (pp. 71–111). Westport, CT: Praeger.

Bertels, S., Papania, L., & Papania. D. (2010). *Embedding sustainability in organizational culture: A systematic review of the body of knowledge.* London, Ontario: Network for Business Sustainability.

Cascio, W. F., & Aguinis, H. (2008). Research in industrial and organizational psychology from 1963 to 2007: Changes, choices, and trends. *Journal of Applied Psychology, 93*, 1062–1081.

Cascio, W. F., & Aguinis, H. (2011). *Applied psychology in human resource management* (7th

Foss, N. J. (2011). Why micro-foundations for resource-based theory are needed and what they may look like. *Journal of Management, 37*, 1413–1428.

Humphrey, S. E., Nahrgang, J. D., & Morgeson, F. P. (2007). Integrating motivational, social, and contextual work design features: A meta-analytic summary and theoretical extension of the work design literature. *Journal of Applied Psychology, 92*, 1332–1356.

Laszlo, C., & Zhexembayeva, N. (2011). *Embedded sustainability: The next big competitive advantage.* Palo Alto, CA: Stanford University Press.

Murphy, K. R. (2004). Conflicting values and interests in banding research and practice. In H. Aguinis (Ed.), *Test-score banding in human resource selection: Legal, technical, and societal issues* (pp. 175–192). Westport, CT: Praeger.

Osterman, P. (2009). *The truth about middle managers.* Boston, MA: Harvard Business School Press.

Palmer, D. (2006). Taking stock of the criteria we use to evaluate one another's work: ASQ fifty years out. *Administrative Science Quarterly, 51,* 535–559.

Pratt, M. G., & Ashforth, B. E. (2003). Fostering meaningfulness in working and meaningfulness at work: An identity perspective. In K. Cameron, J. E. Dutton & R. E. Quinn (Eds), *Positive organizational scholarship* (pp. 309–327). San Francisco, CA: Berrett-Koehler.

Rogelberg, S. G. (2007). Introduction. In S. G. Rogelberg (Ed.), *Encyclopedia of industrial and organizational psychology* (Vol. 1, pp. xxxv–xxxvii). Thousand Oaks, CA: Sage.

Rousseau, D. M. (1995). *Psychological contracts in organizations: Written and unwritten agreements.* Newbury Park, CA: Sage.

Rupp, D. E. (2011). An employee-centered model of organizational justice and social responsibility. *Organizational Psychology Review, 1,* 72–94.

Schmidt, F. L., & Hunter, J. E. (2004). SED banding as a test of scientific values in I/O psychology. In H. Aguinis (Ed.), T*est-score banding in human resource selection: Legal, technical, and societal issues* (pp. 151–173). Westport, CT: Praeger.

Sen, S., & Bhattacharya, C. B. (2001). Does doing good always lead to doing better? Consumer reactions to corporate social responsibility. *Journal of Marketing Research, 38,* 225–243.

Society for Industrial and Organizational Psychology (2012). Mission statement. Retrieved January 29, 2012 from http://www.siop.org/mission.aspx

Swanson, D. L. (1999). Toward an integrative theory of business and society: A research strategy for corporate social performance. *Academy of Management Review, 24,* 506–521.

"The battle for brainpower" (2006, October 5). *The Economist.* Retrieved January 29, 2012, from http://www.economist.com/node/7961894

Turban, D. B. & Greening, D. W. (1997). Corporate social performance and organizational attractiveness to prospective employees. *Academy of Management Journal, 40,* 658–672.

Tushman, M., & O'Reilly, C., (2007). Research and relevance: Implications of Pasteur's quadrant for doctoral programs and faculty development. *Academy of Management Journal, 50,* 769–774.

Vlachos, P. A., Tsamakos, A., Vrechopoulus, A. P., & Avramidis, P. K. (2009). Corporate social responsibility: Attributions, loyalty, and the mediating role of trust. *Journal of the Academy of Marketing Science, 37,* 170–190.

Wrzesniewski, A. (2003). Finding positive meaning in work. In K. S. Cameron, J. E. Dutton, & R. E. Quinn (Eds.), *Positive organizational scholarship: Foundations of a new discipline* (pp. 296–308). San Francisco, CA: Berrett-Koehler.

Wrzesniewski, A., Dutton, J. E., & Debebe, G. (2003). Interpersonal sense making and the meaning of work. *Research in Organizational Behavior, 25,* 93–135.

Zedeck, S. (Ed.) (2011). *APA handbook of industrial and organizational psychology.* Washington, DC: American Psychological Association.

Index